Requiem
of the

Rose ❁ King

1

AYA KANNO

Based on *Henry VI* and *Richard III*
by William Shakespeare

Requiem
of the
Rose

King

Contents

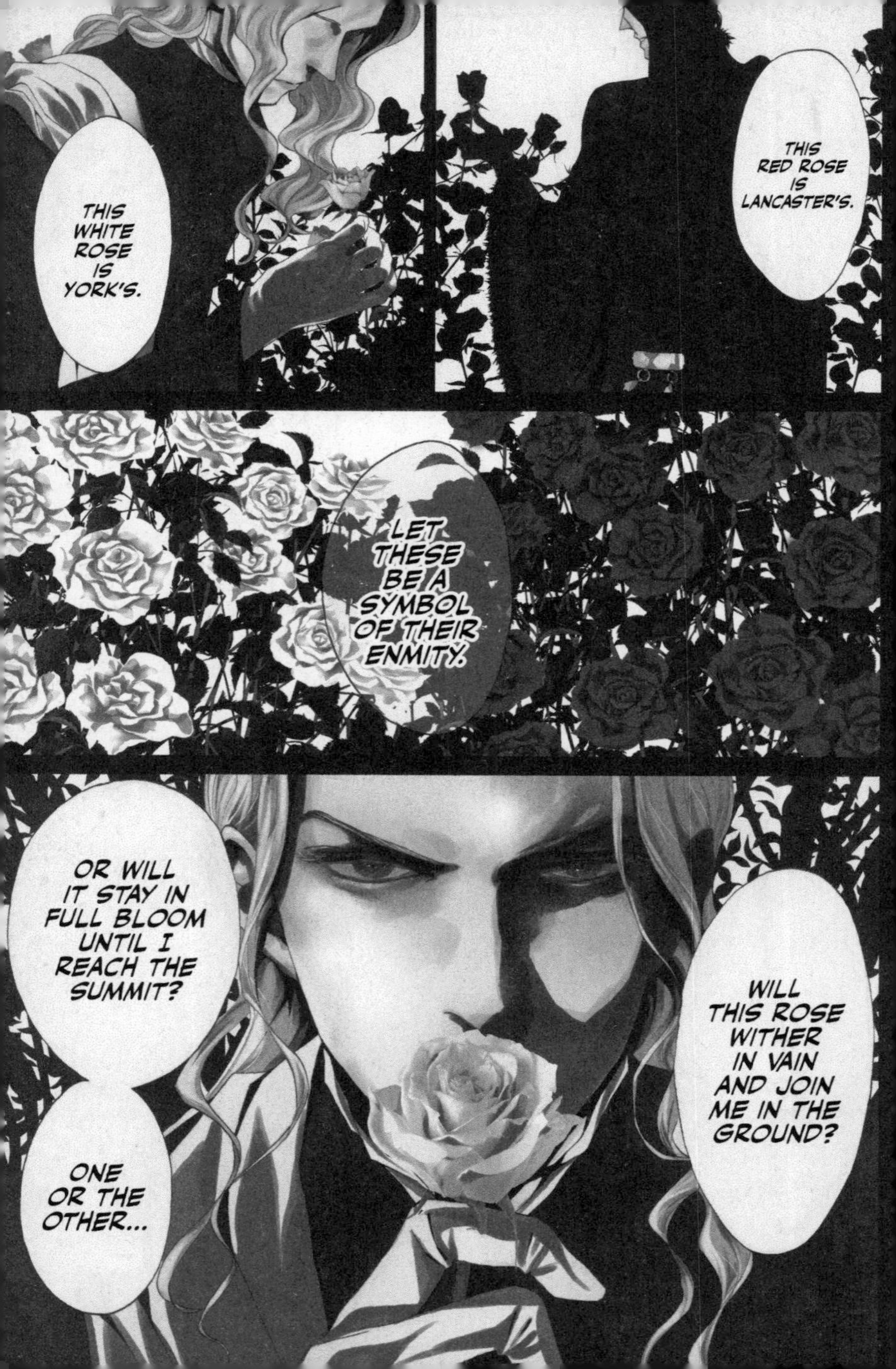
THIS RED ROSE IS LANCASTER'S.
THIS WHITE ROSE IS YORK'S.
LET THESE BE A SYMBOL OF THEIR ENMITY.
WILL THIS ROSE WITHER IN VAIN AND JOIN ME IN THE GROUND?
OR WILL IT STAY IN FULL BLOOM UNTIL I REACH THE SUMMIT?
ONE OR THE OTHER...

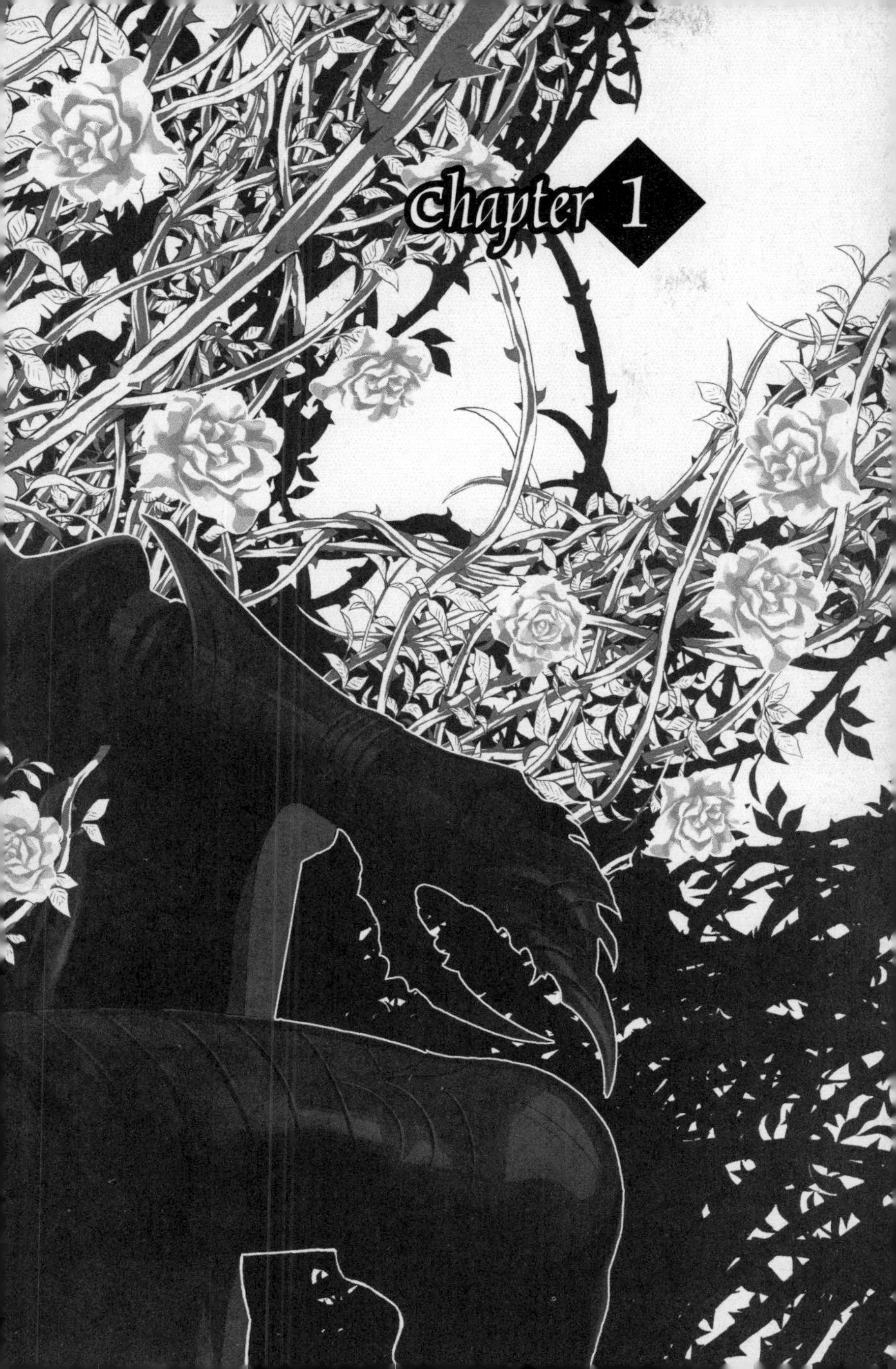
Chapter 1

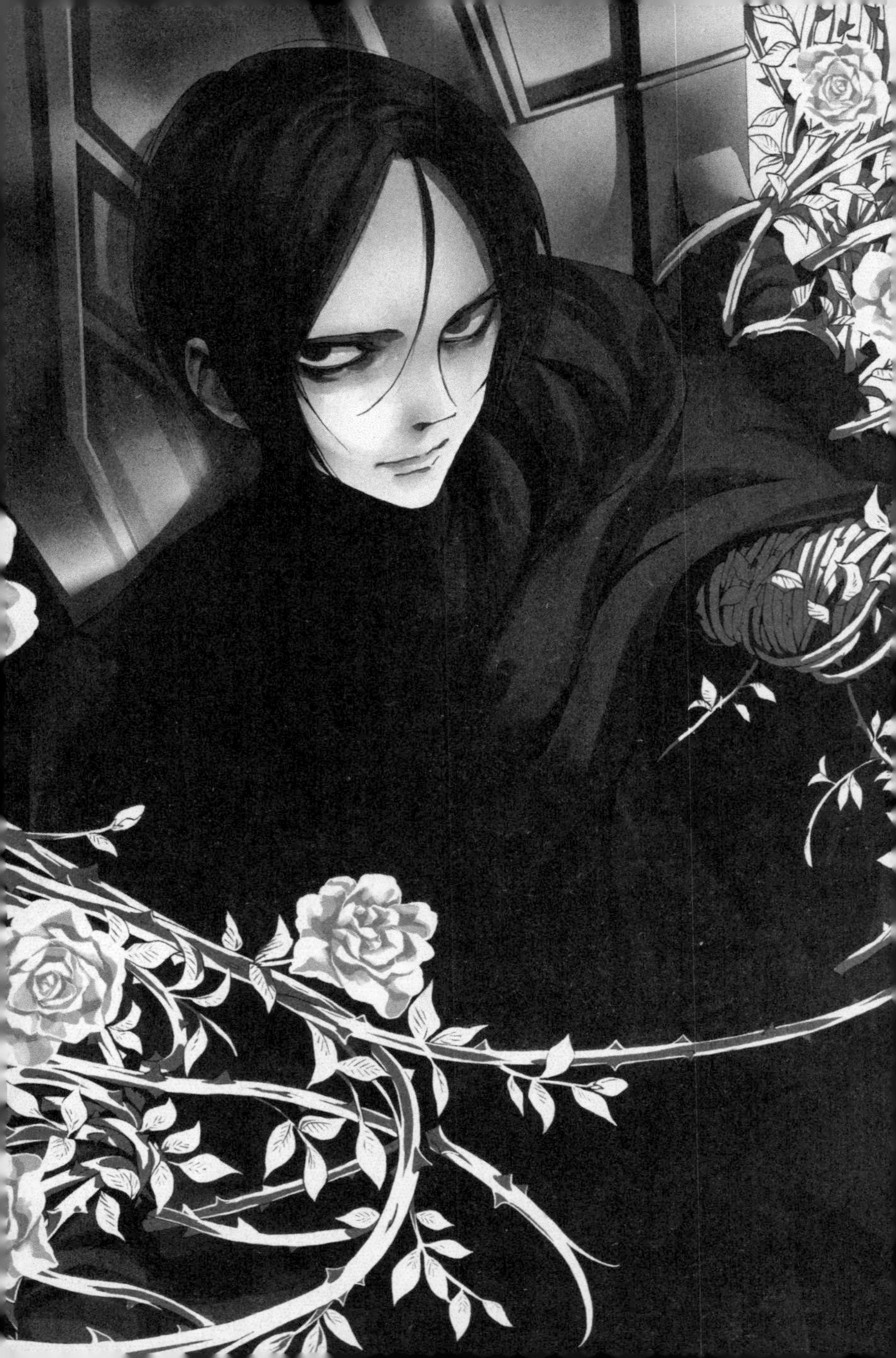

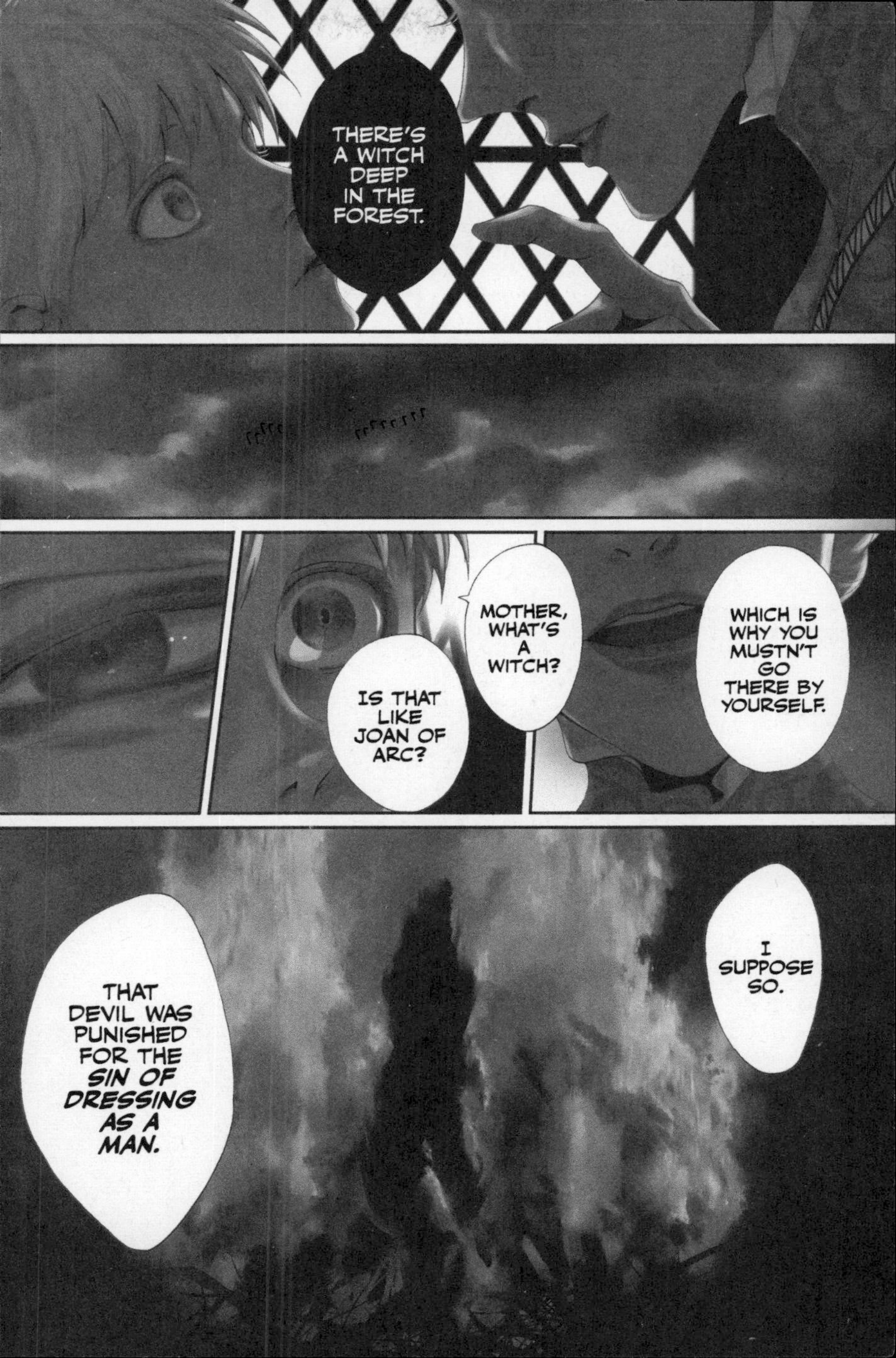
THERE'S A WITCH DEEP IN THE FOREST.
WHICH IS WHY YOU MUSTN'T GO THERE BY YOURSELF.
MOTHER, WHAT'S A WITCH?
IS THAT LIKE JOAN OF ARC?
I SUPPOSE SO.
THAT DEVIL WAS PUNISHED FOR THE *SIN OF DRESSING AS A MAN.*

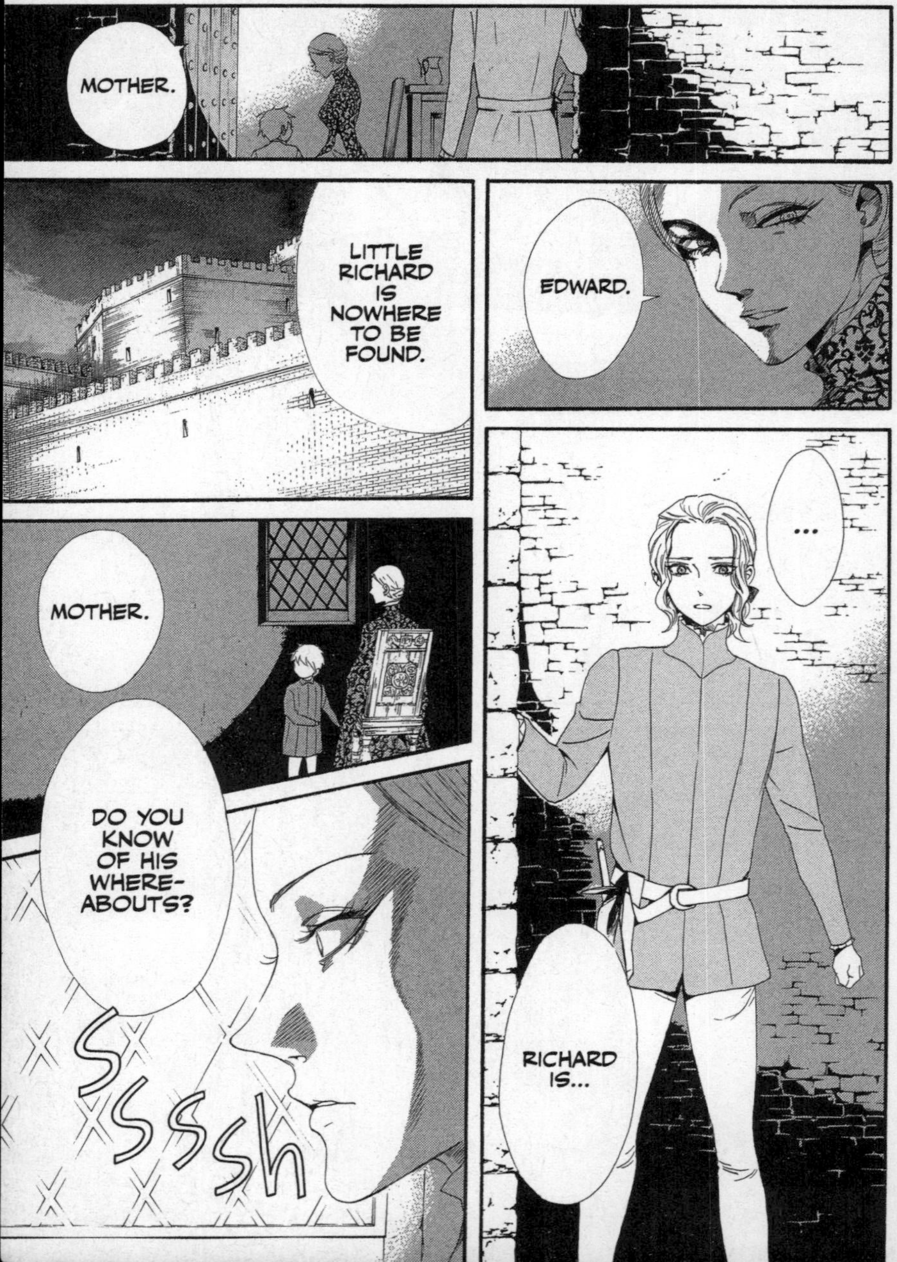
MOTHER.
EDWARD.
LITTLE RICHARD IS NOWHERE TO BE FOUND.
...
RICHARD IS...
MOTHER.
DO YOU KNOW OF HIS WHERE-ABOUTS?
Sssh

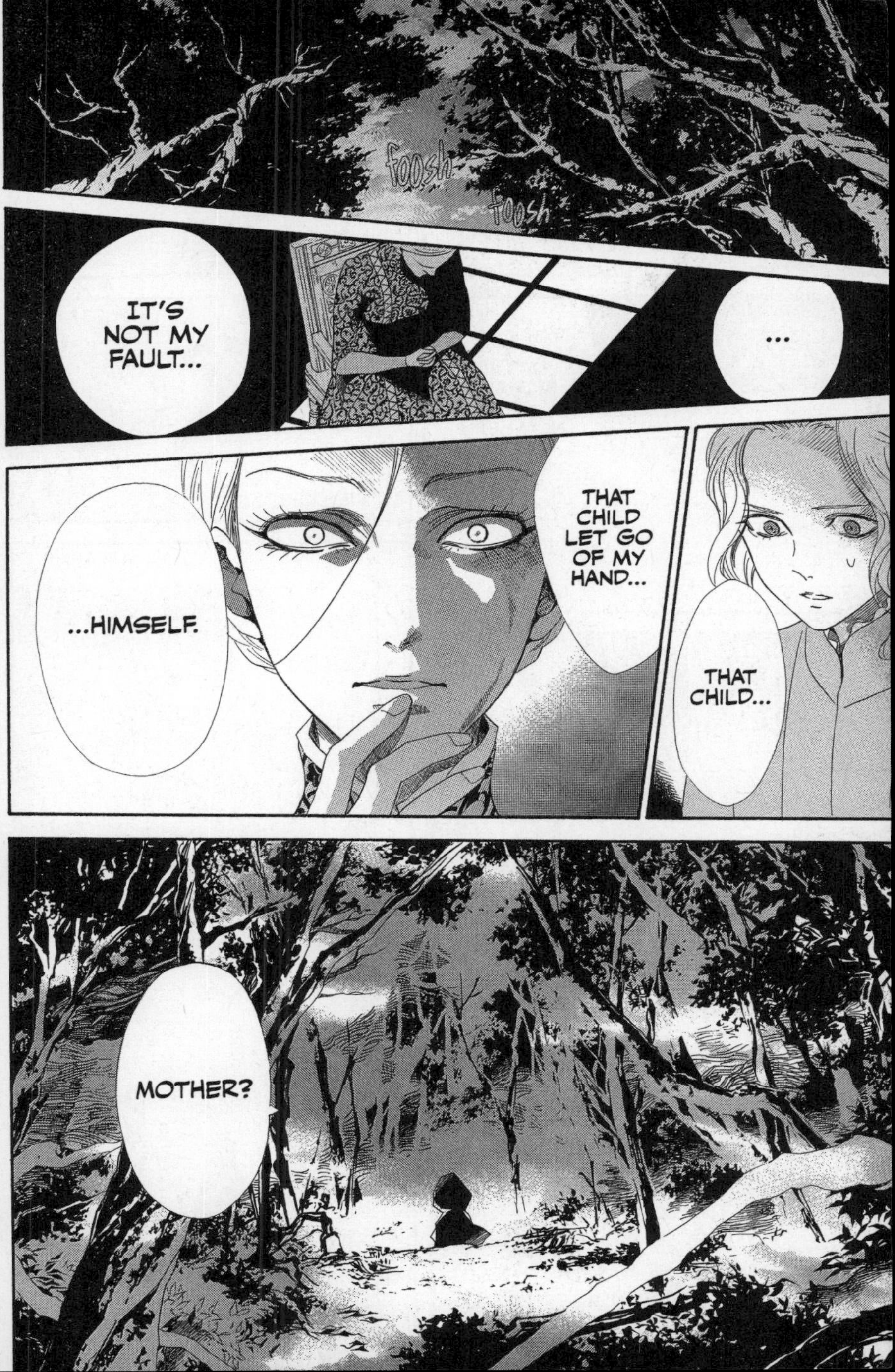
foosh
foosh
...
IT'S NOT MY FAULT...
THAT CHILD...
THAT CHILD LET GO OF MY HAND...
...HIMSELF.
MOTHER?

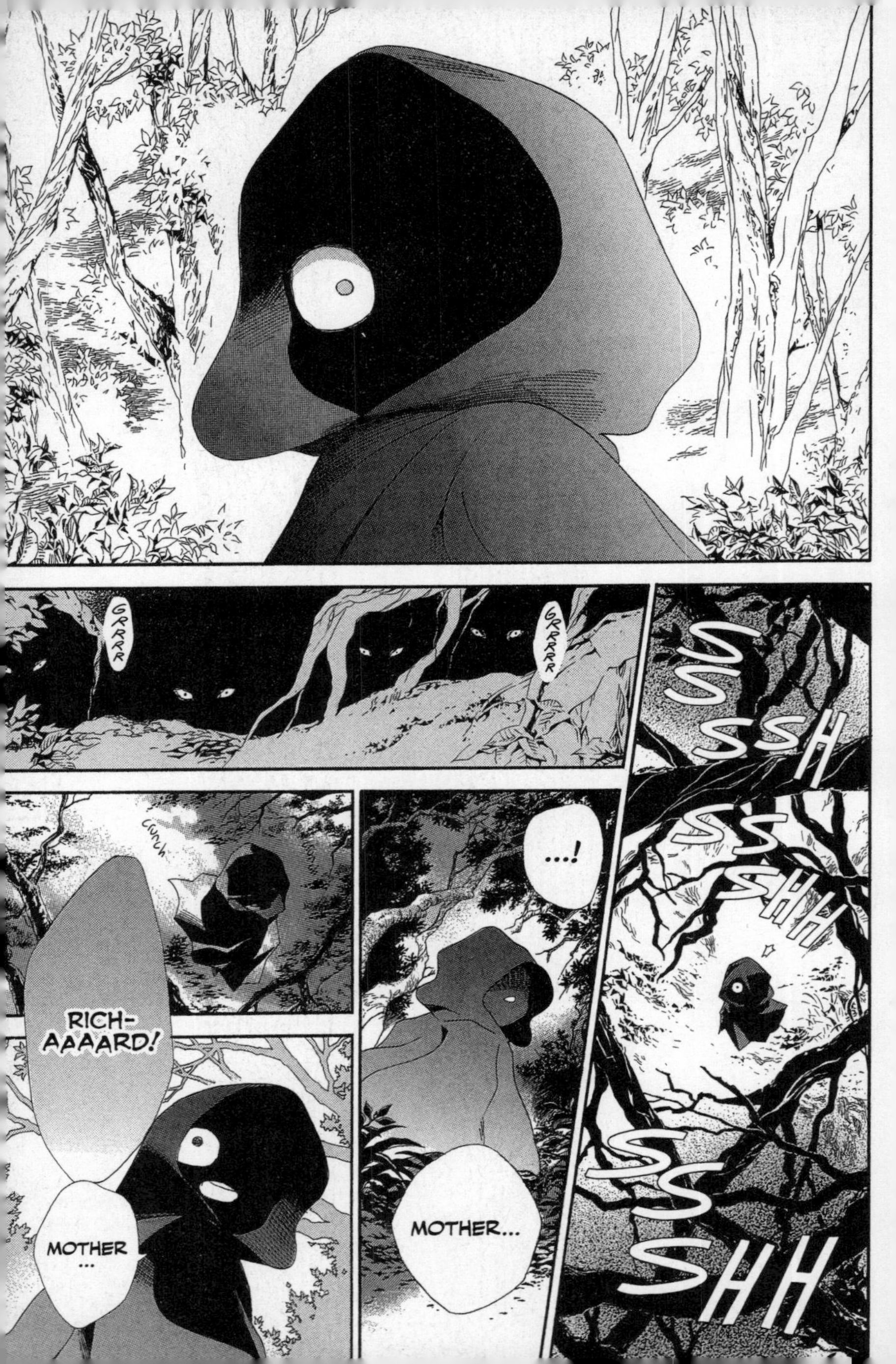

SSSH
SSSHH
SSSHH
GRRRR
GRRRRR
...!
MOTHER...
CRUNCH
RICH-AAAARD!
MOTHER ...

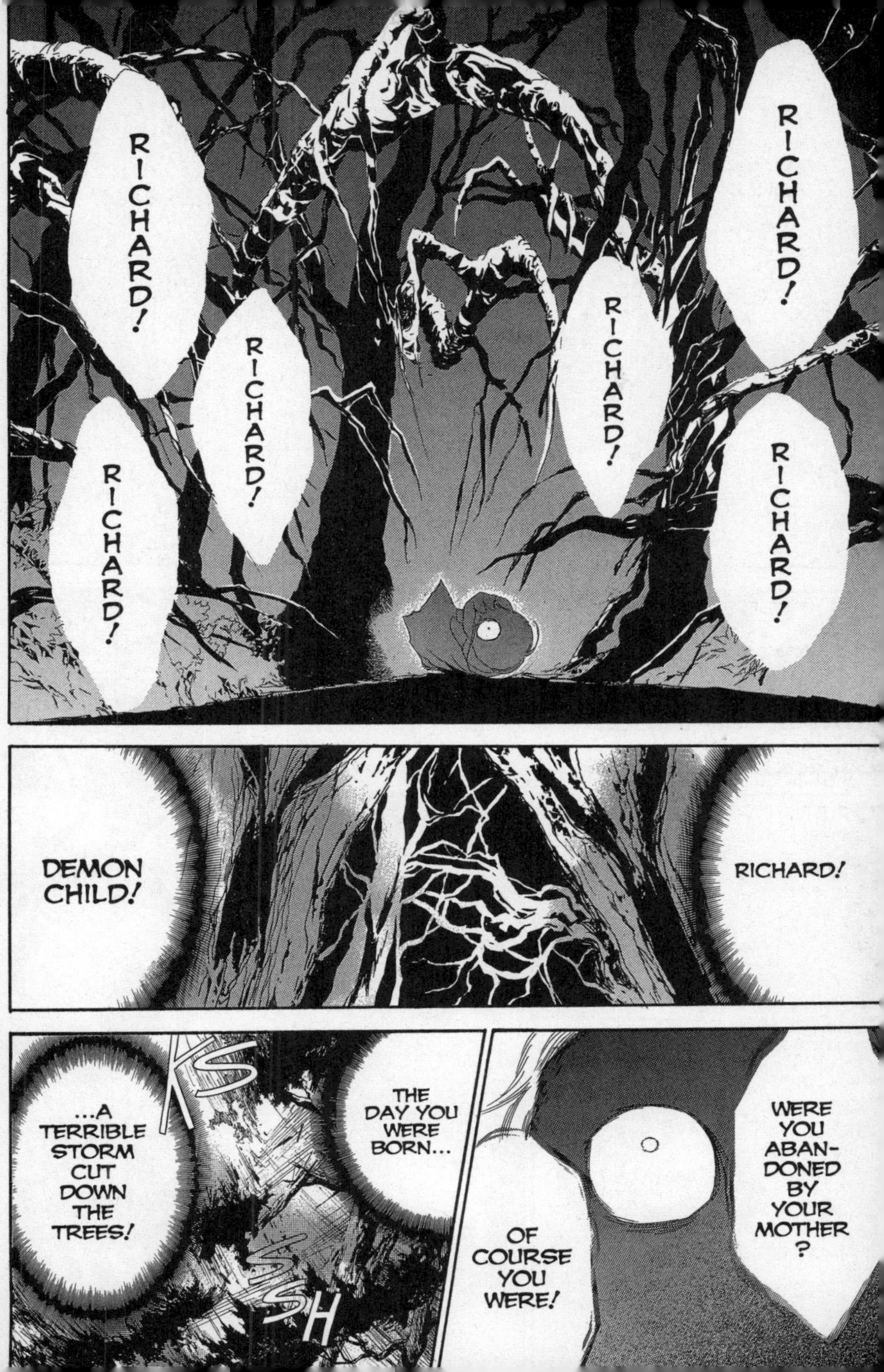
RICHARD!
RICHARD!
RICHARD!
RICHARD!
RICHARD!
RICHARD!
RICHARD!
DEMON CHILD!
WERE YOU ABANDONED BY YOUR MOTHER?
OF COURSE YOU WERE!
THE DAY YOU WERE BORN...
...A TERRIBLE STORM CUT DOWN THE TREES!
KSSH

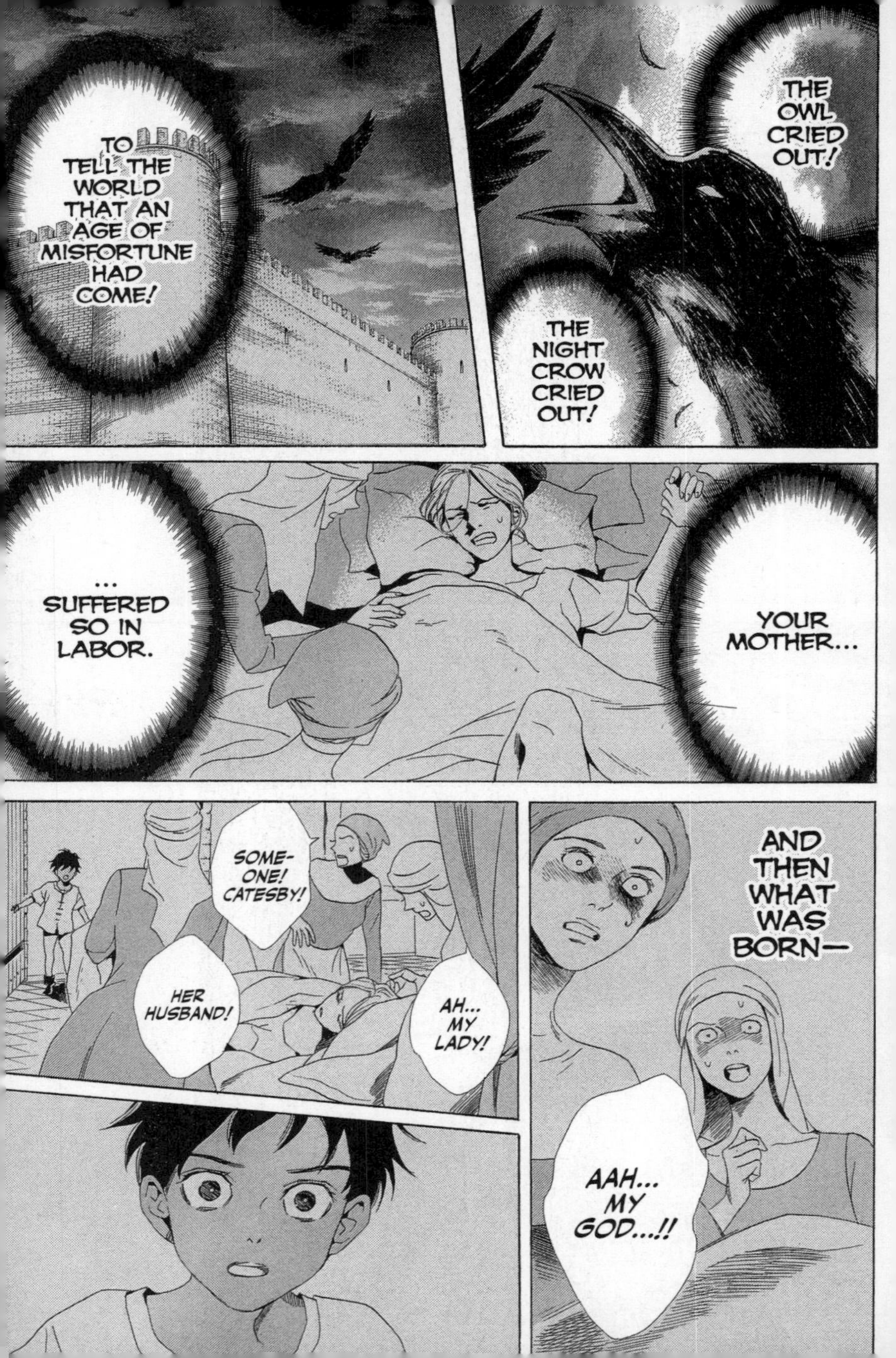
THE OWL CRIED OUT!
THE NIGHT CROW CRIED OUT!
TO TELL THE WORLD THAT AN AGE OF MISFORTUNE HAD COME!
YOUR MOTHER...
... SUFFERED SO IN LABOR.
AND THEN WHAT WAS BORN—
AAH... MY GOD...!!
SOME-ONE! CATESBY!
AH... MY LADY!
HER HUSBAND!

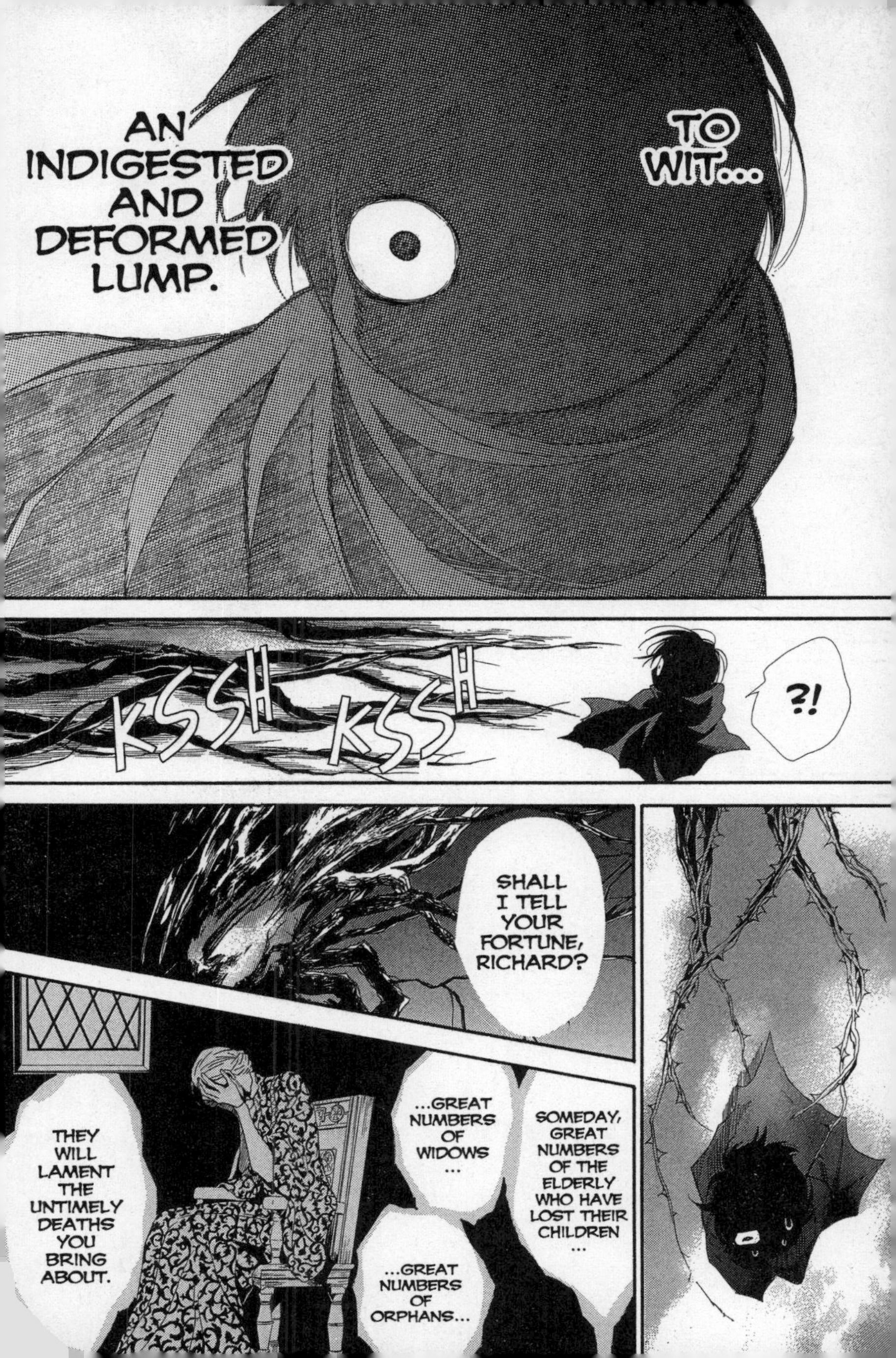
TO WIT...
AN INDIGESTED AND DEFORMED LUMP.
?!
KSSH KSSH
SHALL I TELL YOUR FORTUNE, RICHARD?
SOMEDAY, GREAT NUMBERS OF THE ELDERLY WHO HAVE LOST THEIR CHILDREN...
...GREAT NUMBERS OF WIDOWS...
...GREAT NUMBERS OF ORPHANS...
THEY WILL LAMENT THE UNTIMELY DEATHS YOU BRING ABOUT.

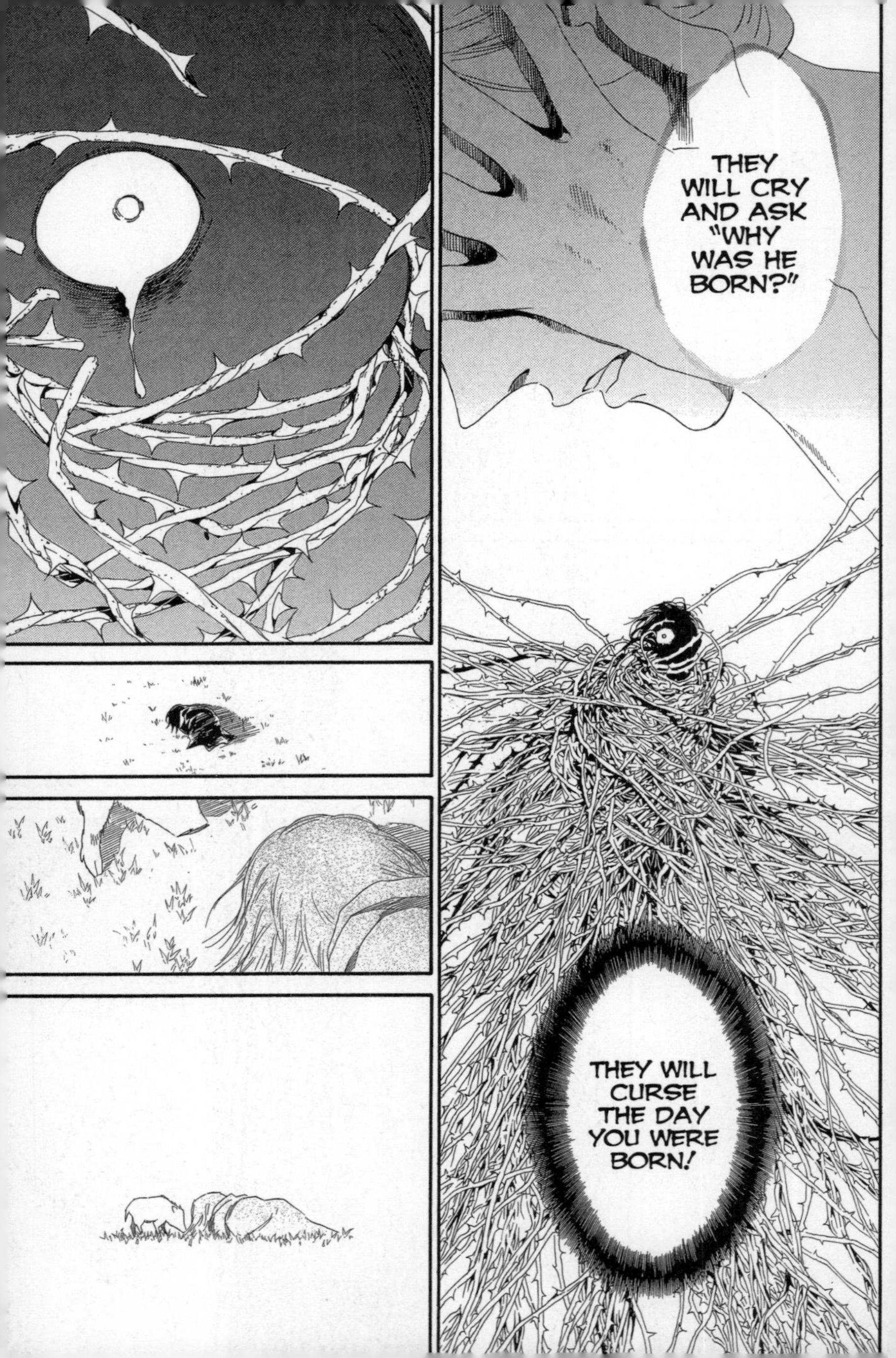
THEY WILL CRY AND ASK "WHY WAS HE BORN?"
THEY WILL CURSE THE DAY YOU WERE BORN!

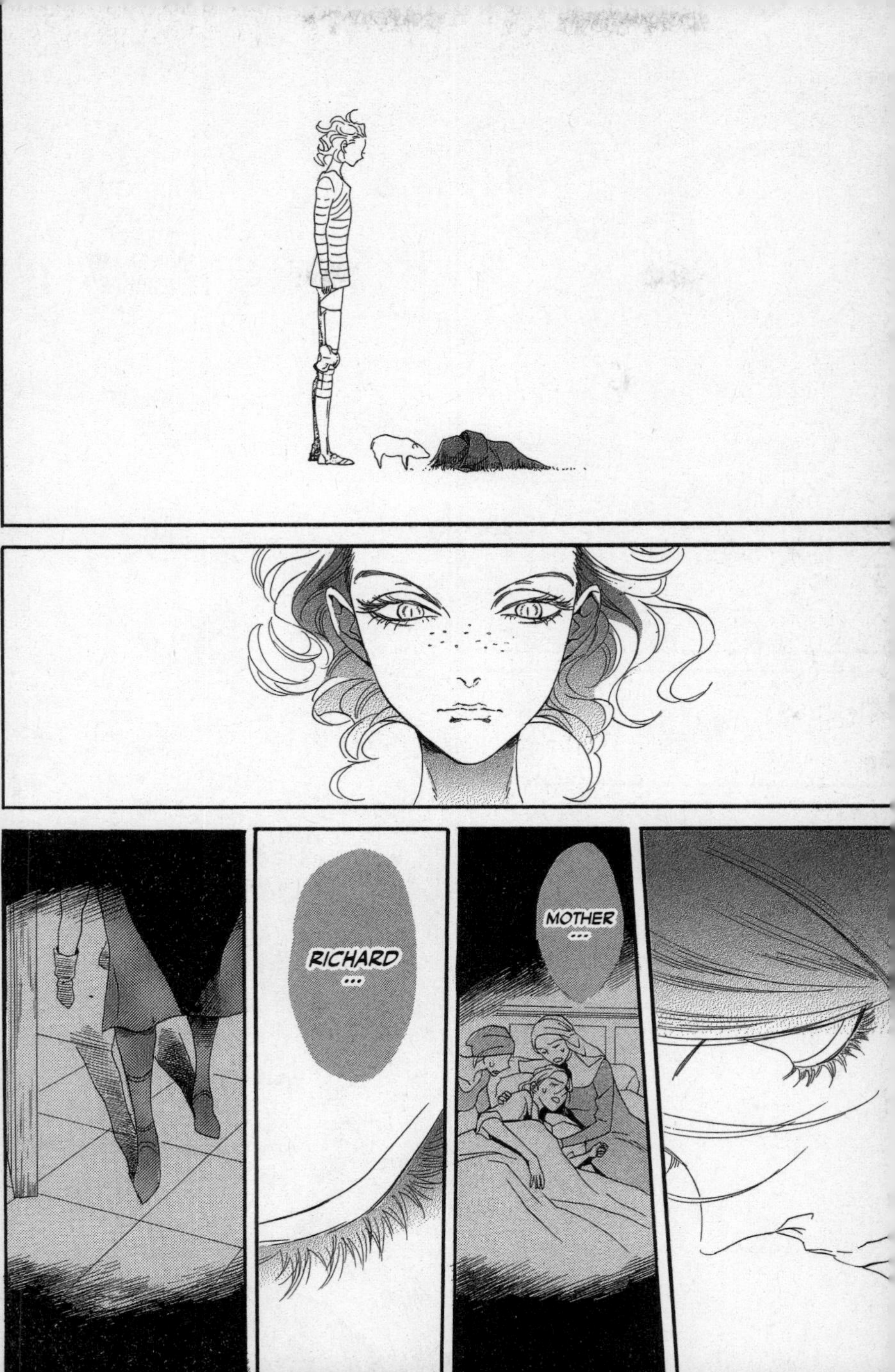
MOTHER ...
RICHARD ...

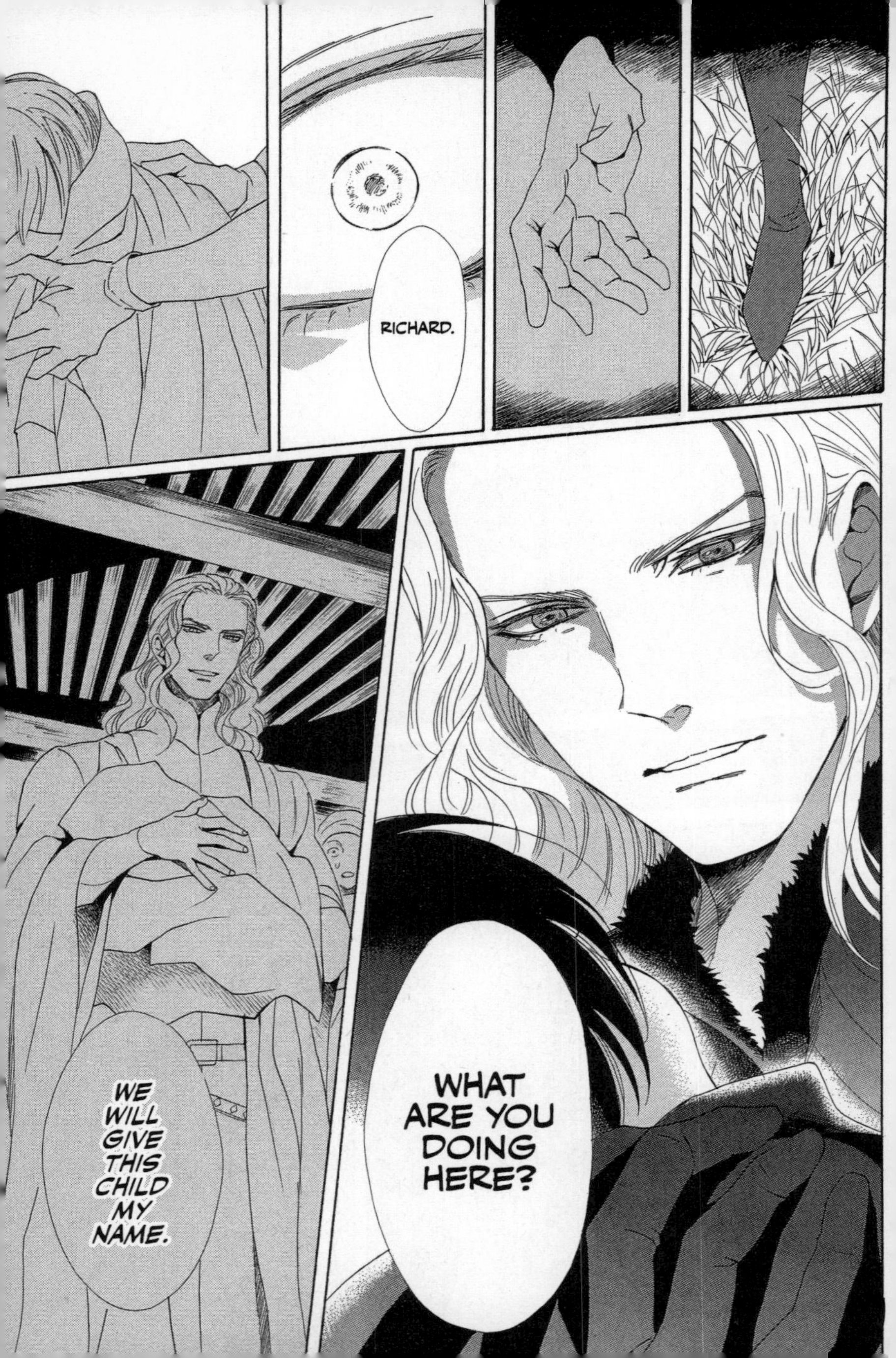
RICHARD.
WHAT ARE YOU DOING HERE?
WE WILL GIVE THIS CHILD MY NAME.

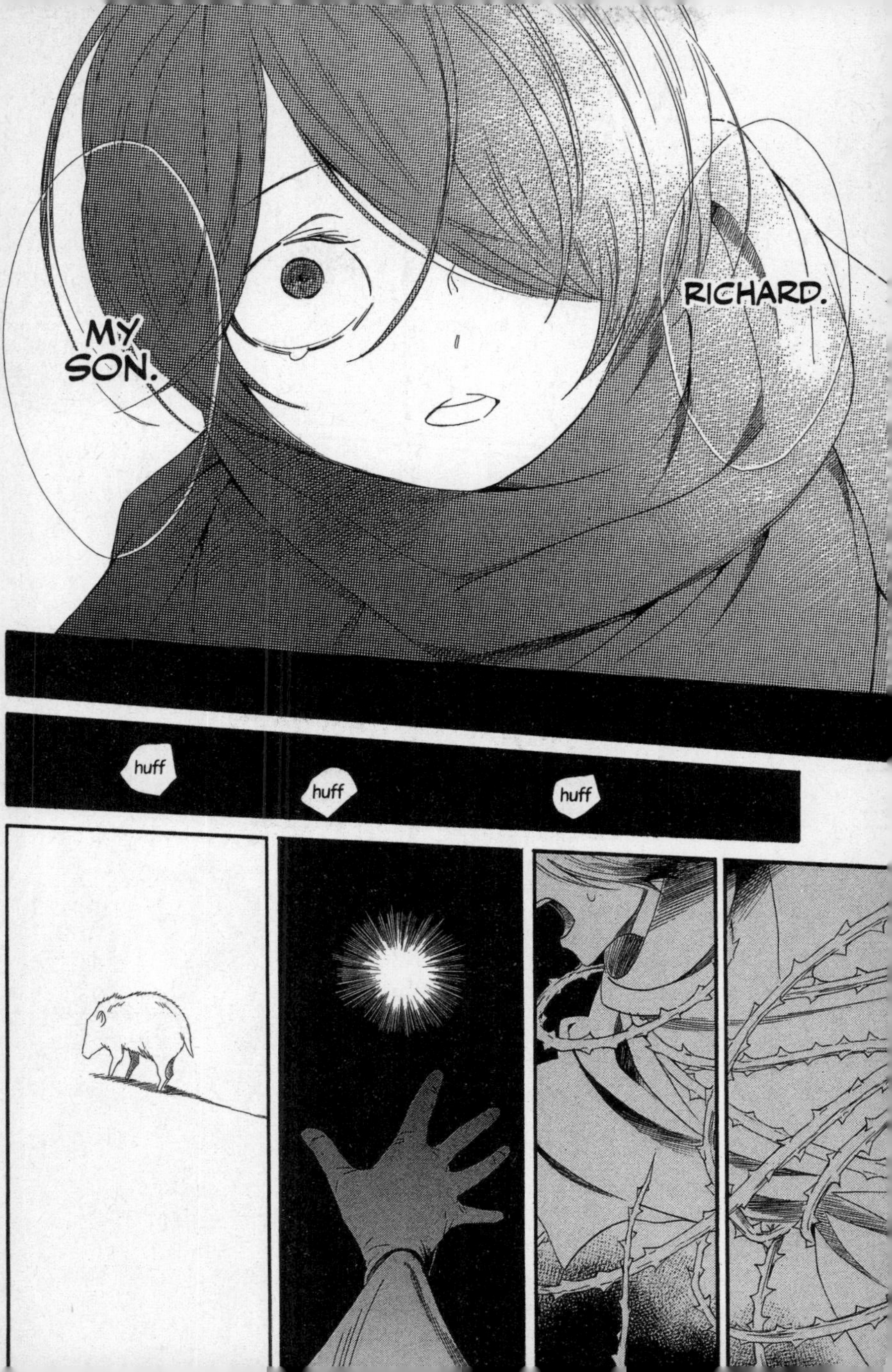
RICHARD.
MY SON.
huff
huff
huff

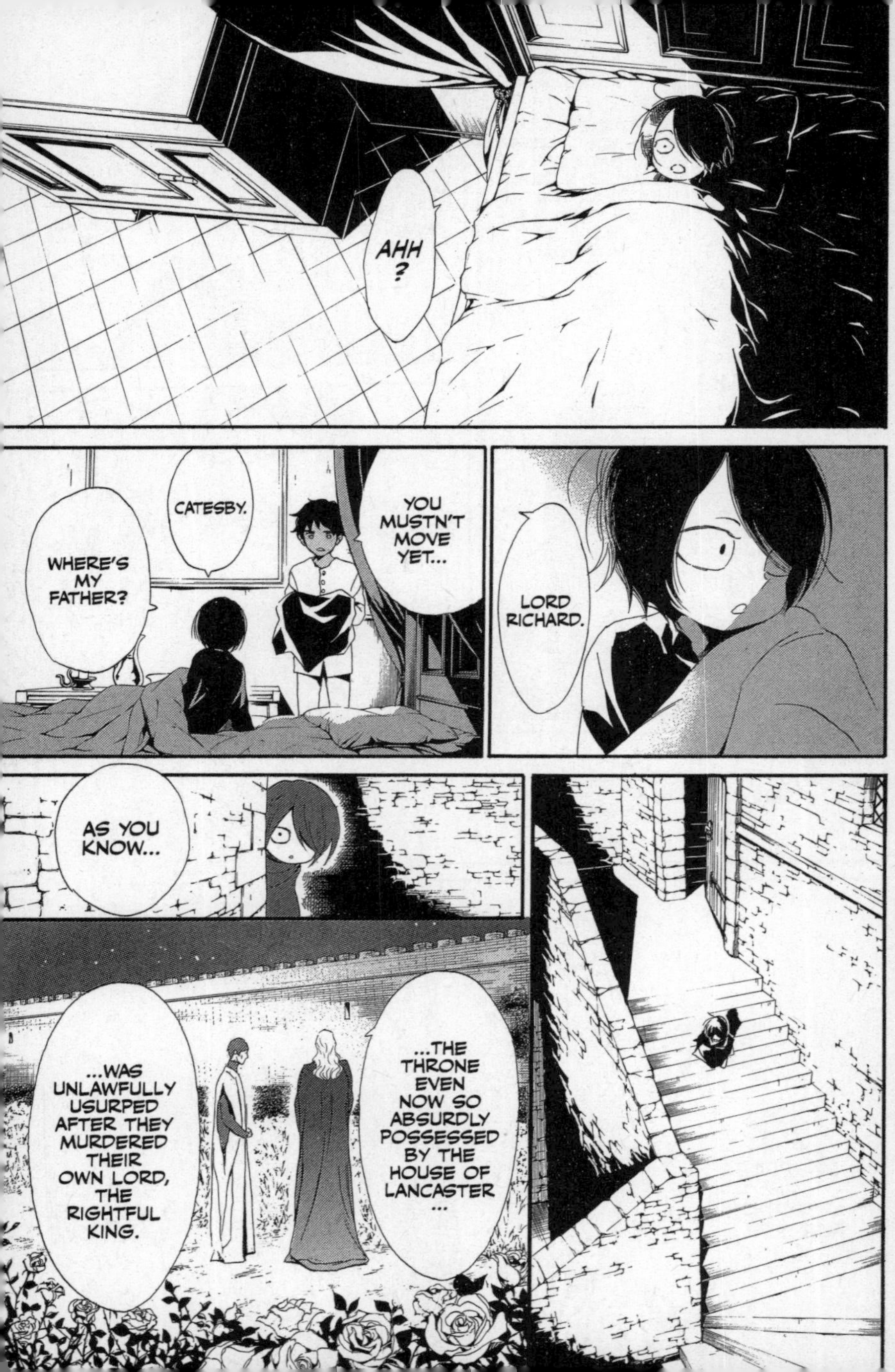
AHH ?
LORD RICHARD.
YOU MUSTN'T MOVE YET...
CATESBY.
WHERE'S MY FATHER?
AS YOU KNOW...
...THE THRONE EVEN NOW SO ABSURDLY POSSESSED BY THE HOUSE OF LANCASTER ...
...WAS UNLAWFULLY USURPED AFTER THEY MURDERED THEIR OWN LORD, THE RIGHTFUL KING.

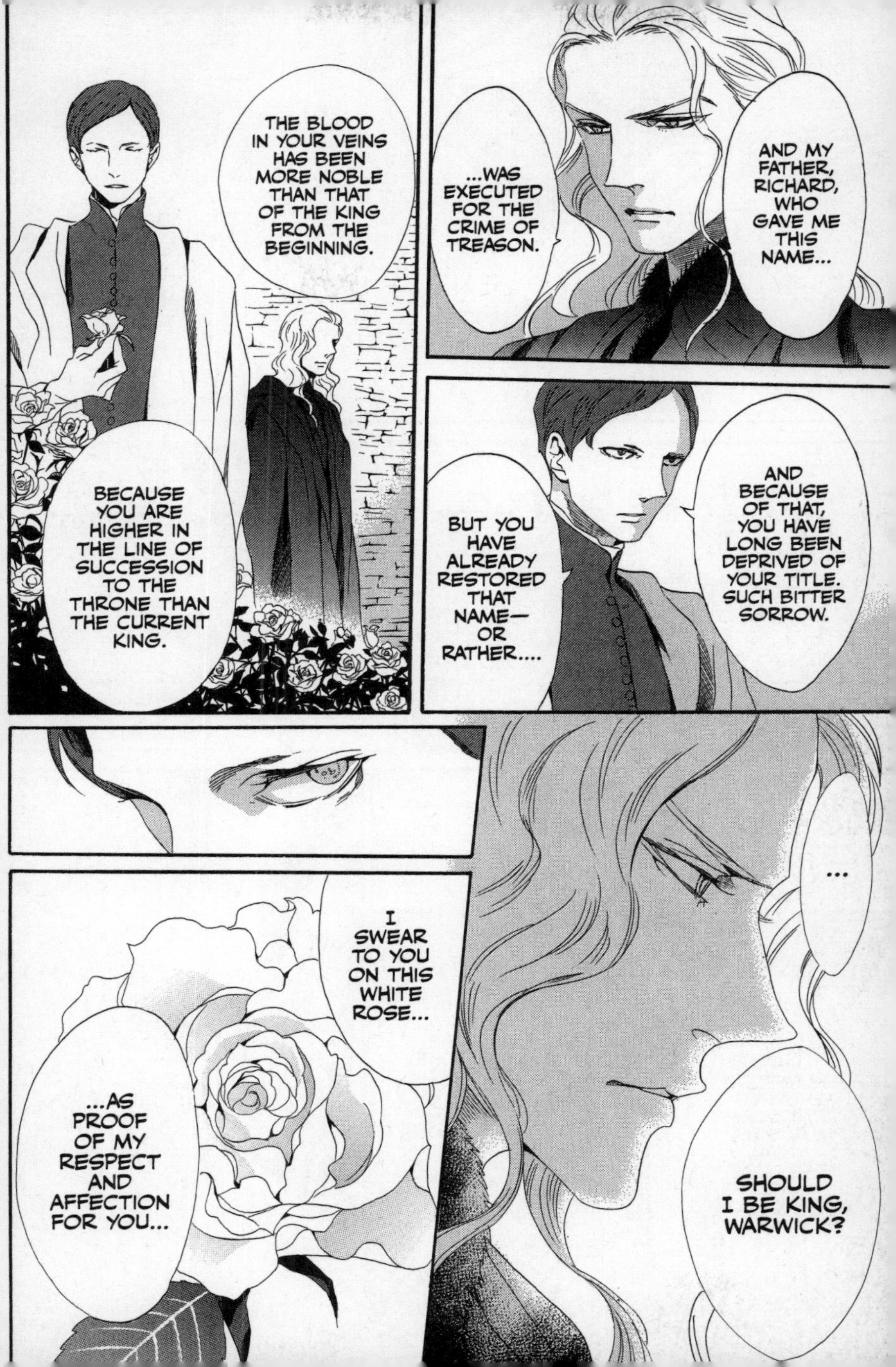
AND MY FATHER, RICHARD, WHO GAVE ME THIS NAME...
...WAS EXECUTED FOR THE CRIME OF TREASON.
AND BECAUSE OF THAT, YOU HAVE LONG BEEN DEPRIVED OF YOUR TITLE. SUCH BITTER SORROW.
BUT YOU HAVE ALREADY RESTORED THAT NAME— OR RATHER....
THE BLOOD IN YOUR VEINS HAS BEEN MORE NOBLE THAN THAT OF THE KING FROM THE BEGINNING.
BECAUSE YOU ARE HIGHER IN THE LINE OF SUCCESSION TO THE THRONE THAN THE CURRENT KING.
...
SHOULD I BE KING, WARWICK?
I SWEAR TO YOU ON THIS WHITE ROSE...
...AS PROOF OF MY RESPECT AND AFFECTION FOR YOU...

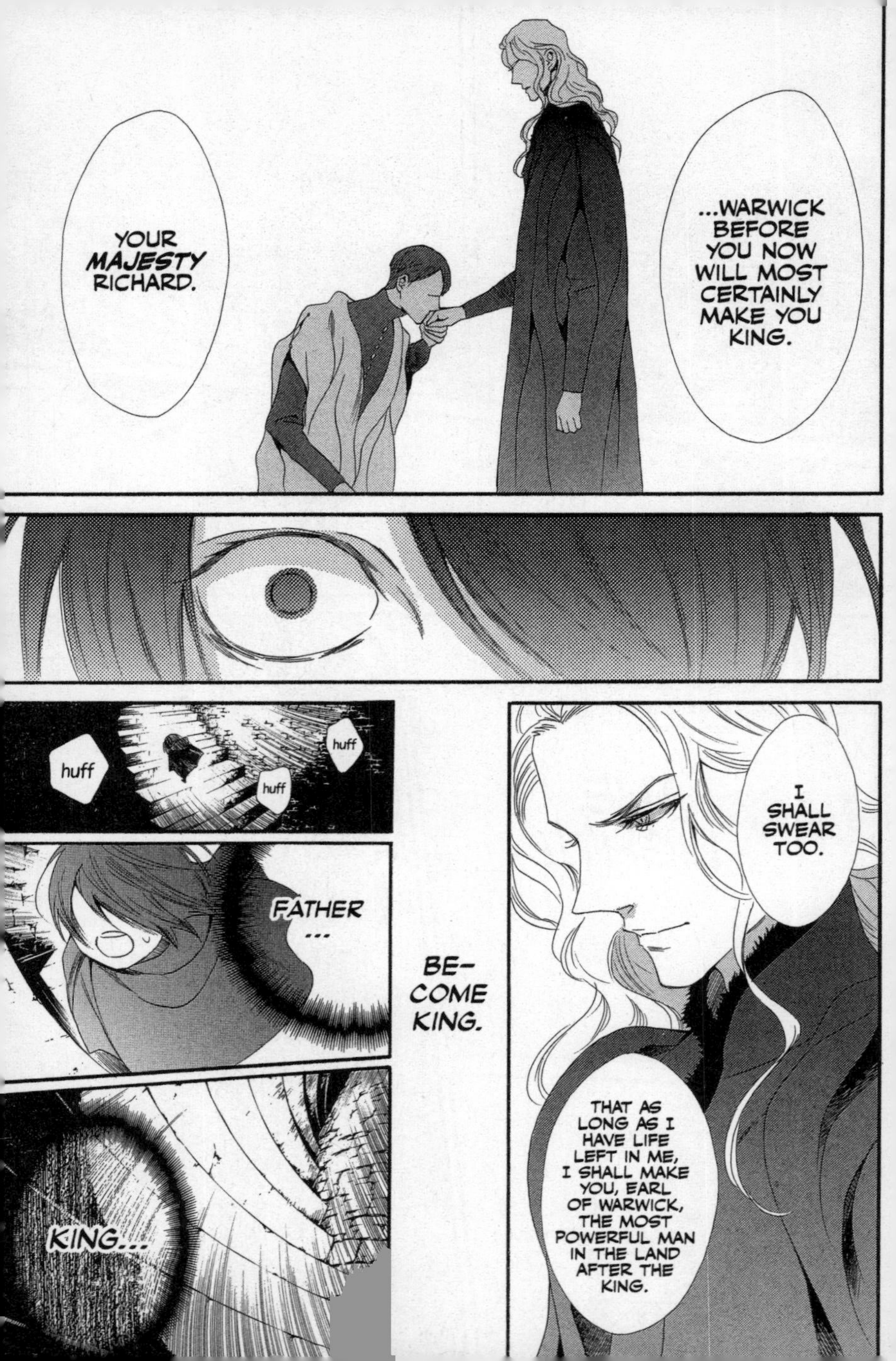
...WARWICK BEFORE YOU NOW WILL MOST CERTAINLY MAKE YOU KING.
YOUR MAJESTY RICHARD.
I SHALL SWEAR TOO.
THAT AS LONG AS I HAVE LIFE LEFT IN ME, I SHALL MAKE YOU, EARL OF WARWICK, THE MOST POWERFUL MAN IN THE LAND AFTER THE KING.
huff
huff
huff
FATHER...
BE-COME KING.
KING...

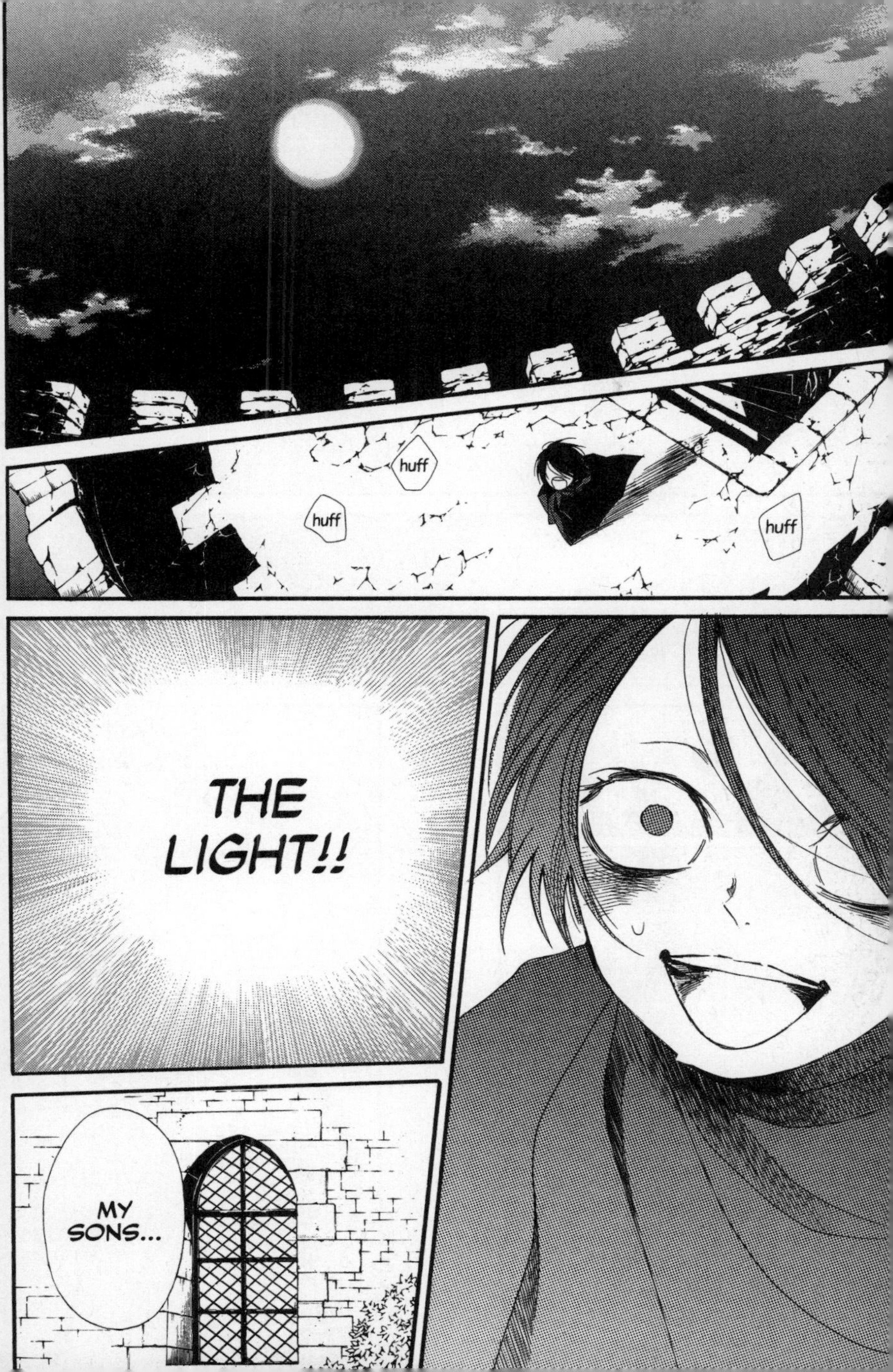
huff
huff
huff
THE LIGHT!!
MY SONS...

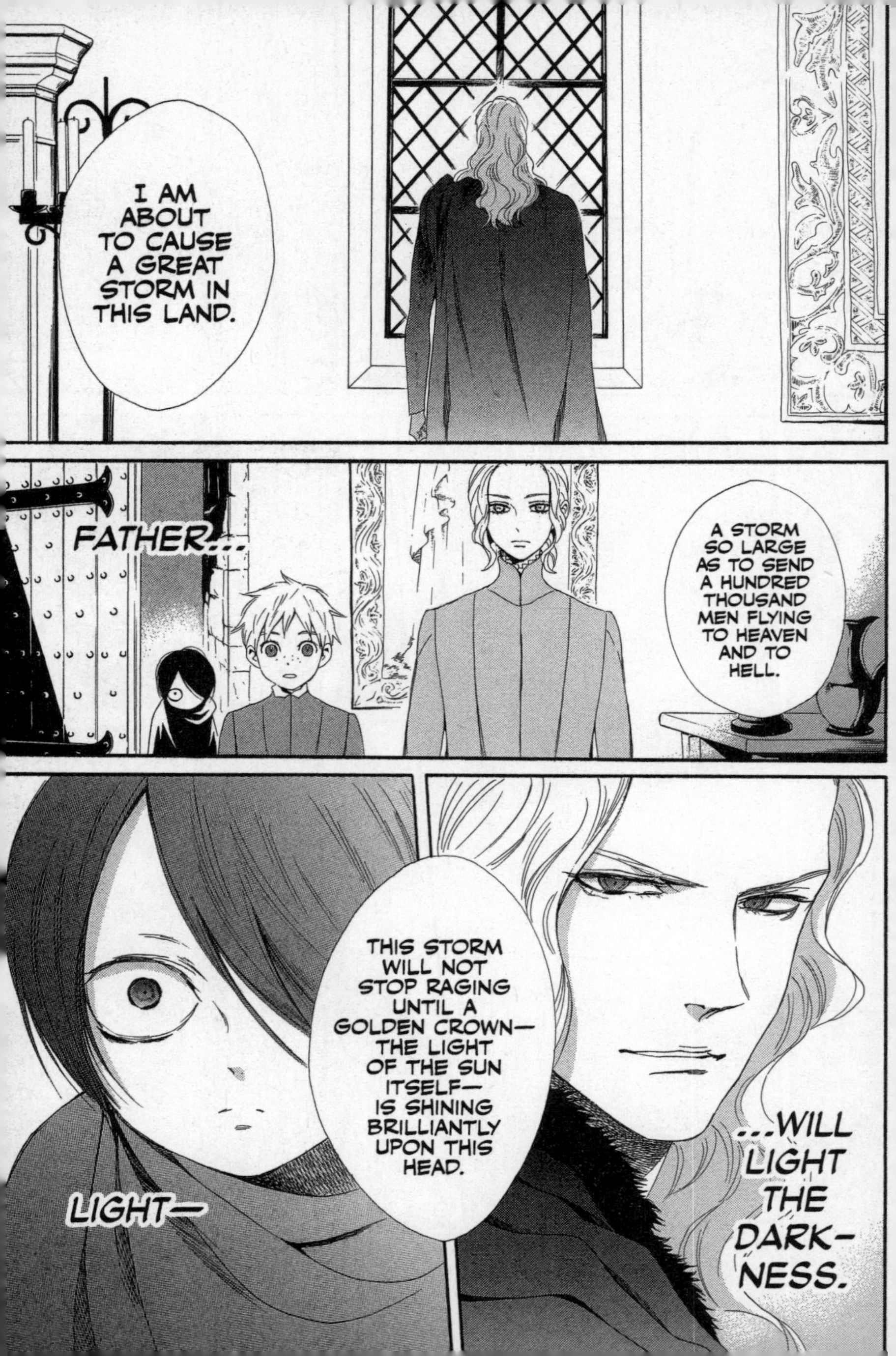
I AM ABOUT TO CAUSE A GREAT STORM IN THIS LAND.
A STORM SO LARGE AS TO SEND A HUNDRED THOUSAND MEN FLYING TO HEAVEN AND TO HELL.
FATHER...
THIS STORM WILL NOT STOP RAGING UNTIL A GOLDEN CROWN—THE LIGHT OF THE SUN ITSELF—IS SHINING BRILLIANTLY UPON THIS HEAD.
...WILL LIGHT THE DARK-NESS.
LIGHT—

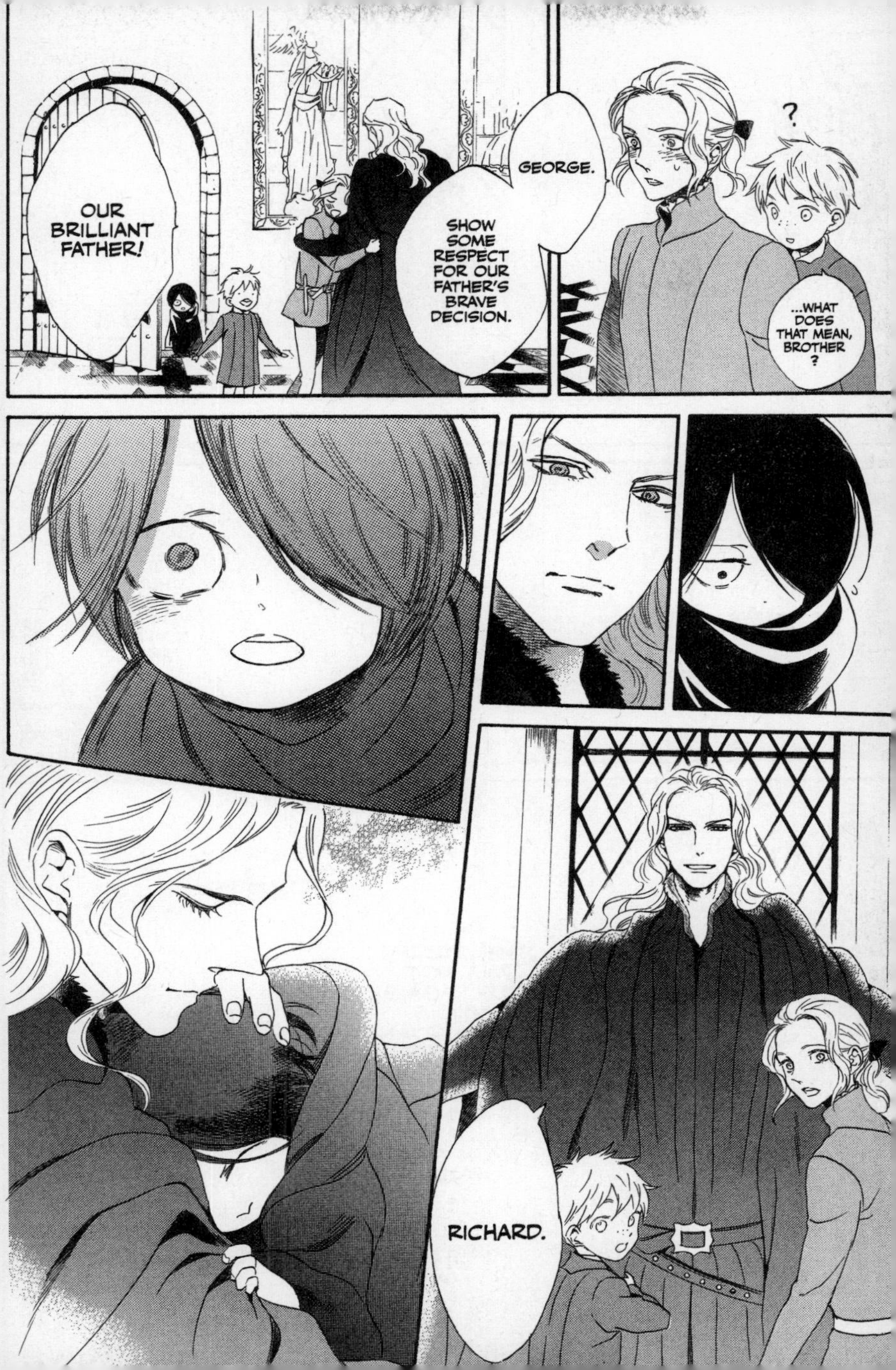
?
GEORGE.
SHOW SOME RESPECT FOR OUR FATHER'S BRAVE DECISION.
...WHAT DOES THAT MEAN, BROTHER?
OUR BRILLIANT FATHER!
RICHARD.

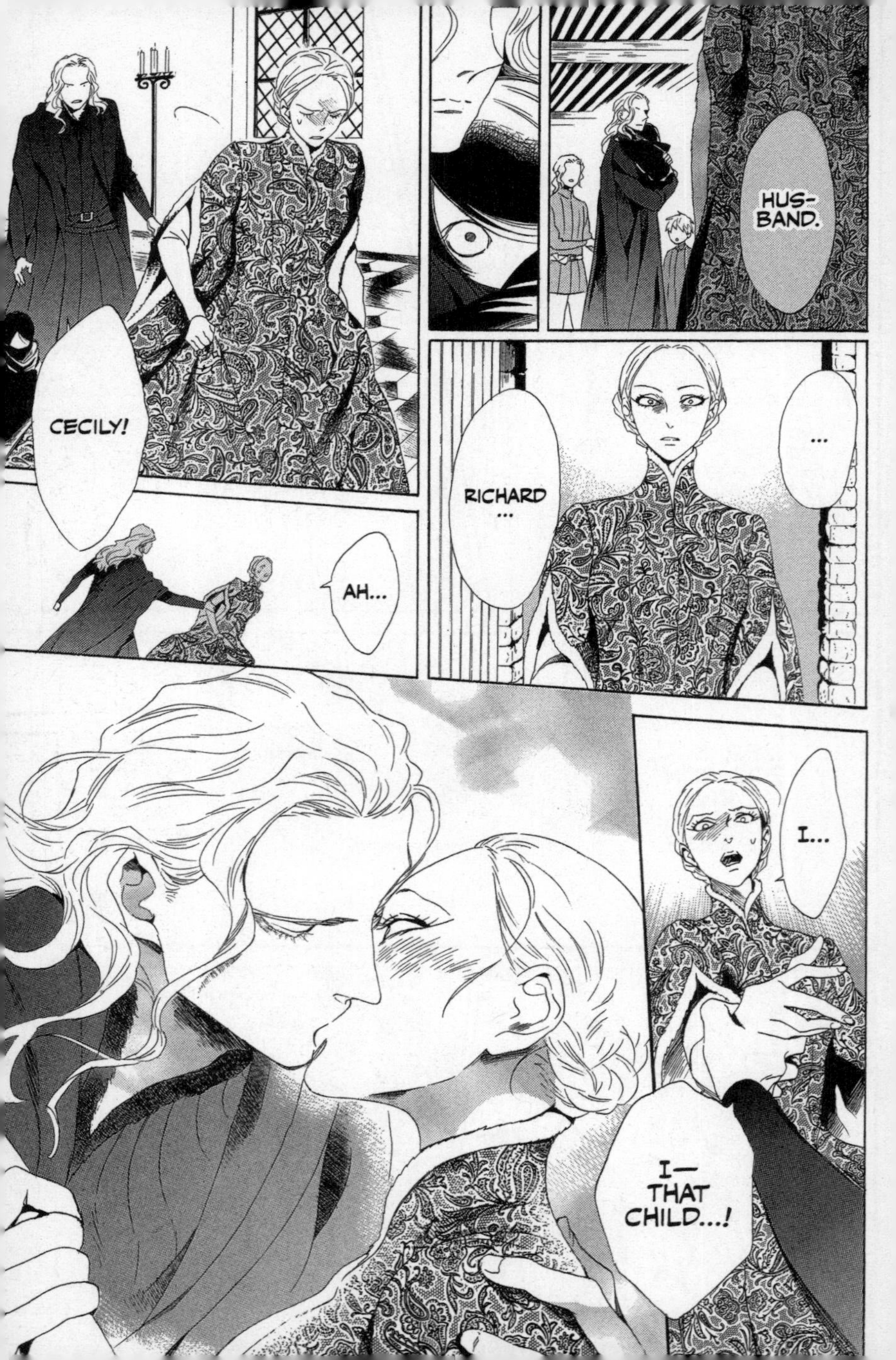
HUS-BAND.
CECILY!
...
RICHARD ...
AH...
I...
I— THAT CHILD...!

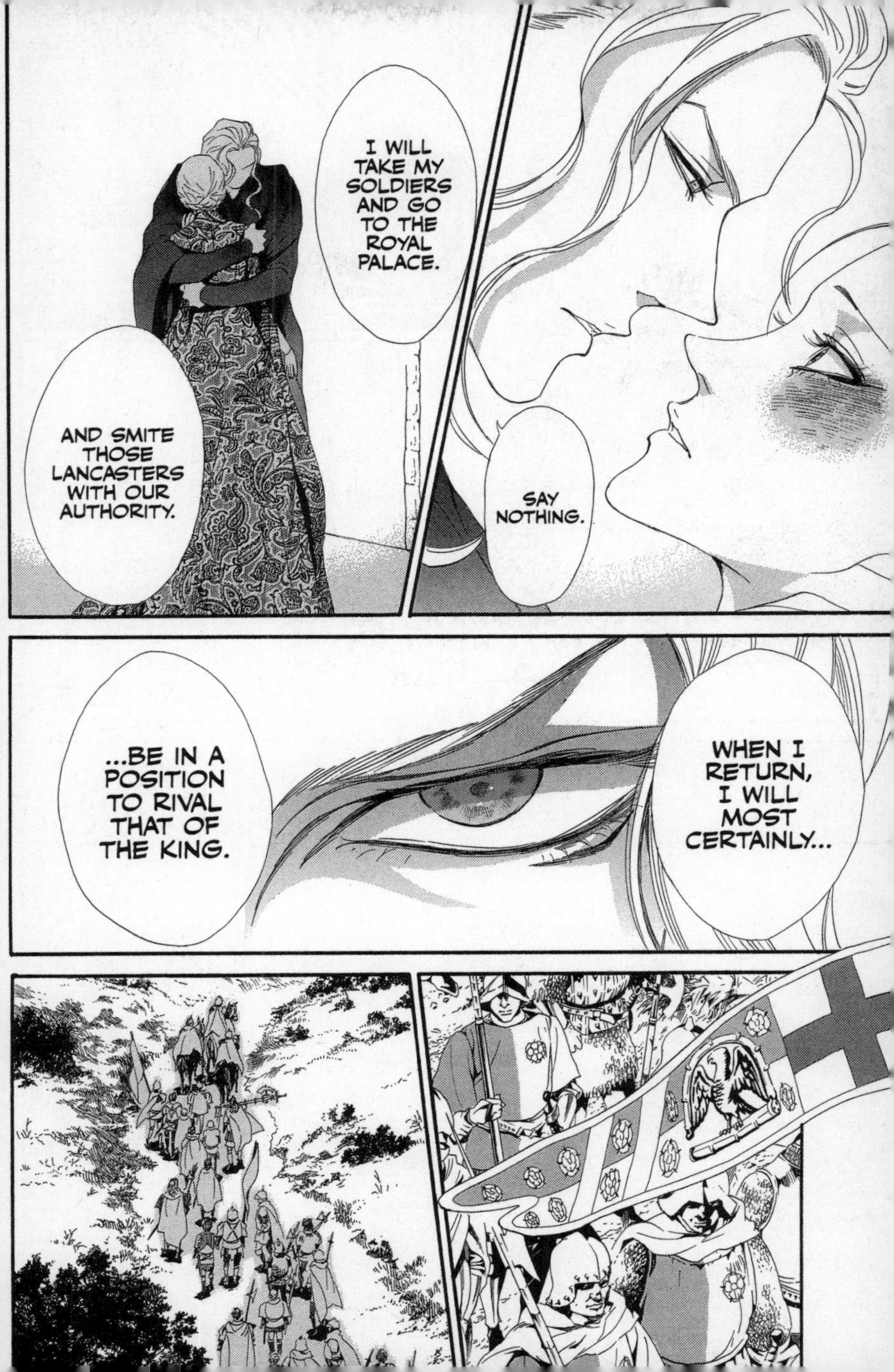
SAY NOTHING.
I WILL TAKE MY SOLDIERS AND GO TO THE ROYAL PALACE.
AND SMITE THOSE LANCASTERS WITH OUR AUTHORITY.
WHEN I RETURN, I WILL MOST CERTAINLY...
...BE IN A POSITION TO RIVAL THAT OF THE KING.

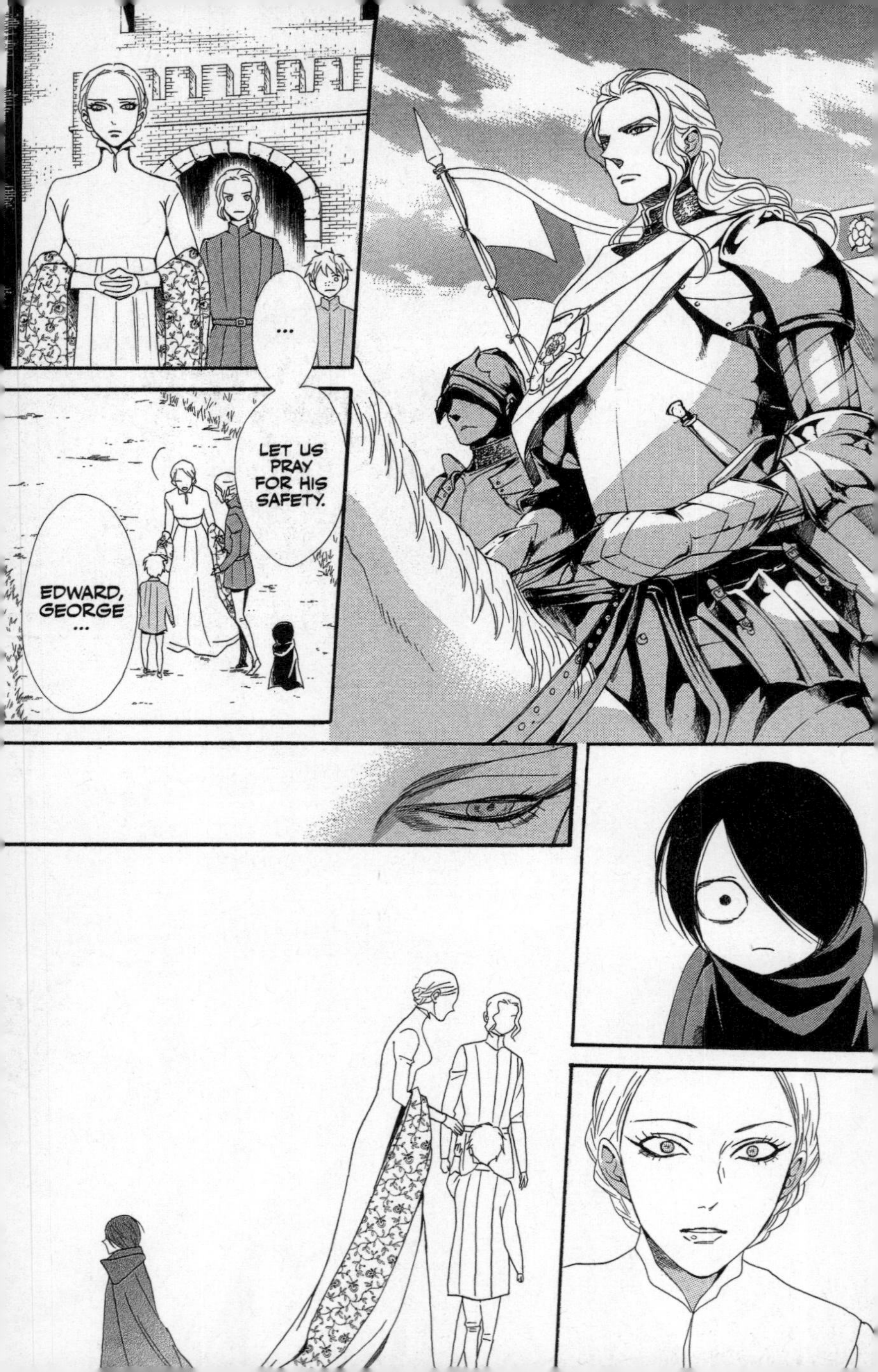
...
LET US PRAY FOR HIS SAFETY.
EDWARD, GEORGE ...

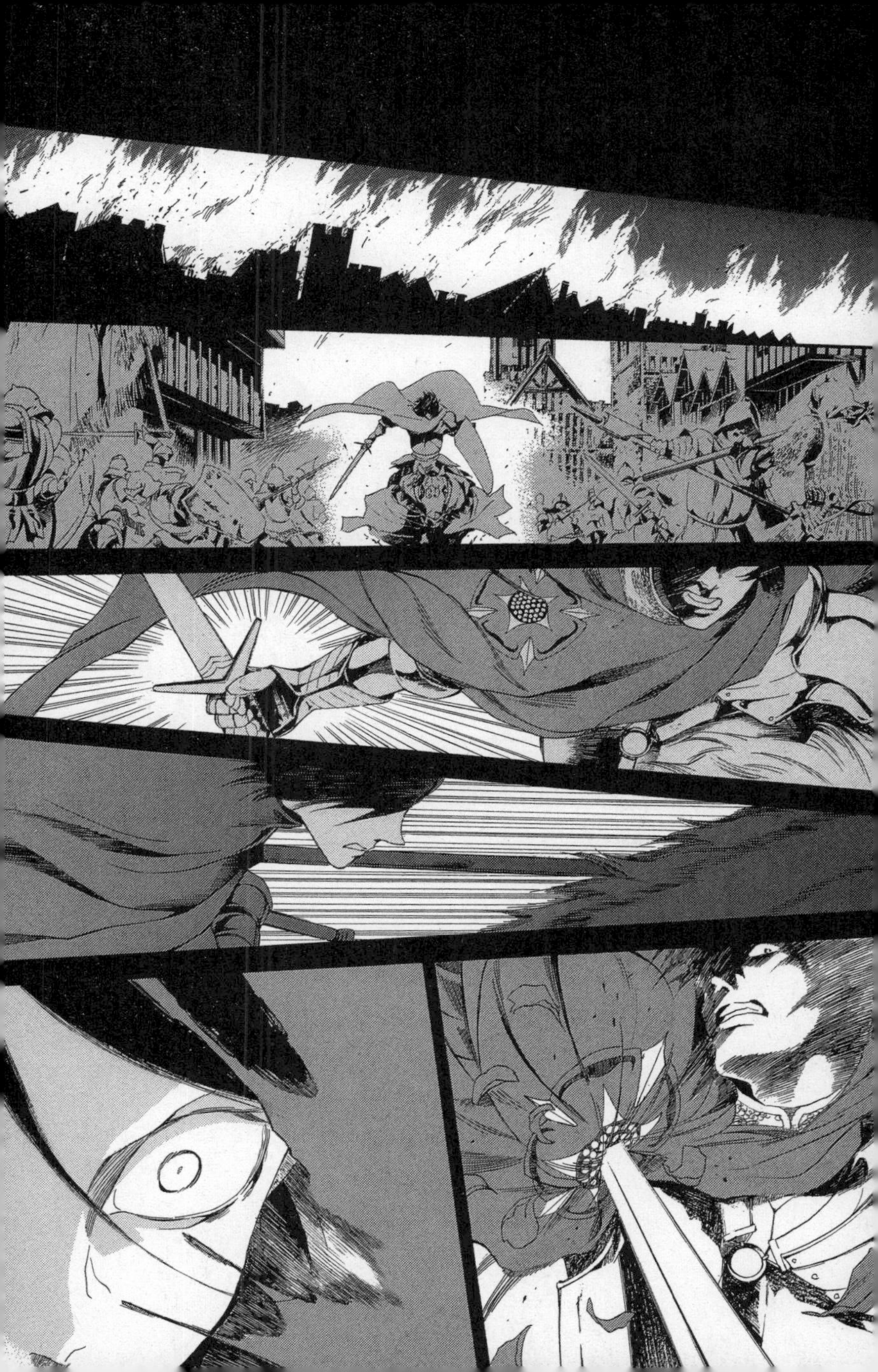

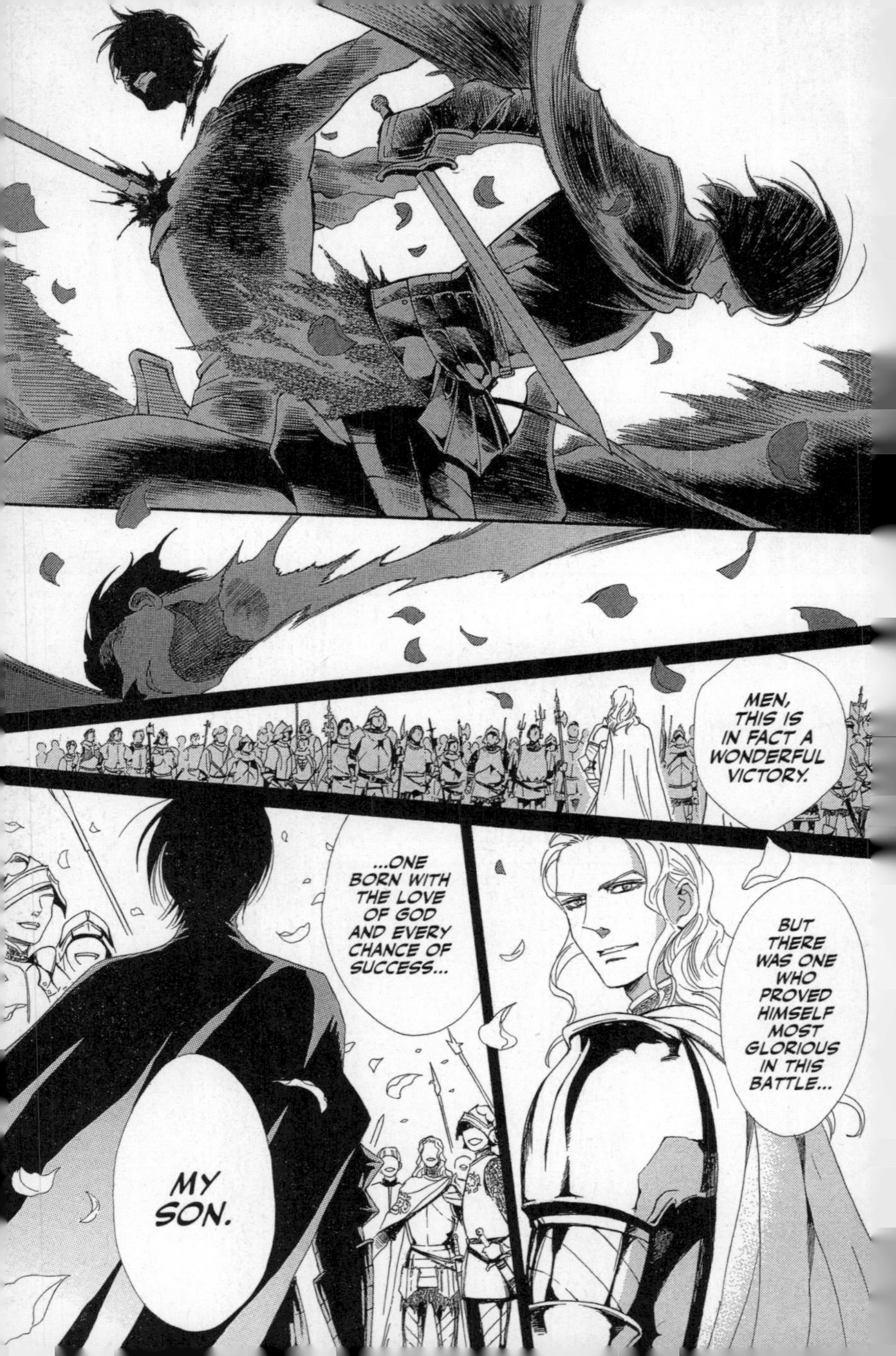
MEN, THIS IS IN FACT A WONDERFUL VICTORY.
BUT THERE WAS ONE WHO PROVED HIMSELF MOST GLORIOUS IN THIS BATTLE...
...ONE BORN WITH THE LOVE OF GOD AND EVERY CHANCE OF SUCCESS...
MY SON.

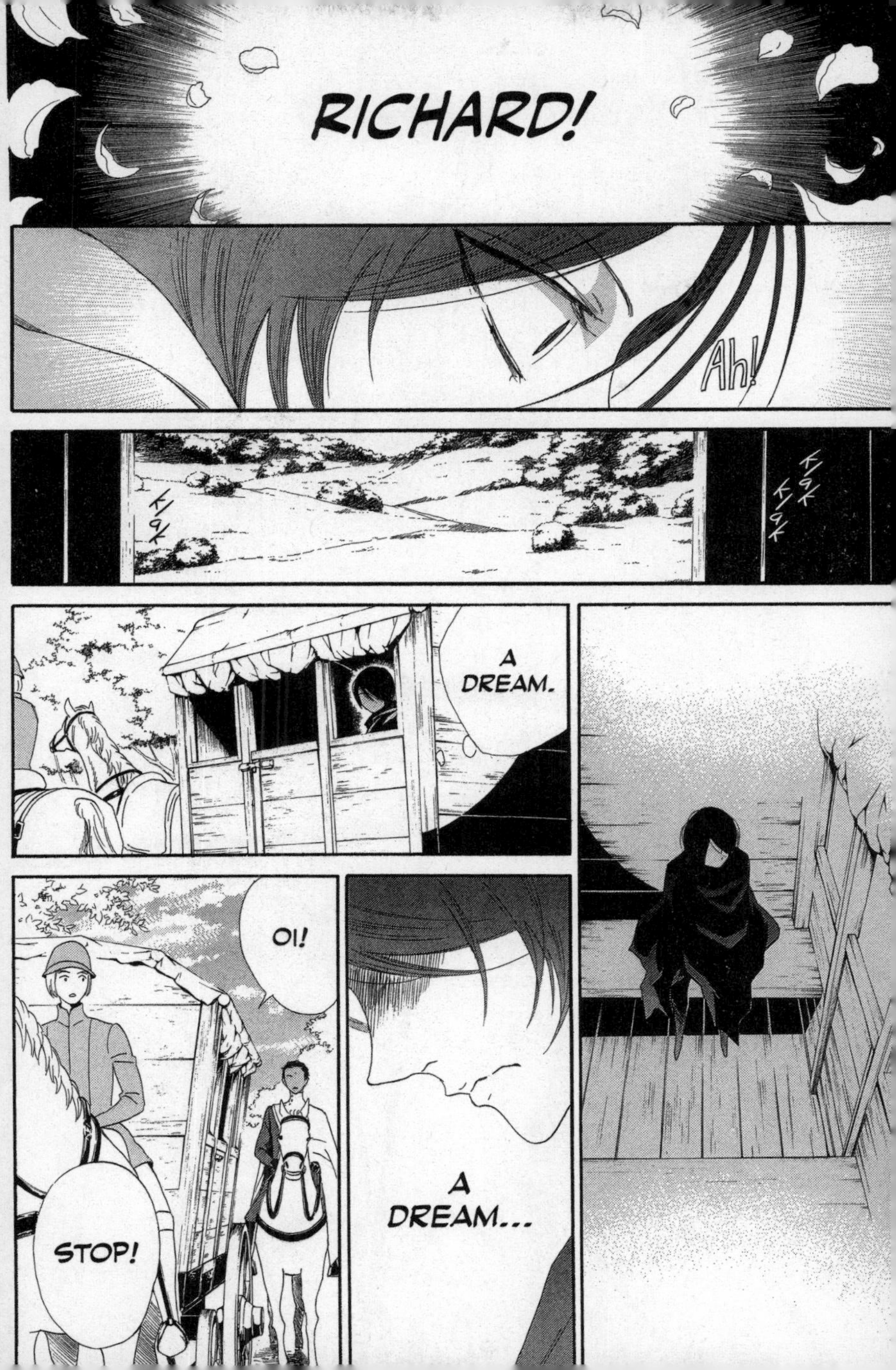
RICHARD!
Ah!
Klak Klak
Klak
A DREAM.
A DREAM...
OI!
STOP!

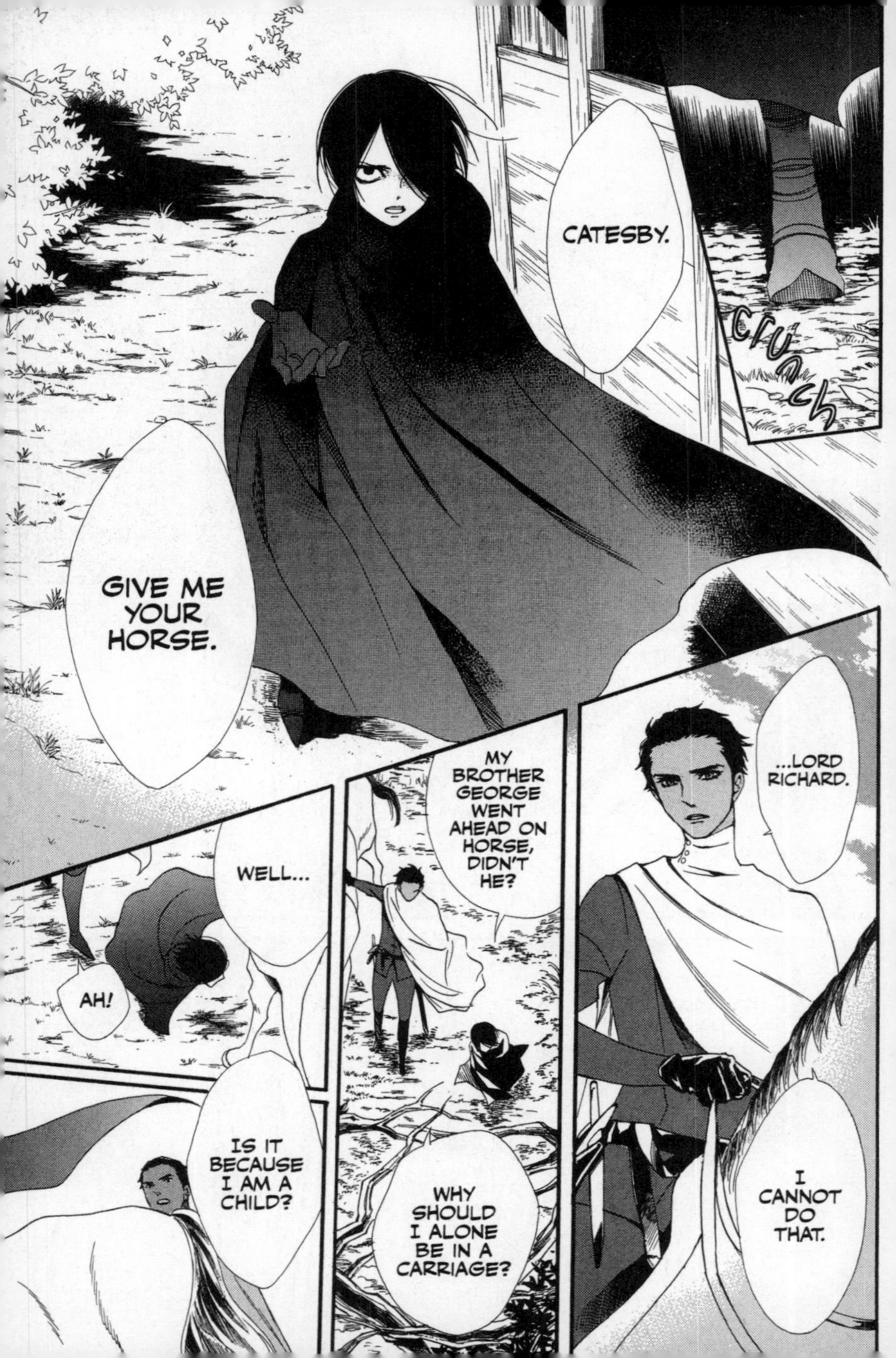
crunch
CATESBY.
GIVE ME YOUR HORSE.
...LORD RICHARD.
I CANNOT DO THAT.
MY BROTHER GEORGE WENT AHEAD ON HORSE, DIDN'T HE?
WHY SHOULD I ALONE BE IN A CARRIAGE?
WELL...
AH!
IS IT BECAUSE I AM A CHILD?

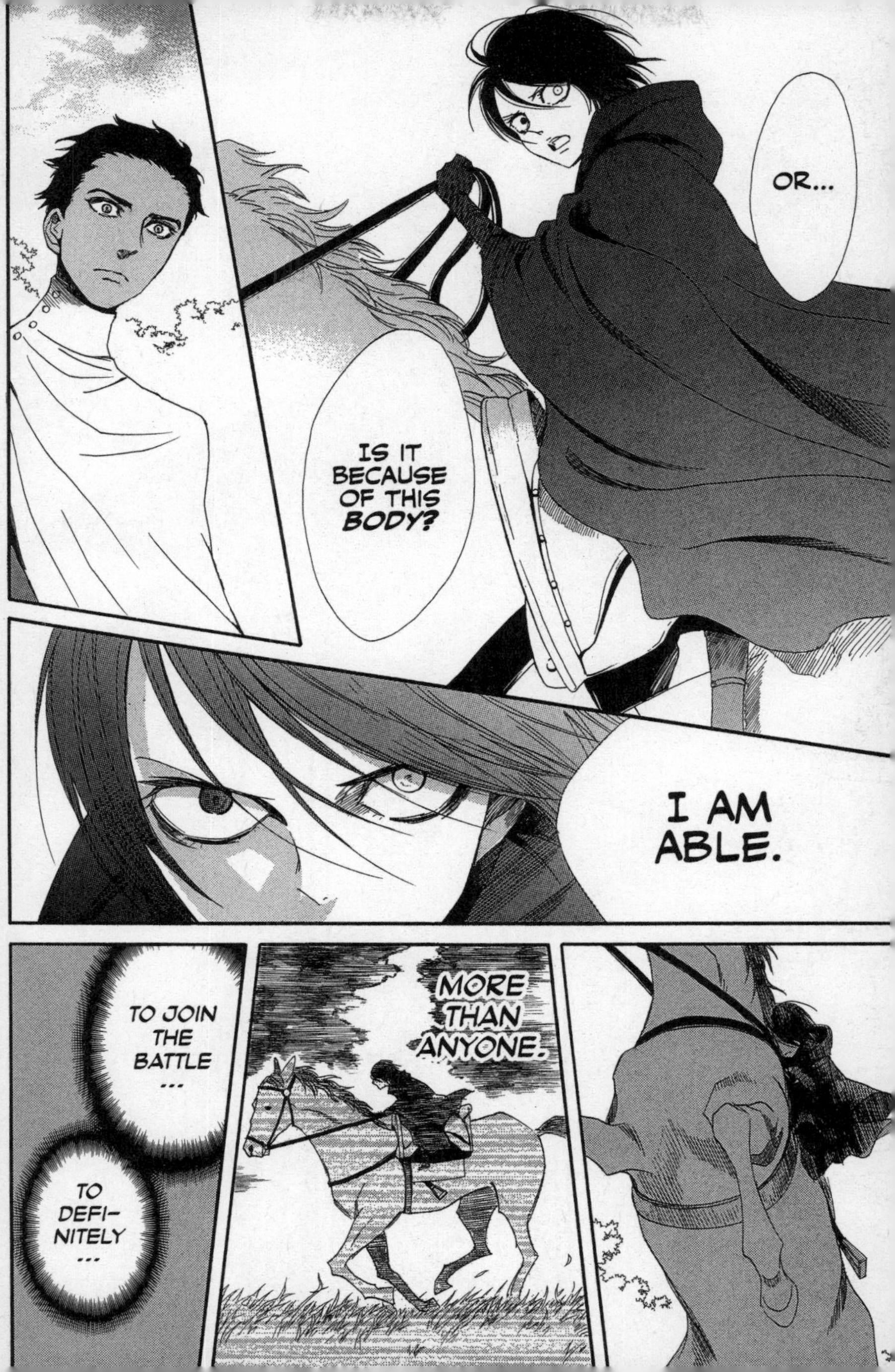
OR...
IS IT BECAUSE OF THIS *BODY?*
I AM ABLE.
MORE THAN ANYONE.
TO JOIN THE BATTLE ...
TO DEFI- NITELY ...

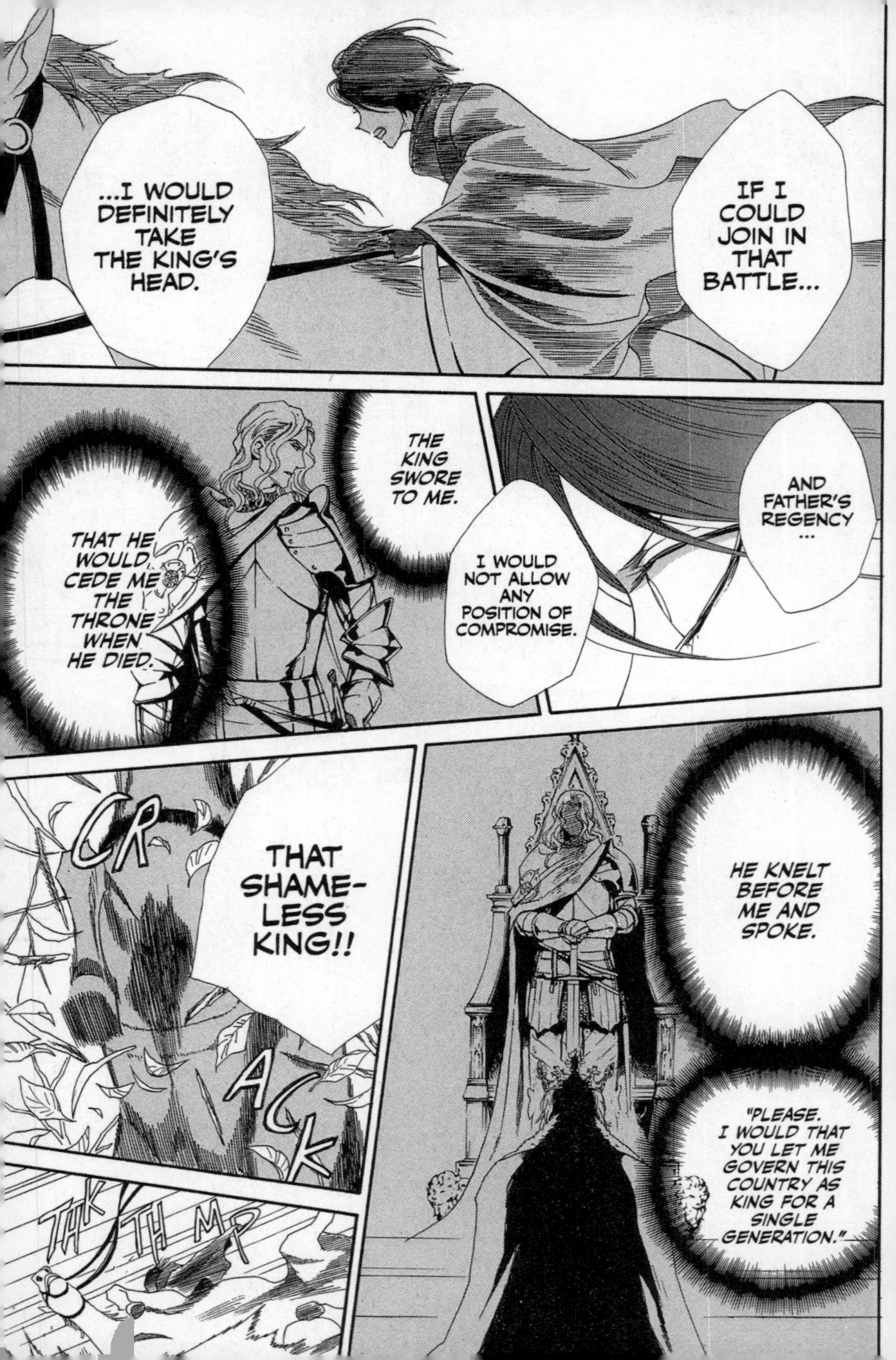
IF I COULD JOIN IN THAT BATTLE...
...I WOULD DEFINITELY TAKE THE KING'S HEAD.
AND FATHER'S REGENCY ...
I WOULD NOT ALLOW ANY POSITION OF COMPROMISE.
THE KING SWORE TO ME.
THAT HE WOULD CEDE ME THE THRONE WHEN HE DIED.
HE KNELT BEFORE ME AND SPOKE.
"PLEASE. I WOULD THAT YOU LET ME GOVERN THIS COUNTRY AS KING FOR A SINGLE GENERATION."
CRACK
THAT SHAME-LESS KING!!
THK
THMP

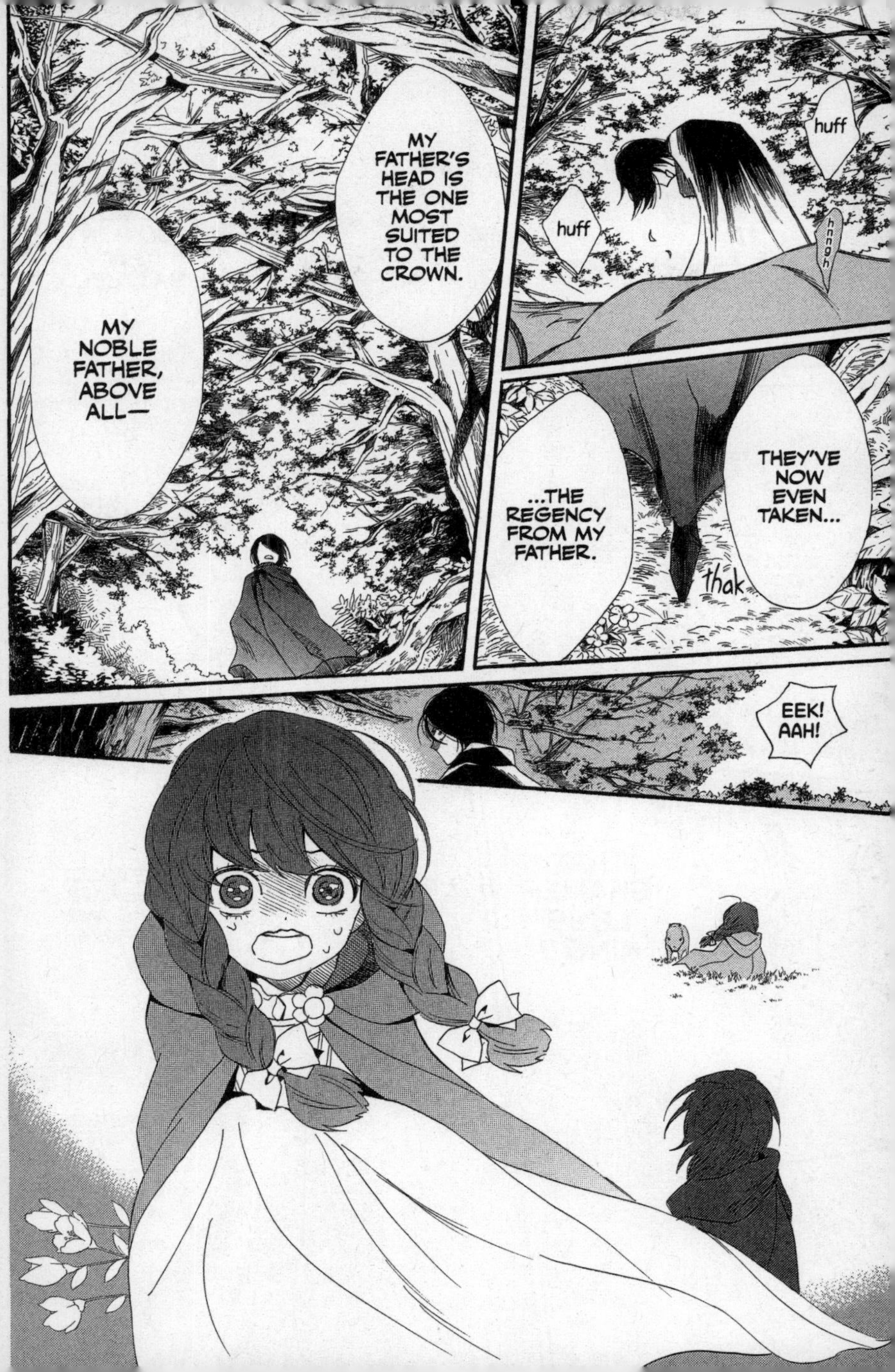
huff
hnngh
huff
THEY'VE NOW EVEN TAKEN...
thak
...THE REGENCY FROM MY FATHER.
MY FATHER'S HEAD IS THE ONE MOST SUITED TO THE CROWN.
MY NOBLE FATHER, ABOVE ALL—
EEK! AAH!

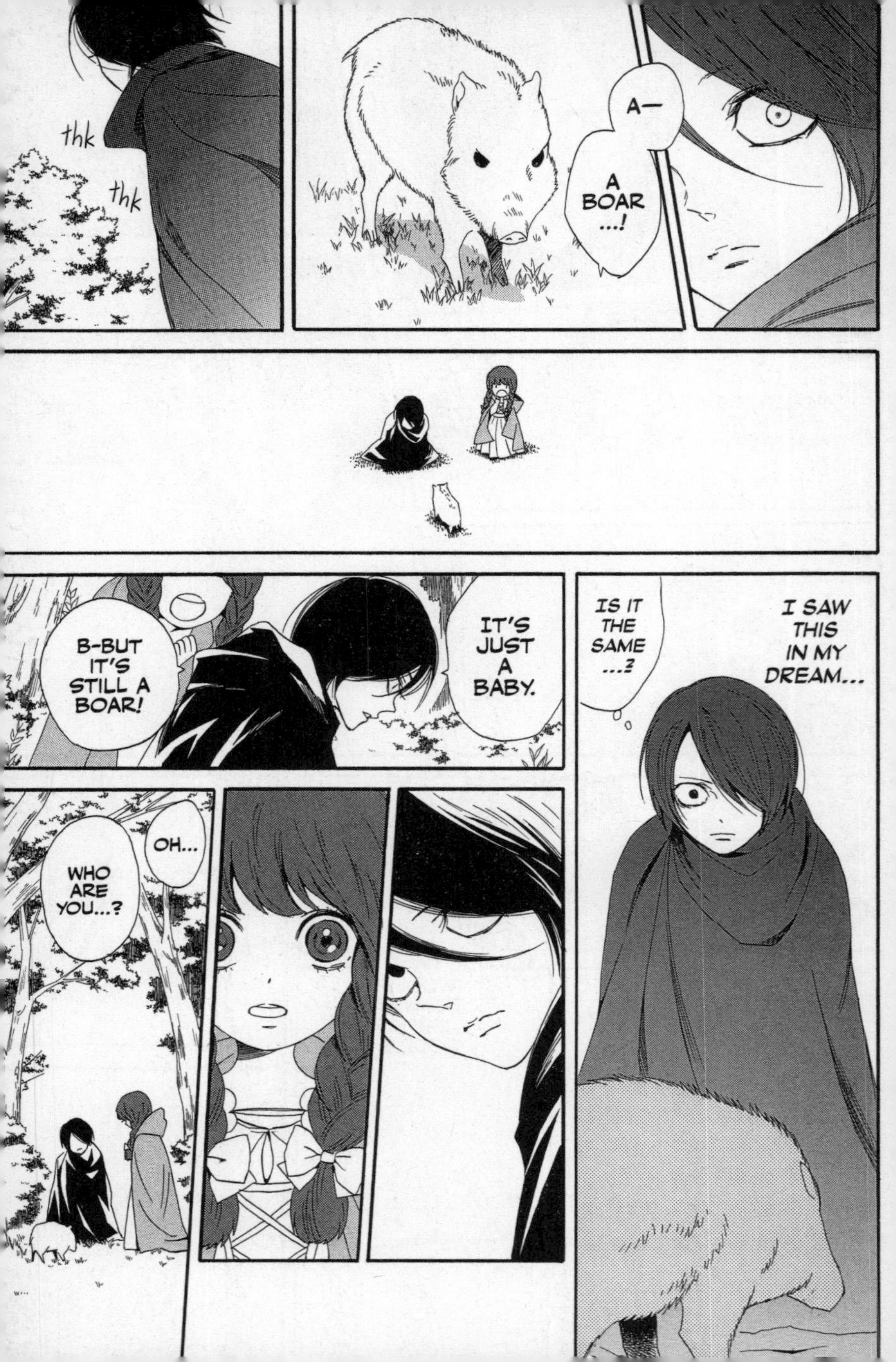
A—
A BOAR ...!
thk
thk
I SAW THIS IN MY DREAM...
IS IT THE SAME ...?
IT'S JUST A BABY.
B-BUT IT'S STILL A BOAR!
OH...
WHO ARE YOU...?

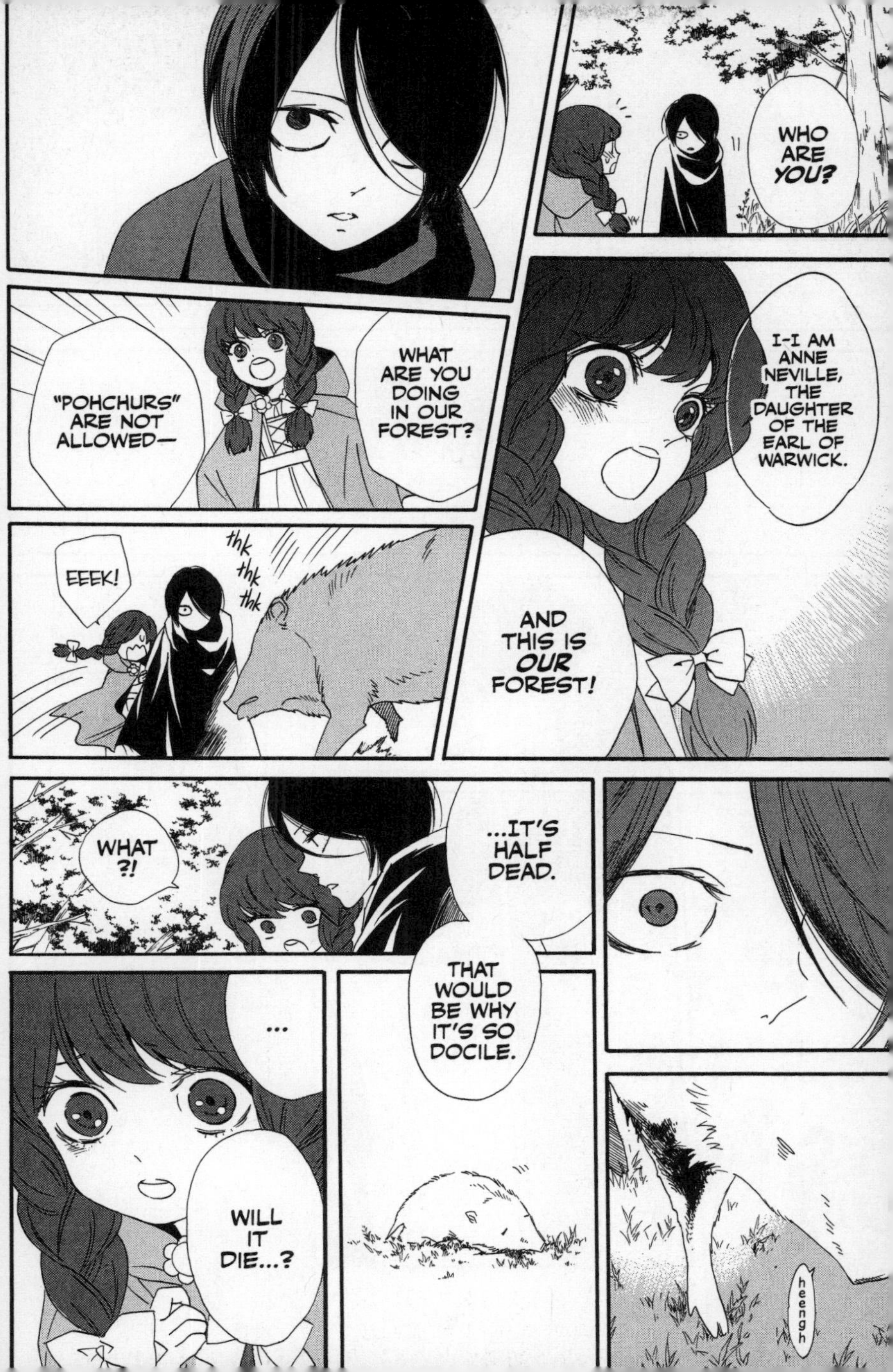
WHO ARE YOU?
I-I AM ANNE NEVILLE, THE DAUGHTER OF THE EARL OF WARWICK.
AND THIS IS OUR FOREST!
WHAT ARE YOU DOING IN OUR FOREST?
"POHCHURS" ARE NOT ALLOWED—
thk thk thk
EEEK!
...IT'S HALF DEAD.
WHAT ?!
heengh
THAT WOULD BE WHY IT'S SO DOCILE.
...
WILL IT DIE...?

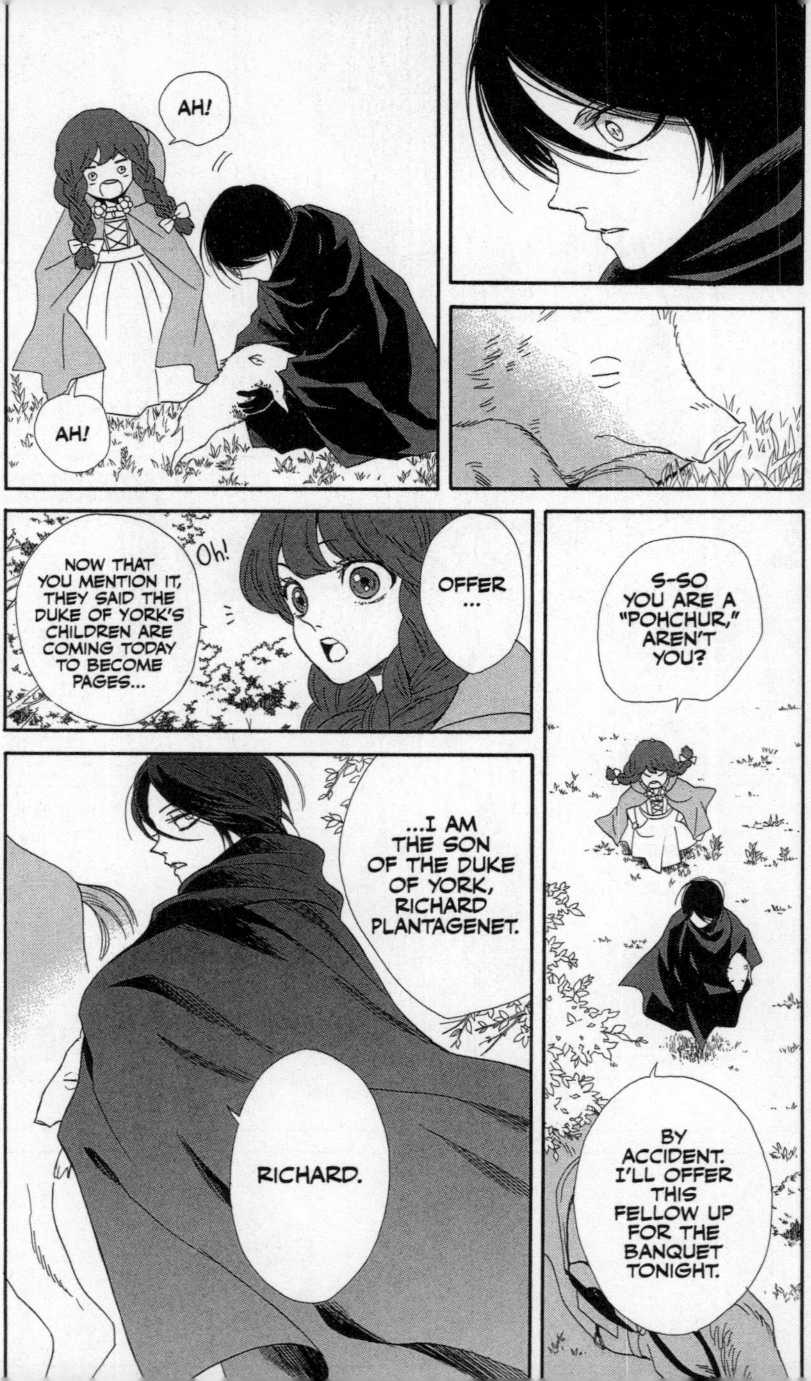
AH!
AH!
S-SO YOU ARE A "POHCHUR," AREN'T YOU?
BY ACCIDENT. I'LL OFFER THIS FELLOW UP FOR THE BANQUET TONIGHT.
OFFER ...
Oh!
NOW THAT YOU MENTION IT, THEY SAID THE DUKE OF YORK'S CHILDREN ARE COMING TODAY TO BECOME PAGES...
...I AM THE SON OF THE DUKE OF YORK, RICHARD PLANTAGENET.
RICHARD.

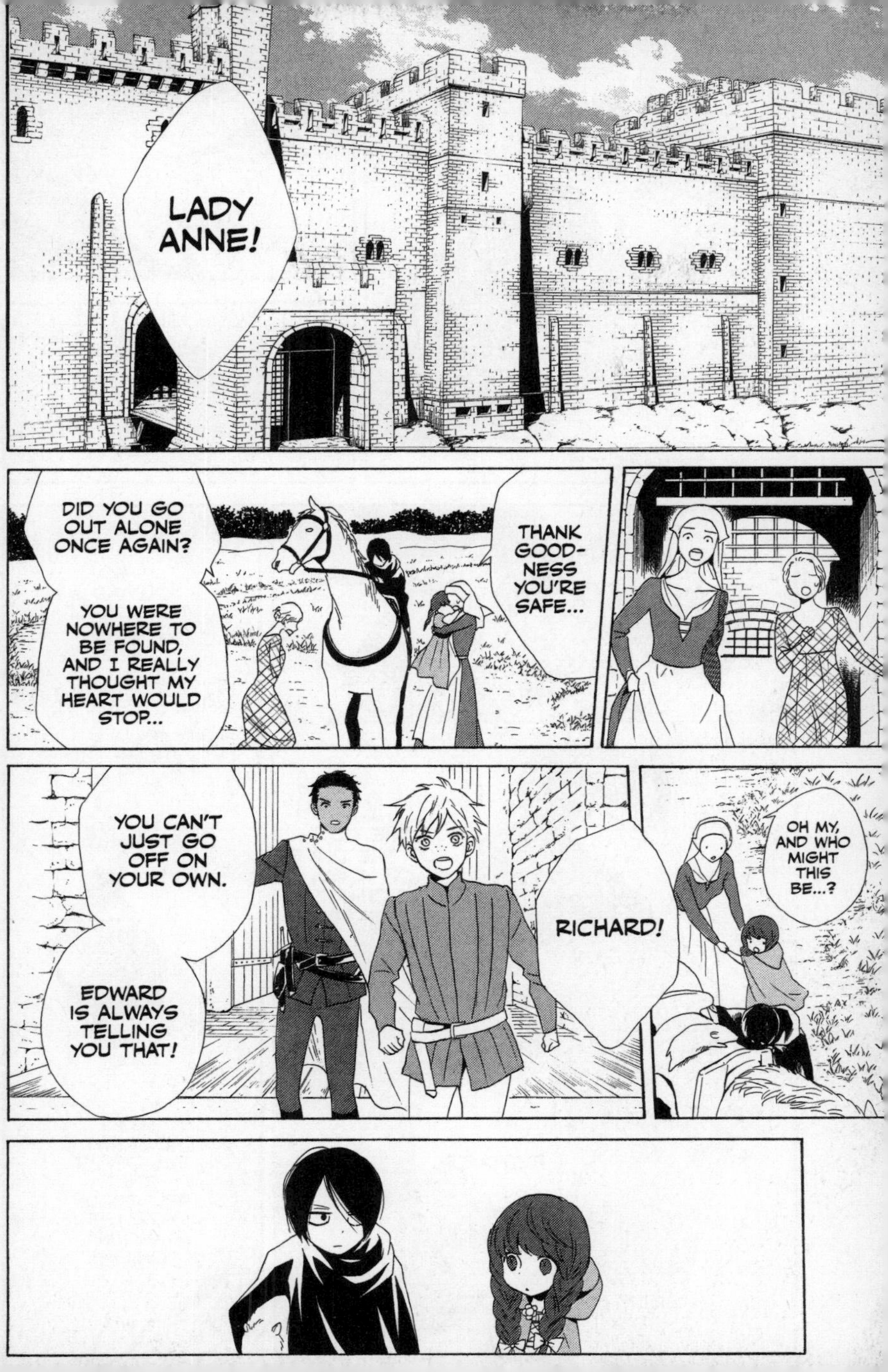
LADY ANNE!
THANK GOOD-NESS YOU'RE SAFE...
DID YOU GO OUT ALONE ONCE AGAIN?
YOU WERE NOWHERE TO BE FOUND, AND I REALLY THOUGHT MY HEART WOULD STOP...
OH MY, AND WHO MIGHT THIS BE...?
RICHARD!
YOU CAN'T JUST GO OFF ON YOUR OWN.
EDWARD IS ALWAYS TELLING YOU THAT!

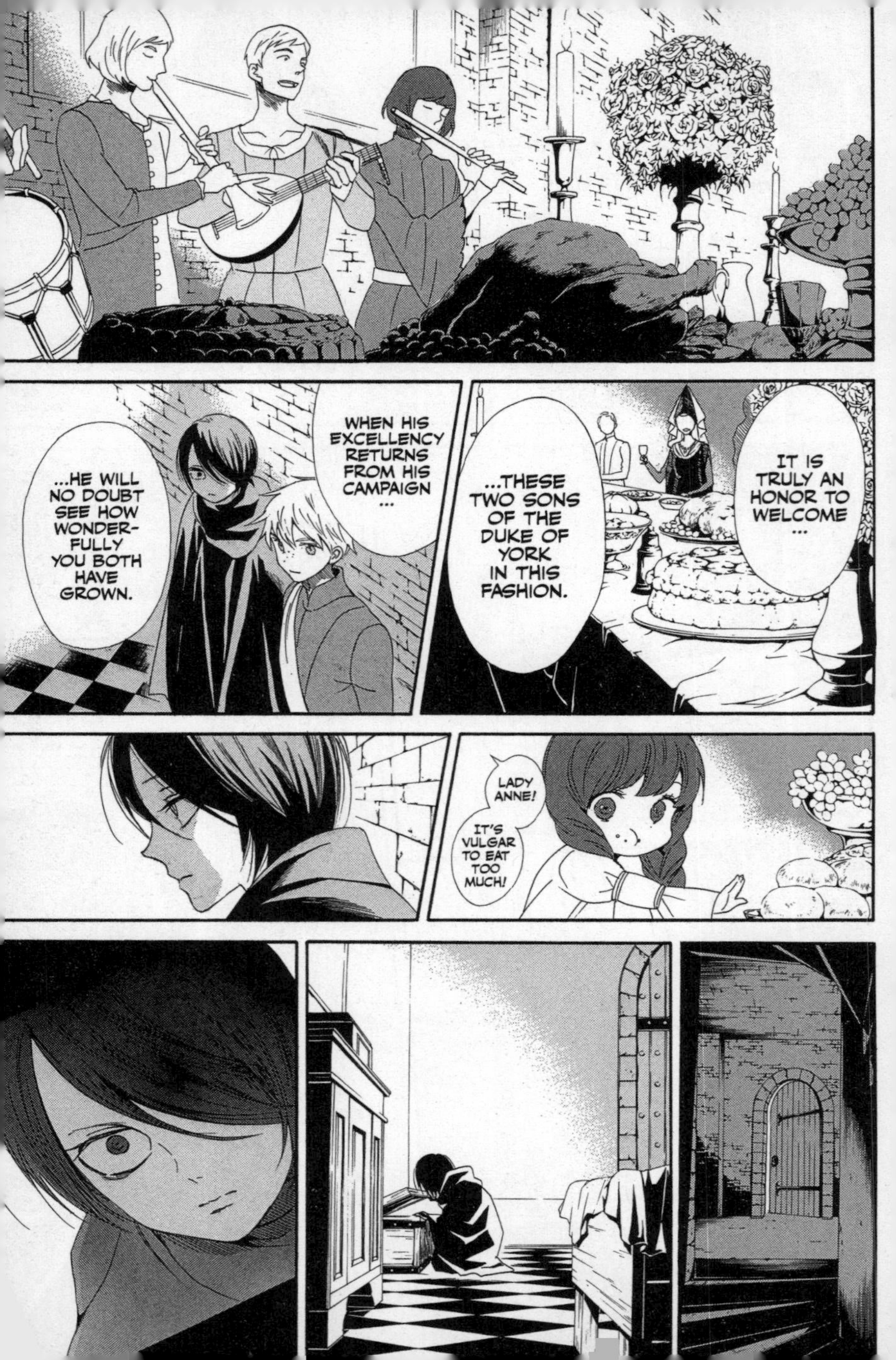
IT IS TRULY AN HONOR TO WELCOME ...
...THESE TWO SONS OF THE DUKE OF YORK IN THIS FASHION.
WHEN HIS EXCELLENCY RETURNS FROM HIS CAMPAIGN ...
...HE WILL NO DOUBT SEE HOW WONDER-FULLY YOU BOTH HAVE GROWN.
LADY ANNE!
IT'S VULGAR TO EAT TOO MUCH!

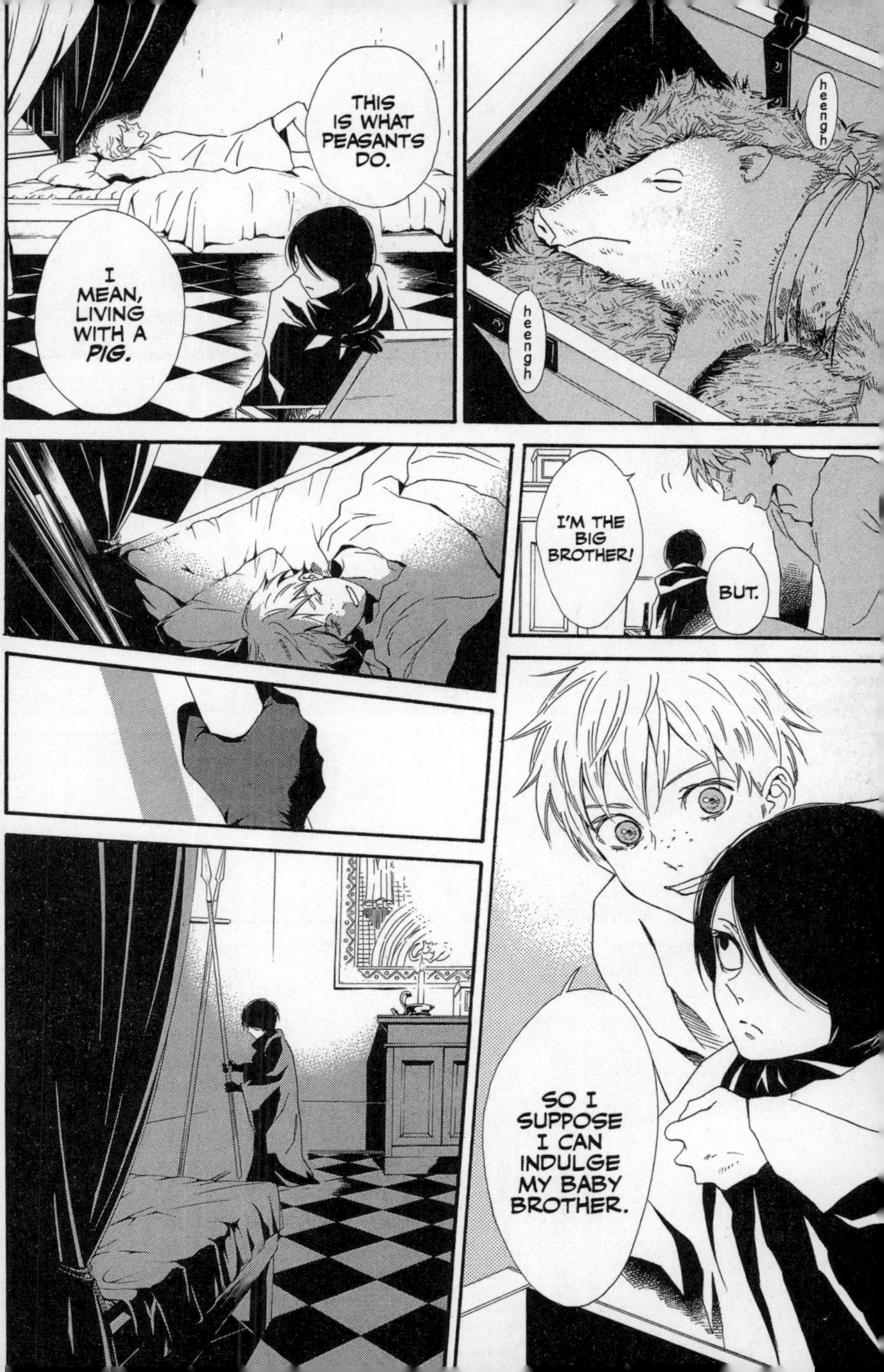
heengh
heengh
THIS IS WHAT PEASANTS DO.
I MEAN, LIVING WITH A *PIG*.
BUT.
I'M THE BIG BROTHER!
SO I SUPPOSE I CAN INDULGE MY BABY BROTHER.

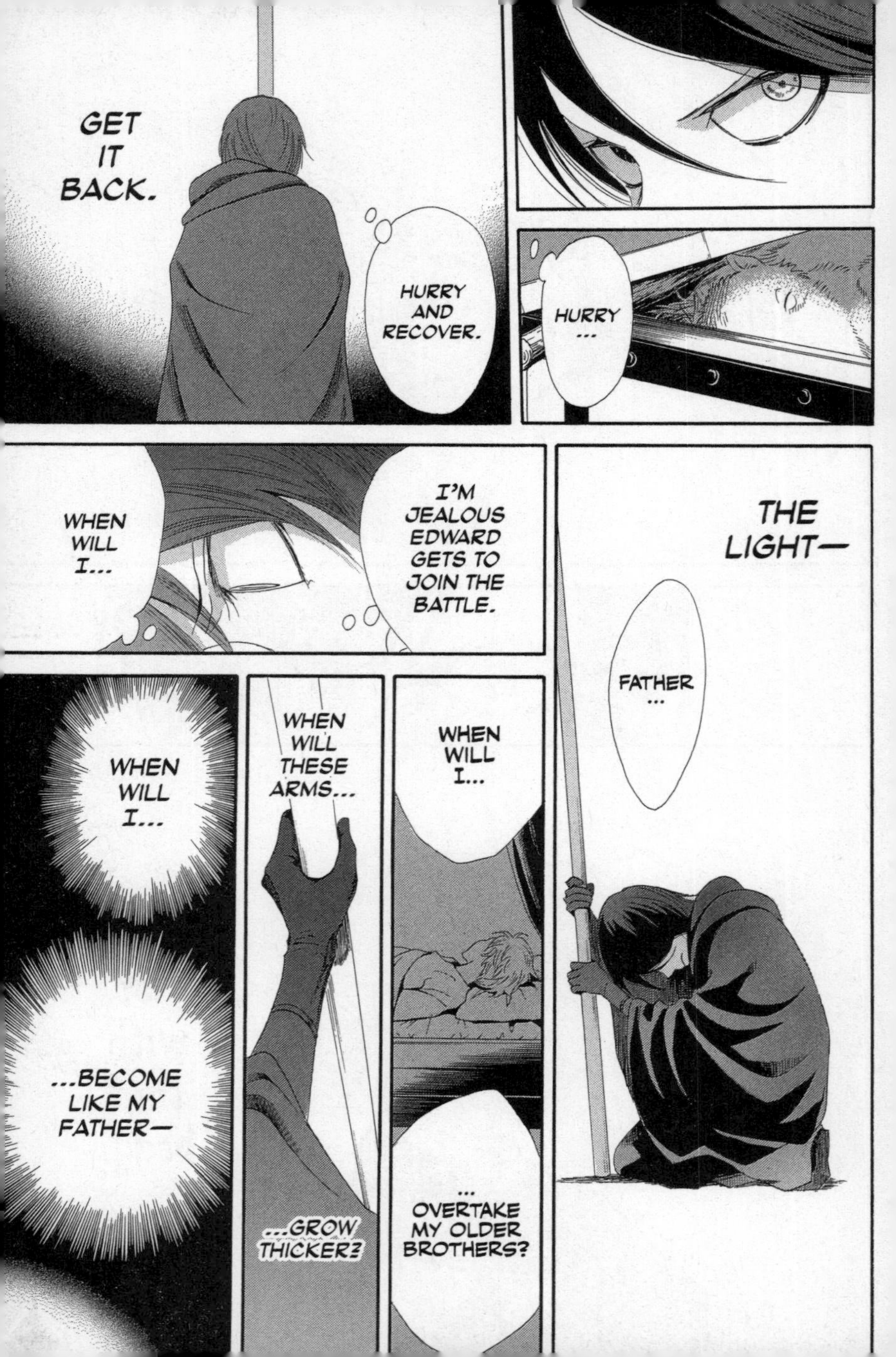
HURRY...
HURRY AND RECOVER.
GET IT BACK.
THE LIGHT—
FATHER...
I'M JEALOUS EDWARD GETS TO JOIN THE BATTLE.
WHEN WILL I...
WHEN WILL I...
...OVERTAKE MY OLDER BROTHERS?
WHEN WILL THESE ARMS...
...GROW THICKER?
WHEN WILL I...
...BECOME LIKE MY FATHER—

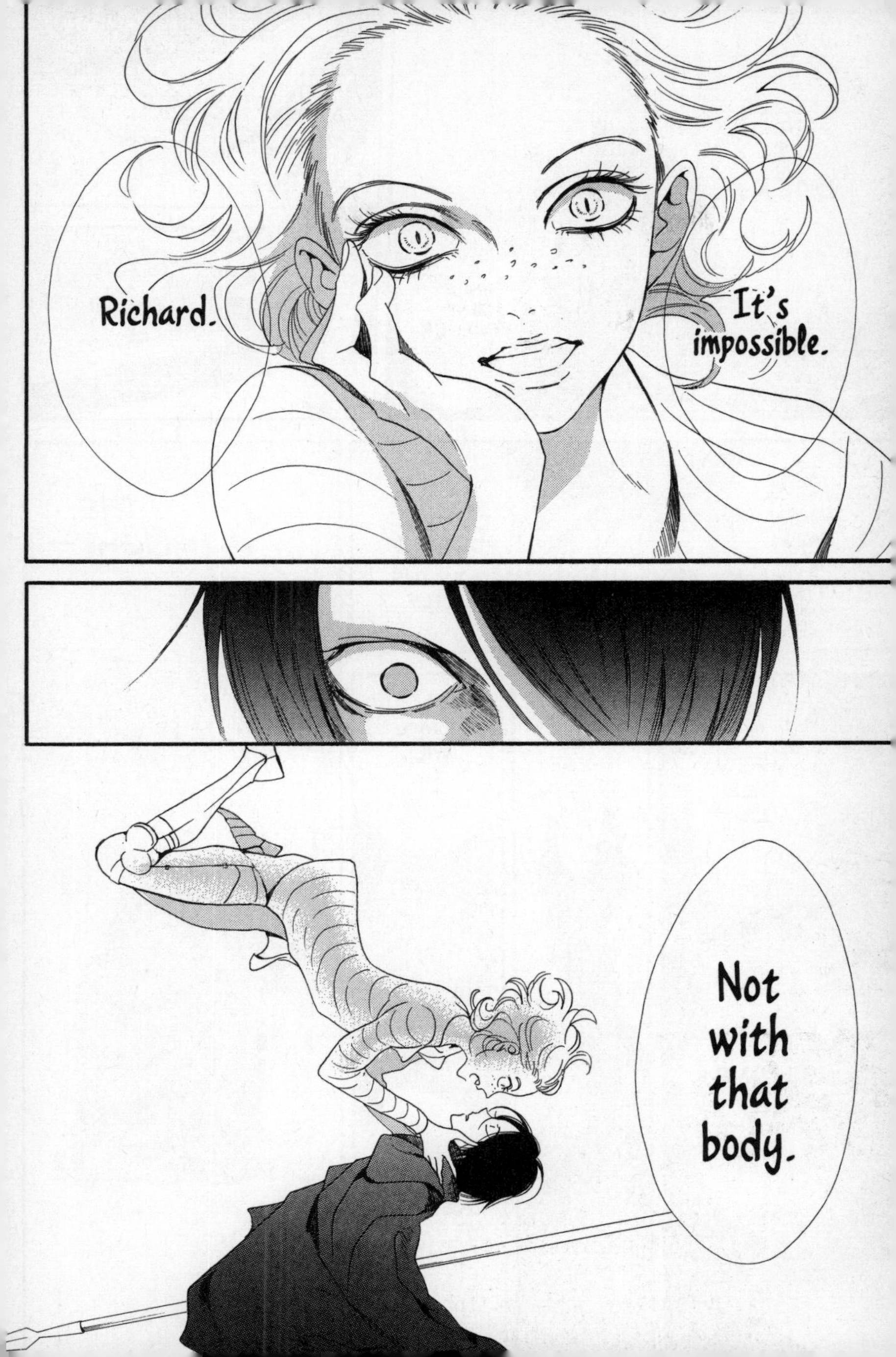
It's impossible.
Richard.
Not with that body.

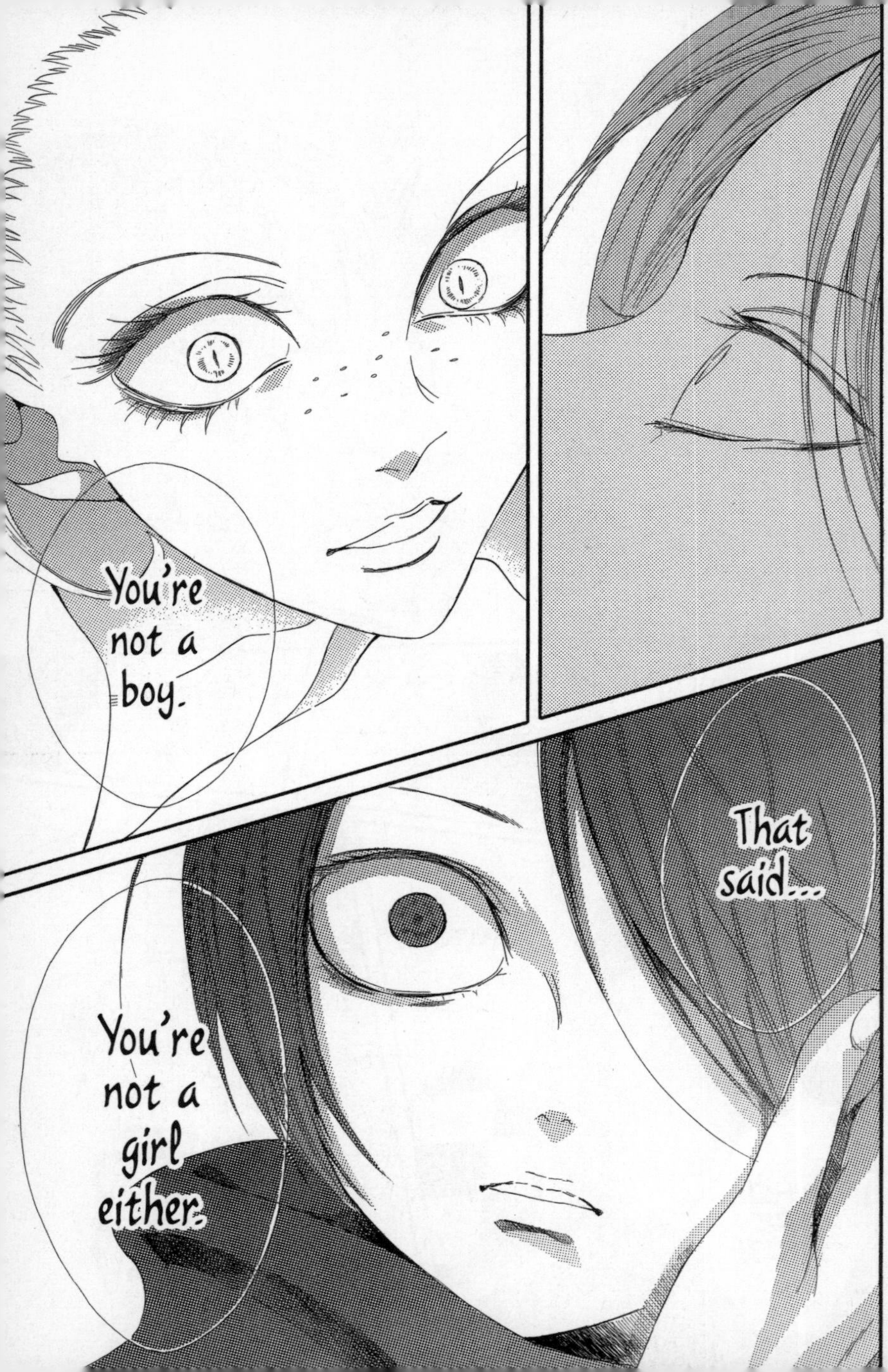
You're not a boy.
That said...
You're not a girl either.

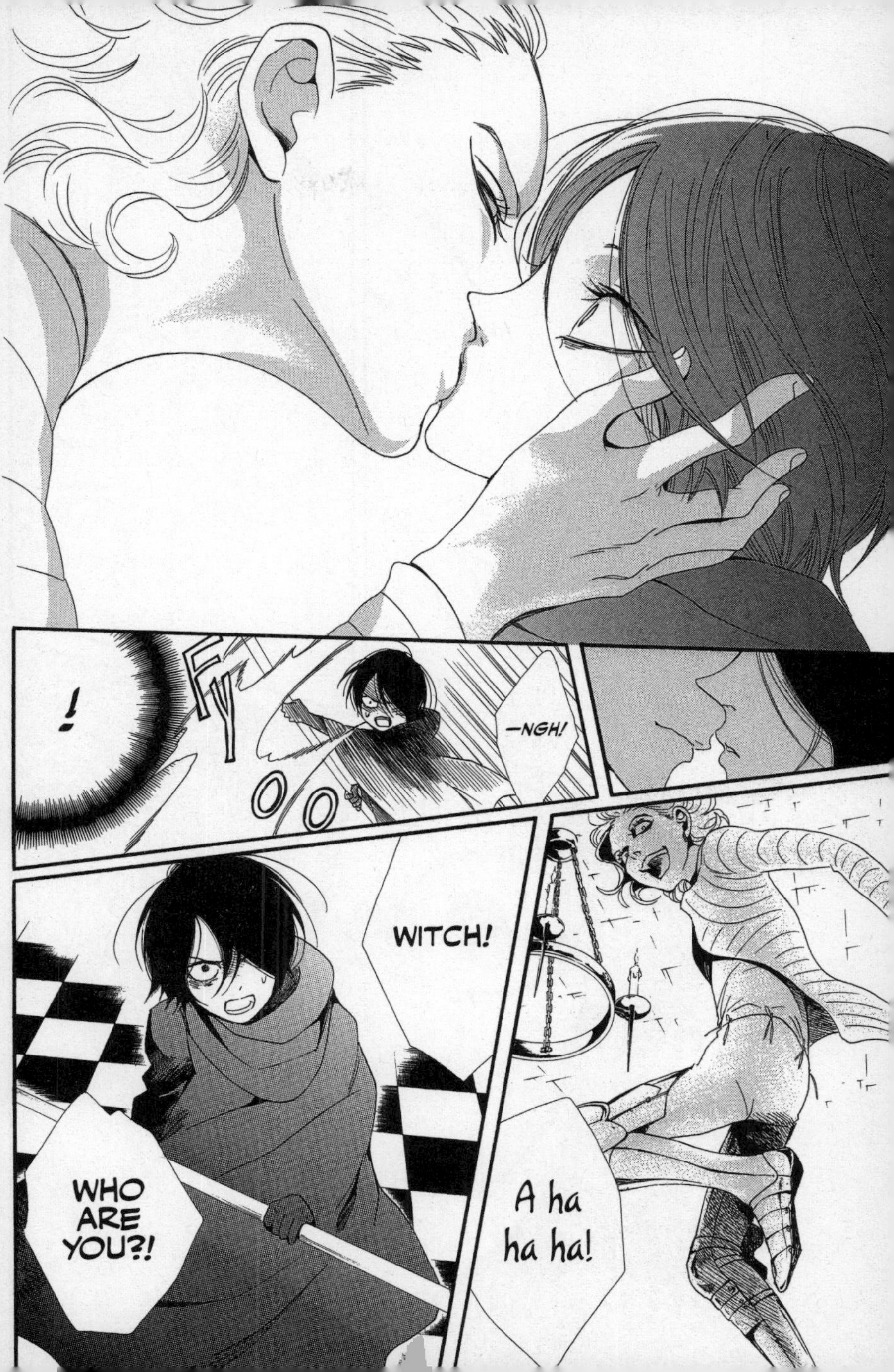

—NGH!
FYOOO
!
A ha ha ha!
WITCH!
WHO ARE YOU?!

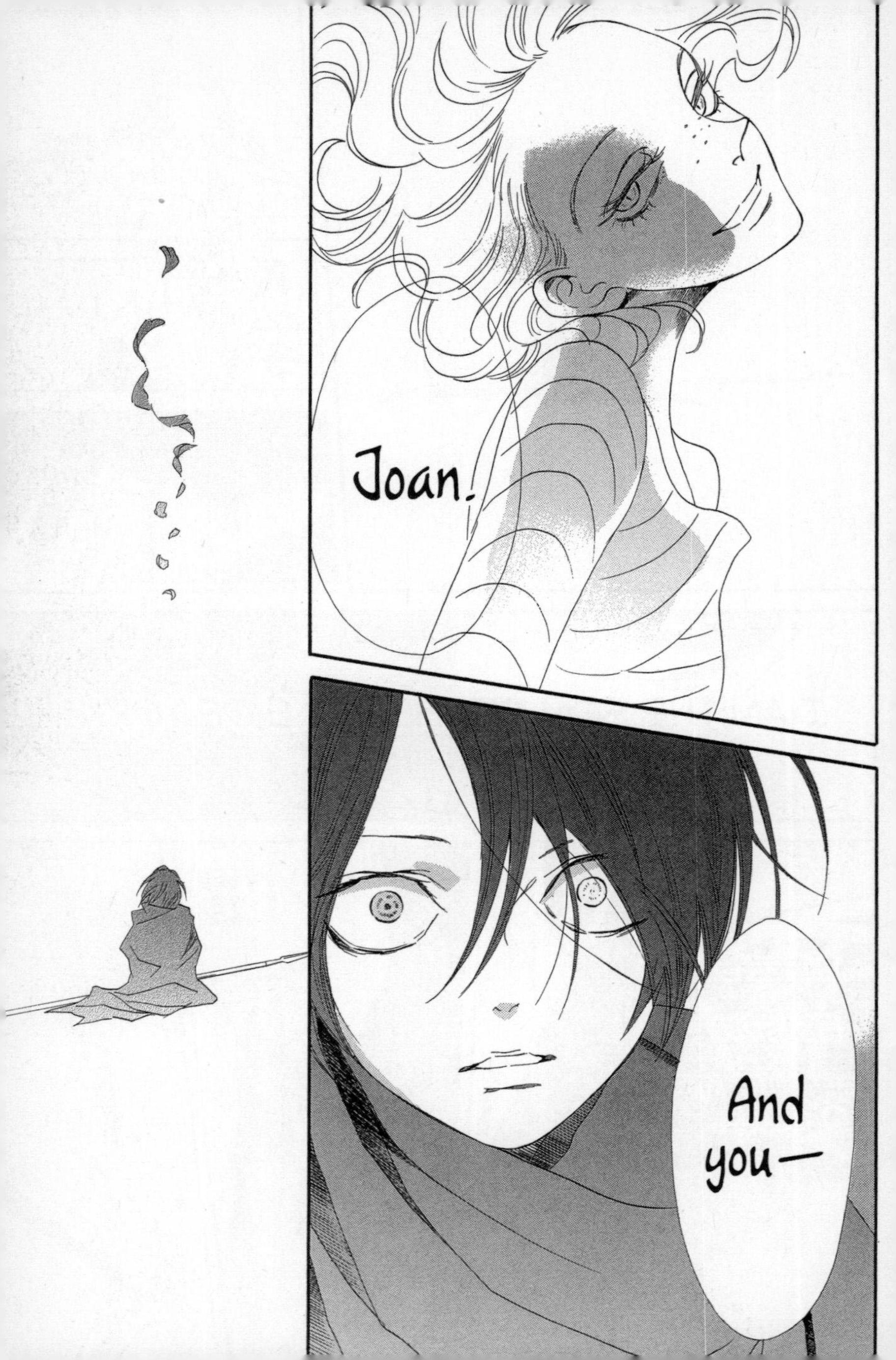
Joan.
And you—

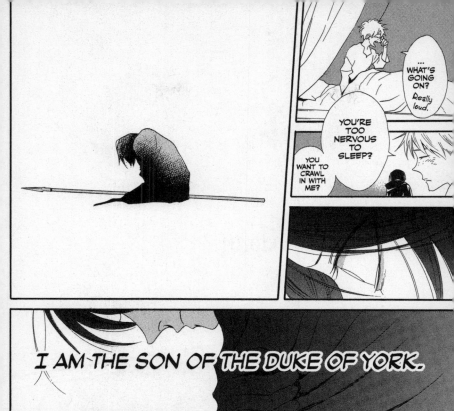

...
WHAT'S GOING ON? *Really loud.*

YOU'RE TOO NERVOUS TO SLEEP?

YOU WANT TO CRAWL IN WITH ME?

I AM THE SON OF THE DUKE OF YORK.

THERE'S NO REASON I SHOULDN'T BE ABLE.

HERE WE GO!

ARE YOU READY?

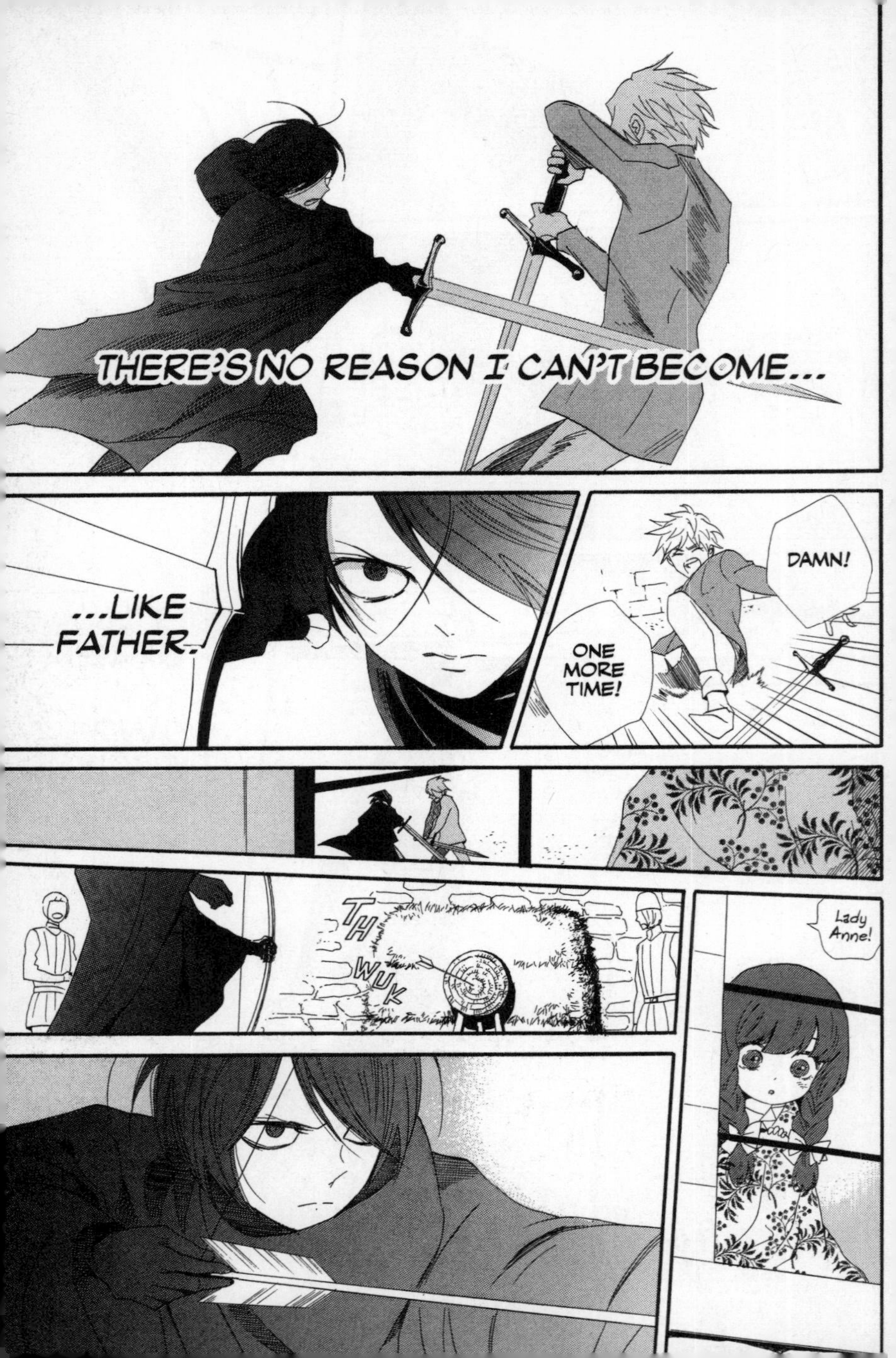
THERE'S NO REASON I CAN'T BECOME...
DAMN!
ONE MORE TIME!
...LIKE FATHER.
Lady Anne!
THWUK

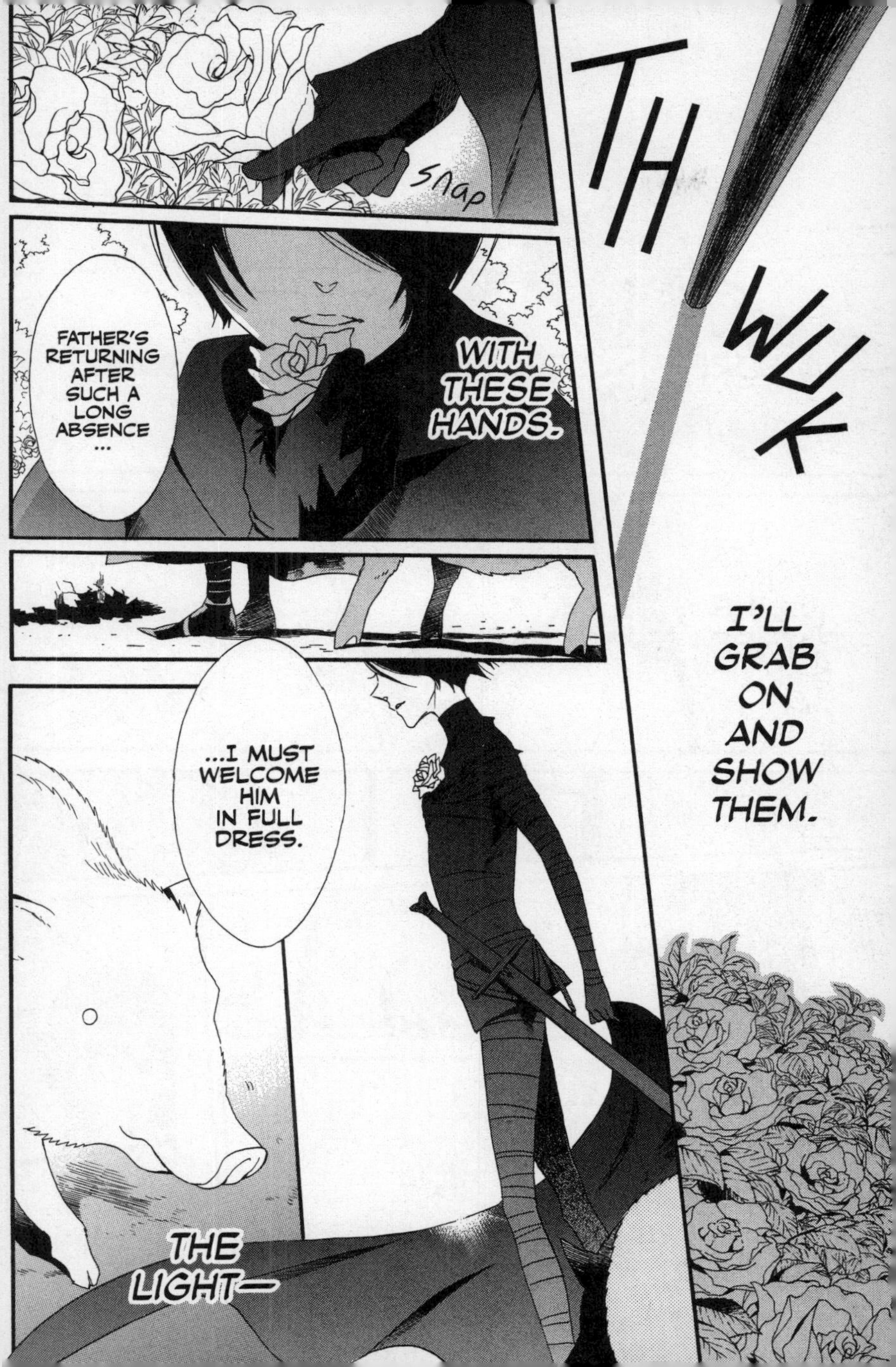
THWUK
I'LL GRAB ON AND SHOW THEM.
SNAP
WITH THESE HANDS.
FATHER'S RETURNING AFTER SUCH A LONG ABSENCE...
...I MUST WELCOME HIM IN FULL DRESS.
THE LIGHT—

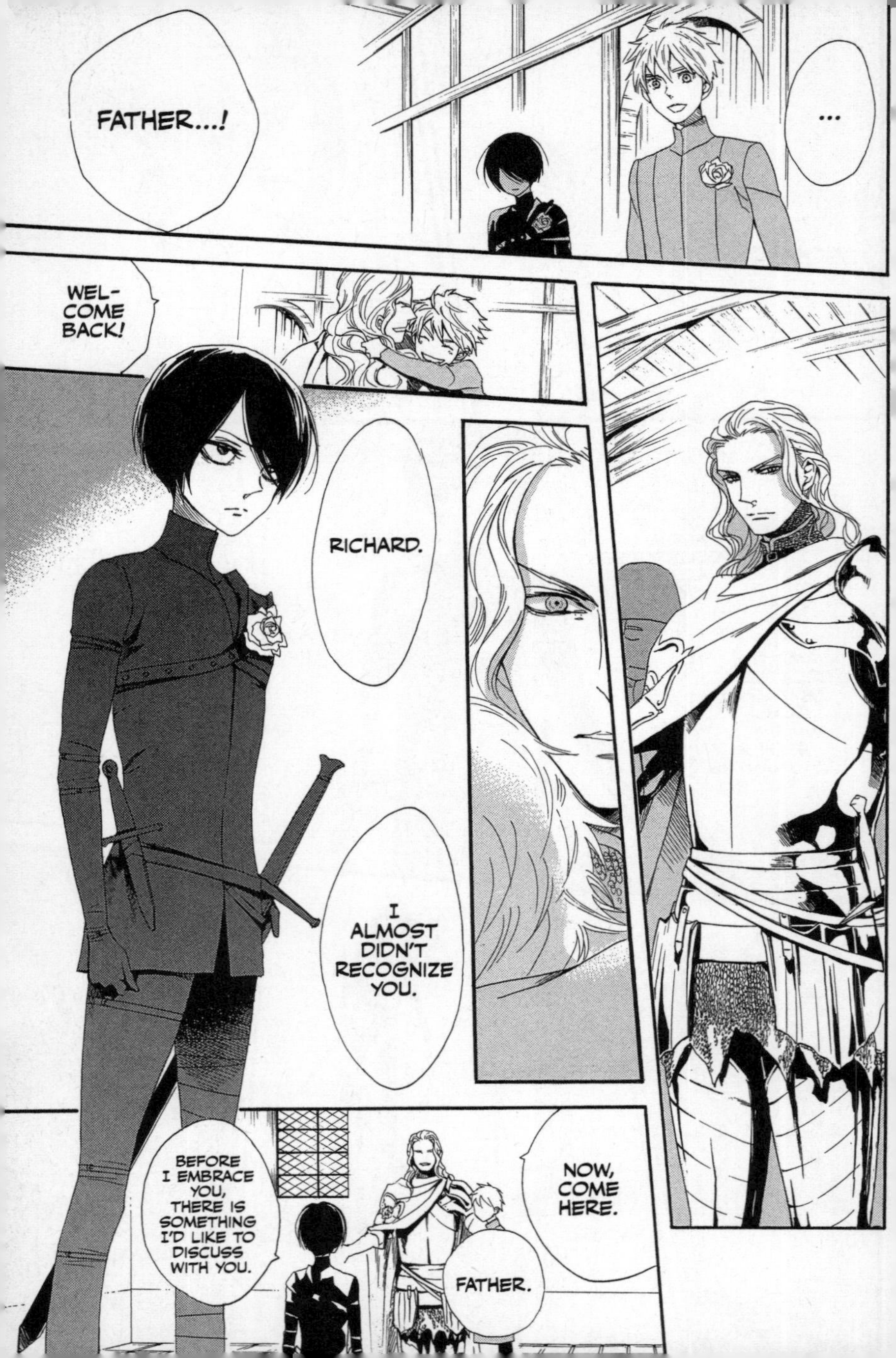
...
FATHER...!
WEL-COME BACK!
RICHARD.
I ALMOST DIDN'T RECOGNIZE YOU.
NOW, COME HERE.
FATHER.
BEFORE I EMBRACE YOU, THERE IS SOMETHING I'D LIKE TO DISCUSS WITH YOU.

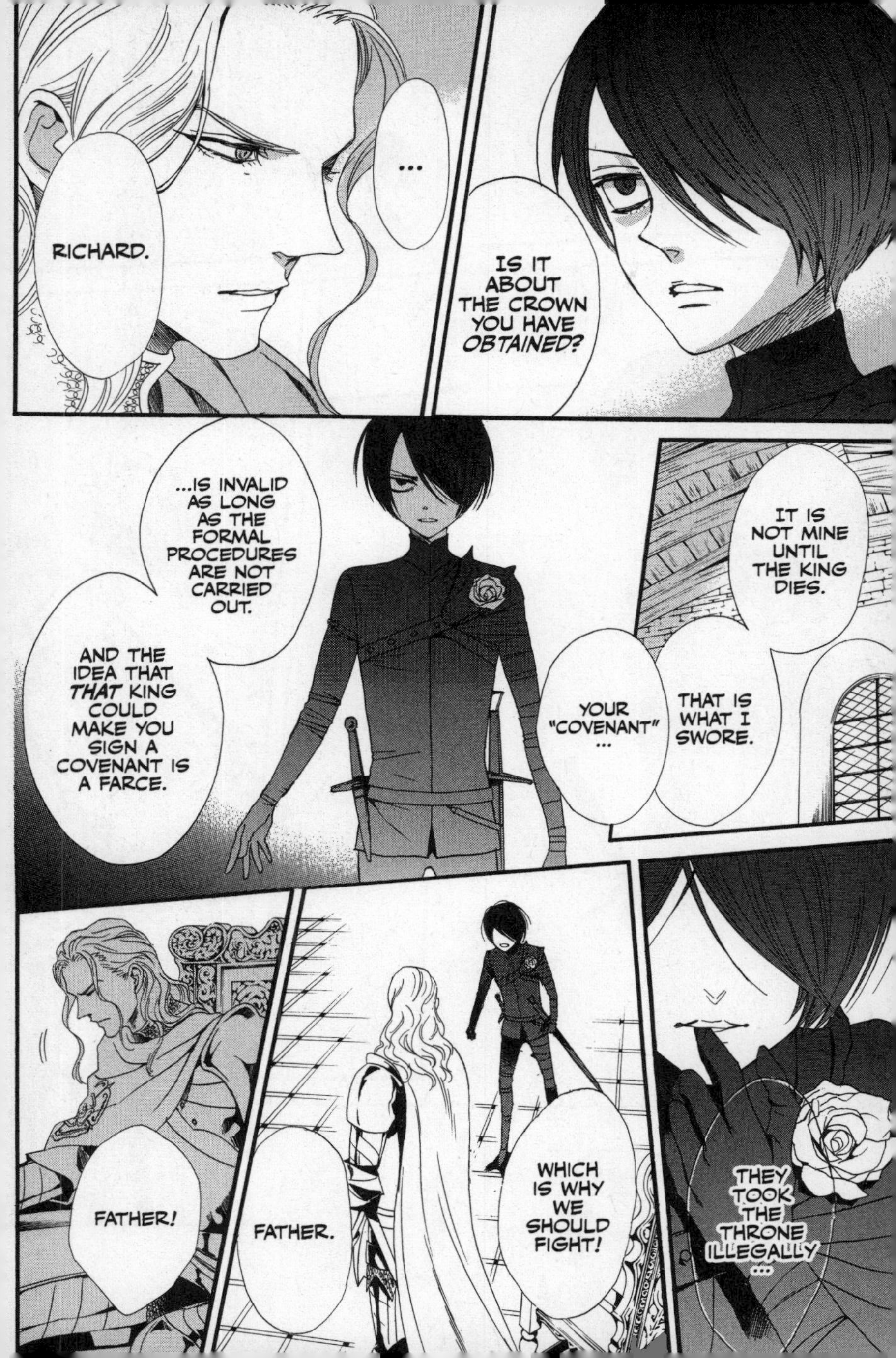
IS IT ABOUT THE CROWN YOU HAVE *OBTAINED*?
...
RICHARD.
IT IS NOT MINE UNTIL THE KING DIES.
THAT IS WHAT I SWORE.
YOUR "COVENANT"...
...IS INVALID AS LONG AS THE FORMAL PROCEDURES ARE NOT CARRIED OUT.
AND THE IDEA THAT *THAT* KING COULD MAKE YOU SIGN A COVENANT IS A FARCE.
THEY TOOK THE THRONE ILLEGALLY...
WHICH IS WHY WE SHOULD FIGHT!
FATHER.
FATHER!

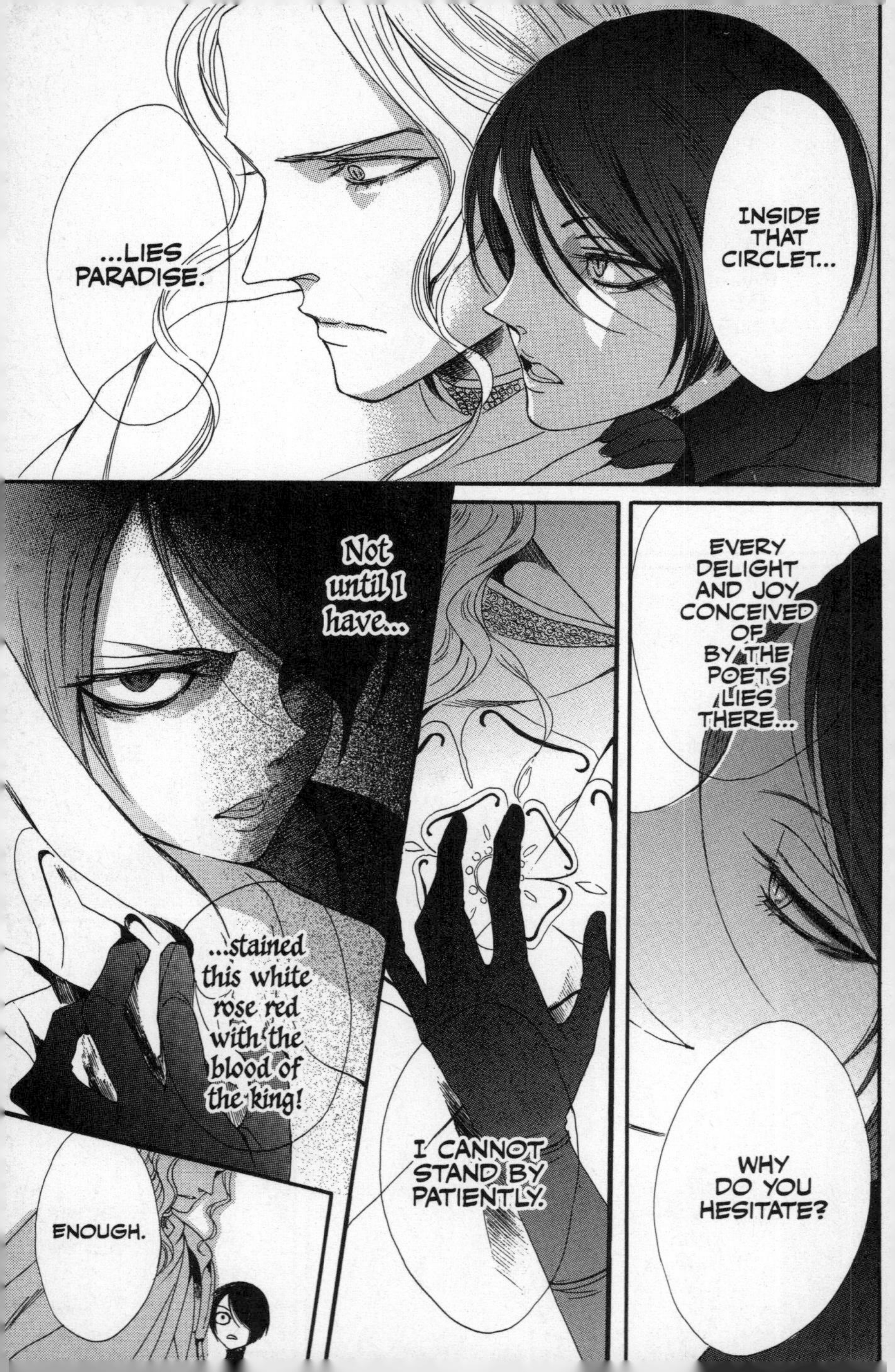
INSIDE THAT CIRCLET...
...LIES PARADISE.
EVERY DELIGHT AND JOY CONCEIVED OF BY THE POETS LIES THERE...
WHY DO YOU HESITATE?
I CANNOT STAND BY PATIENTLY.
Not until I have...
...stained this white rose red with the blood of the king!
ENOUGH.

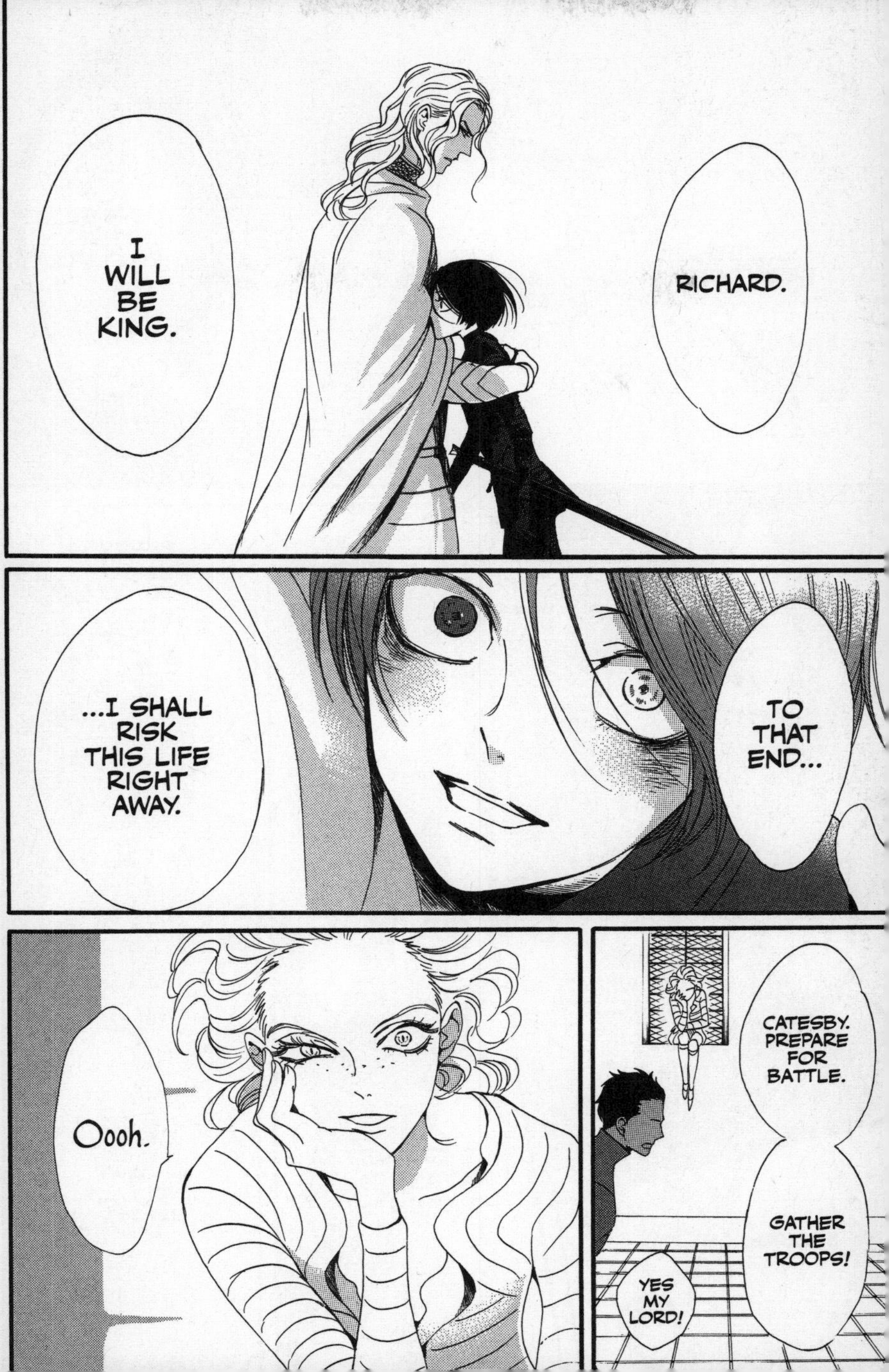
RICHARD.
I WILL BE KING.
TO THAT END...
...I SHALL RISK THIS LIFE RIGHT AWAY.
CATESBY. PREPARE FOR BATTLE.
GATHER THE TROOPS!
YES MY LORD!
Oooh.

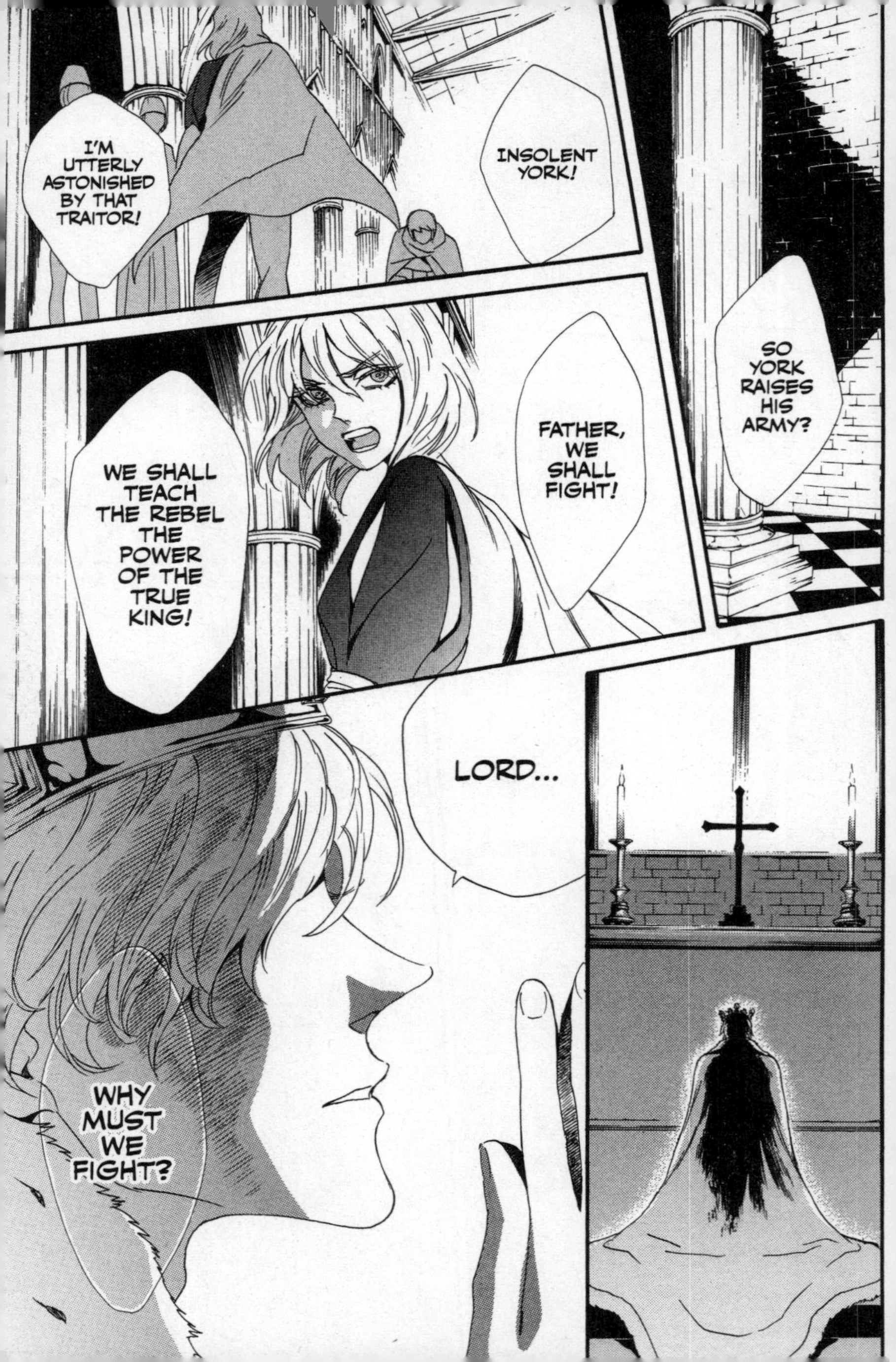
SO YORK RAISES HIS ARMY?
INSOLENT YORK!
I'M UTTERLY ASTONISHED BY THAT TRAITOR!
FATHER, WE SHALL FIGHT!
WE SHALL TEACH THE REBEL THE POWER OF THE TRUE KING!
LORD...
WHY MUST WE FIGHT?

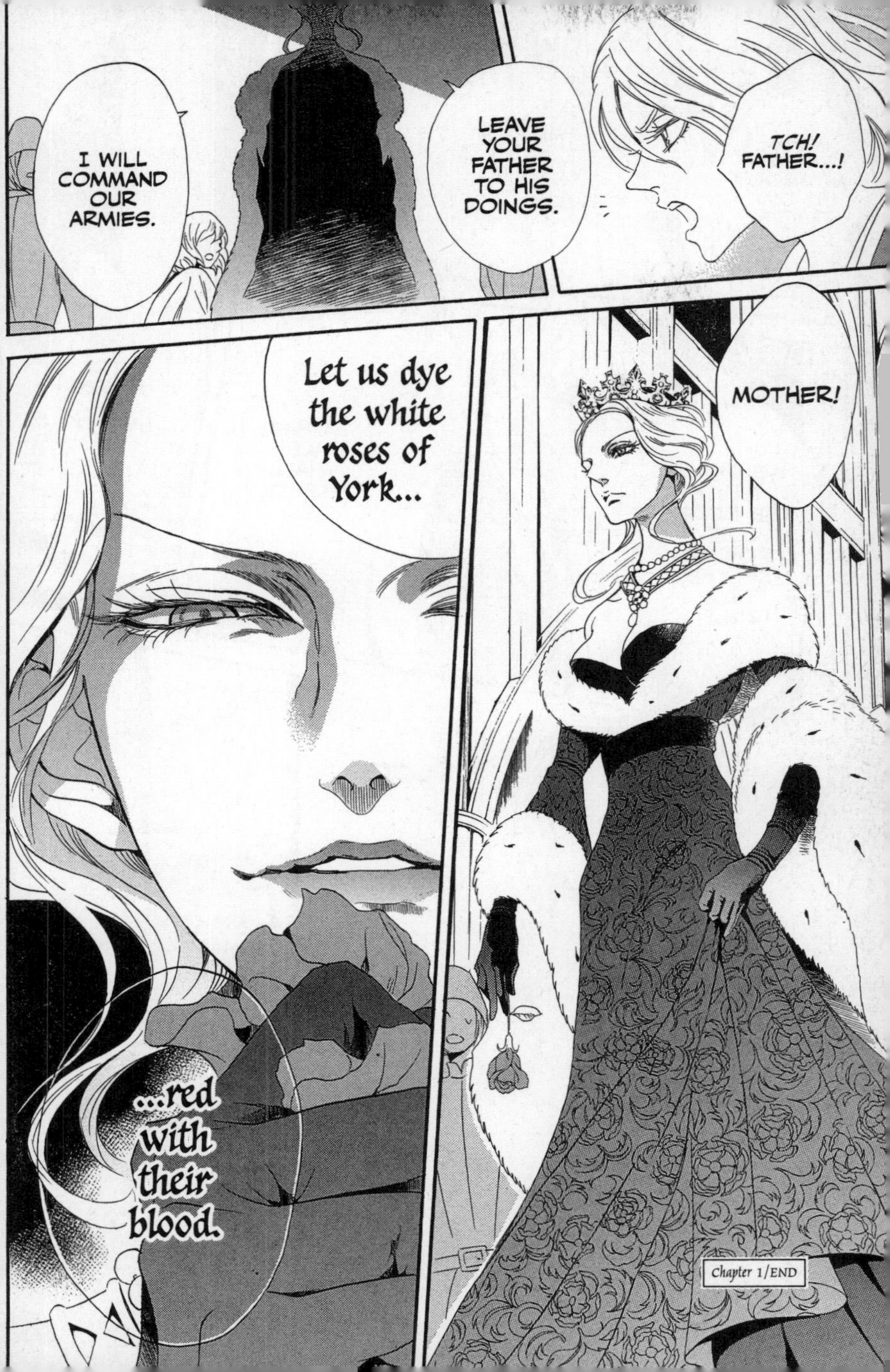
TCH! FATHER...!
LEAVE YOUR FATHER TO HIS DOINGS.
I WILL COMMAND OUR ARMIES.
MOTHER!
Let us dye the white roses of York...
...red with their blood.
Chapter 1/END

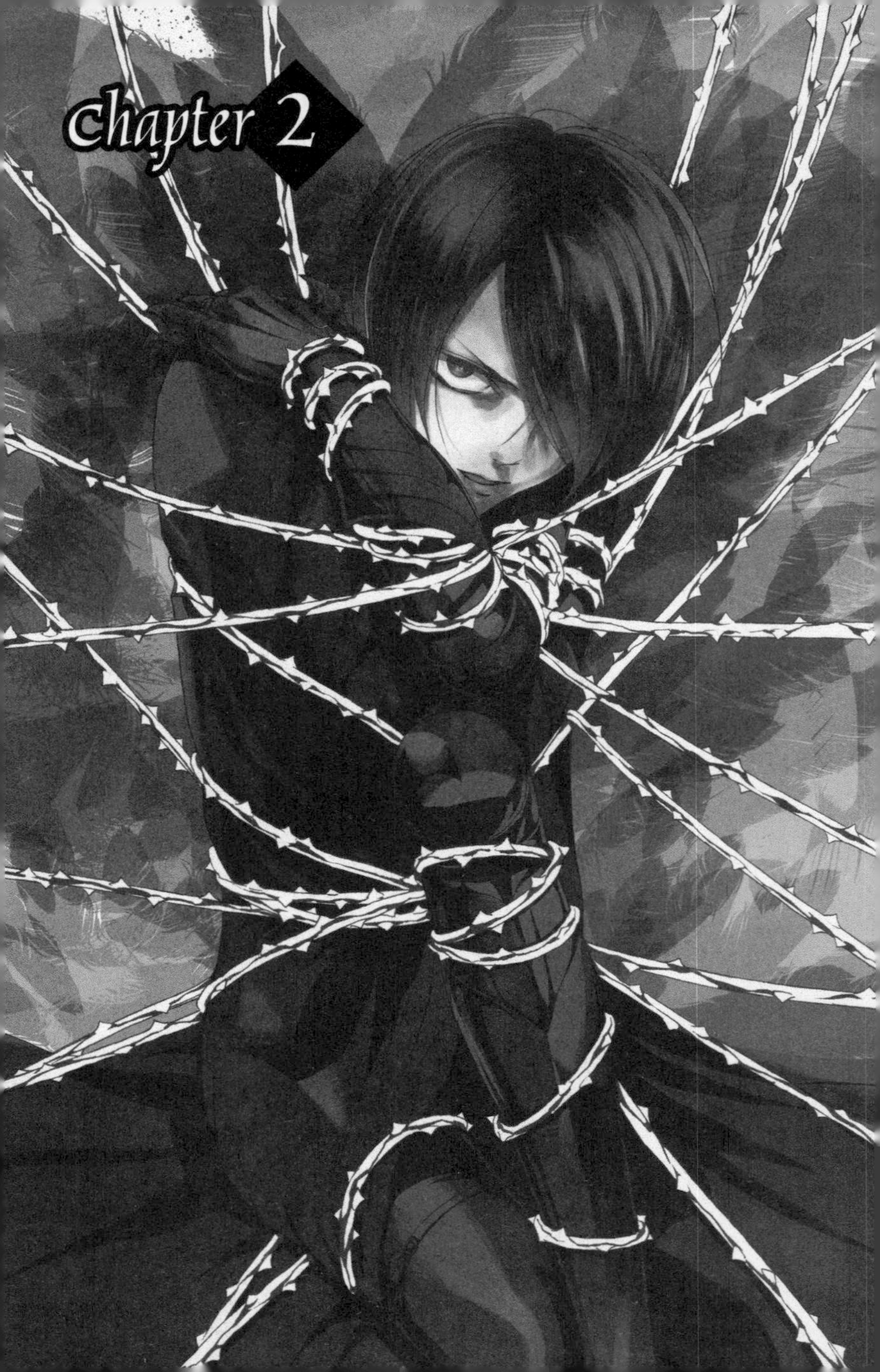
Chapter 2

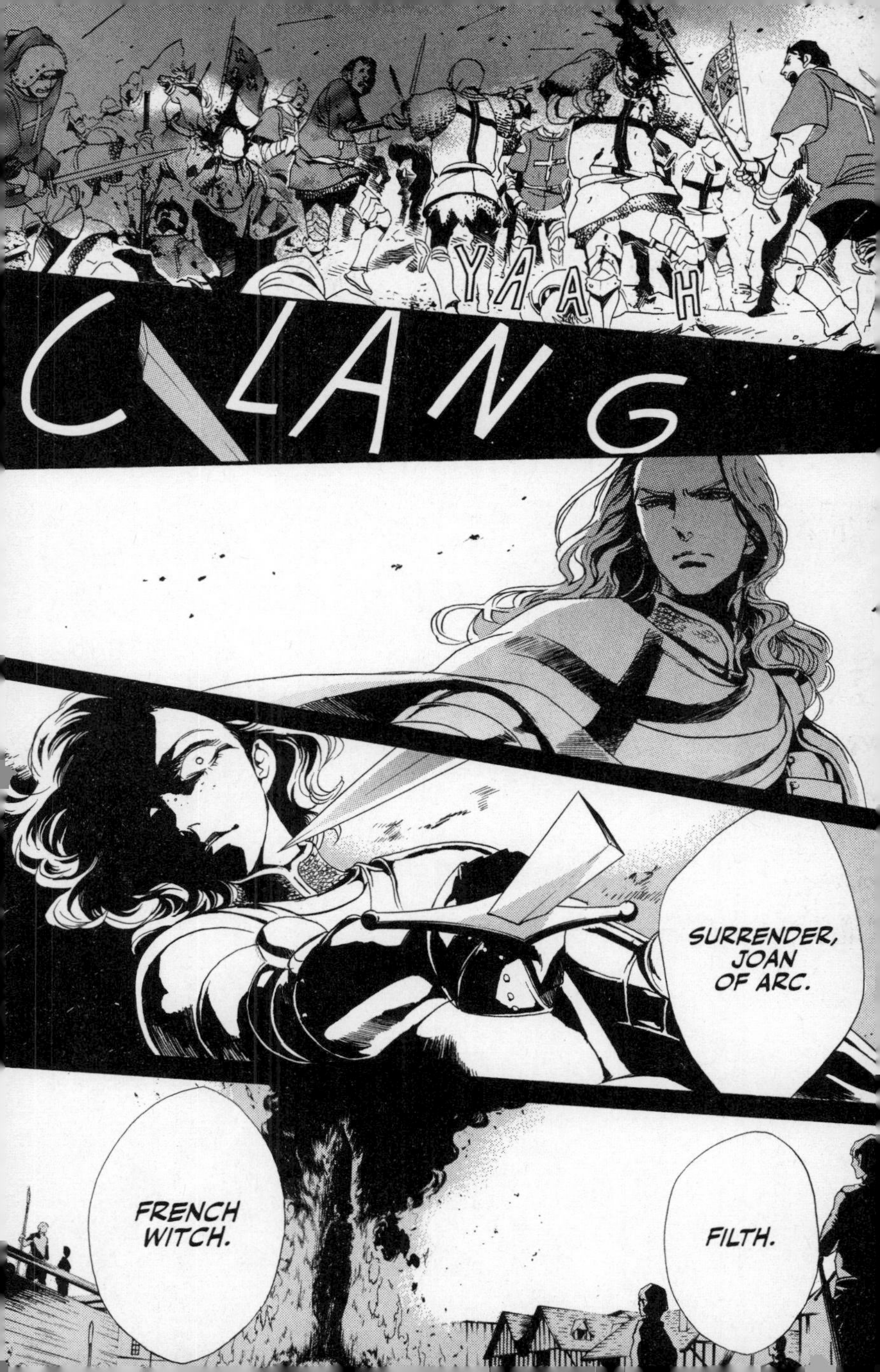
YAAH
CLANG
SURRENDER, JOAN OF ARC.
FILTH.
FRENCH WITCH.

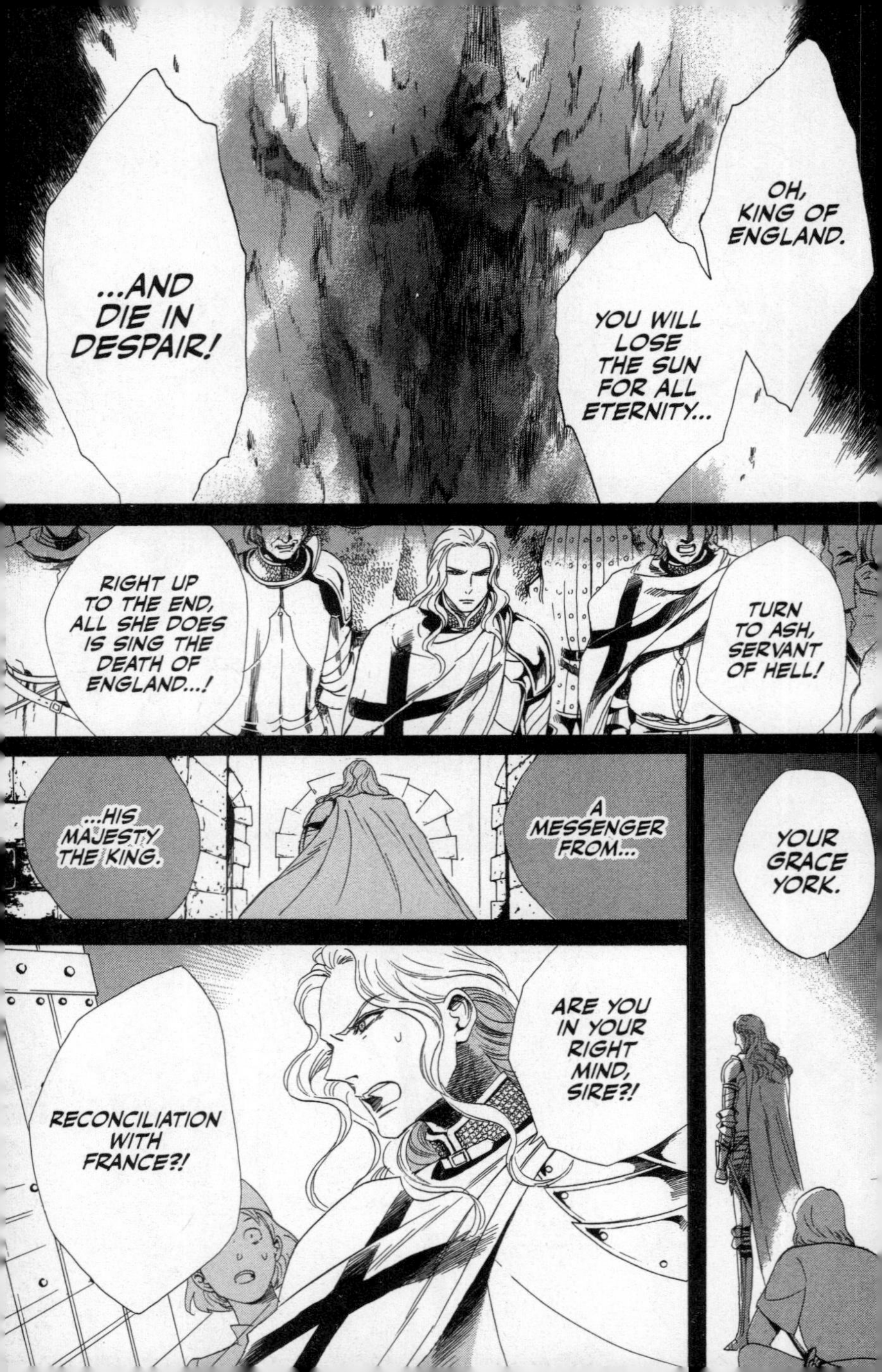
OH, KING OF ENGLAND.
YOU WILL LOSE THE SUN FOR ALL ETERNITY...
...AND DIE IN DESPAIR!
TURN TO ASH, SERVANT OF HELL!
RIGHT UP TO THE END, ALL SHE DOES IS SING THE DEATH OF ENGLAND...!
YOUR GRACE YORK.
A MESSENGER FROM...
...HIS MAJESTY THE KING.
ARE YOU IN YOUR RIGHT MIND, SIRE?!
RECONCILIATION WITH FRANCE?!

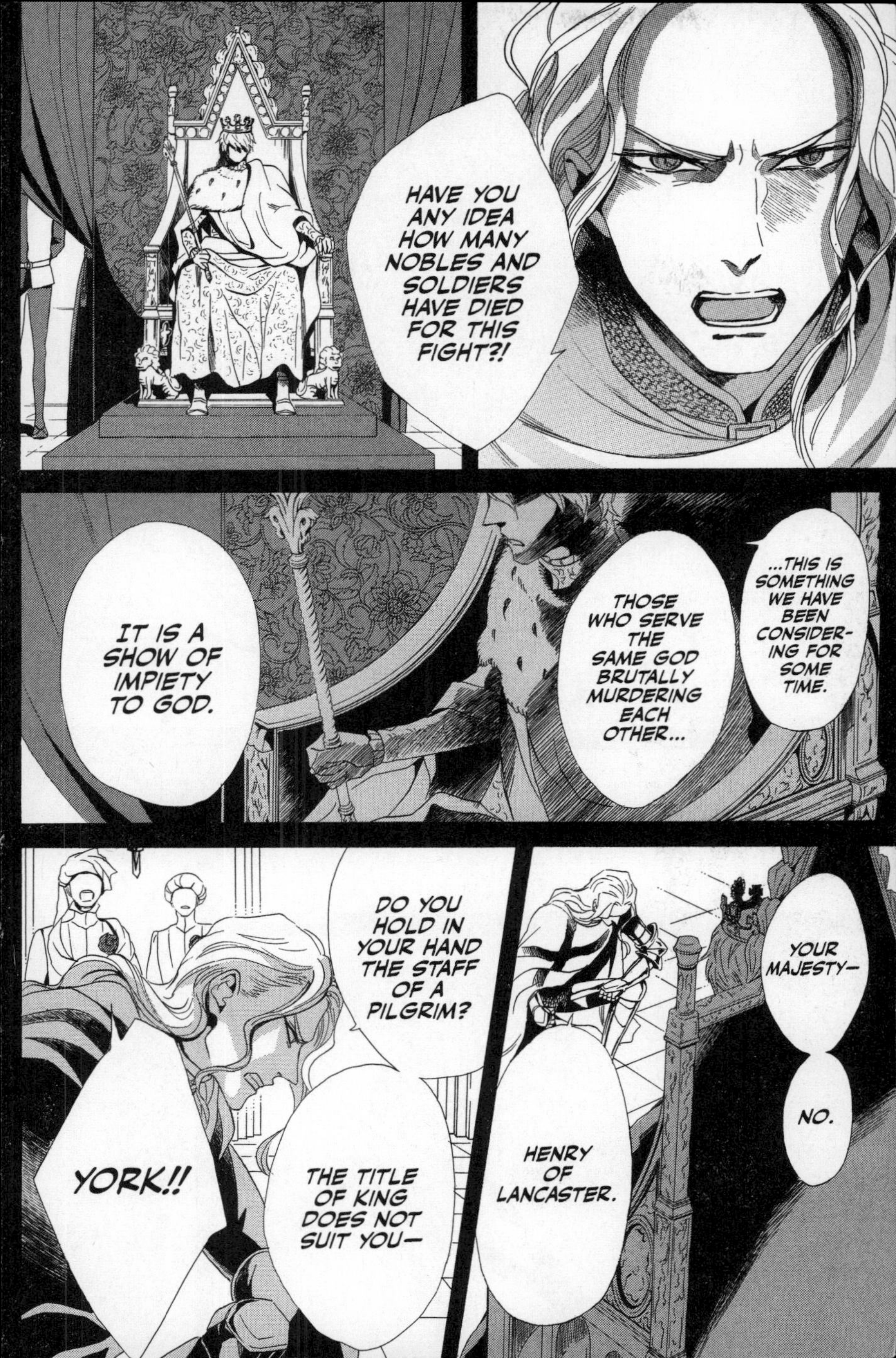
HAVE YOU ANY IDEA HOW MANY NOBLES AND SOLDIERS HAVE DIED FOR THIS FIGHT?!
...THIS IS SOMETHING WE HAVE BEEN CONSIDER-ING FOR SOME TIME.
THOSE WHO SERVE THE SAME GOD BRUTALLY MURDERING EACH OTHER...
IT IS A SHOW OF IMPIETY TO GOD.
YOUR MAJESTY—
NO.
HENRY OF LANCASTER.
DO YOU HOLD IN YOUR HAND THE STAFF OF A PILGRIM?
THE TITLE OF KING DOES NOT SUIT YOU—
YORK!!

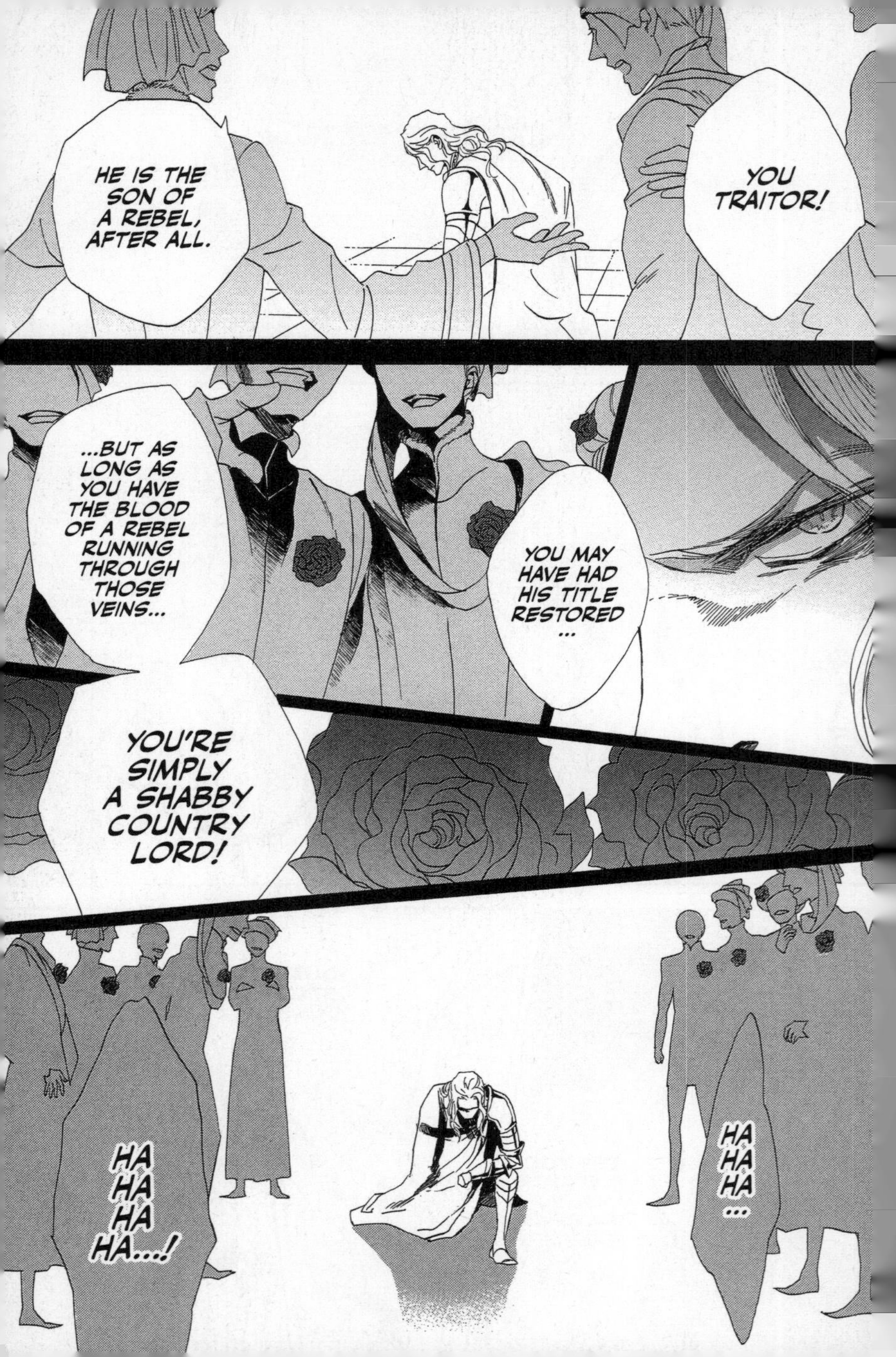
YOU TRAITOR!
HE IS THE SON OF A REBEL, AFTER ALL.
YOU MAY HAVE HAD HIS TITLE RESTORED ...
...BUT AS LONG AS YOU HAVE THE BLOOD OF A REBEL RUNNING THROUGH THOSE VEINS...
YOU'RE SIMPLY A SHABBY COUNTRY LORD!
HA HA HA ...
HA HA HA HA...!

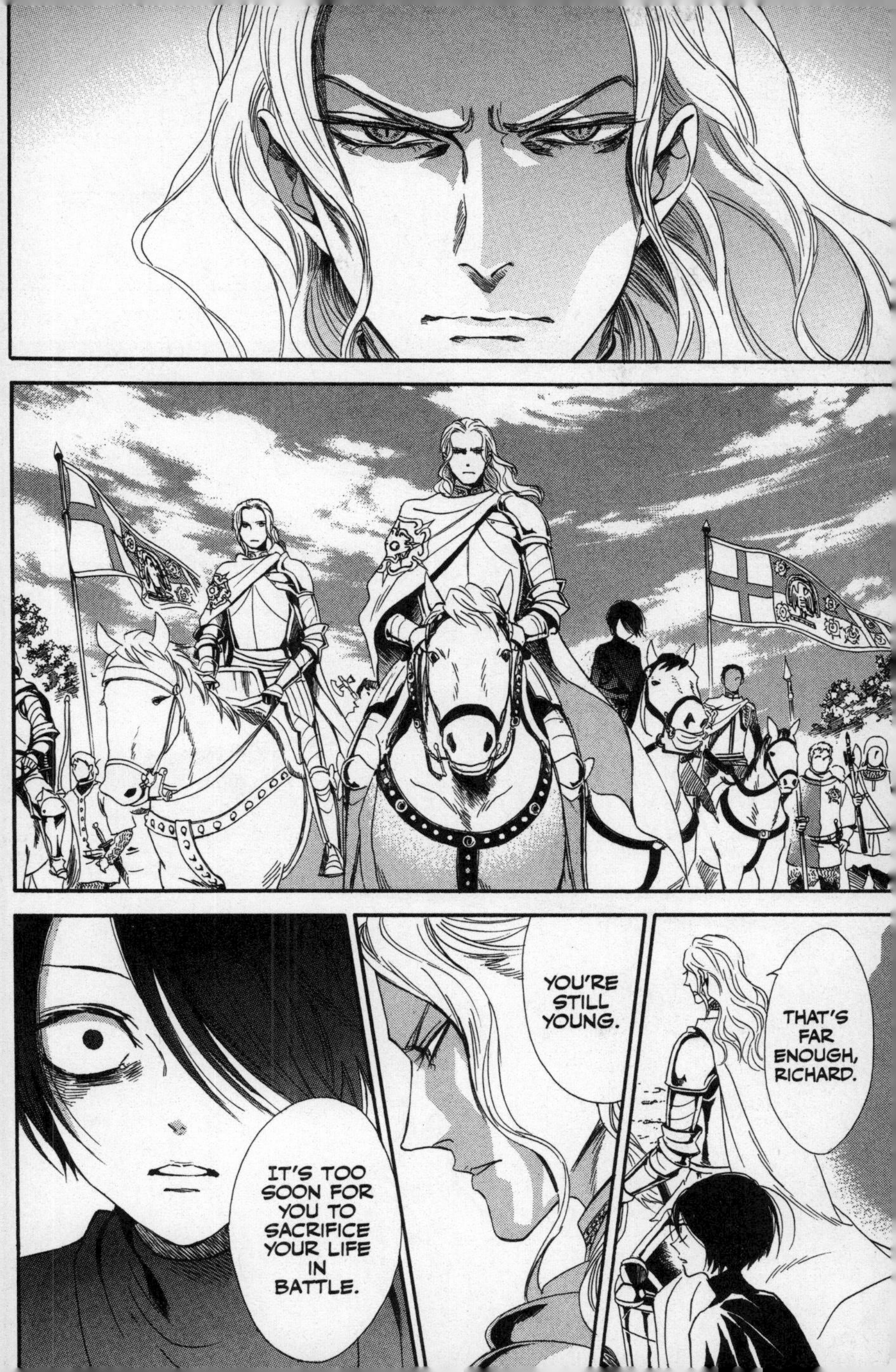
THAT'S FAR ENOUGH, RICHARD.
YOU'RE STILL YOUNG.
IT'S TOO SOON FOR YOU TO SACRIFICE YOUR LIFE IN BATTLE.

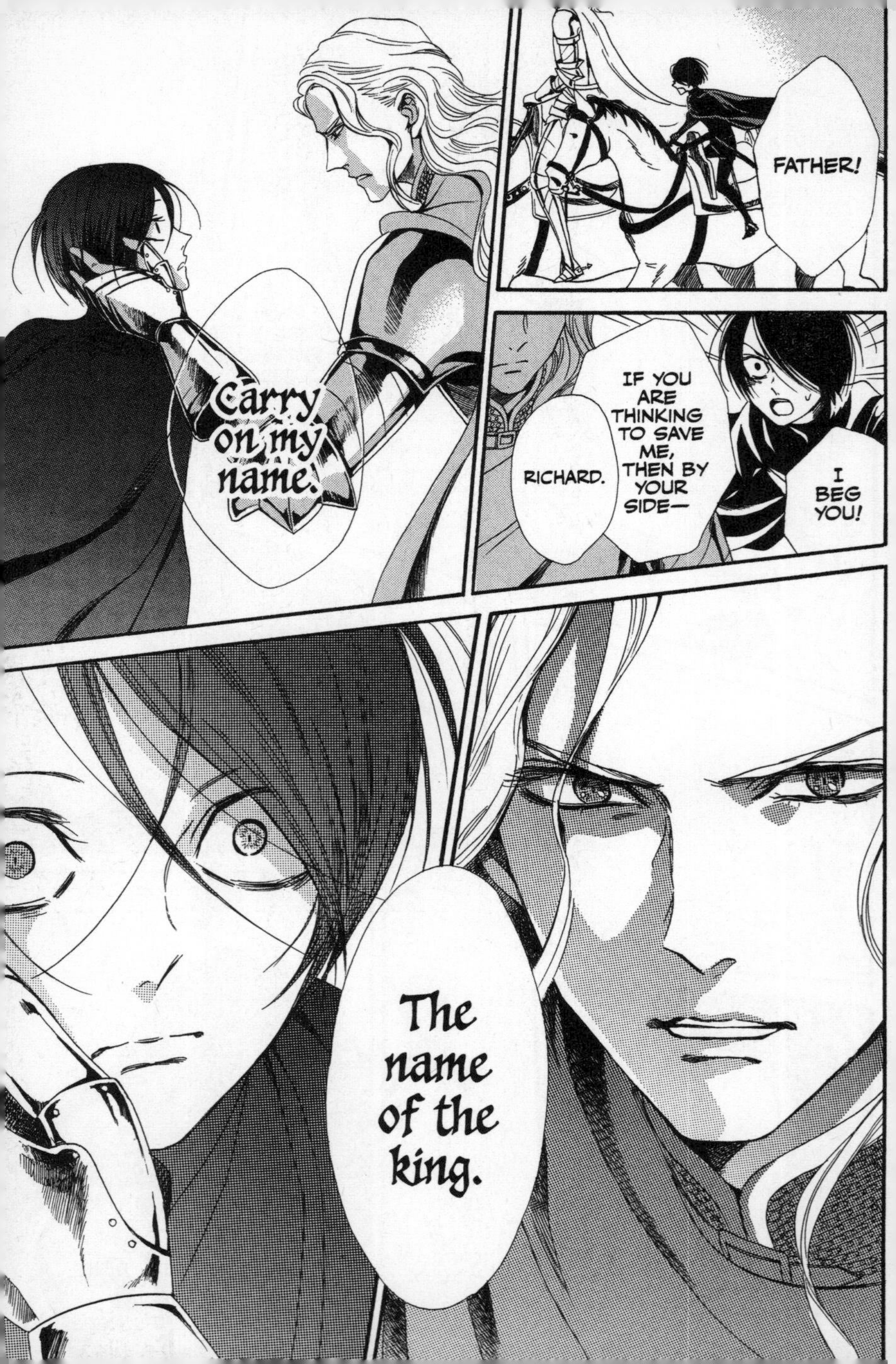
FATHER!
IF YOU ARE THINKING TO SAVE ME, THEN BY YOUR SIDE—
I BEG YOU!
RICHARD.
Carry on my name.
The name of the king.

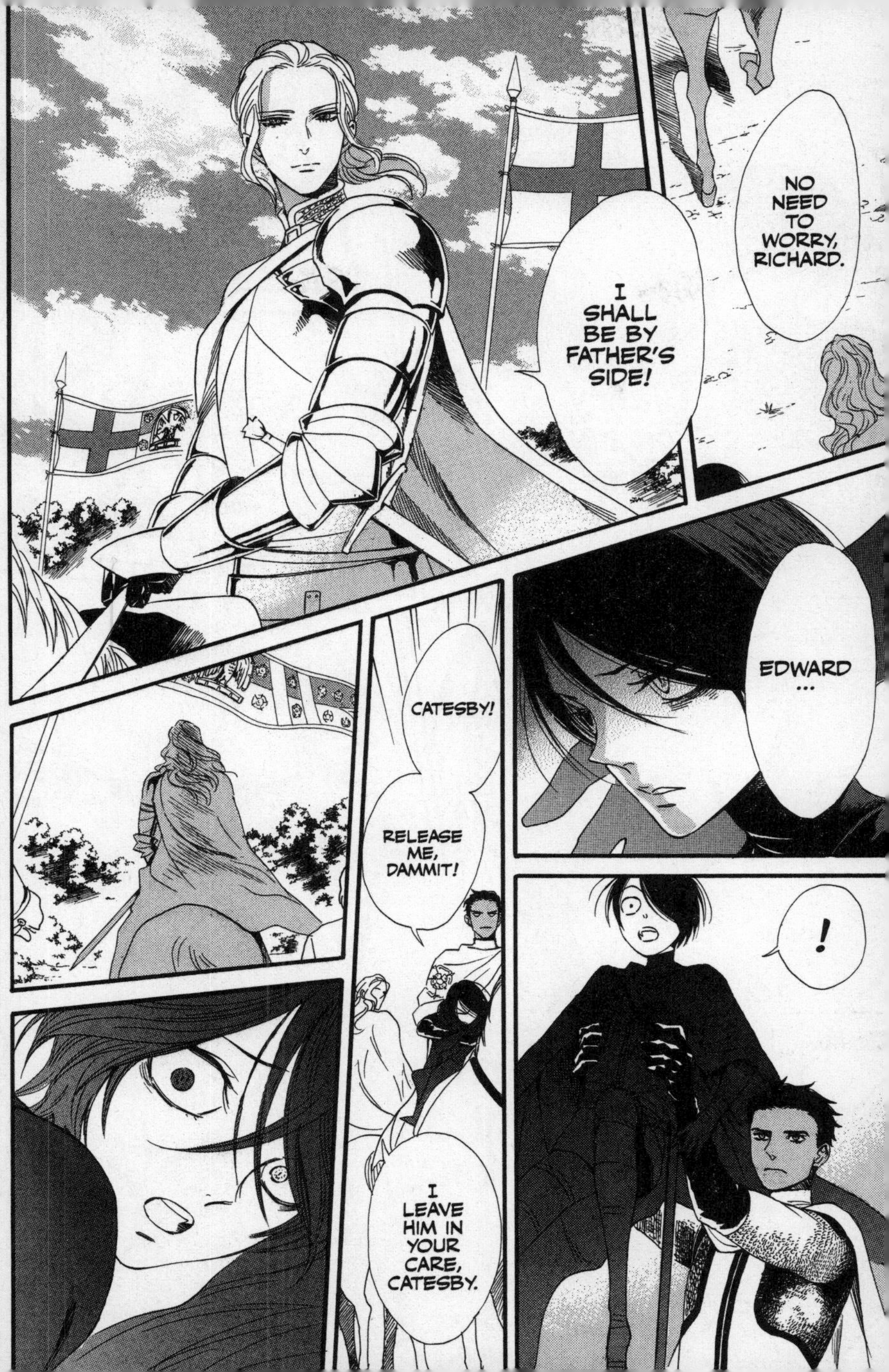
NO NEED TO WORRY, RICHARD.
I SHALL BE BY FATHER'S SIDE!
EDWARD ...
!
CATESBY!
RELEASE ME, DAMMIT!
I LEAVE HIM IN YOUR CARE, CATESBY.

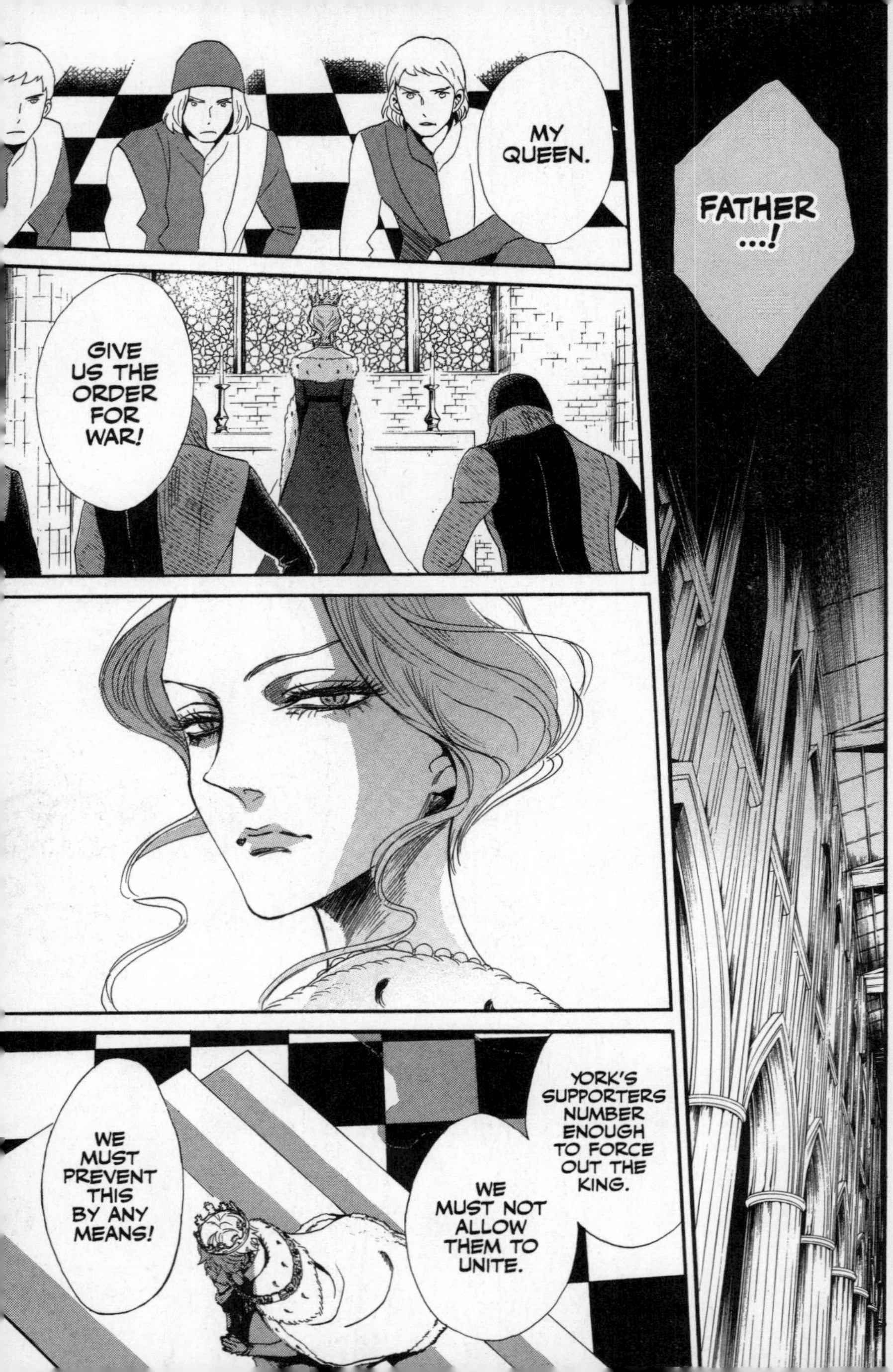
FATHER ...!
MY QUEEN.
GIVE US THE ORDER FOR WAR!
YORK'S SUPPORTERS NUMBER ENOUGH TO FORCE OUT THE KING.
WE MUST NOT ALLOW THEM TO UNITE.
WE MUST PREVENT THIS BY ANY MEANS!

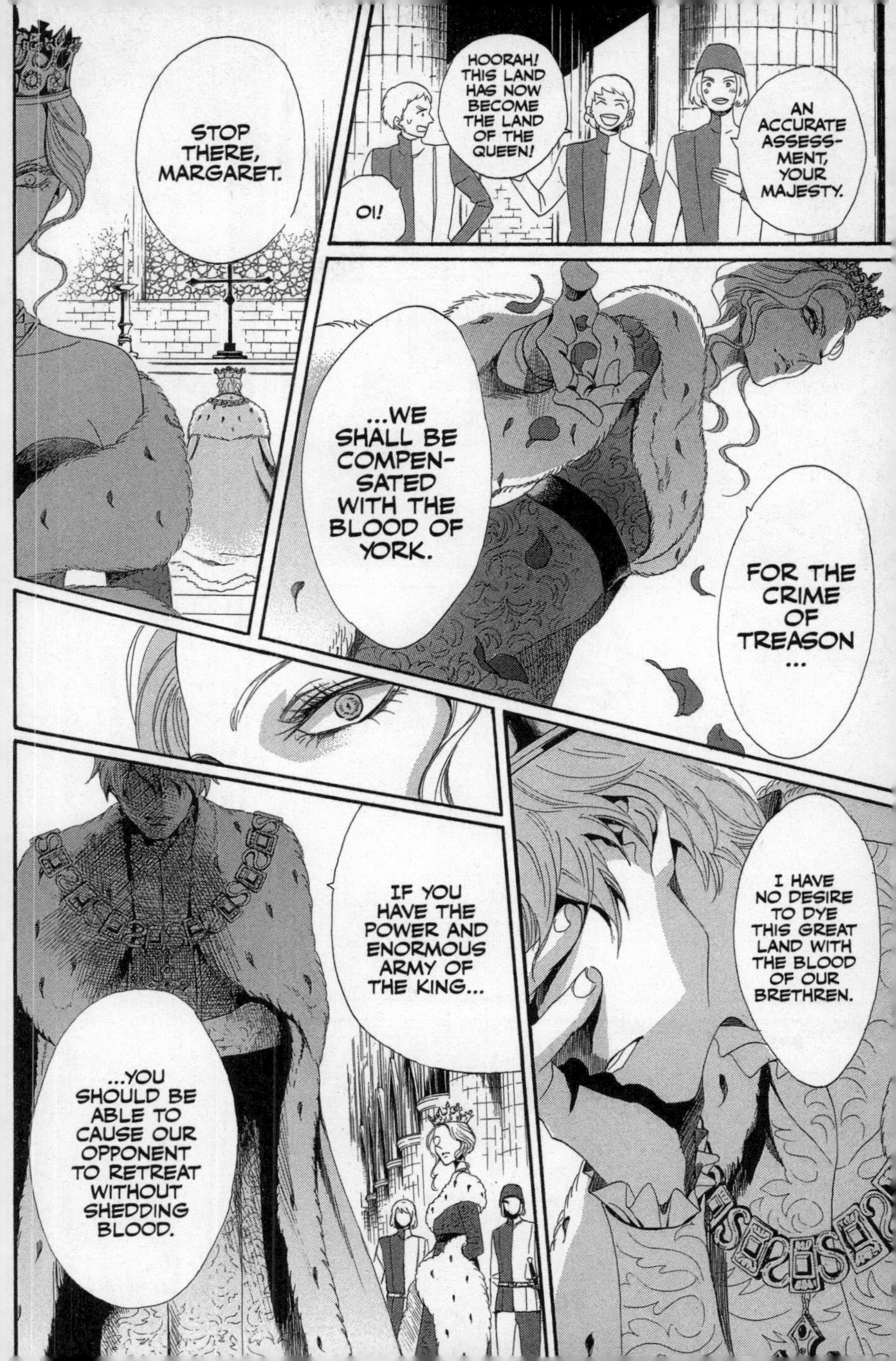
HOORAH! THIS LAND HAS NOW BECOME THE LAND OF THE QUEEN!
AN ACCURATE ASSESS-MENT, YOUR MAJESTY.
OI!
FOR THE CRIME OF TREASON...
...WE SHALL BE COMPEN-SATED WITH THE BLOOD OF YORK.
STOP THERE, MARGARET.
I HAVE NO DESIRE TO DYE THIS GREAT LAND WITH THE BLOOD OF OUR BRETHREN.
IF YOU HAVE THE POWER AND ENORMOUS ARMY OF THE KING...
...YOU SHOULD BE ABLE TO CAUSE OUR OPPONENT TO RETREAT WITHOUT SHEDDING BLOOD.

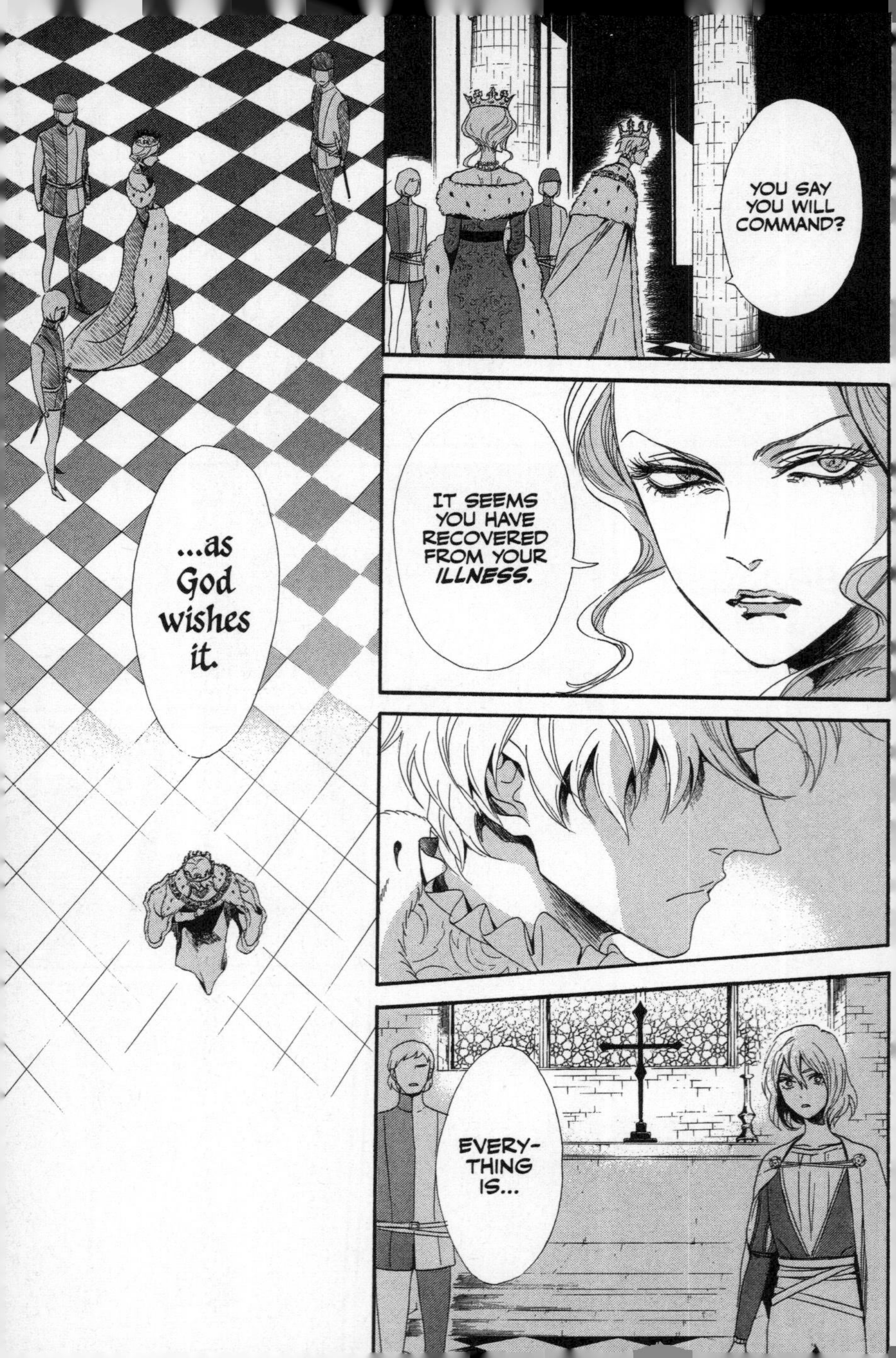
YOU SAY YOU WILL COMMAND?
IT SEEMS YOU HAVE RECOVERED FROM YOUR *ILLNESS.*
EVERY-THING IS...
...as God wishes it.

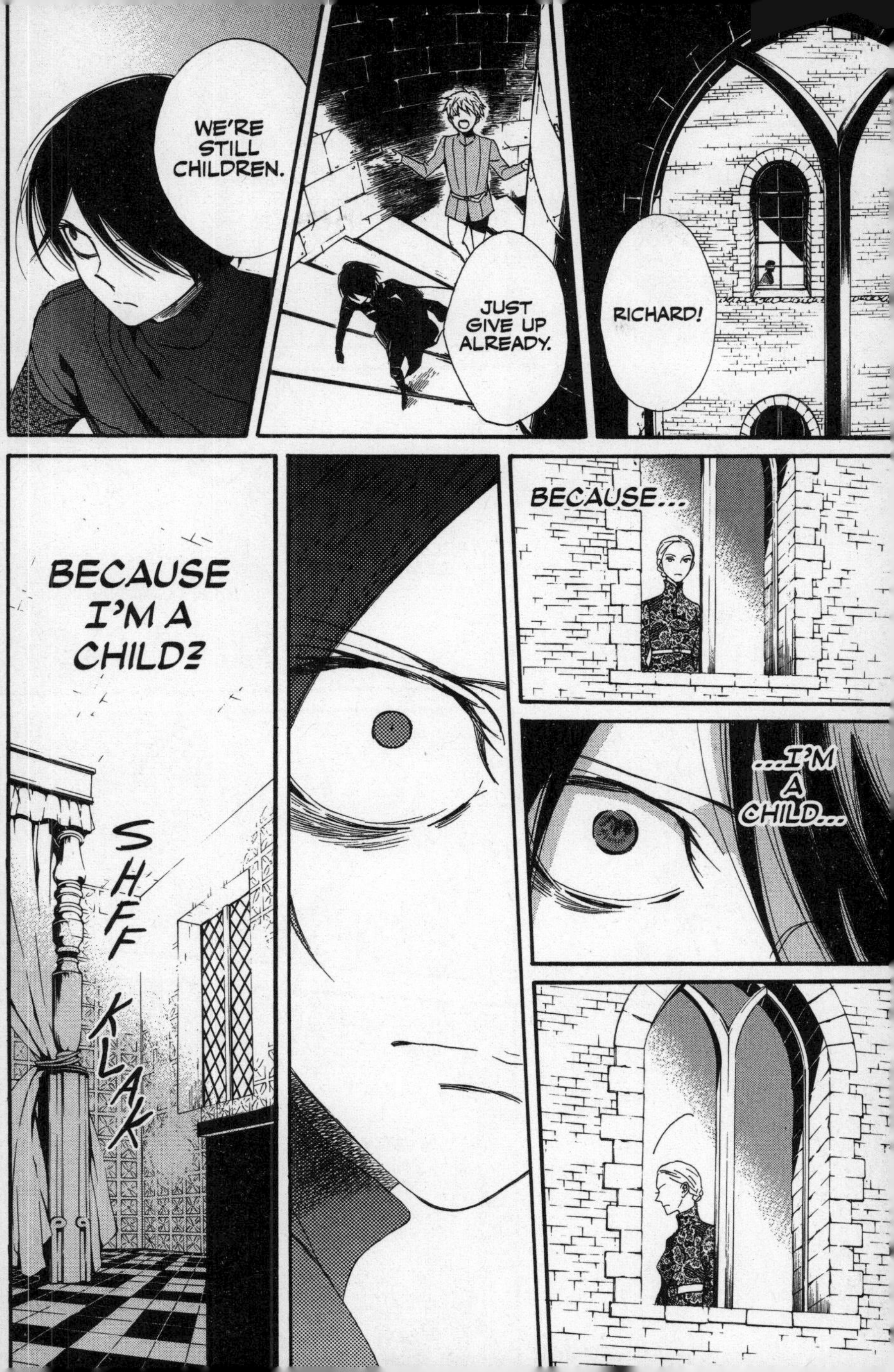
RICHARD!
JUST GIVE UP ALREADY.
WE'RE STILL CHILDREN.
BECAUSE...
...I'M A CHILD...
BECAUSE I'M A CHILD?
SHFF
KLAK

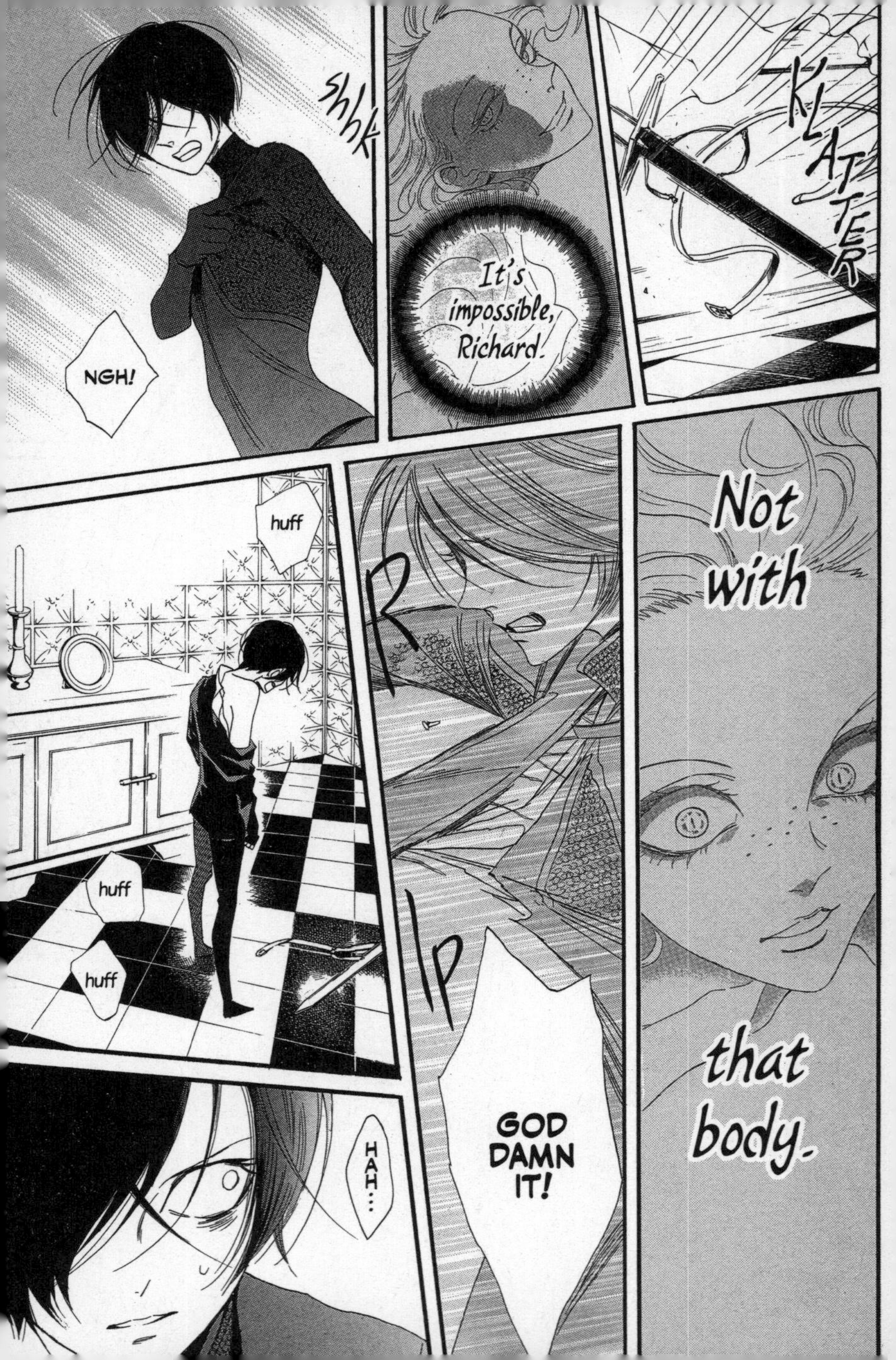
KLATTER
It's impossible, Richard.
SHHK
NGH!
Not with that body.
RIP
GOD DAMN IT!
huff
huff
huff
HAH...

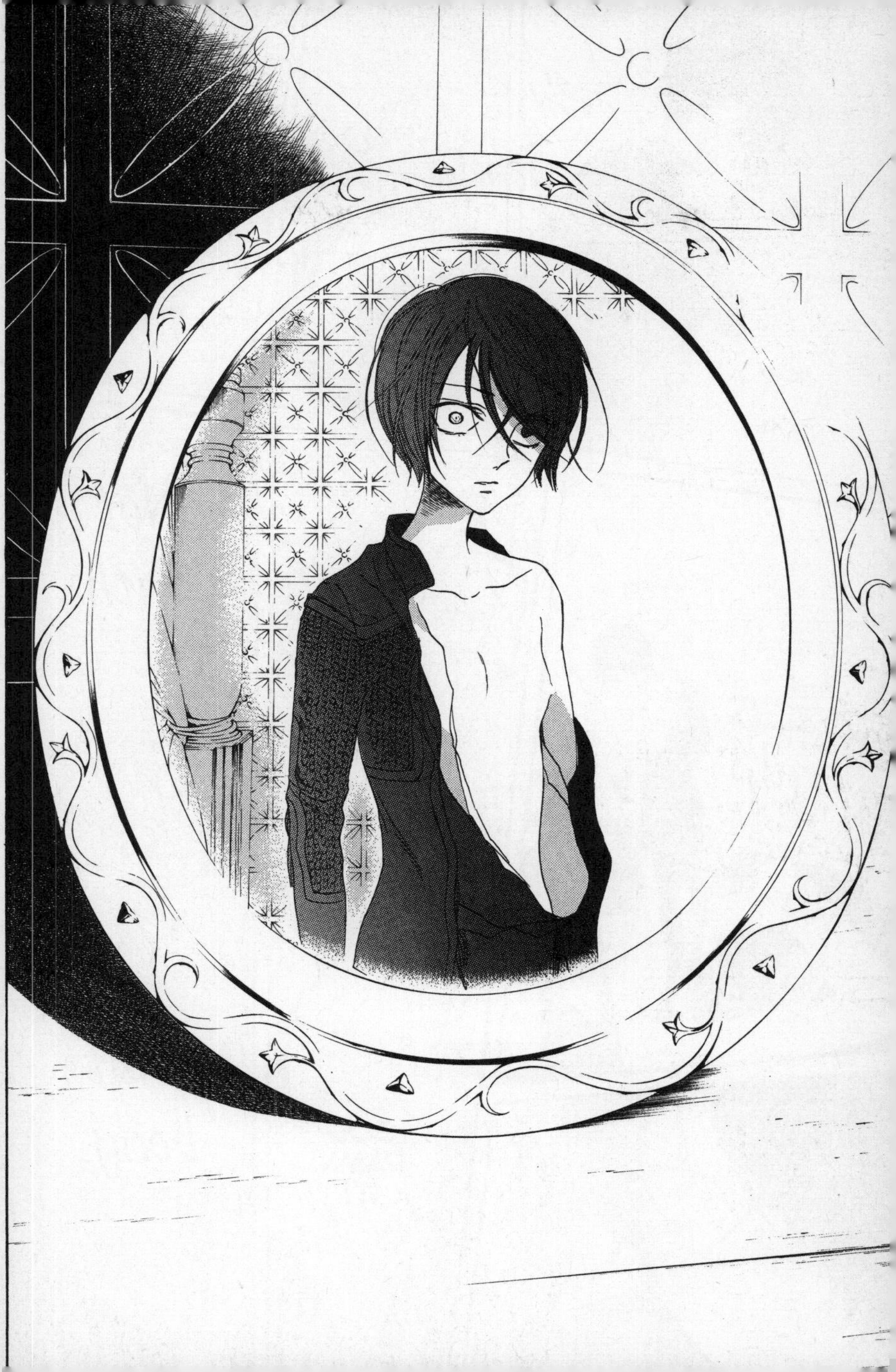

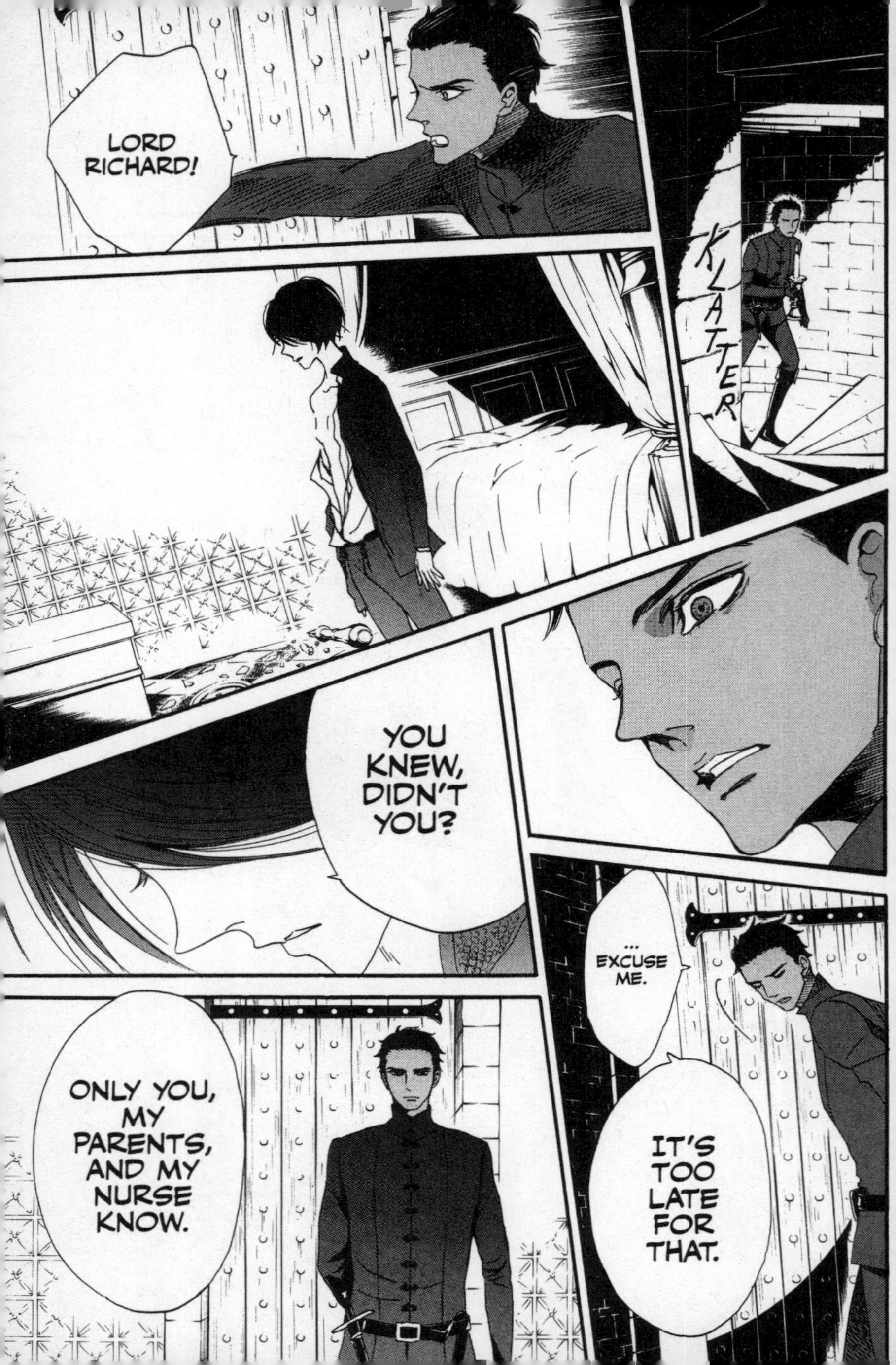
KLATTER
LORD RICHARD!
YOU KNEW, DIDN'T YOU?
... EXCUSE ME.
IT'S TOO LATE FOR THAT.
ONLY YOU, MY PARENTS, AND MY NURSE KNOW.

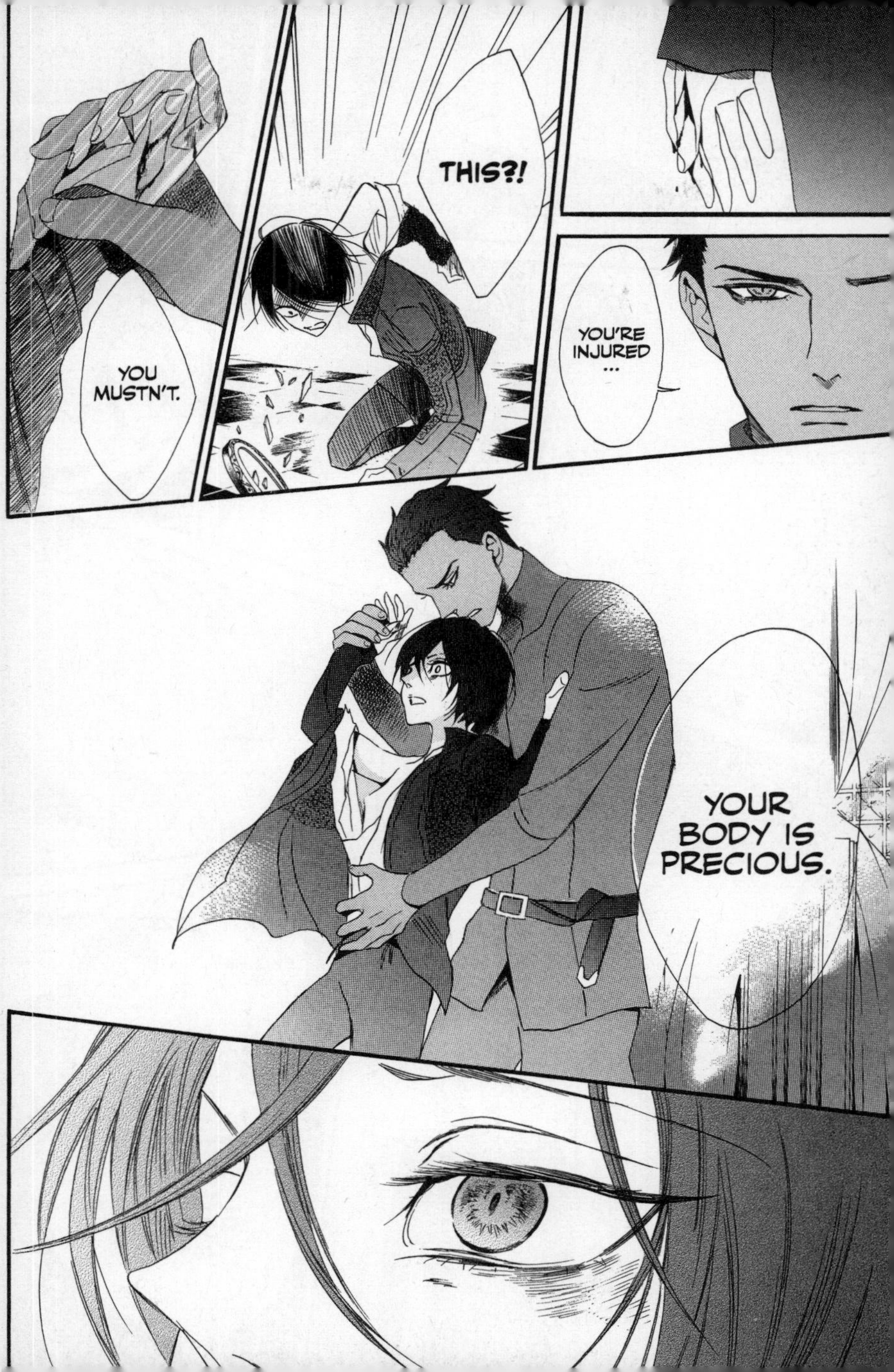
YOU'RE INJURED ...
THIS?!
YOU MUSTN'T.
YOUR BODY IS PRECIOUS.

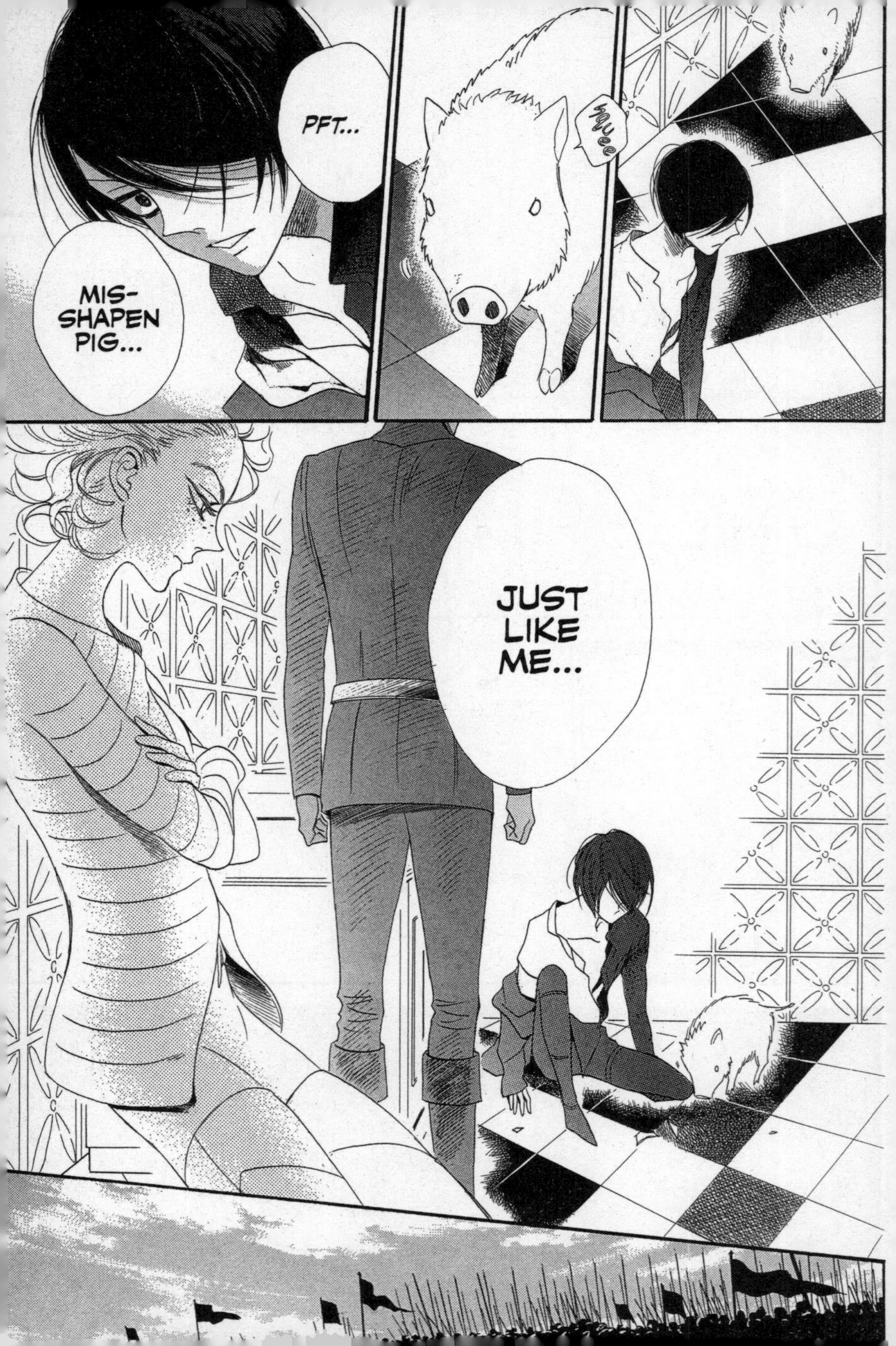
squee
PFT...
MIS-SHAPEN PIG...
JUST LIKE ME...

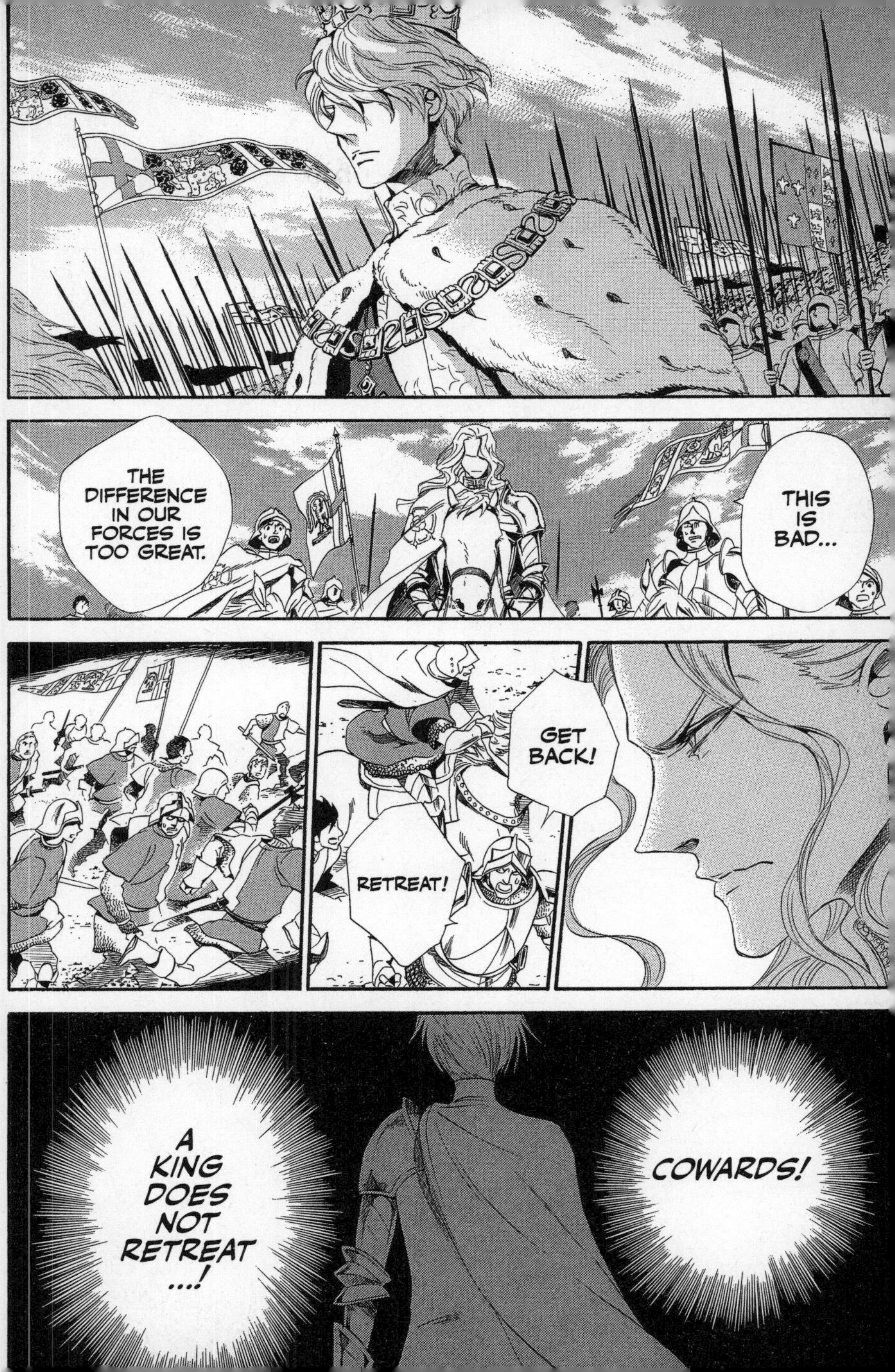
THIS IS BAD...
THE DIFFERENCE IN OUR FORCES IS TOO GREAT.
GET BACK!
RETREAT!
COWARDS!
A KING DOES NOT RETREAT ...!

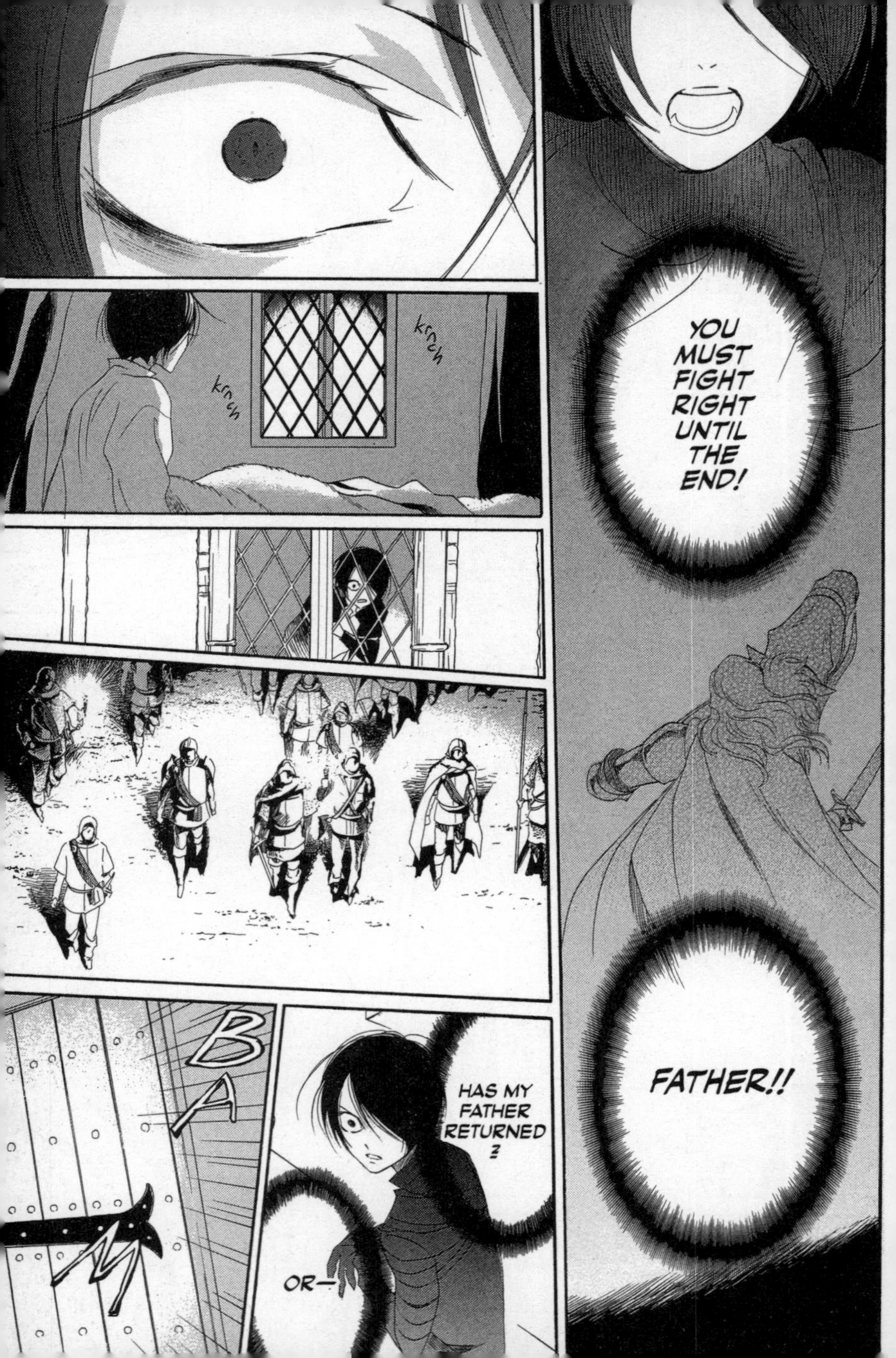
YOU MUST FIGHT RIGHT UNTIL THE END!
FATHER!!
krnch
krnch
HAS MY FATHER RETURNED?
OR—
BAM

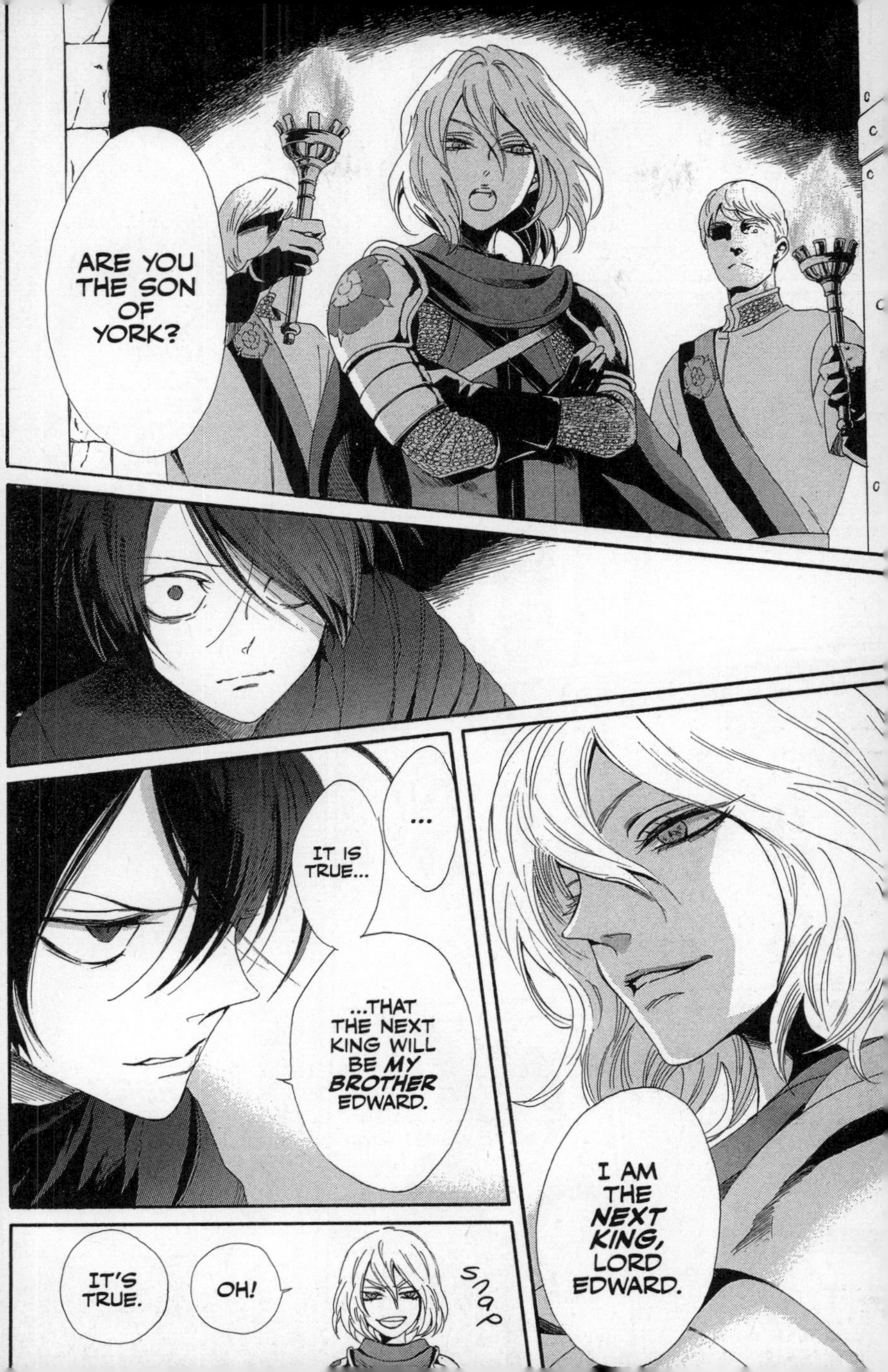

ARE YOU THE SON OF YORK?
I AM THE NEXT KING, LORD EDWARD.
...
IT IS TRUE...
...THAT THE NEXT KING WILL BE MY BROTHER EDWARD.
snap
OH!
IT'S TRUE.

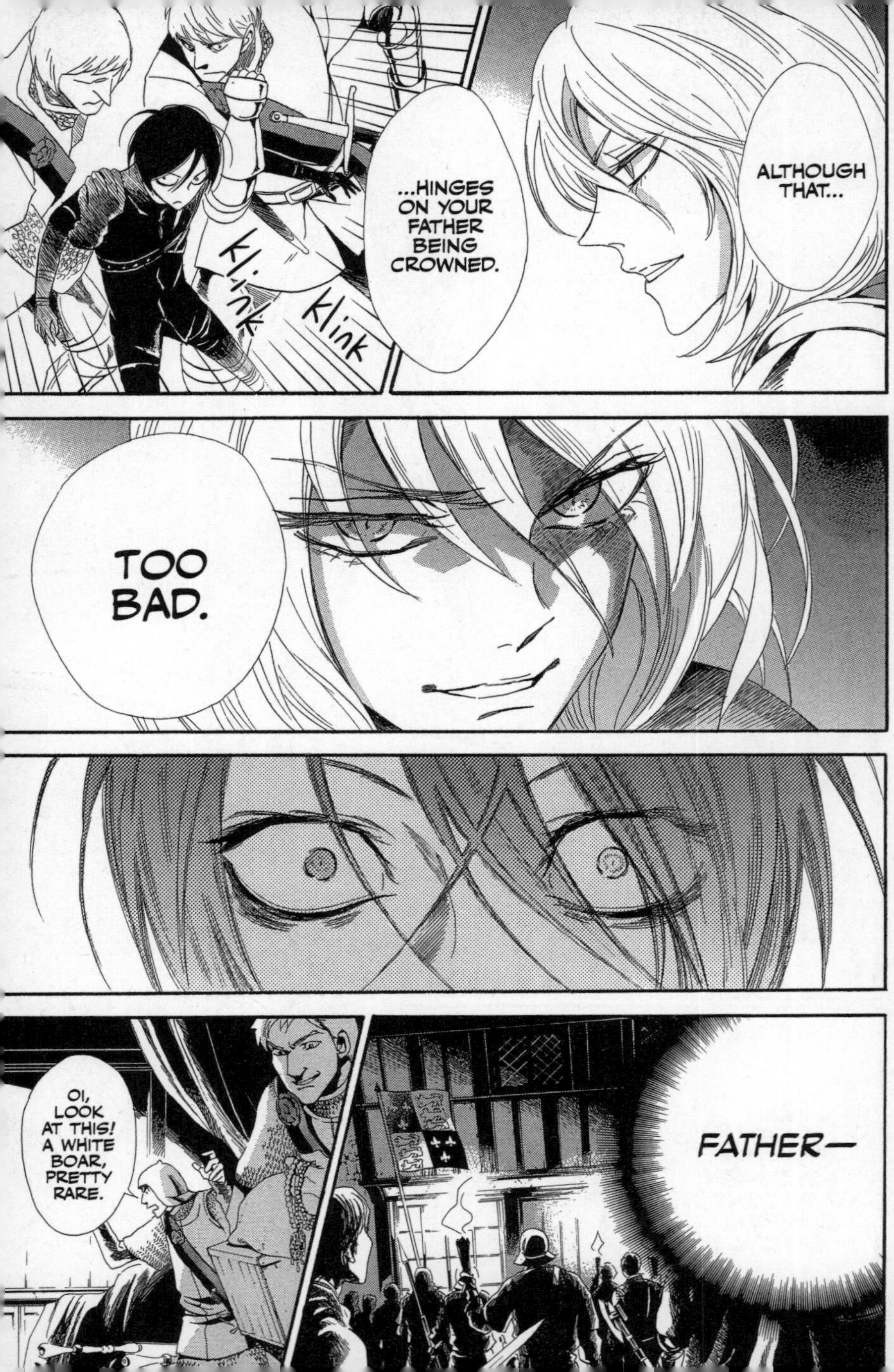

ALTHOUGH THAT...
...HINGES ON YOUR FATHER BEING CROWNED.
klink
klink
TOO BAD.
FATHER—
OI, LOOK AT THIS! A WHITE BOAR, PRETTY RARE.

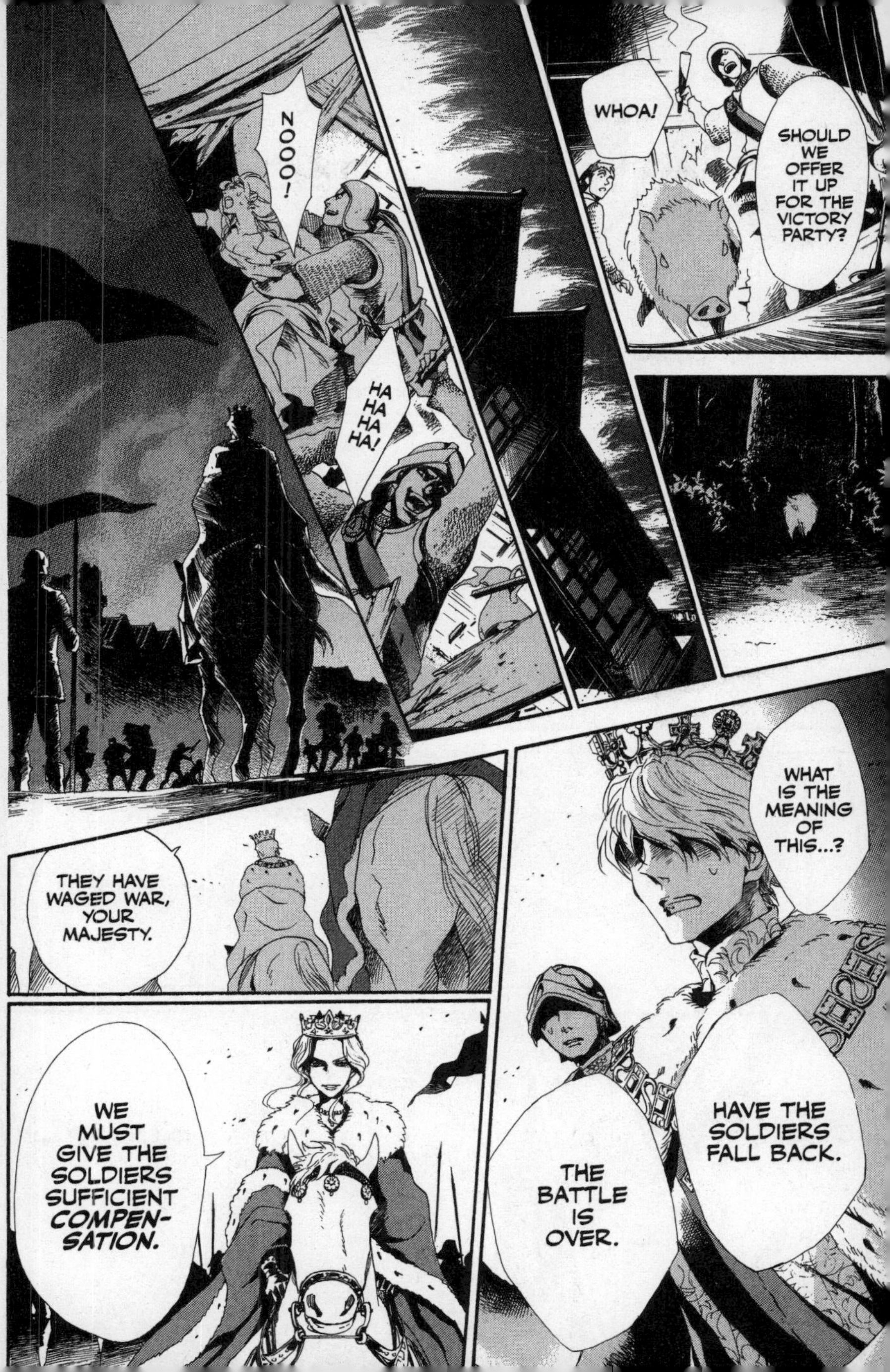
WHOA!
SHOULD WE OFFER IT UP FOR THE VICTORY PARTY?
NOOOO!
HA HA HA HA!
WHAT IS THE MEANING OF THIS...?
THEY HAVE WAGED WAR, YOUR MAJESTY.
HAVE THE SOLDIERS FALL BACK.
THE BATTLE IS OVER.
WE MUST GIVE THE SOLDIERS SUFFICIENT *COMPENSATION.*

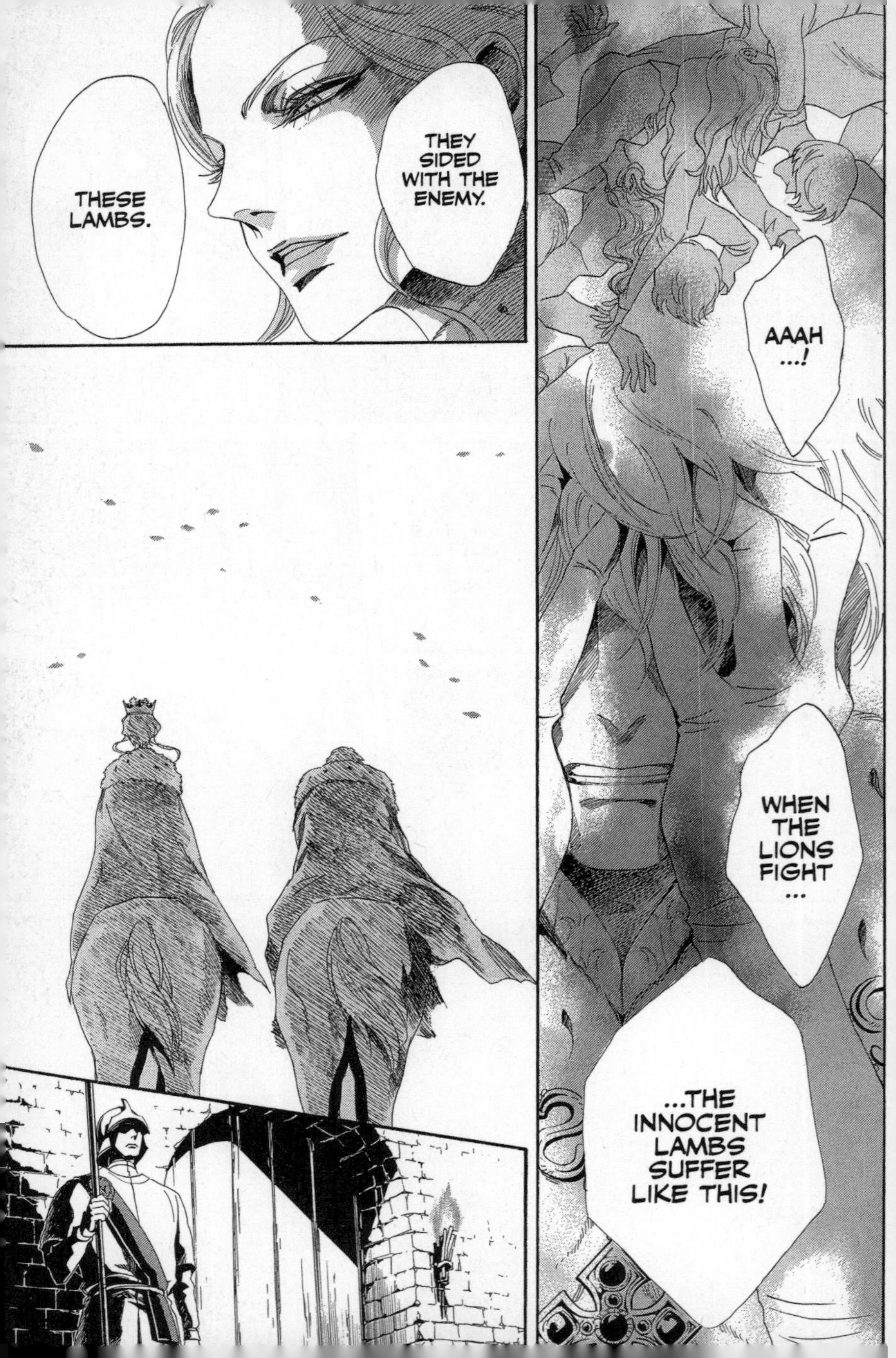
AAAH ...!
WHEN THE LIONS FIGHT ...
...THE INNOCENT LAMBS SUFFER LIKE THIS!
THEY SIDED WITH THE ENEMY.
THESE LAMBS.

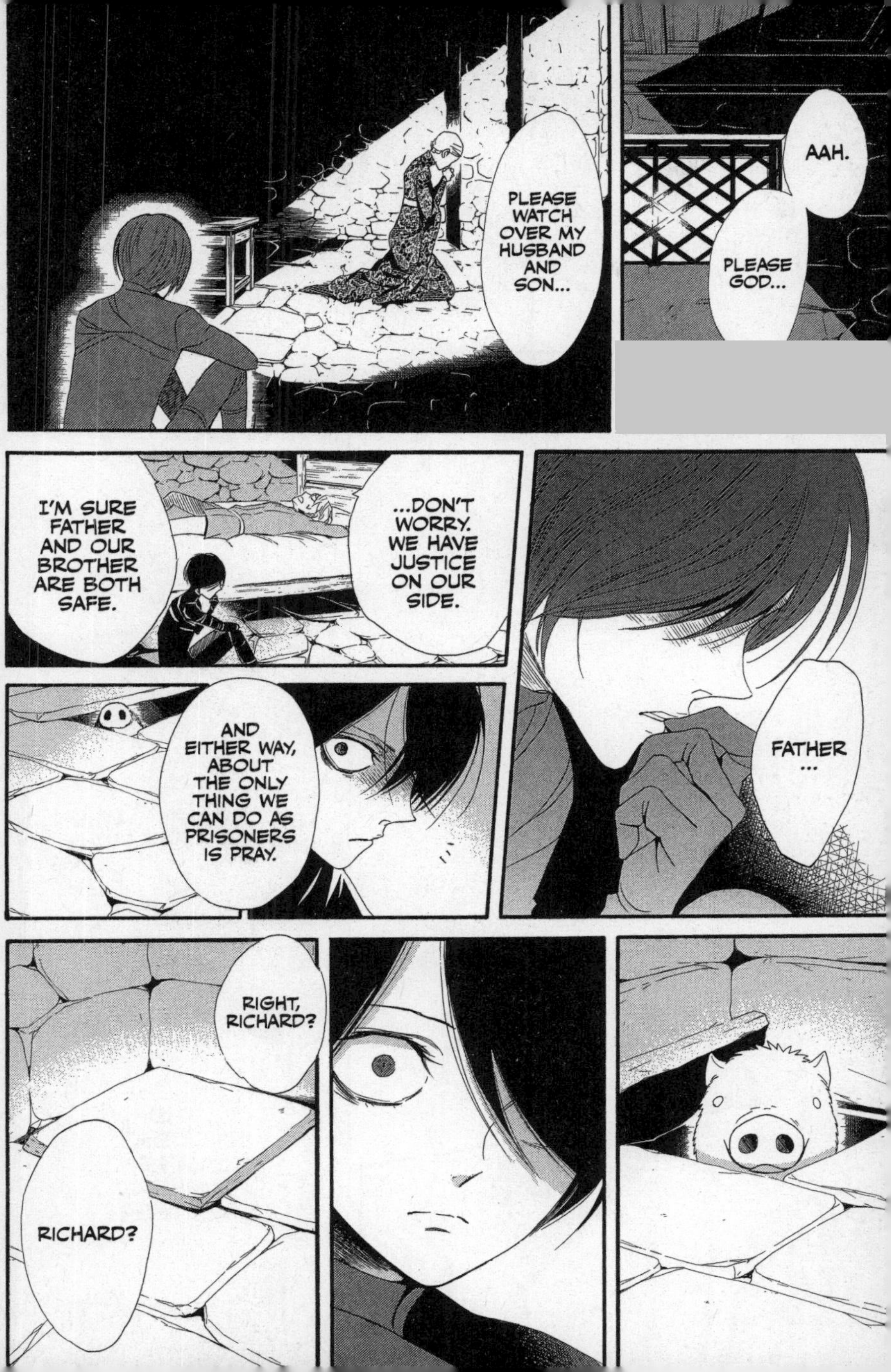
AAH.
PLEASE GOD...
PLEASE WATCH OVER MY HUSBAND AND SON...
FATHER ...
...DON'T WORRY. WE HAVE JUSTICE ON OUR SIDE.
I'M SURE FATHER AND OUR BROTHER ARE BOTH SAFE.
AND EITHER WAY, ABOUT THE ONLY THING WE CAN DO AS PRISONERS IS PRAY.
RIGHT, RICHARD?
RICHARD?

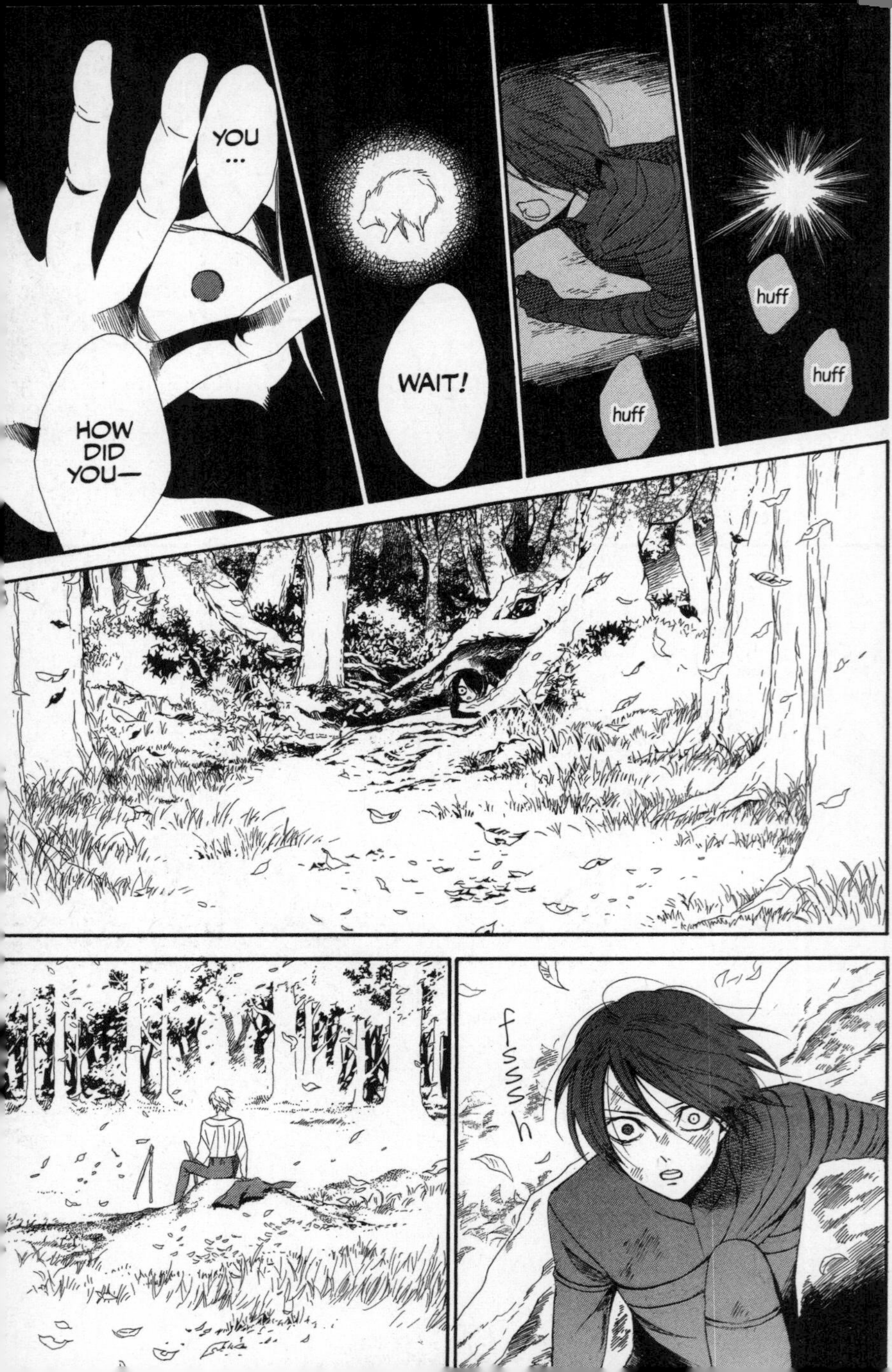
huff
huff
huff
WAIT!
YOU ...
HOW DID YOU—
fsssh

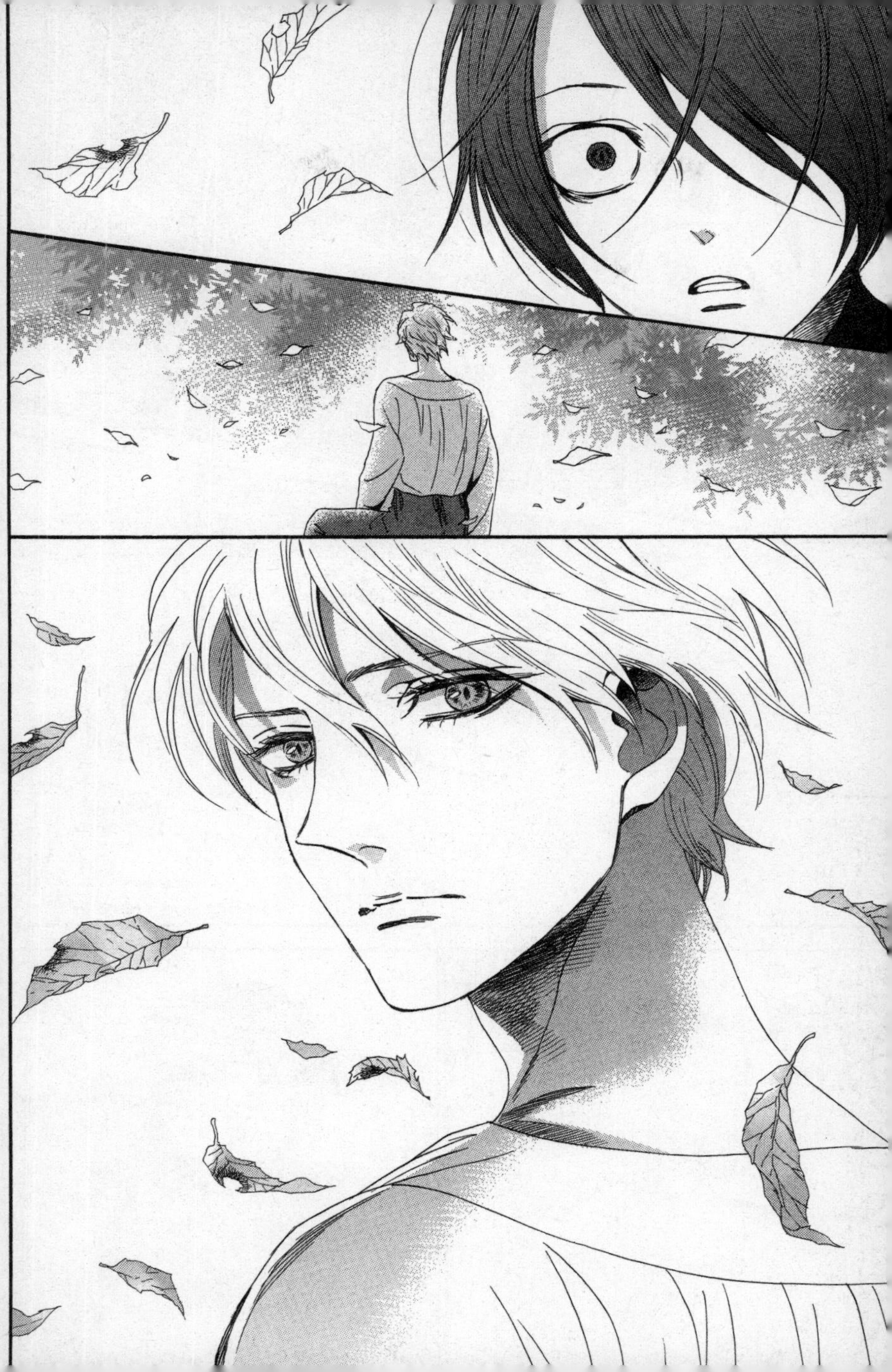

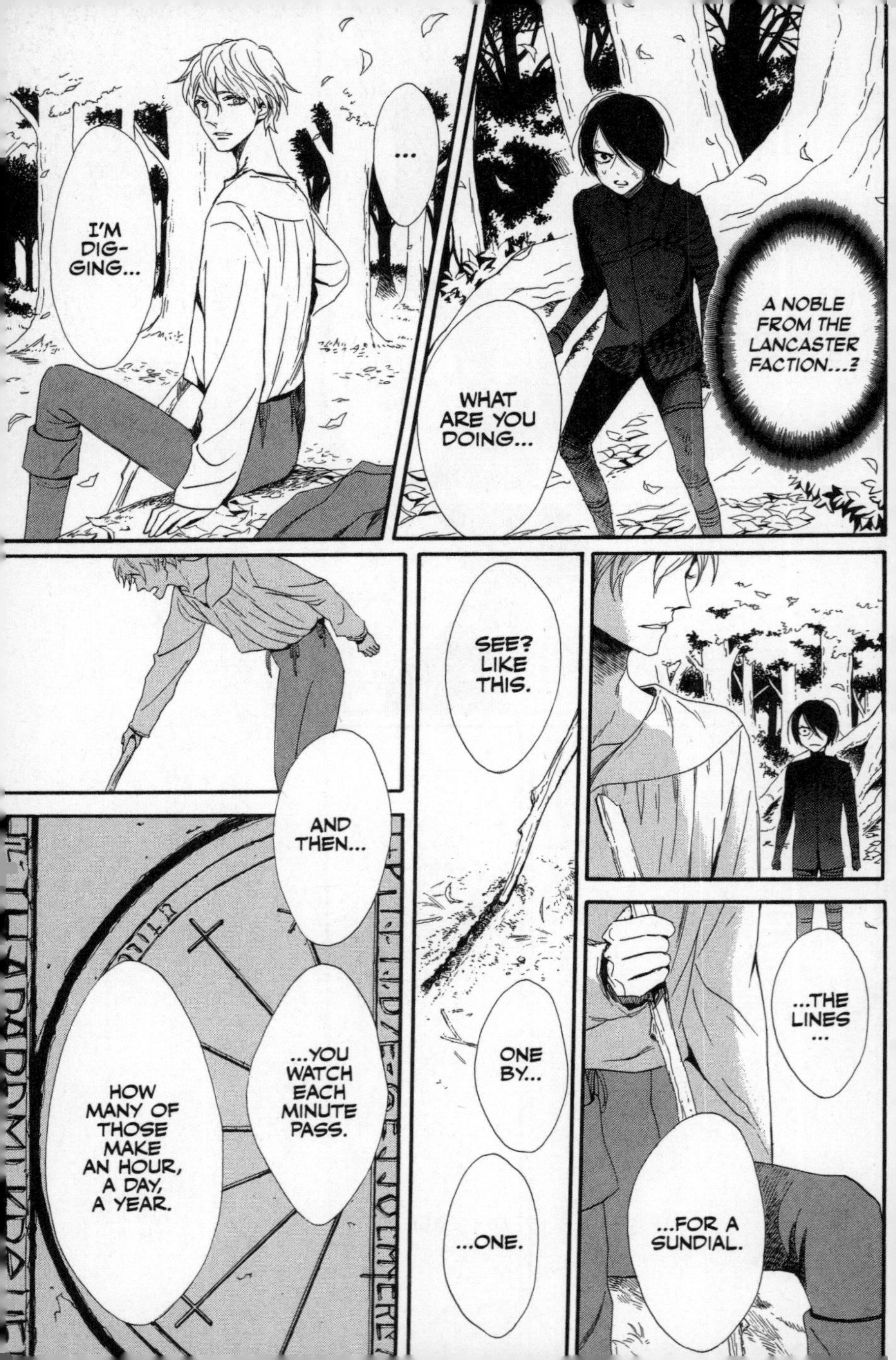
A NOBLE FROM THE LANCASTER FACTION...?
WHAT ARE YOU DOING...
...
I'M DIG-GING...
...THE LINES...
...FOR A SUNDIAL.
SEE? LIKE THIS.
ONE BY...
...ONE.
AND THEN...
...YOU WATCH EACH MINUTE PASS.
HOW MANY OF THOSE MAKE AN HOUR, A DAY, A YEAR.

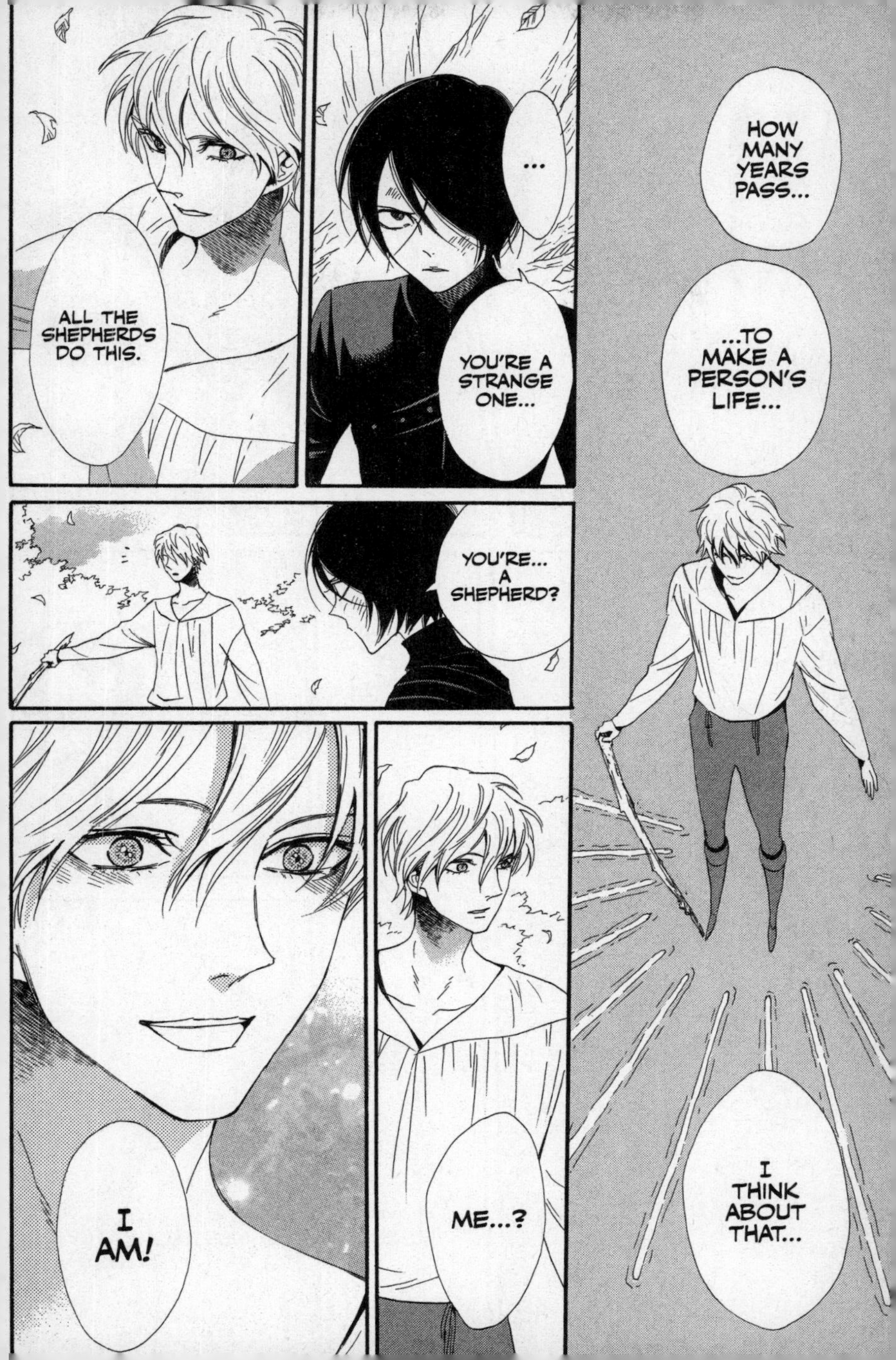
HOW MANY YEARS PASS...
...TO MAKE A PERSON'S LIFE...
I THINK ABOUT THAT...
...
YOU'RE A STRANGE ONE...
ALL THE SHEPHERDS DO THIS.
YOU'RE... A SHEPHERD?
ME...?
I AM!

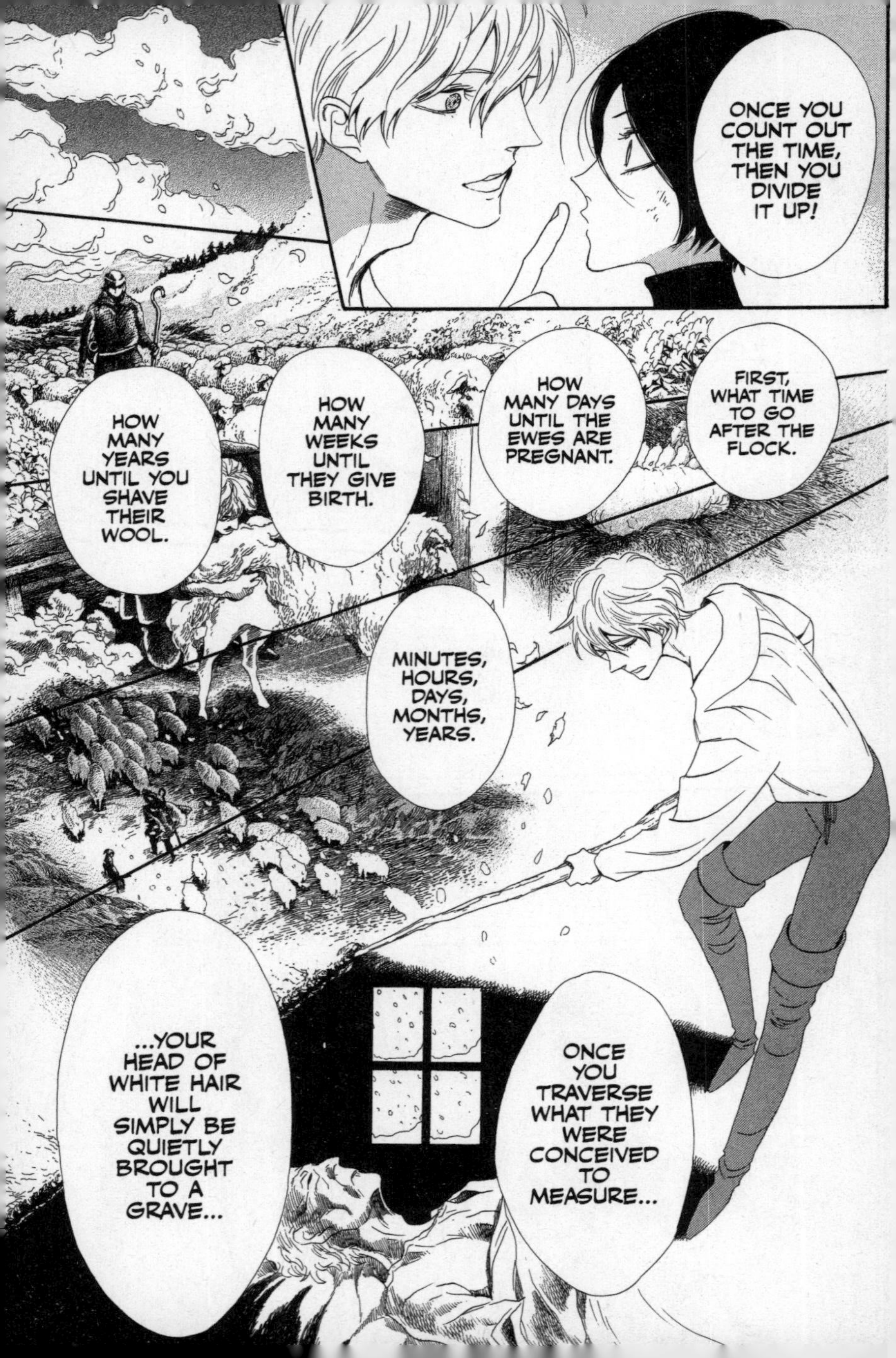
ONCE YOU COUNT OUT THE TIME, THEN YOU DIVIDE IT UP!
FIRST, WHAT TIME TO GO AFTER THE FLOCK.
HOW MANY DAYS UNTIL THE EWES ARE PREGNANT.
HOW MANY WEEKS UNTIL THEY GIVE BIRTH.
HOW MANY YEARS UNTIL YOU SHAVE THEIR WOOL.
MINUTES, HOURS, DAYS, MONTHS, YEARS.
ONCE YOU TRAVERSE WHAT THEY WERE CONCEIVED TO MEASURE...
...YOUR HEAD OF WHITE HAIR WILL SIMPLY BE QUIETLY BROUGHT TO A GRAVE...

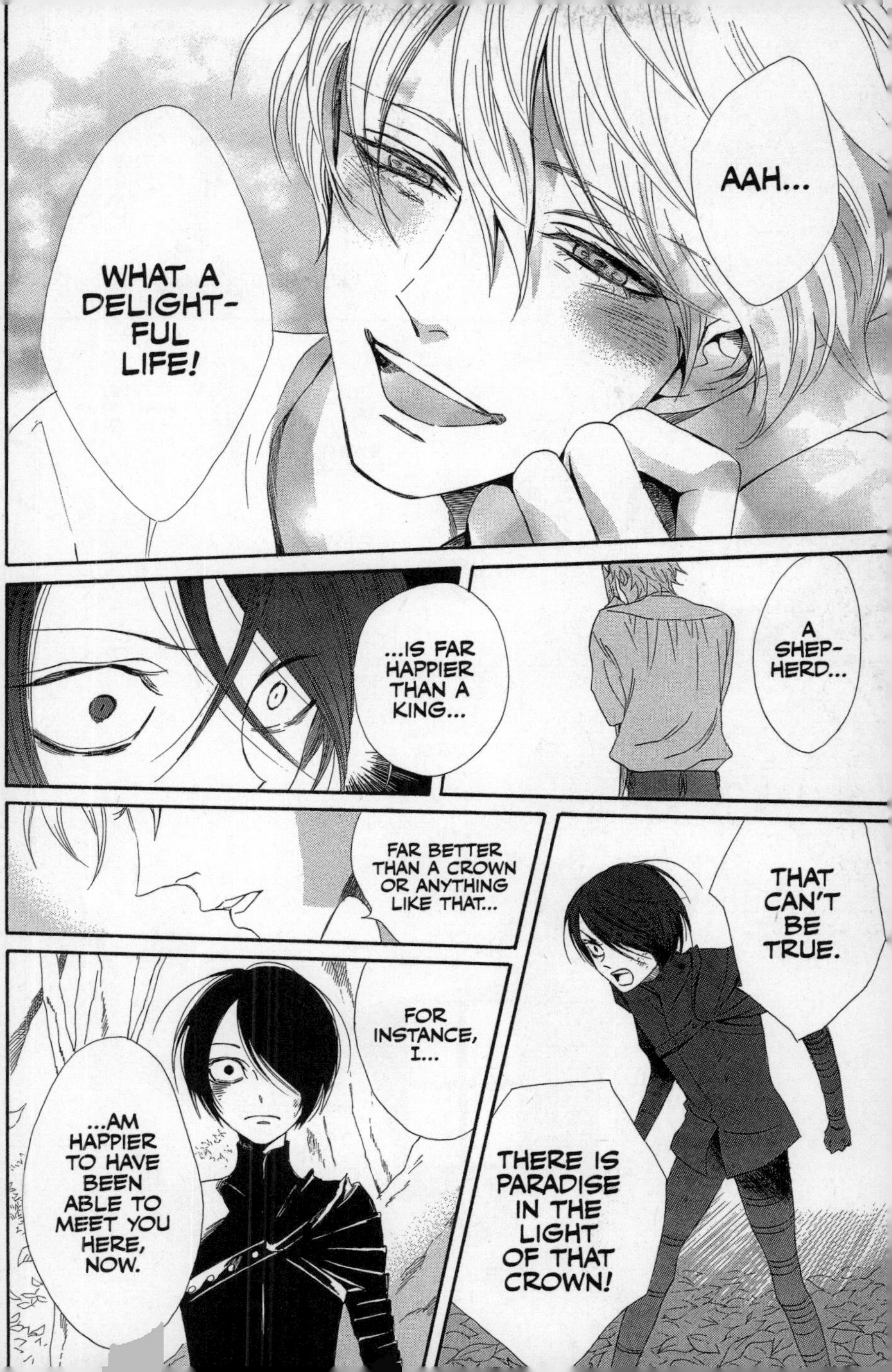
AAH...
WHAT A DELIGHT-FUL LIFE!
A SHEP-HERD...
...IS FAR HAPPIER THAN A KING...
THAT CAN'T BE TRUE.
THERE IS PARADISE IN THE LIGHT OF THAT CROWN!
FAR BETTER THAN A CROWN OR ANYTHING LIKE THAT...
FOR INSTANCE, I...
...AM HAPPIER TO HAVE BEEN ABLE TO MEET YOU HERE, NOW.

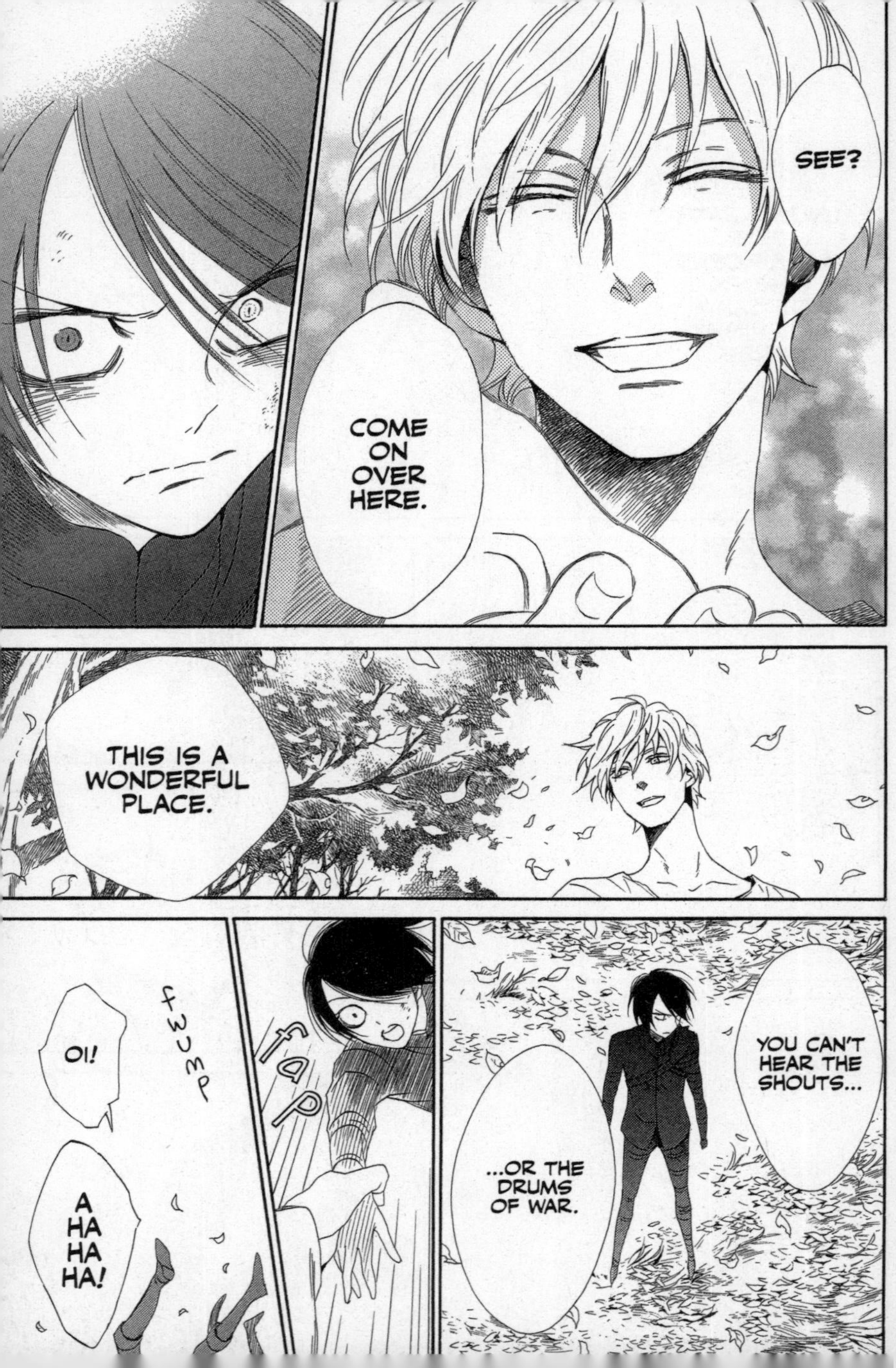
SEE?
COME ON OVER HERE.
THIS IS A WONDERFUL PLACE.
YOU CAN'T HEAR THE SHOUTS...
...OR THE DRUMS OF WAR.
fap
FWUMP
OI!
A HA HA HA!

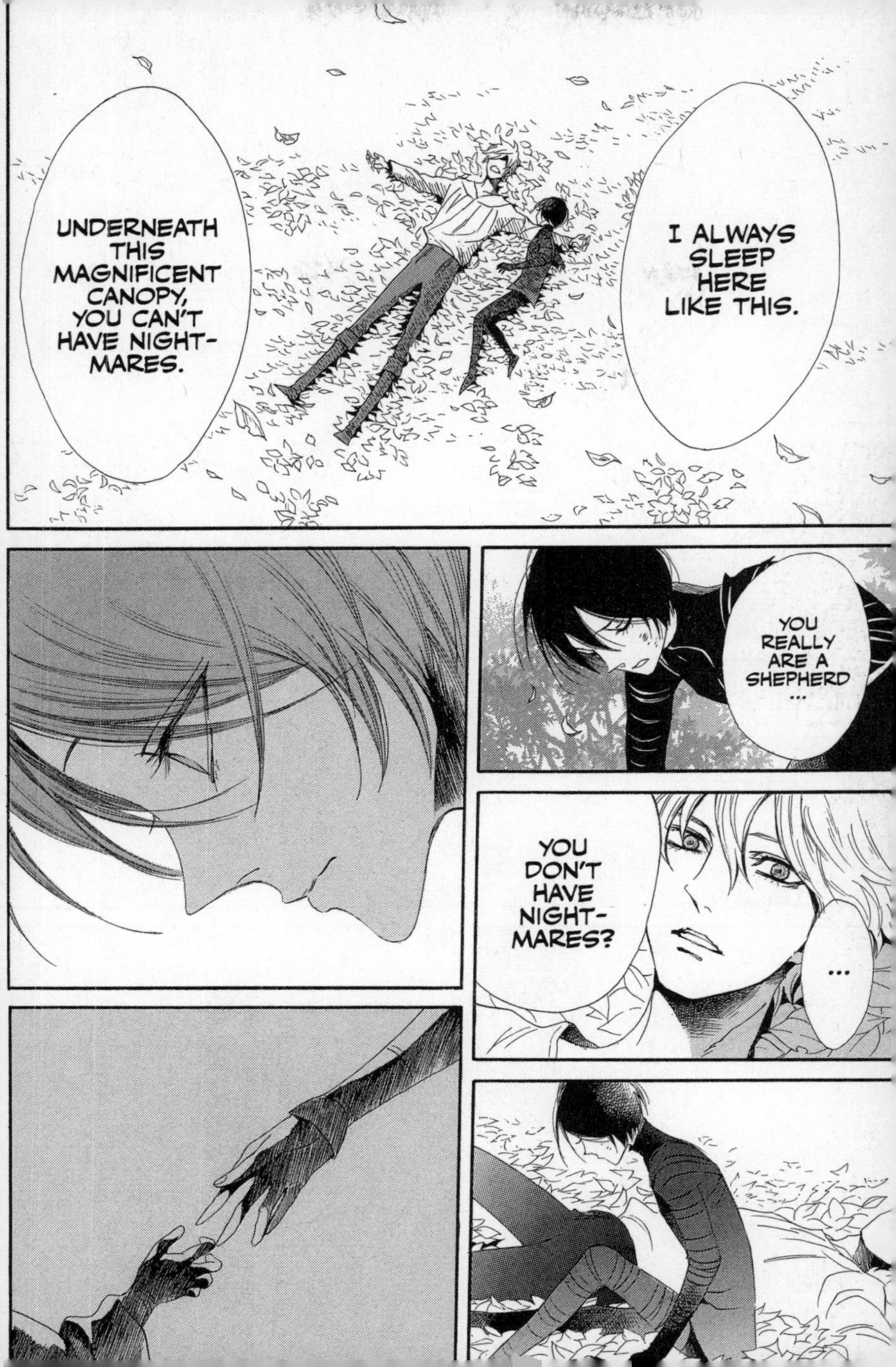
I ALWAYS SLEEP HERE LIKE THIS.
UNDERNEATH THIS MAGNIFICENT CANOPY, YOU CAN'T HAVE NIGHTMARES.
YOU REALLY ARE A SHEPHERD ...
YOU DON'T HAVE NIGHTMARES?
...

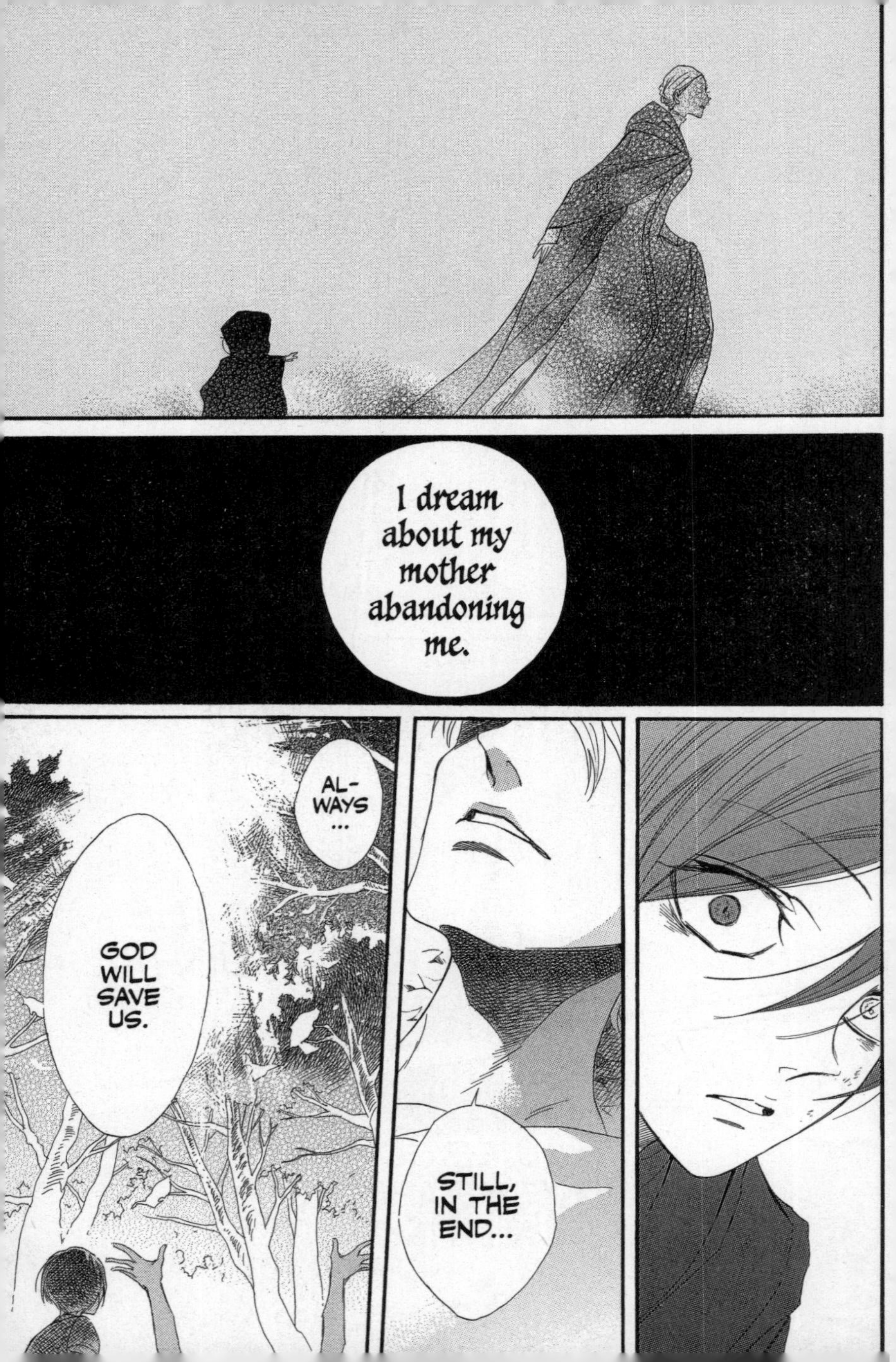

I dream about my mother abandoning me.
STILL, IN THE END...
AL-WAYS...
GOD WILL SAVE US.

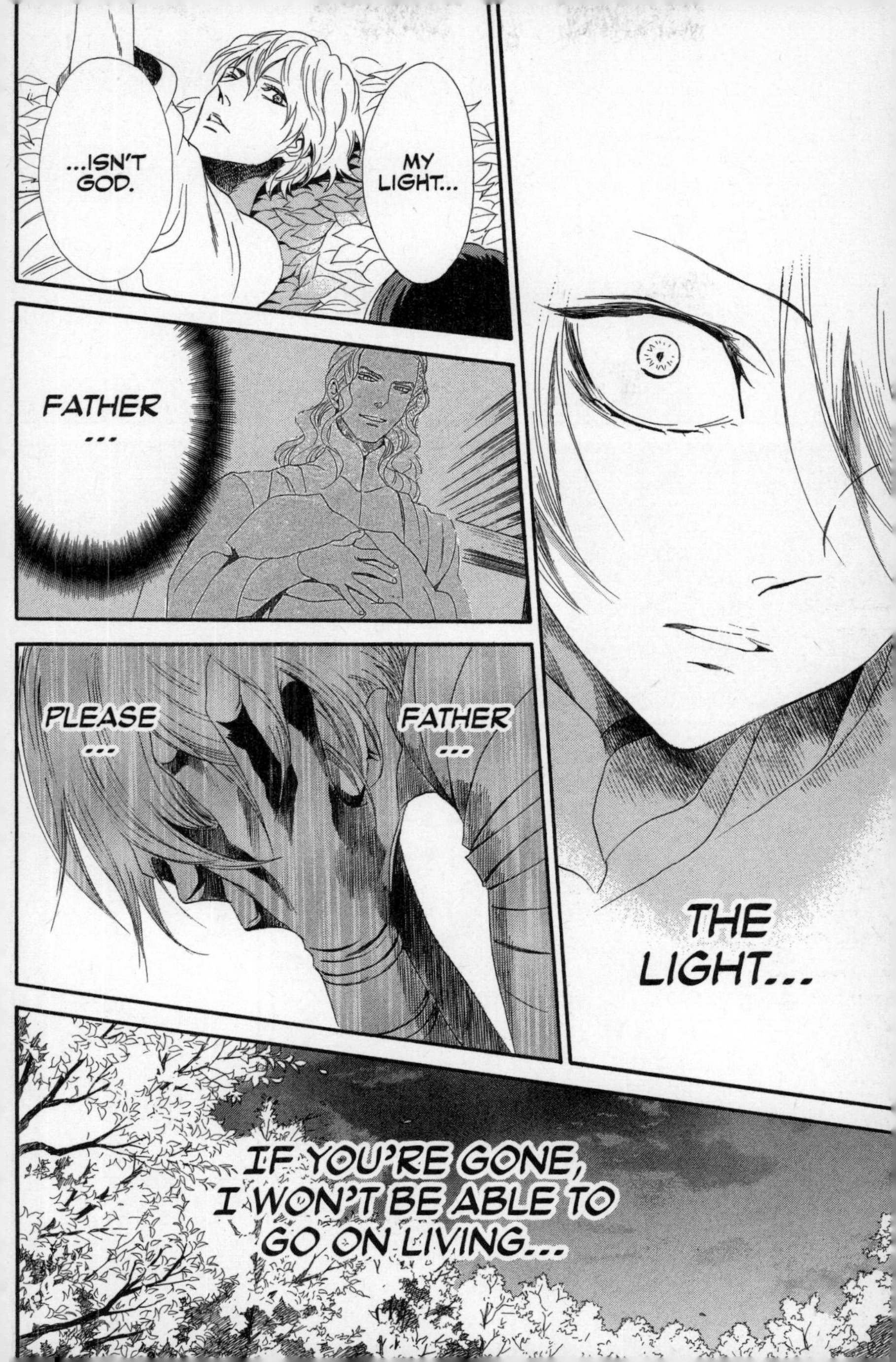
THE LIGHT...
MY LIGHT...
...ISN'T GOD.
FATHER ...
FATHER ...
PLEASE ...
IF YOU'RE GONE, I WON'T BE ABLE TO GO ON LIVING...

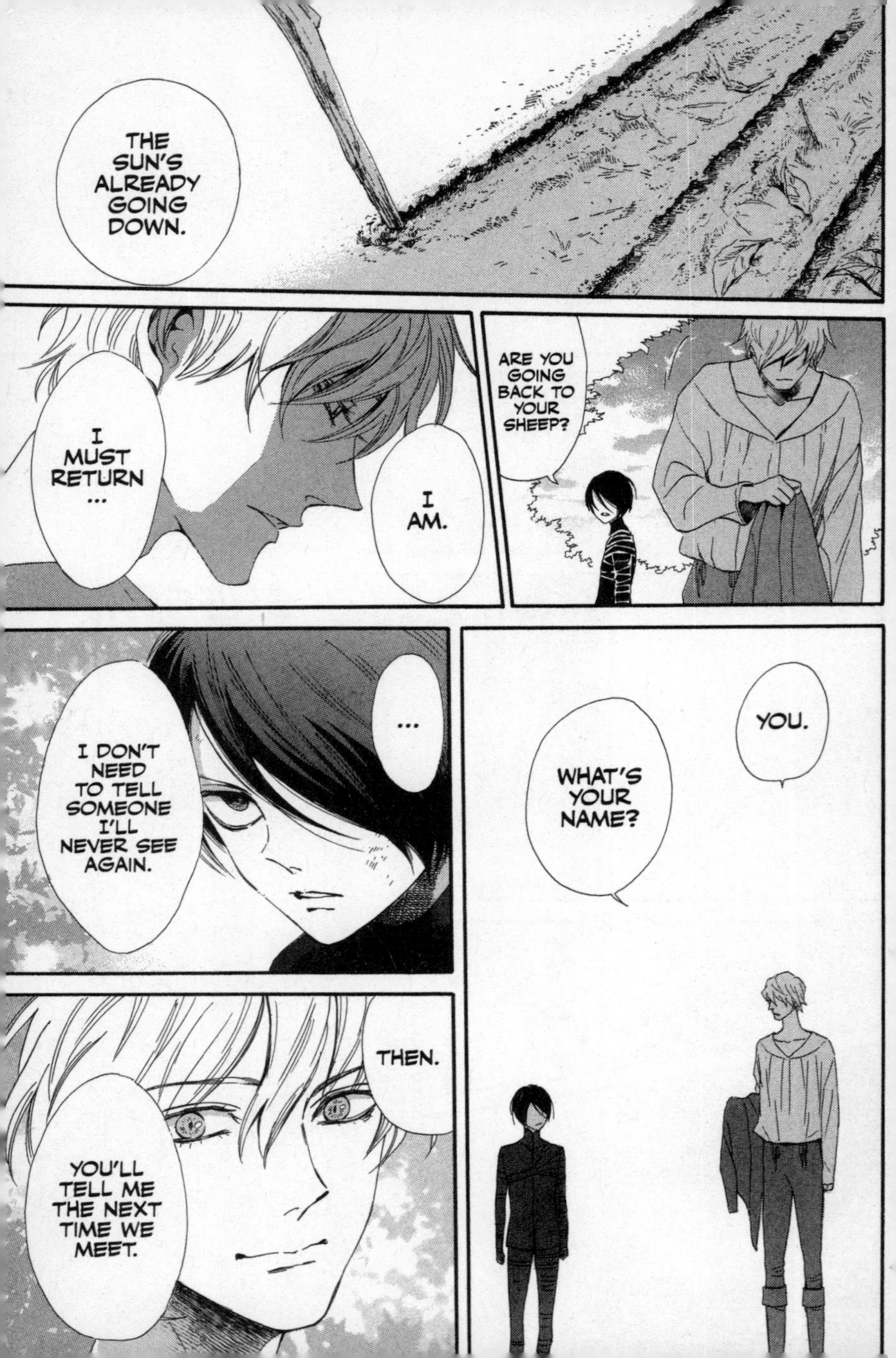
THE SUN'S ALREADY GOING DOWN.
ARE YOU GOING BACK TO YOUR SHEEP?
I AM.
I MUST RETURN ...
YOU.
WHAT'S YOUR NAME?
...
I DON'T NEED TO TELL SOMEONE I'LL NEVER SEE AGAIN.
THEN.
YOU'LL TELL ME THE NEXT TIME WE MEET.

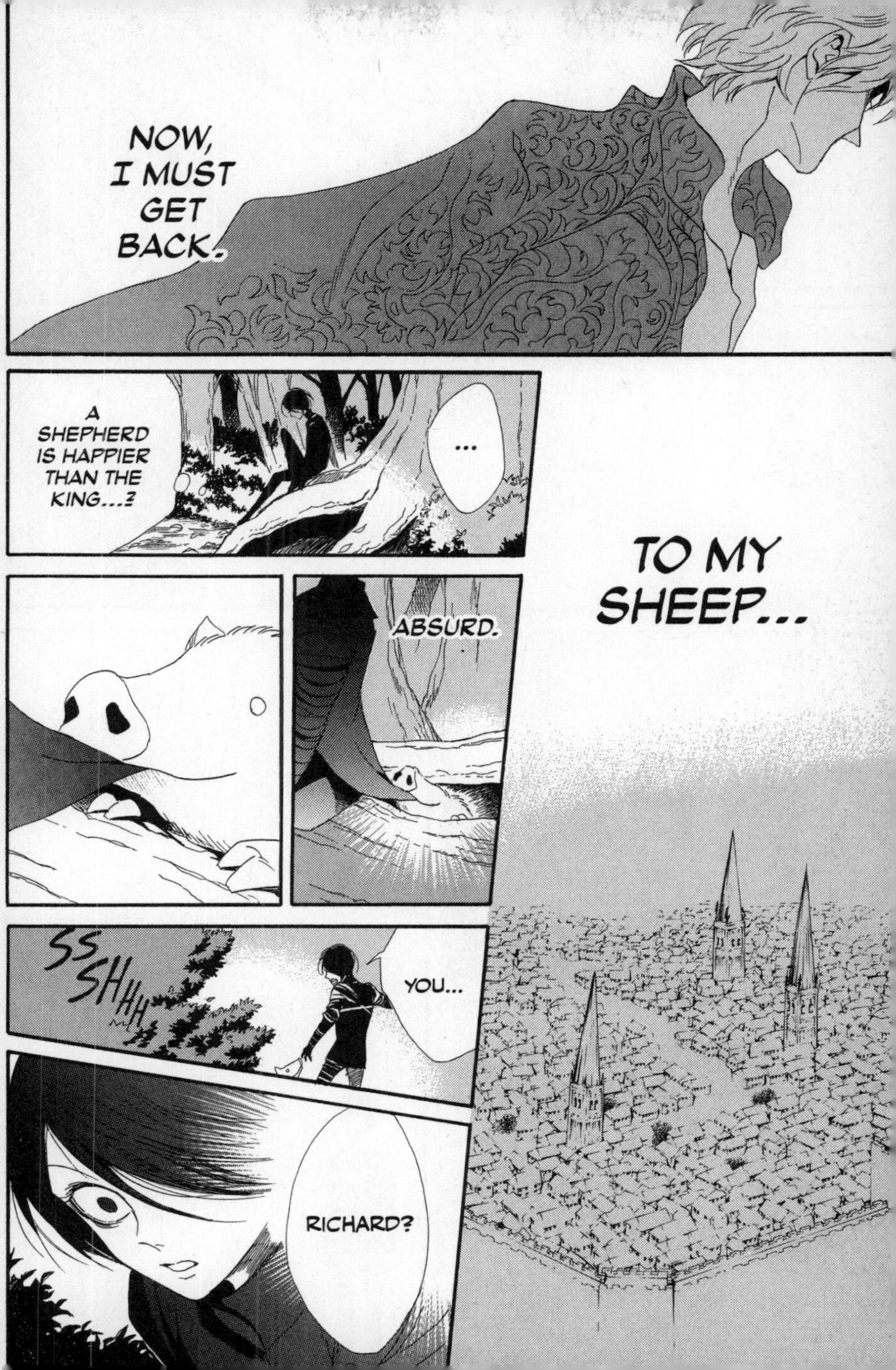
NOW, I MUST GET BACK.
TO MY SHEEP...
...
A SHEPHERD IS HAPPIER THAN THE KING...?
ABSURD.
YOU...
SSSHHH
RICHARD?

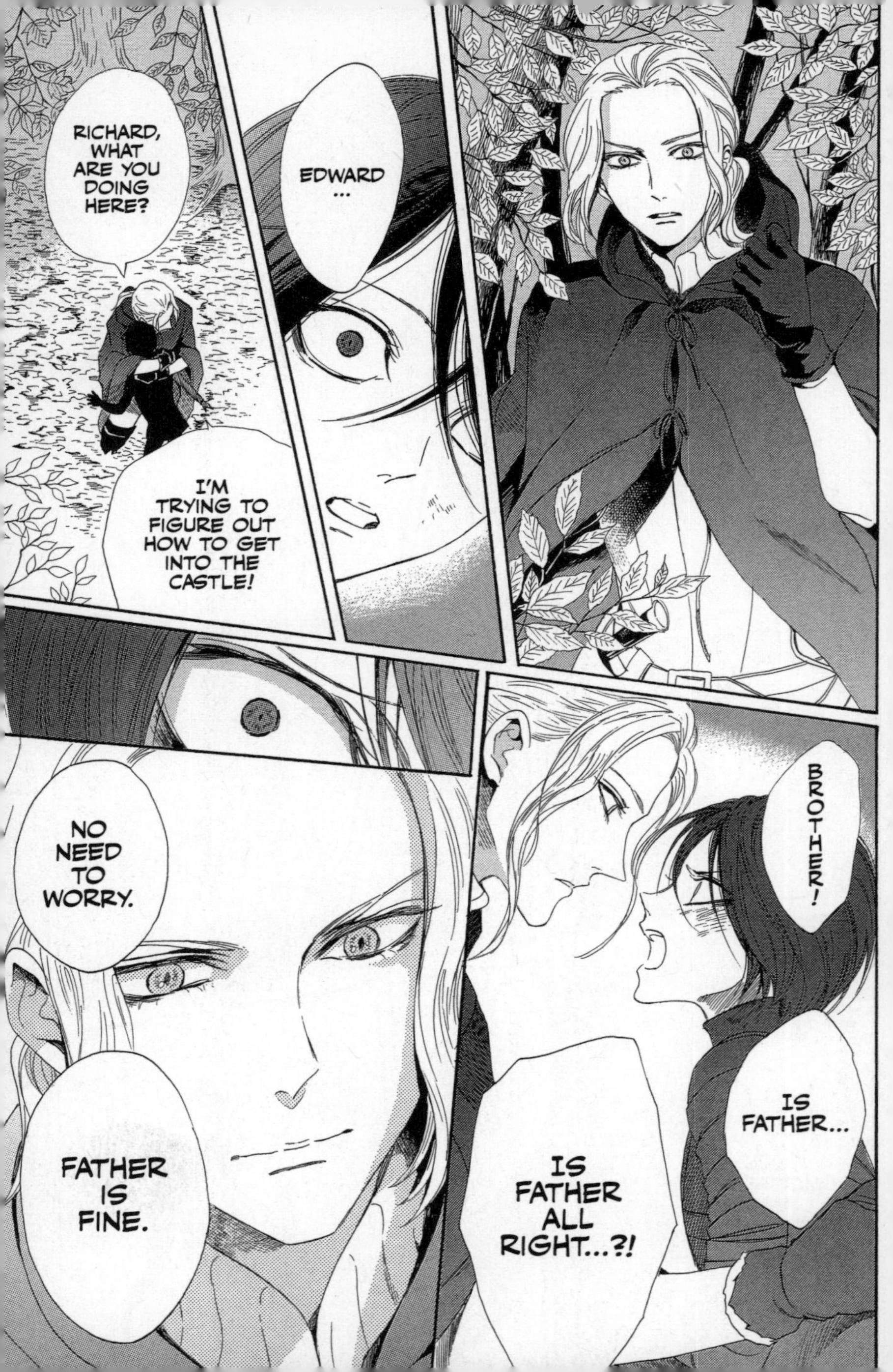
EDWARD ...
RICHARD, WHAT ARE YOU DOING HERE?
I'M TRYING TO FIGURE OUT HOW TO GET INTO THE CASTLE!
BROTHER!
IS FATHER...
IS FATHER ALL RIGHT...?!
NO NEED TO WORRY.
FATHER IS FINE.

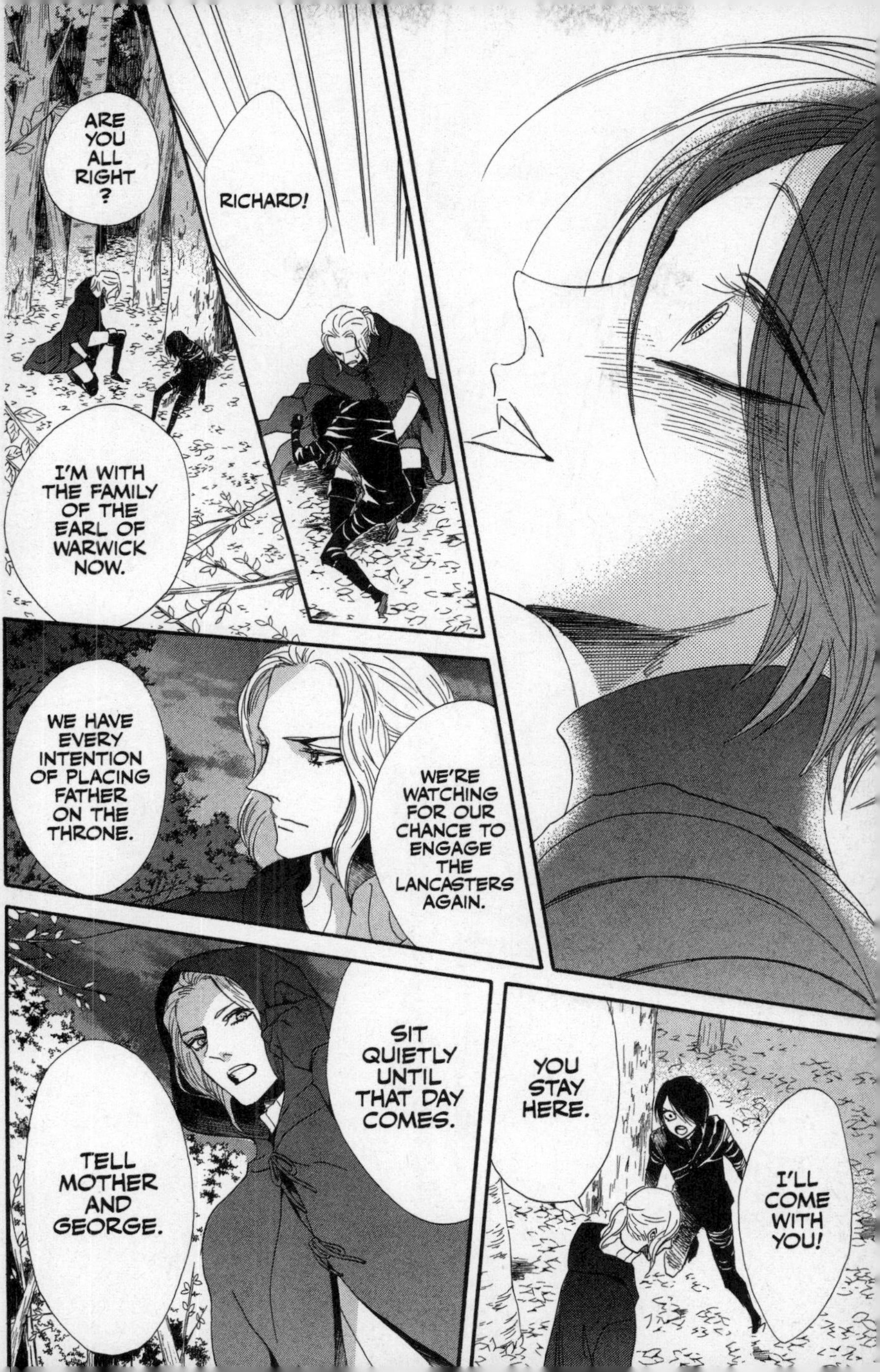
RICHARD!
ARE YOU ALL RIGHT?
I'M WITH THE FAMILY OF THE EARL OF WARWICK NOW.
WE'RE WATCHING FOR OUR CHANCE TO ENGAGE THE LANCASTERS AGAIN.
WE HAVE EVERY INTENTION OF PLACING FATHER ON THE THRONE.
I'LL COME WITH YOU!
YOU STAY HERE.
SIT QUIETLY UNTIL THAT DAY COMES.
TELL MOTHER AND GEORGE.

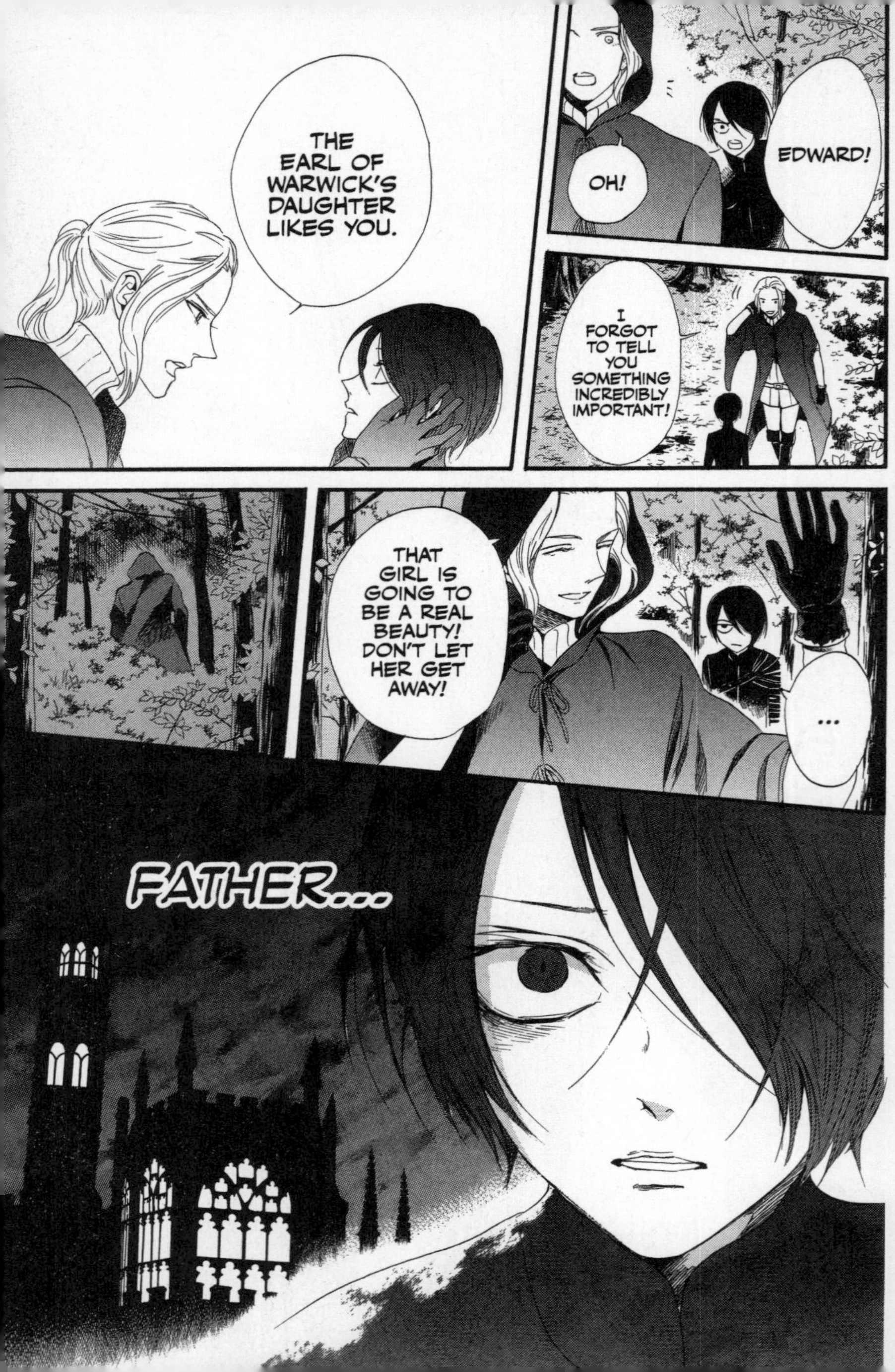
EDWARD!
OH!
I FORGOT TO TELL YOU SOMETHING INCREDIBLY IMPORTANT!
THE EARL OF WARWICK'S DAUGHTER LIKES YOU.
THAT GIRL IS GOING TO BE A REAL BEAUTY! DON'T LET HER GET AWAY!
...
FATHER...

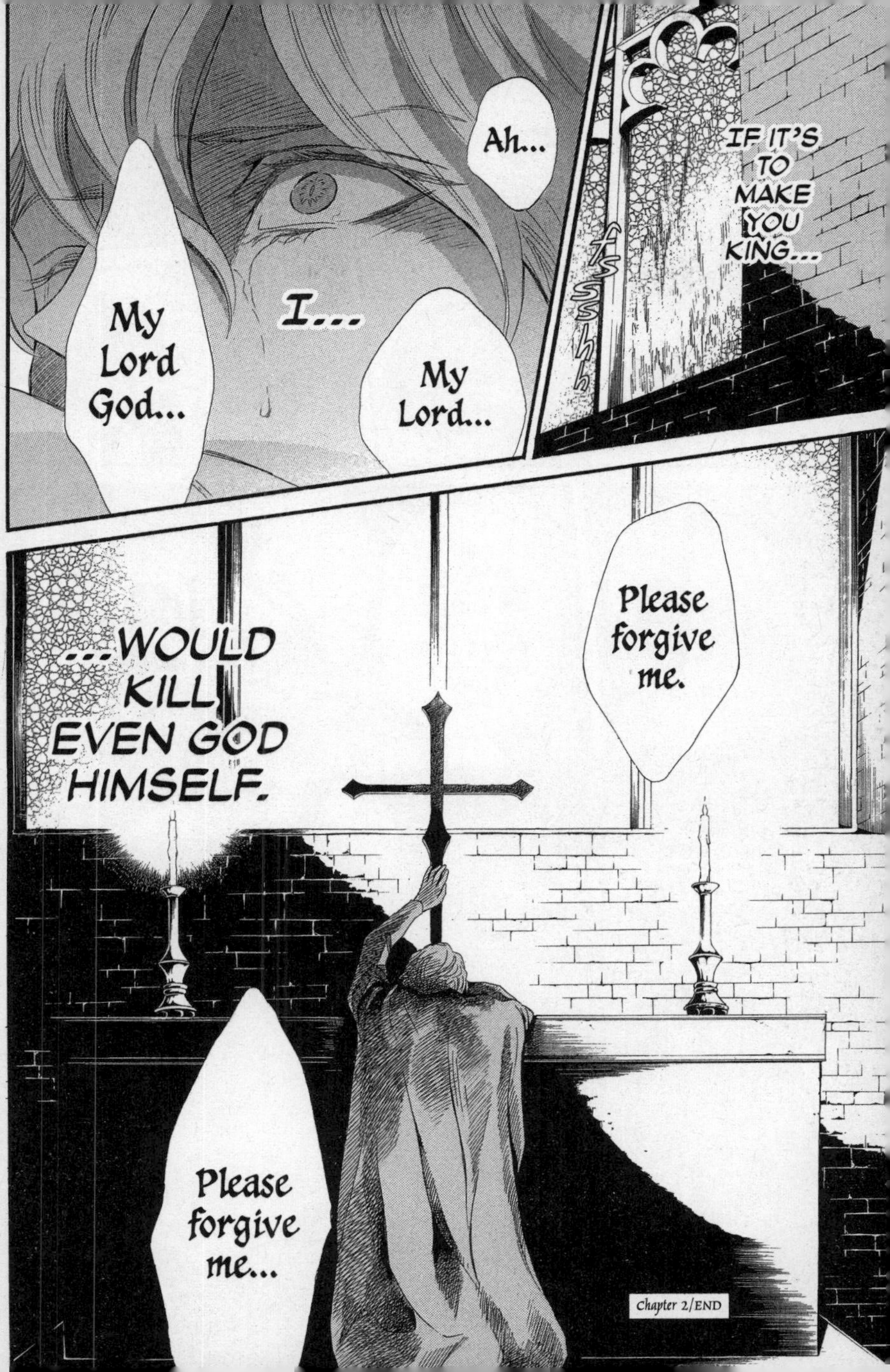
IF IT'S TO MAKE YOU KING...
fssshh
Ah...
My Lord...
I...
My Lord God...
Please forgive me.
...WOULD KILL EVEN GOD HIMSELF.
Please forgive me...
Chapter 2/END

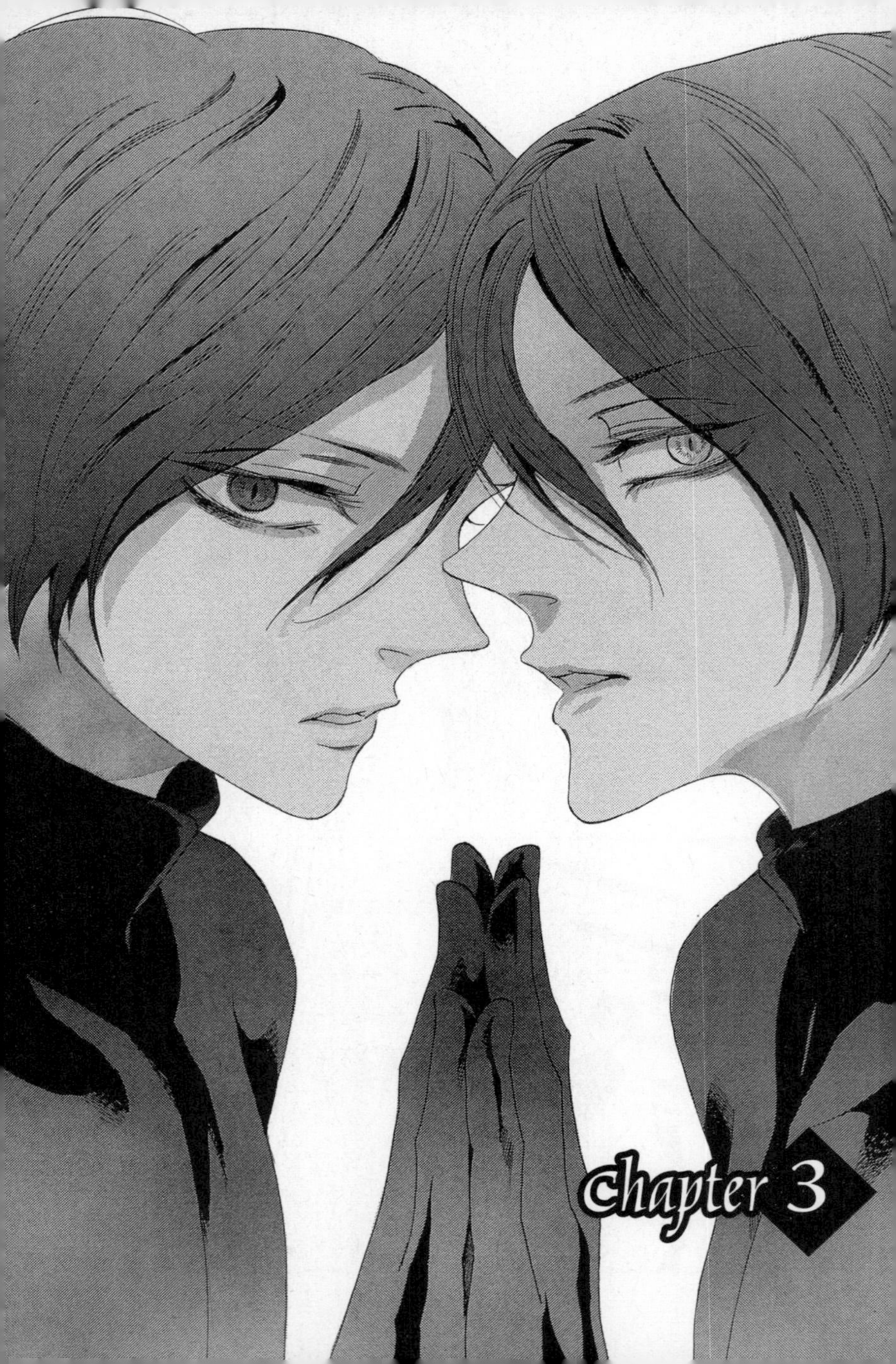
Chapter 3

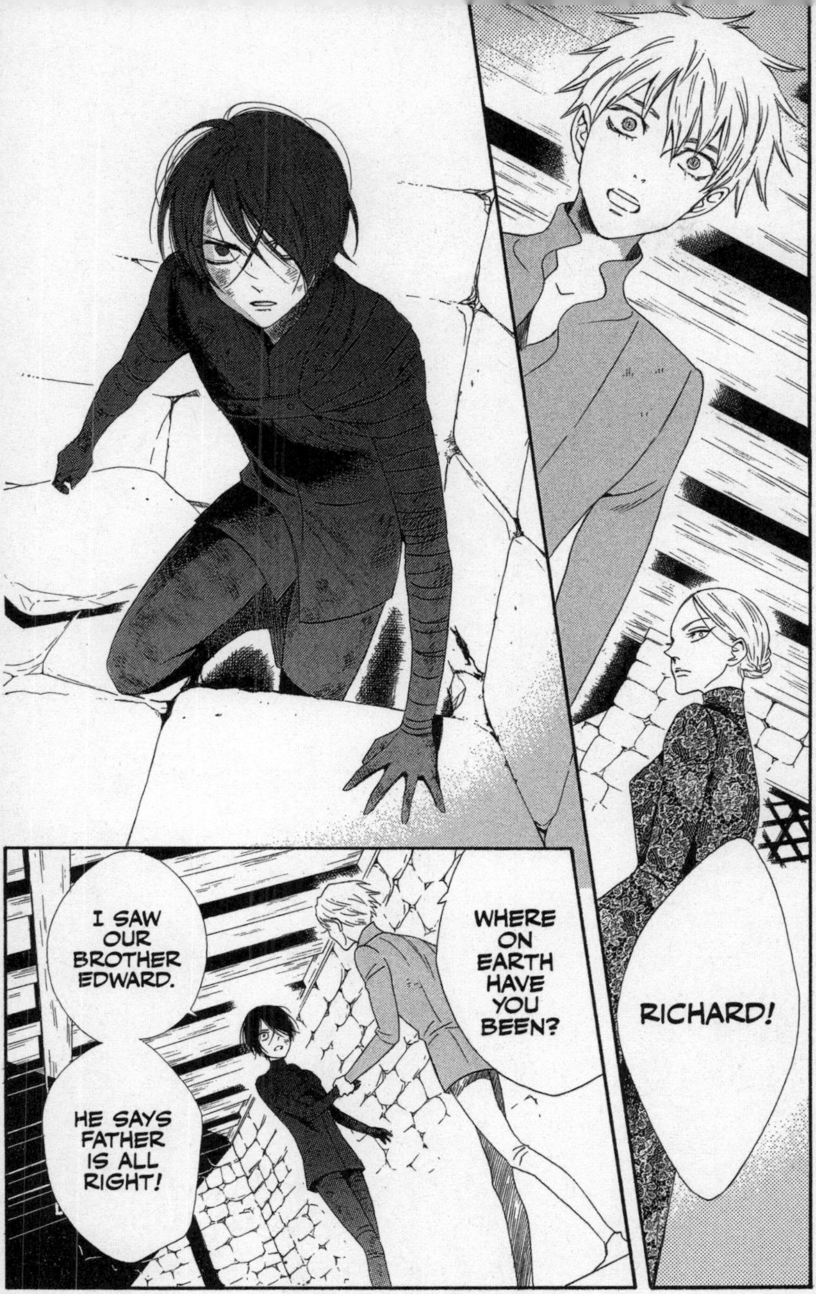
RICHARD!
WHERE ON EARTH HAVE YOU BEEN?
I SAW OUR BROTHER EDWARD.
HE SAYS FATHER IS ALL RIGHT!

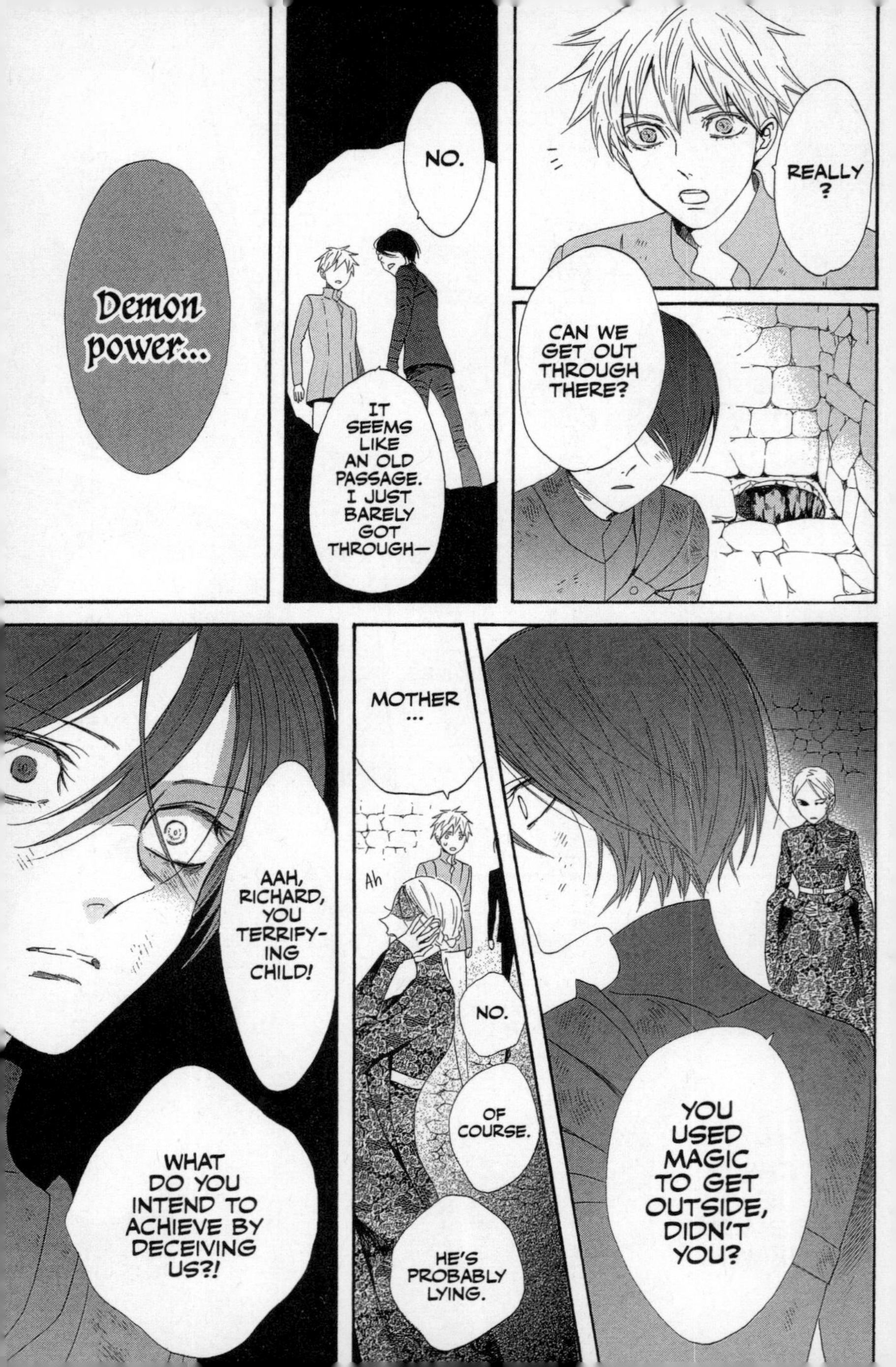
REALLY?
CAN WE GET OUT THROUGH THERE?
NO.
IT SEEMS LIKE AN OLD PASSAGE. I JUST BARELY GOT THROUGH—
Demon power...
YOU USED MAGIC TO GET OUTSIDE, DIDN'T YOU?
MOTHER...
Ah
NO.
OF COURSE.
HE'S PROBABLY LYING.
AAH, RICHARD, YOU TERRIFYING-ING CHILD!
WHAT DO YOU INTEND TO ACHIEVE BY DECEIVING US?!

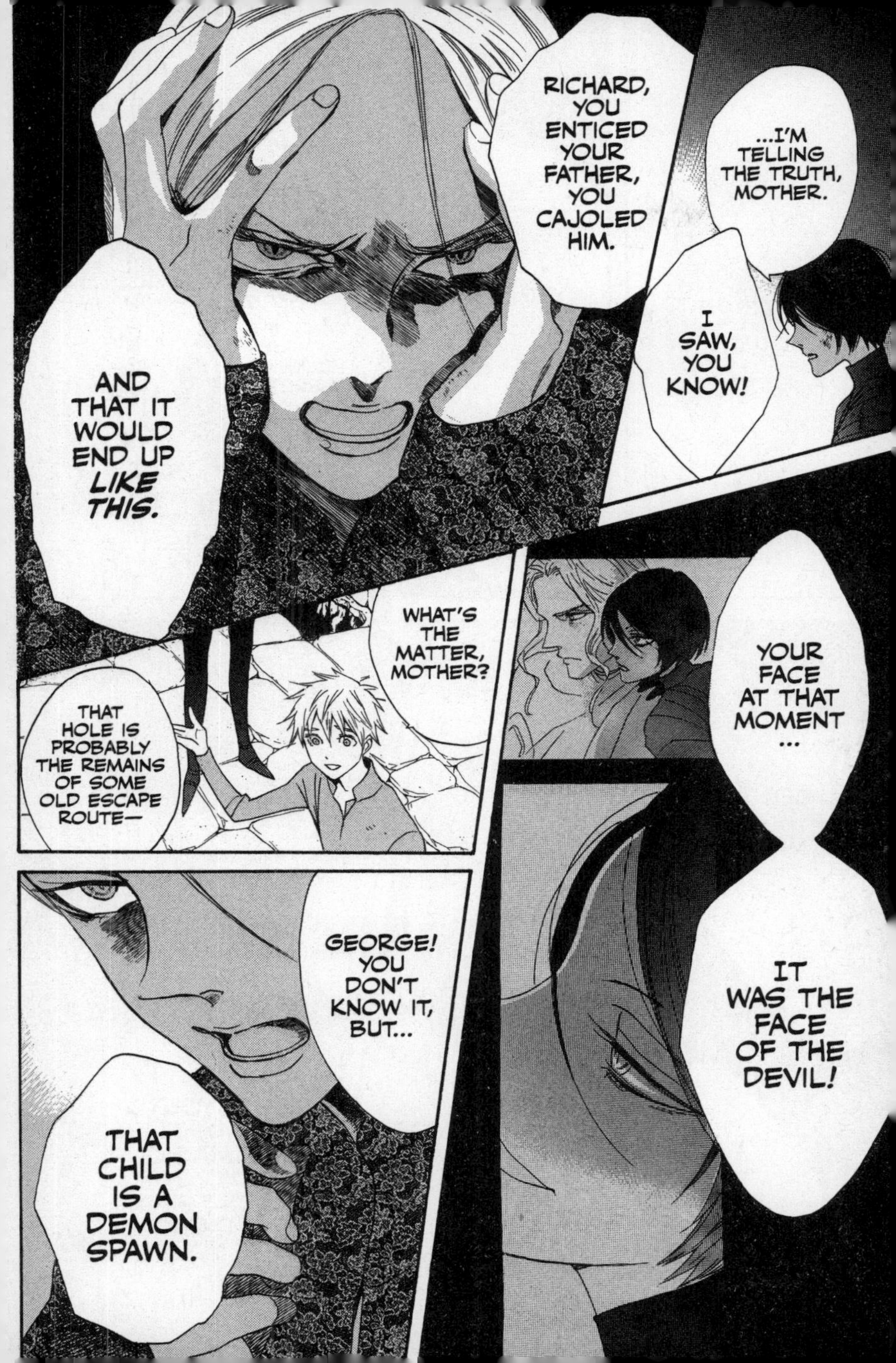
...I'M TELLING THE TRUTH, MOTHER.
I SAW, YOU KNOW!
RICHARD, YOU ENTICED YOUR FATHER, YOU CAJOLED HIM.
AND THAT IT WOULD END UP *LIKE THIS.*
YOUR FACE AT THAT MOMENT...
WHAT'S THE MATTER, MOTHER?
THAT HOLE IS PROBABLY THE REMAINS OF SOME OLD ESCAPE ROUTE—
IT WAS THE FACE OF THE DEVIL!
GEORGE! YOU DON'T KNOW IT, BUT...
THAT CHILD IS A DEMON SPAWN.

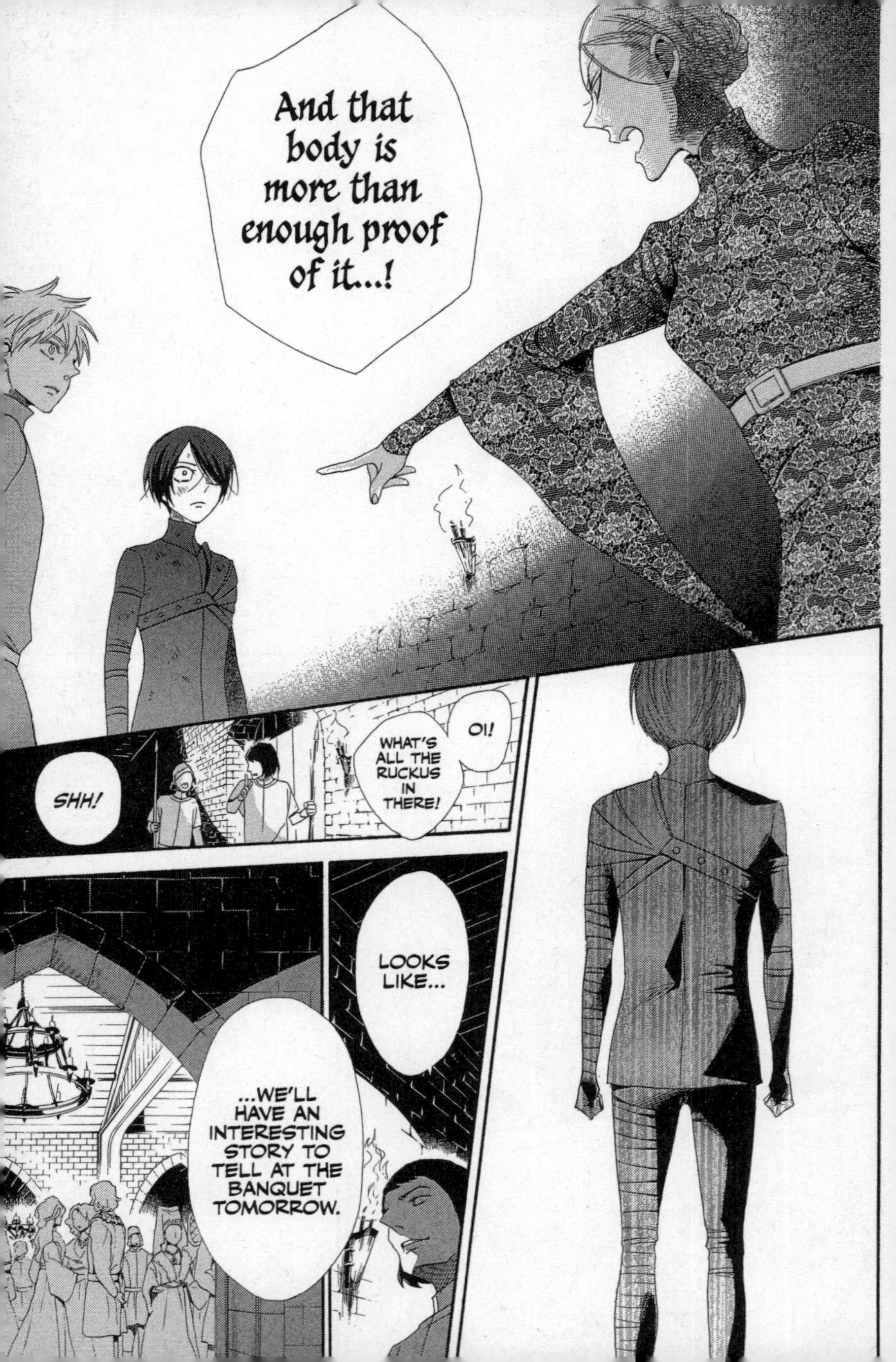
And that body is more than enough proof of it...!
OI!
WHAT'S ALL THE RUCKUS IN THERE!
SHH!
LOOKS LIKE...
...WE'LL HAVE AN INTERESTING STORY TO TELL AT THE BANQUET TOMORROW.

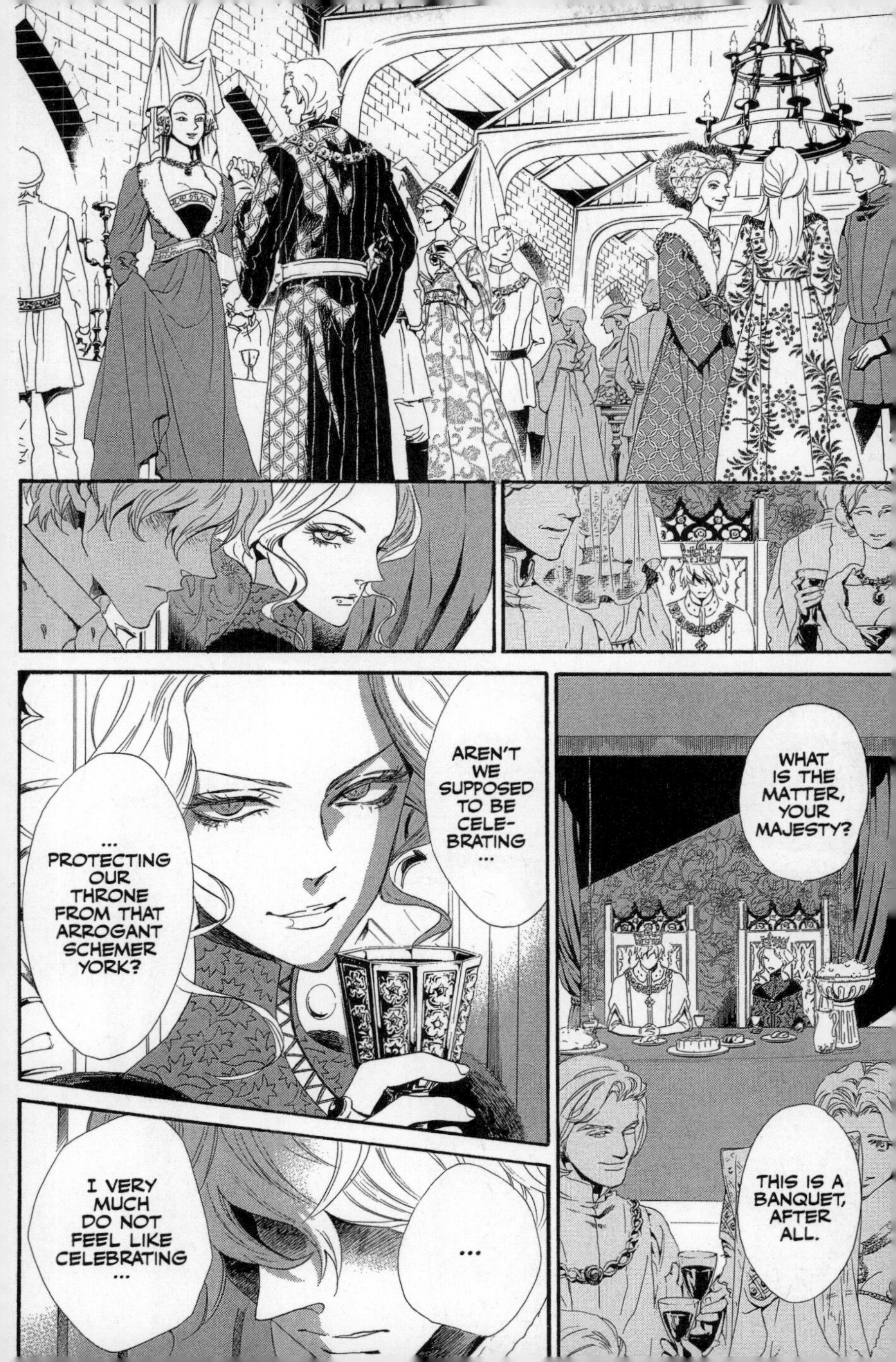
WHAT IS THE MATTER, YOUR MAJESTY?
THIS IS A BANQUET, AFTER ALL.
AREN'T WE SUPPOSED TO BE CELE-BRATING ...
... PROTECTING OUR THRONE FROM THAT ARROGANT SCHEMER YORK?
...
I VERY MUCH DO NOT FEEL LIKE CELEBRATING ...

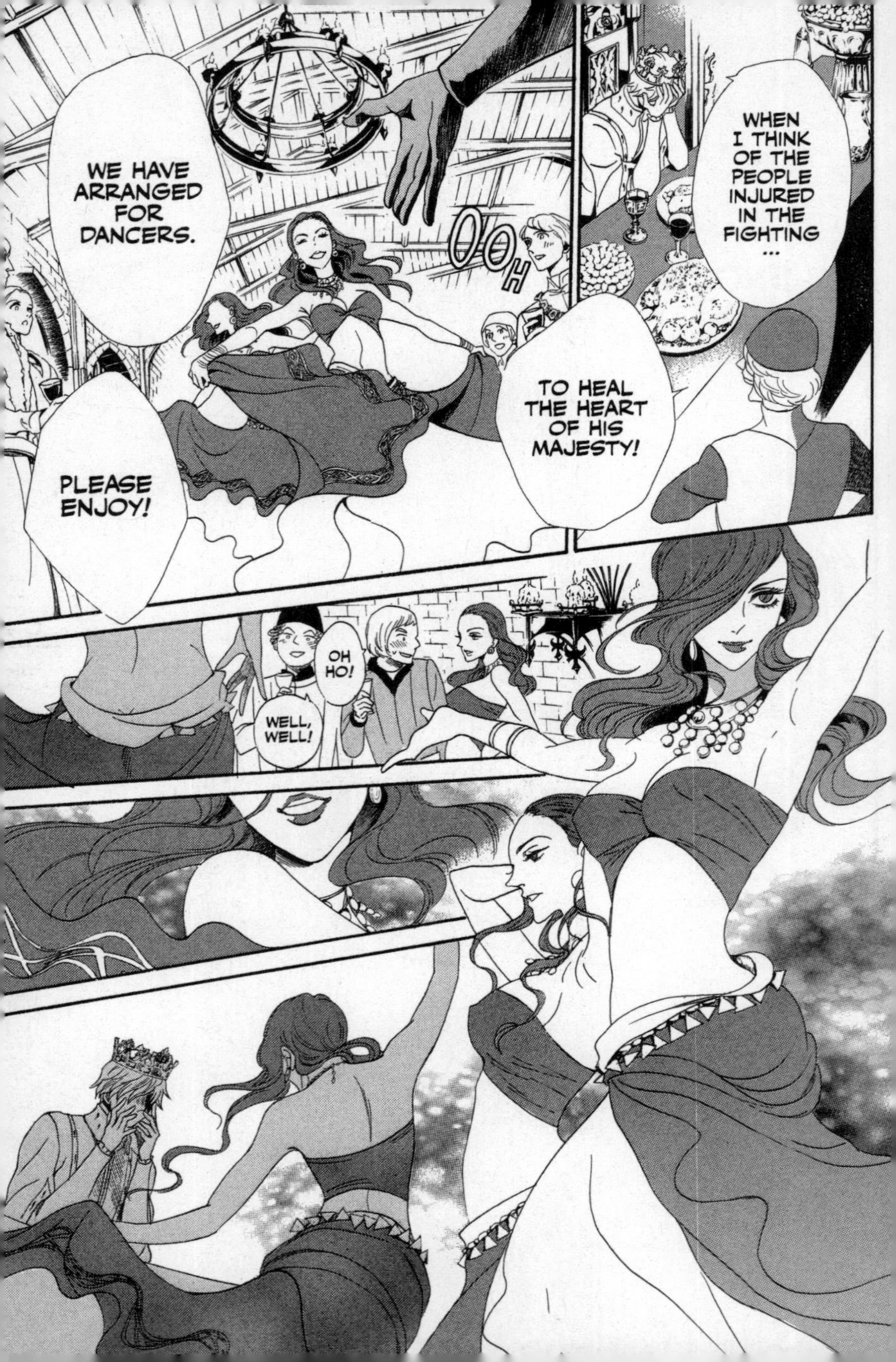
WHEN I THINK OF THE PEOPLE INJURED IN THE FIGHTING ...
WE HAVE ARRANGED FOR DANCERS.
OOH
TO HEAL THE HEART OF HIS MAJESTY!
PLEASE ENJOY!
OH HO!
WELL, WELL!

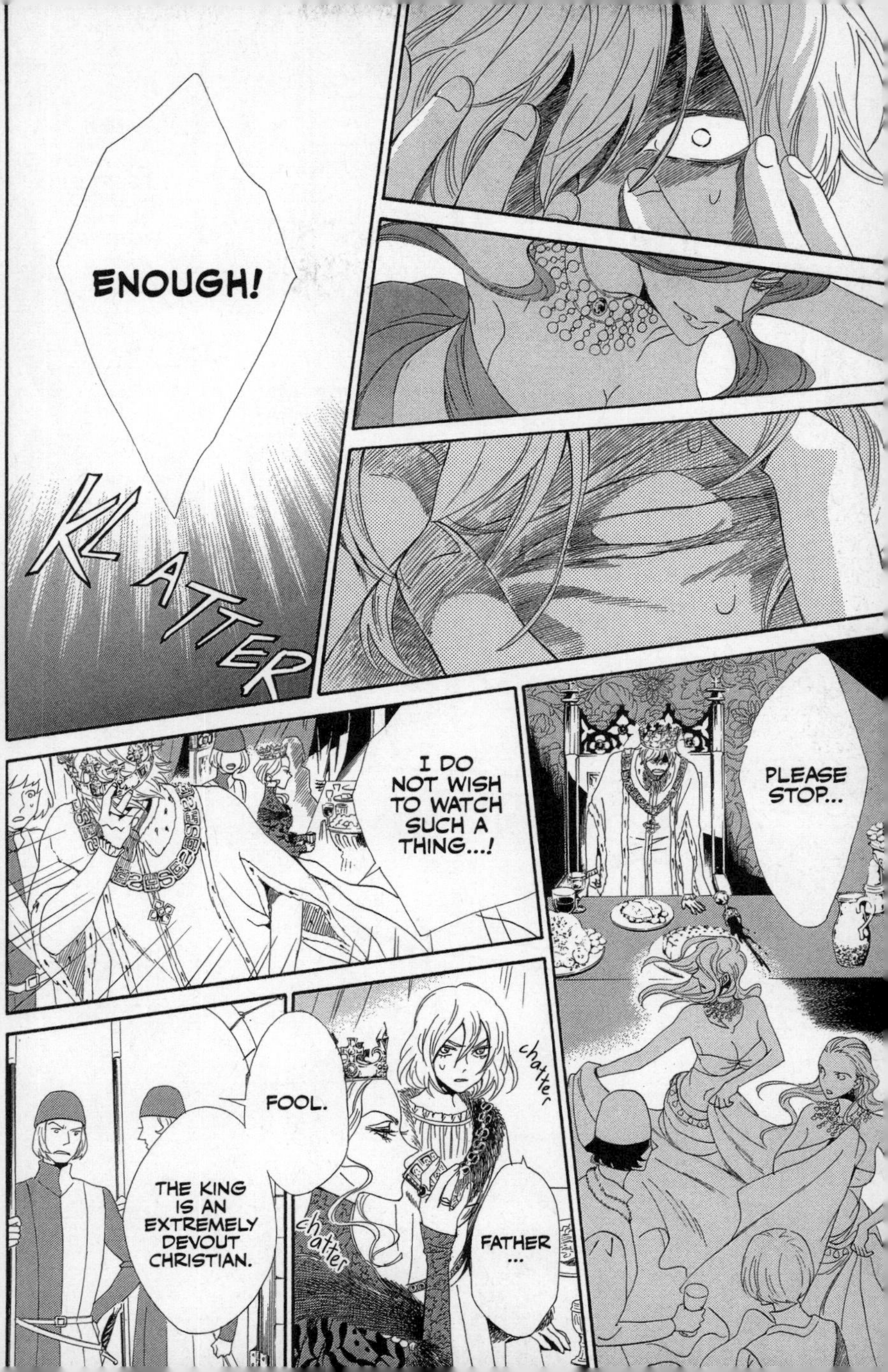
ENOUGH!
KLATTER
PLEASE STOP...
I DO NOT WISH TO WATCH SUCH A THING...!
chatter
FOOL.
FATHER ...
chatter
THE KING IS AN EXTREMELY DEVOUT CHRISTIAN.

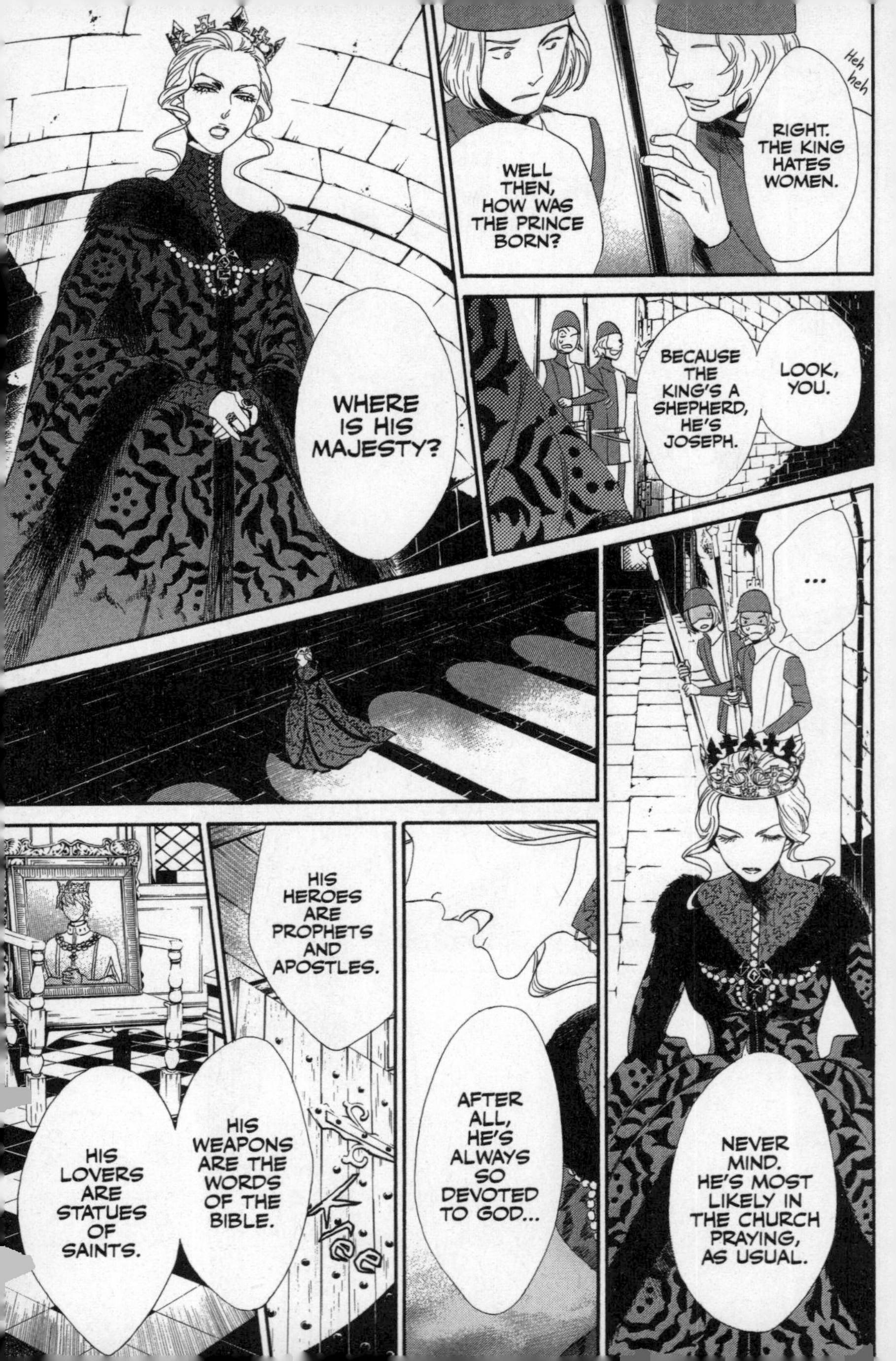
Heh heh
RIGHT. THE KING HATES WOMEN.
WELL THEN, HOW WAS THE PRINCE BORN?
LOOK, YOU.
BECAUSE THE KING'S A SHEPHERD, HE'S JOSEPH.
WHERE IS HIS MAJESTY?
...
NEVER MIND. HE'S MOST LIKELY IN THE CHURCH PRAYING, AS USUAL.
AFTER ALL, HE'S ALWAYS SO DEVOTED TO GOD...
HIS HEROES ARE PROPHETS AND APOSTLES.
HIS WEAPONS ARE THE WORDS OF THE BIBLE.
HIS LOVERS ARE STATUES OF SAINTS.

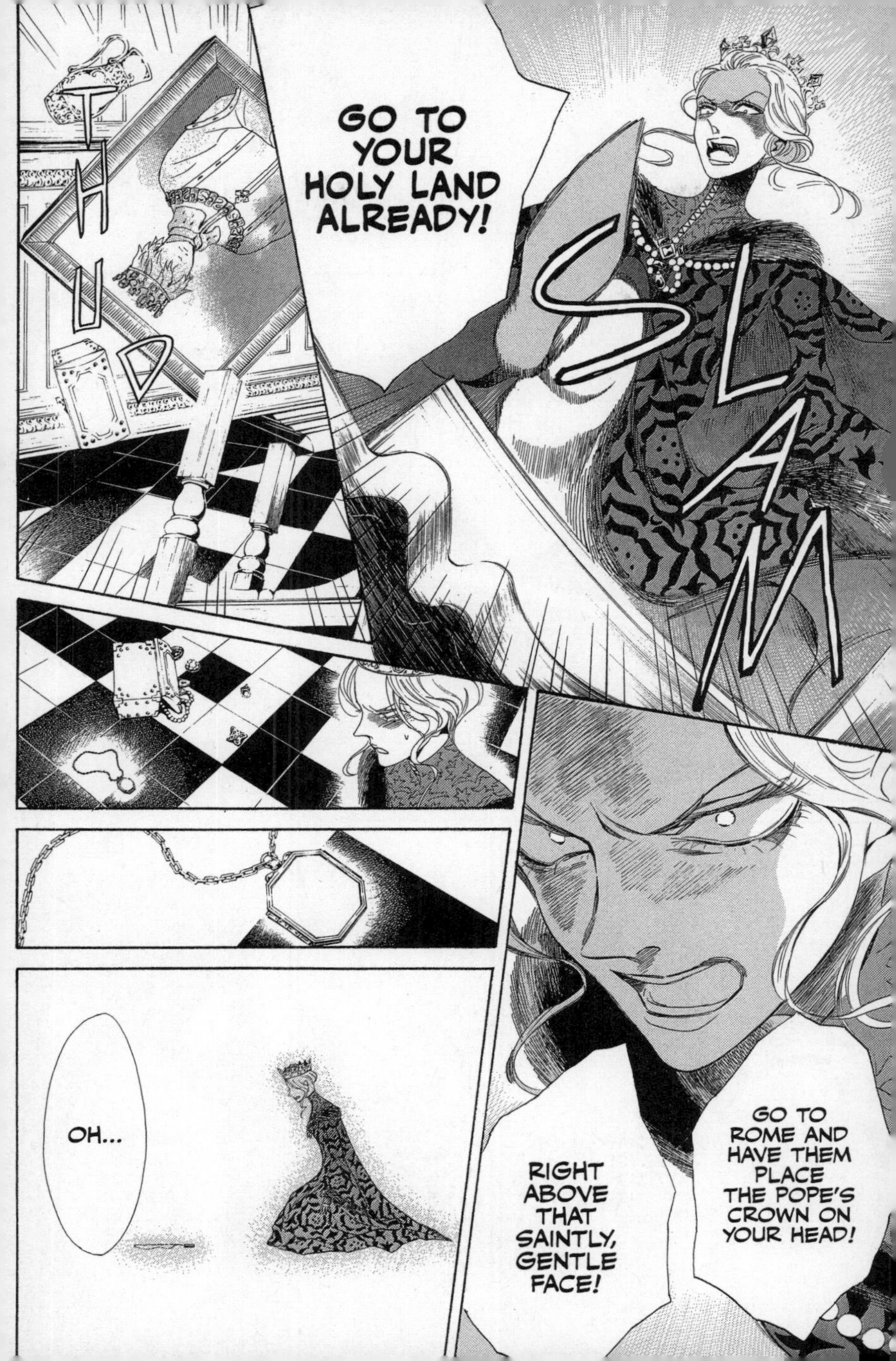
GO TO YOUR HOLY LAND ALREADY!
SLAM
THUD
GO TO ROME AND HAVE THEM PLACE THE POPE'S CROWN ON YOUR HEAD!
RIGHT ABOVE THAT SAINTLY, GENTLE FACE!
OH...

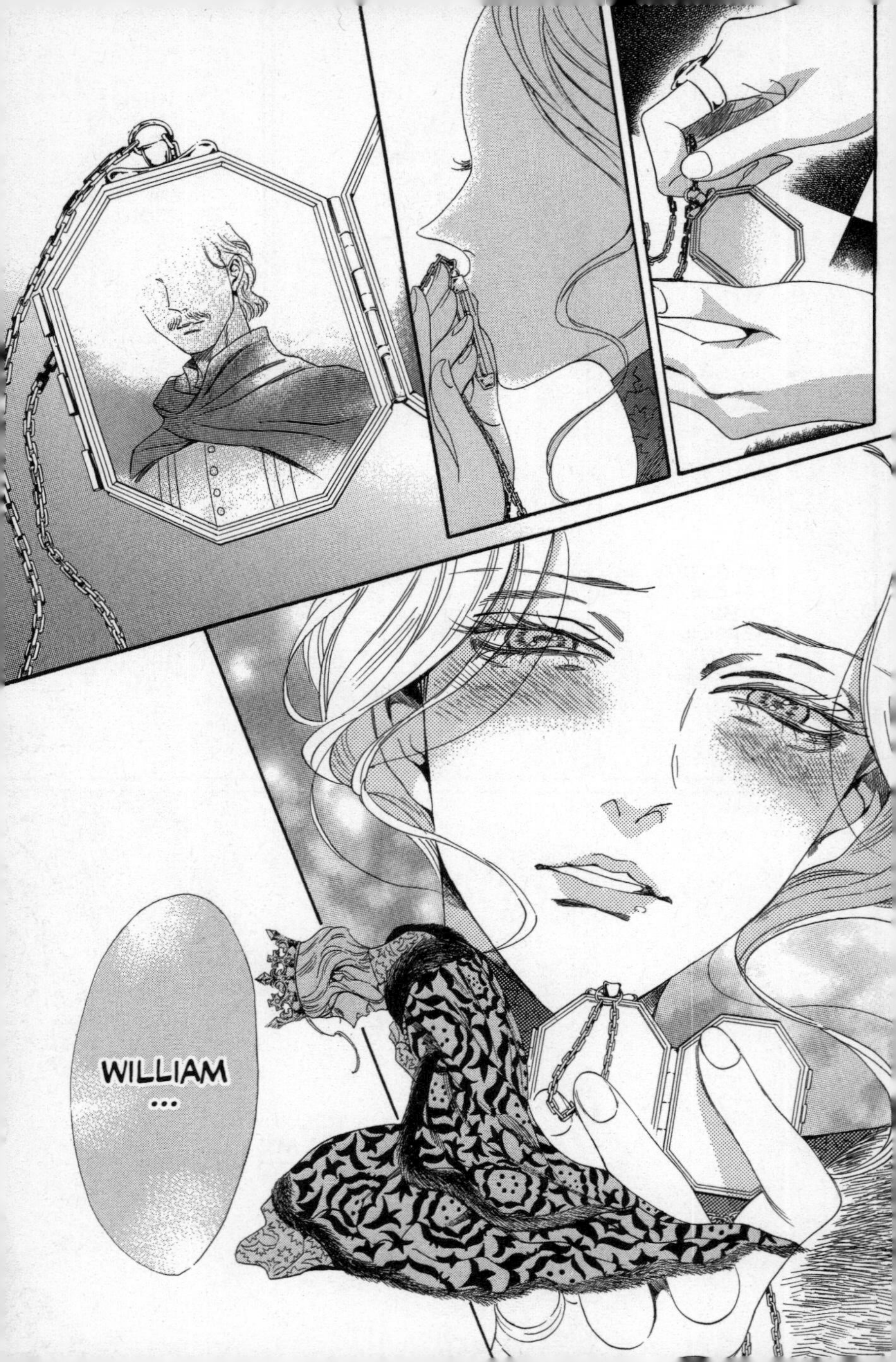
WILLIAM
...

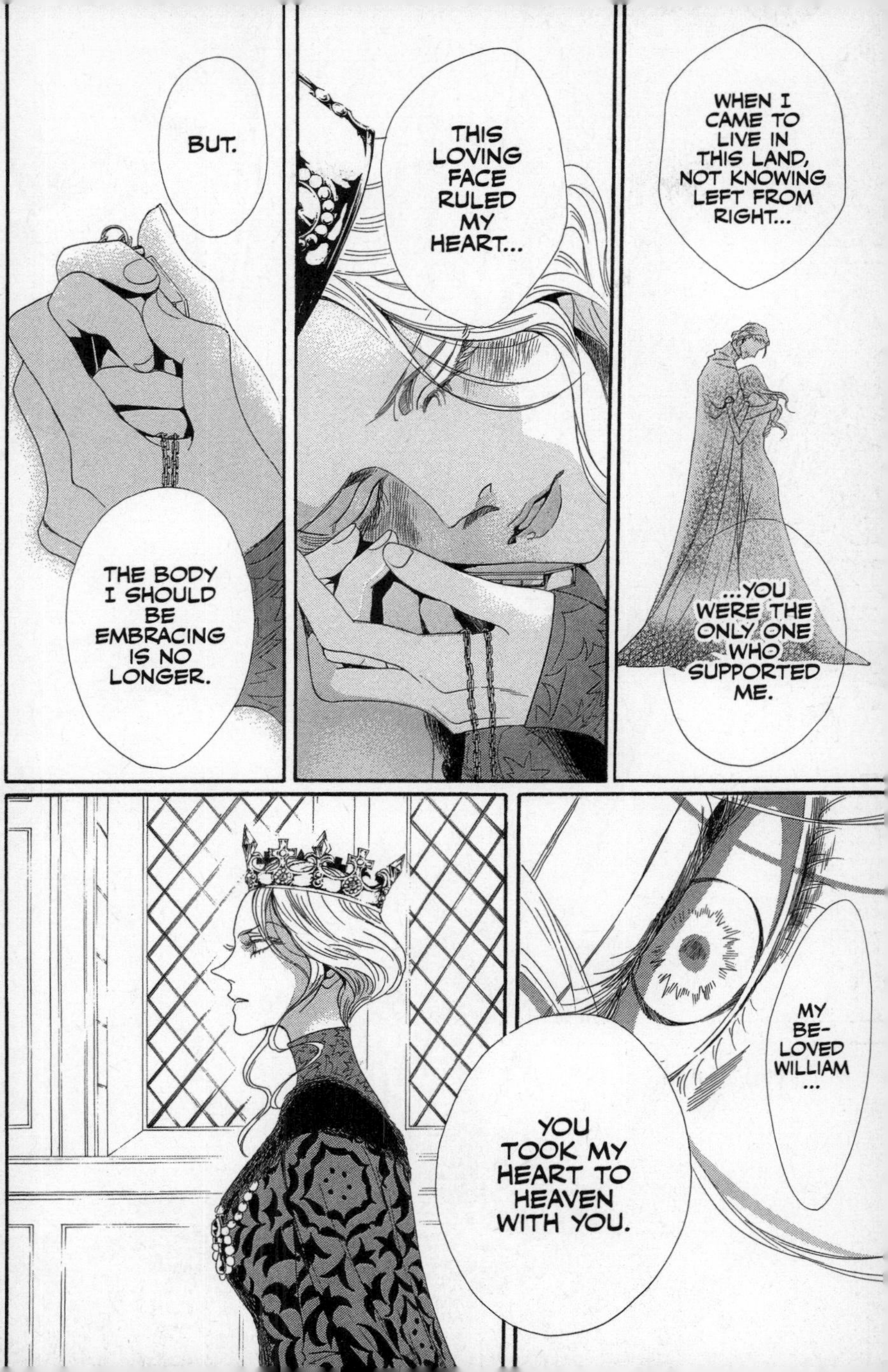
WHEN I CAME TO LIVE IN THIS LAND, NOT KNOWING LEFT FROM RIGHT...
...YOU WERE THE ONLY ONE WHO SUPPORTED ME.
THIS LOVING FACE RULED MY HEART...
BUT.
THE BODY I SHOULD BE EMBRACING IS NO LONGER.
MY BE-LOVED WILLIAM ...
YOU TOOK MY HEART TO HEAVEN WITH YOU.

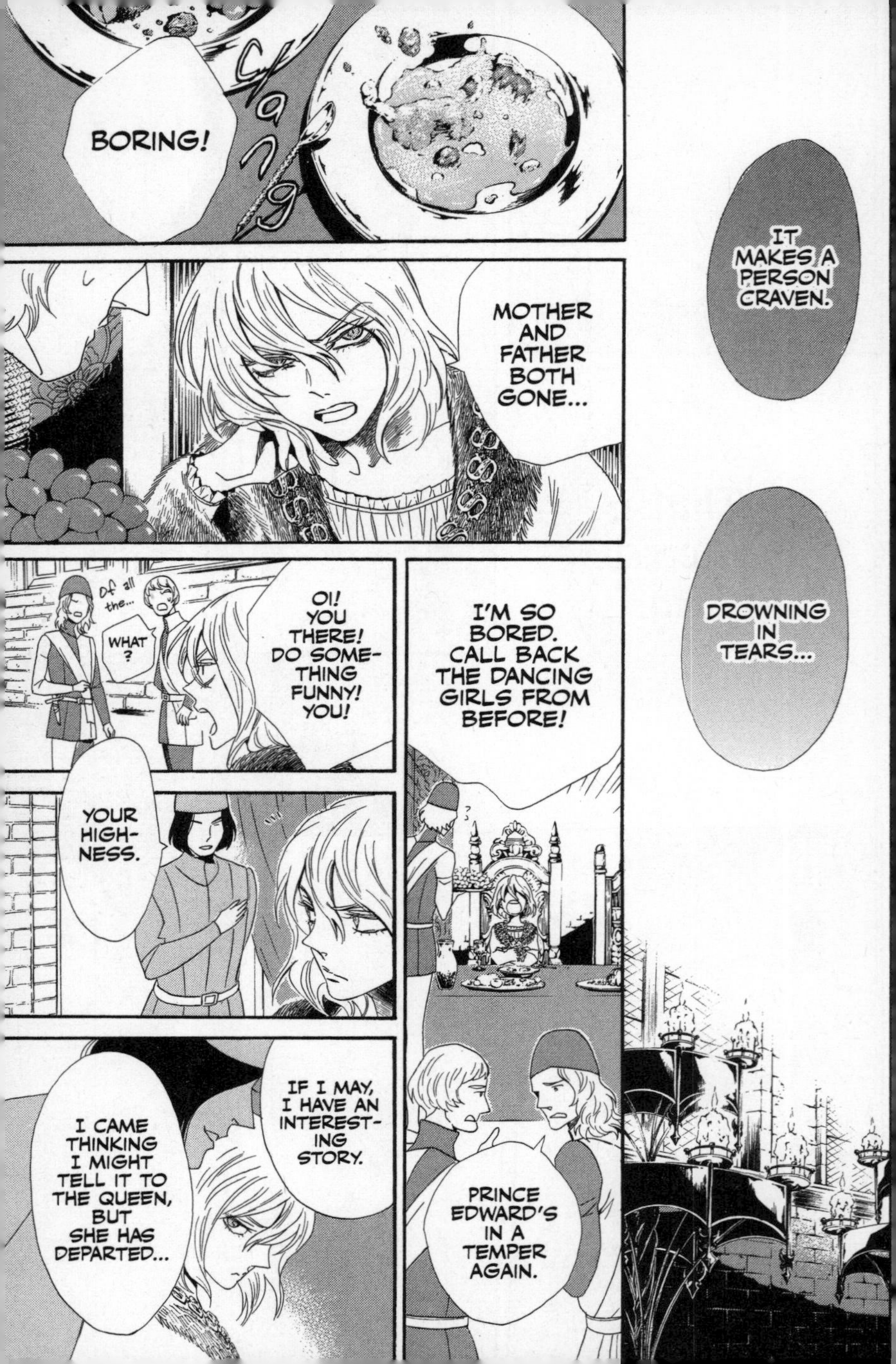
IT MAKES A PERSON CRAVEN.
DROWNING IN TEARS...
BORING!
Clang
MOTHER AND FATHER BOTH GONE...
I'M SO BORED. CALL BACK THE DANCING GIRLS FROM BEFORE!
PRINCE EDWARD'S IN A TEMPER AGAIN.
Of all the...
WHAT?
OI! YOU THERE! DO SOME-THING FUNNY! YOU!
YOUR HIGH-NESS.
IF I MAY, I HAVE AN INTEREST-ING STORY.
I CAME THINKING I MIGHT TELL IT TO THE QUEEN, BUT SHE HAS DEPARTED...

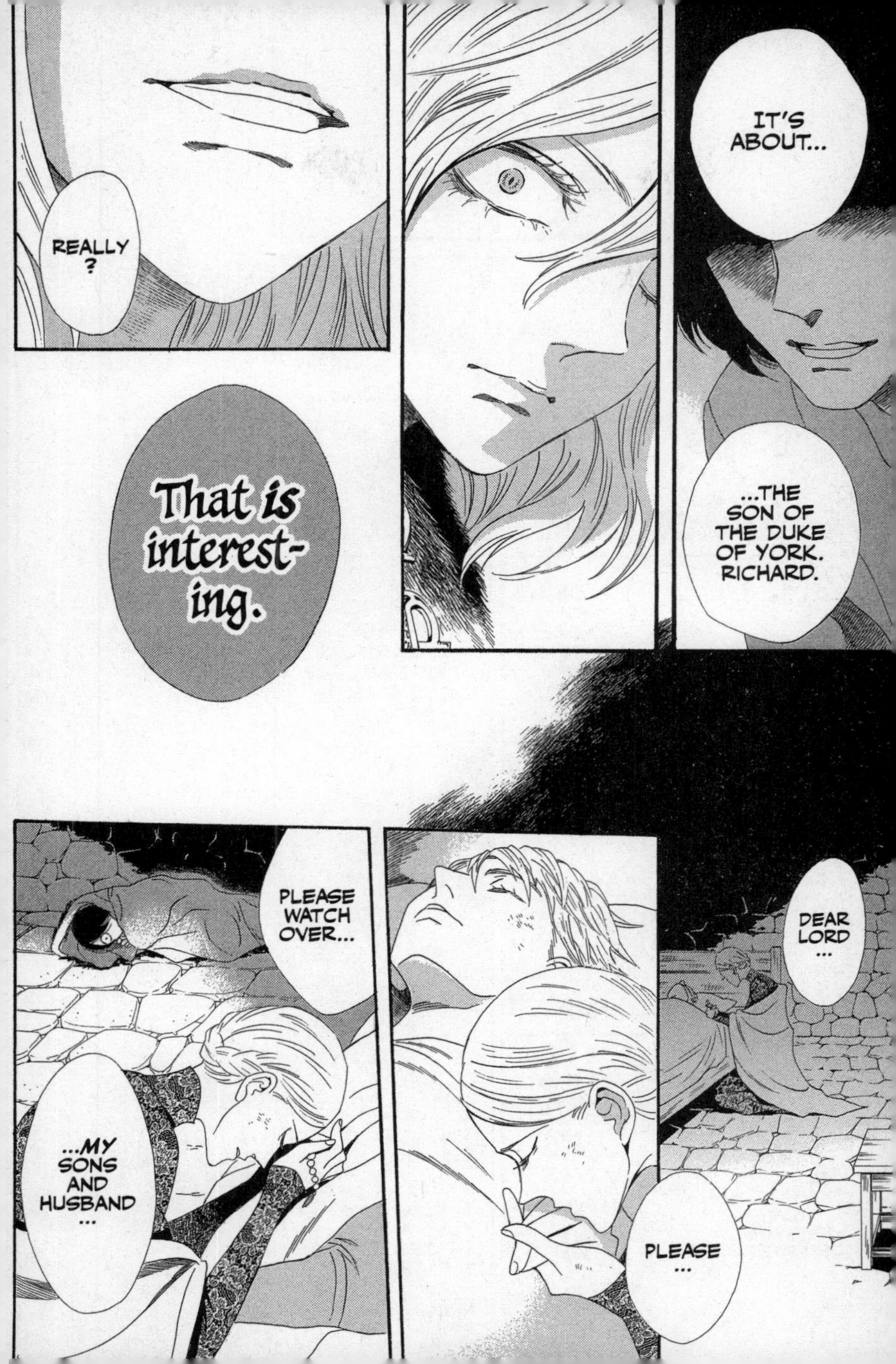
IT'S ABOUT...
...THE SON OF THE DUKE OF YORK. RICHARD.
REALLY ?
That is interesting.
DEAR LORD ...
PLEASE ...
PLEASE WATCH OVER...
...MY SONS AND HUSBAND ...

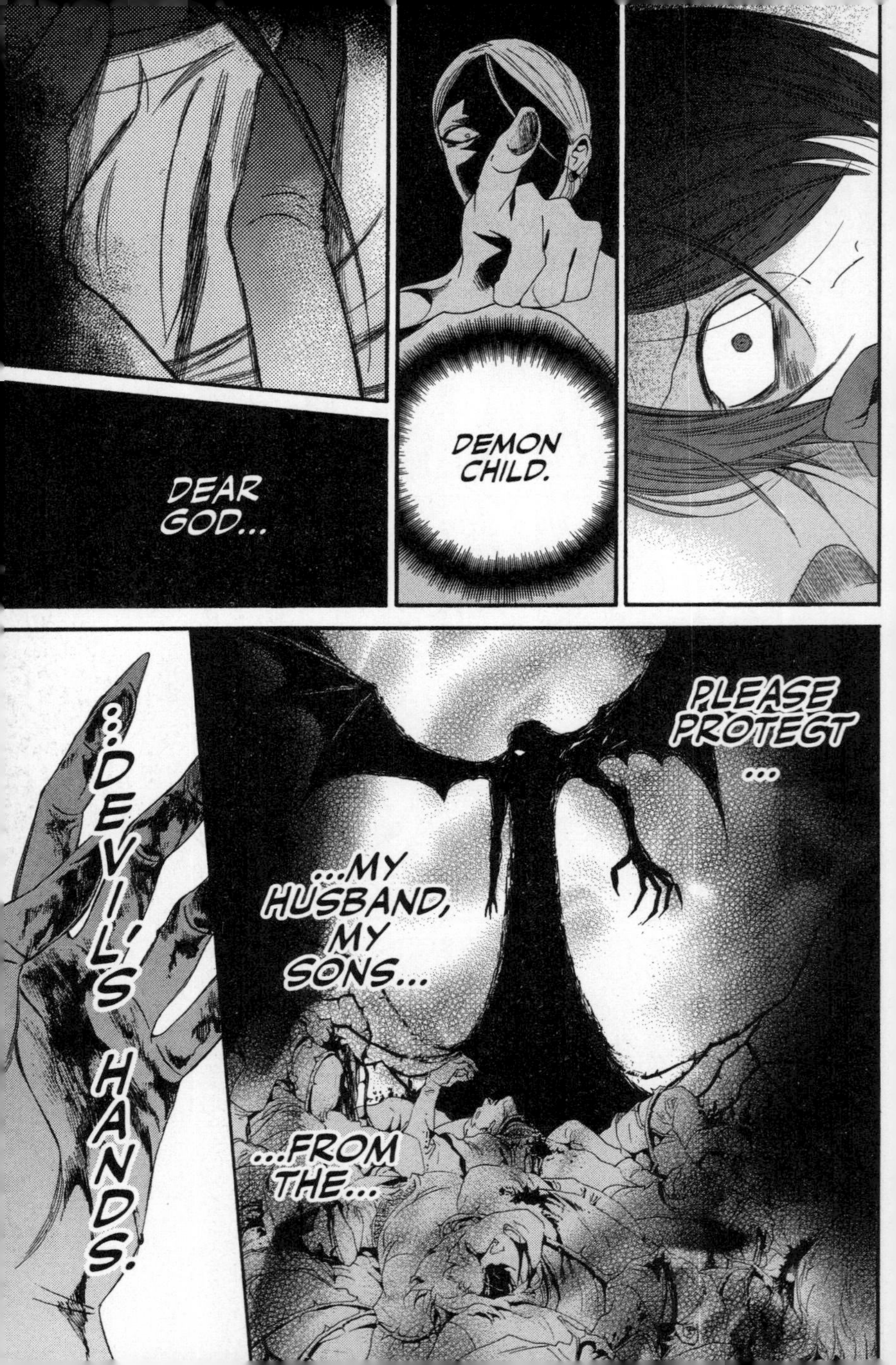
DEMON CHILD.
DEAR GOD...
PLEASE PROTECT ...
...MY HUSBAND, MY SONS...
...FROM THE...
...DEVIL'S HANDS.

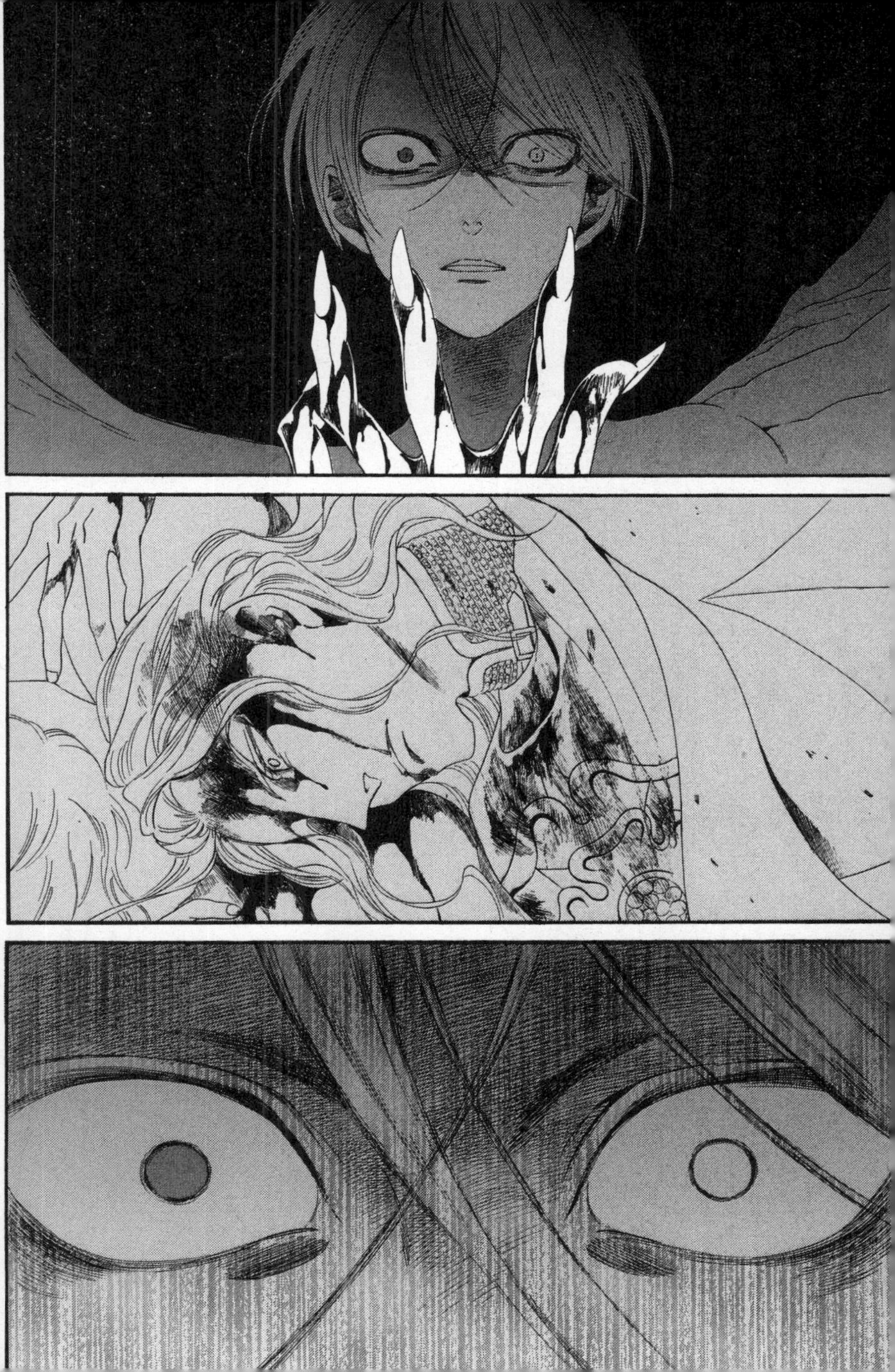

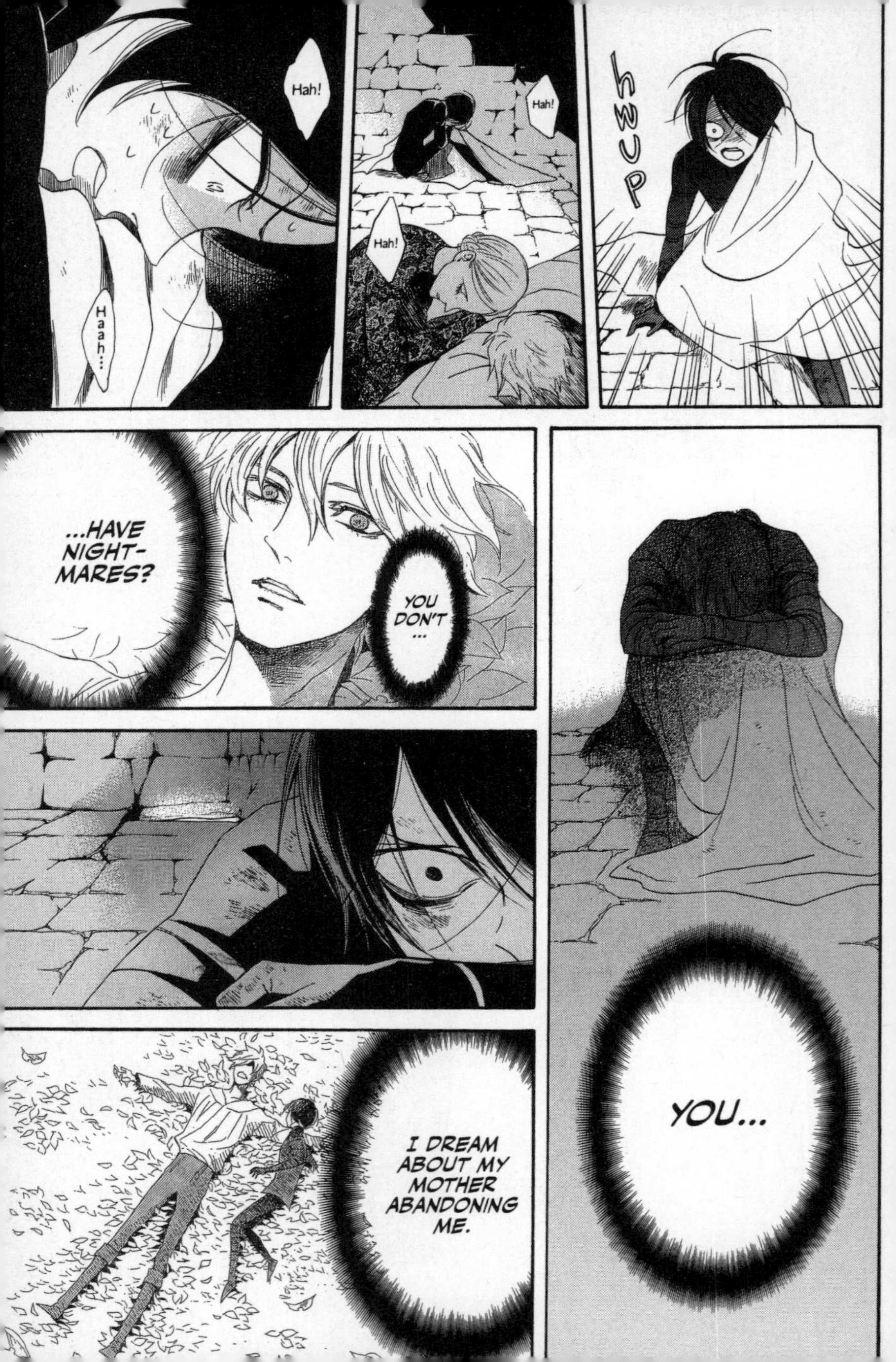
hwup
Hah!
Hah!
Hah!
Haah...
YOU...
YOU DON'T ...
...HAVE NIGHT-MARES?
I DREAM ABOUT MY MOTHER ABANDONING ME.

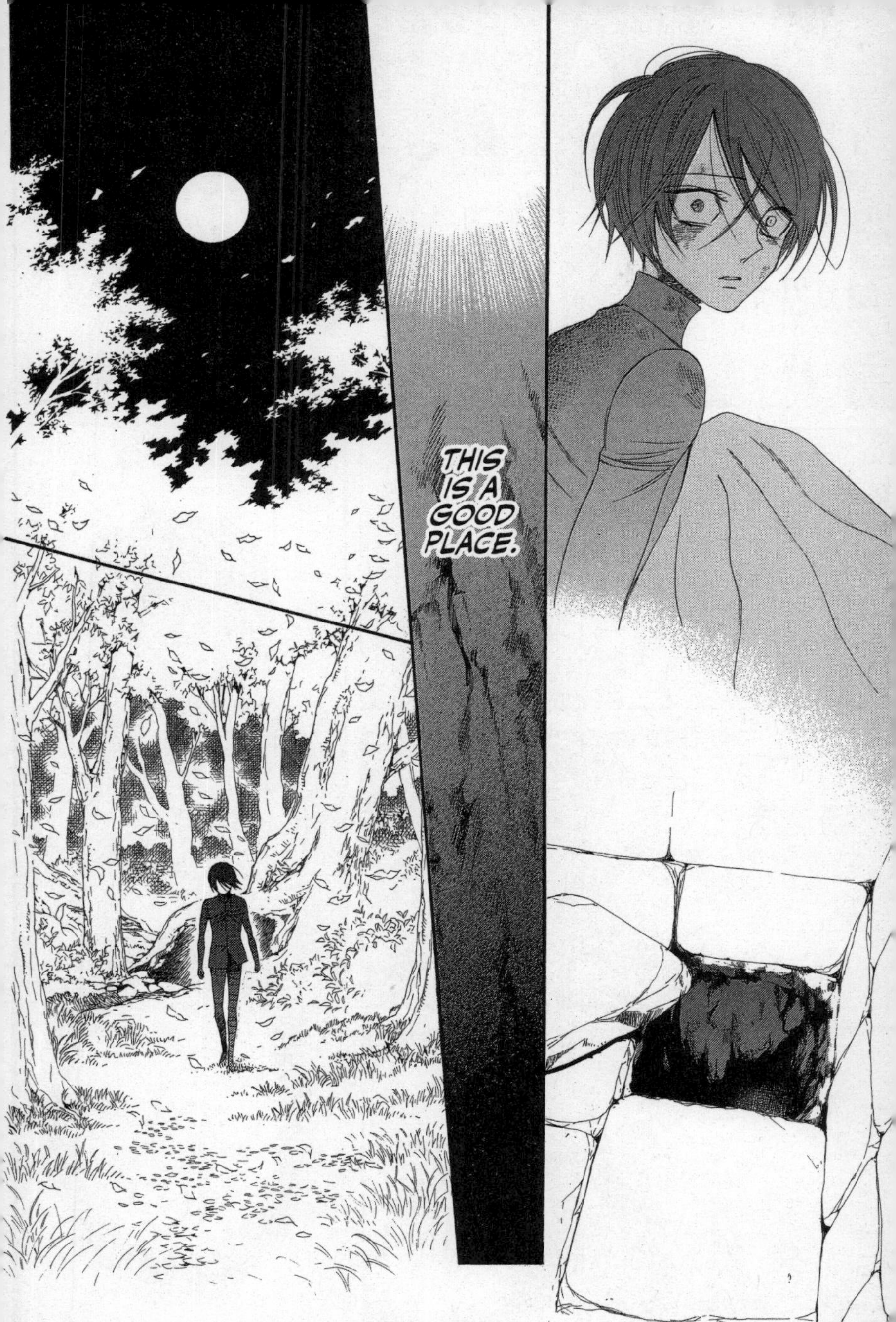
THIS IS A GOOD PLACE.

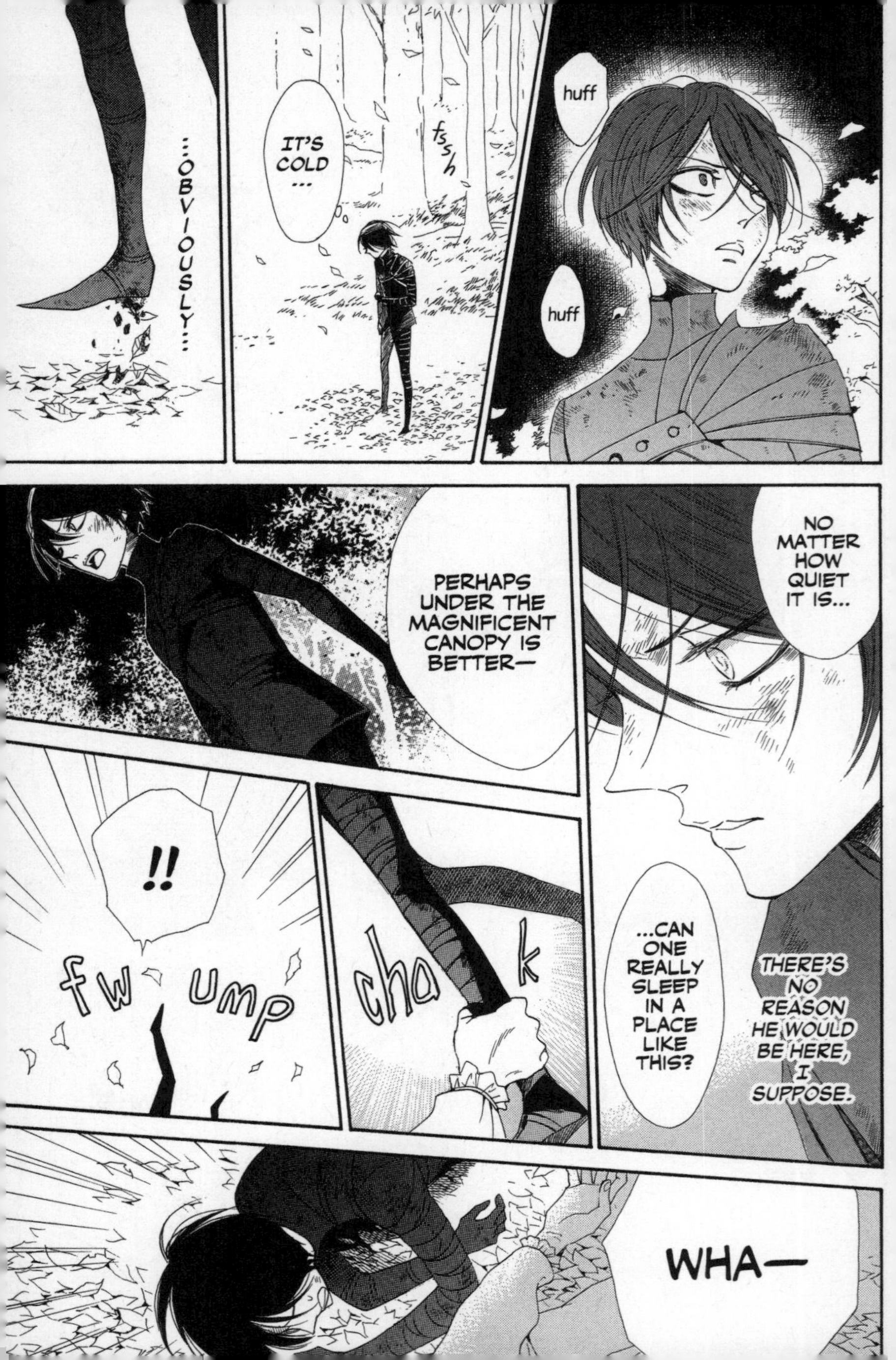
huff
huff
IT'S COLD...
fssh
...OBVIOUSLY...
NO MATTER HOW QUIET IT IS...
...CAN ONE REALLY SLEEP IN A PLACE LIKE THIS?
THERE'S NO REASON HE WOULD BE HERE, I SUPPOSE.
PERHAPS UNDER THE MAGNIFICENT CANOPY IS BETTER—
chak
!!
fwump
WHA—

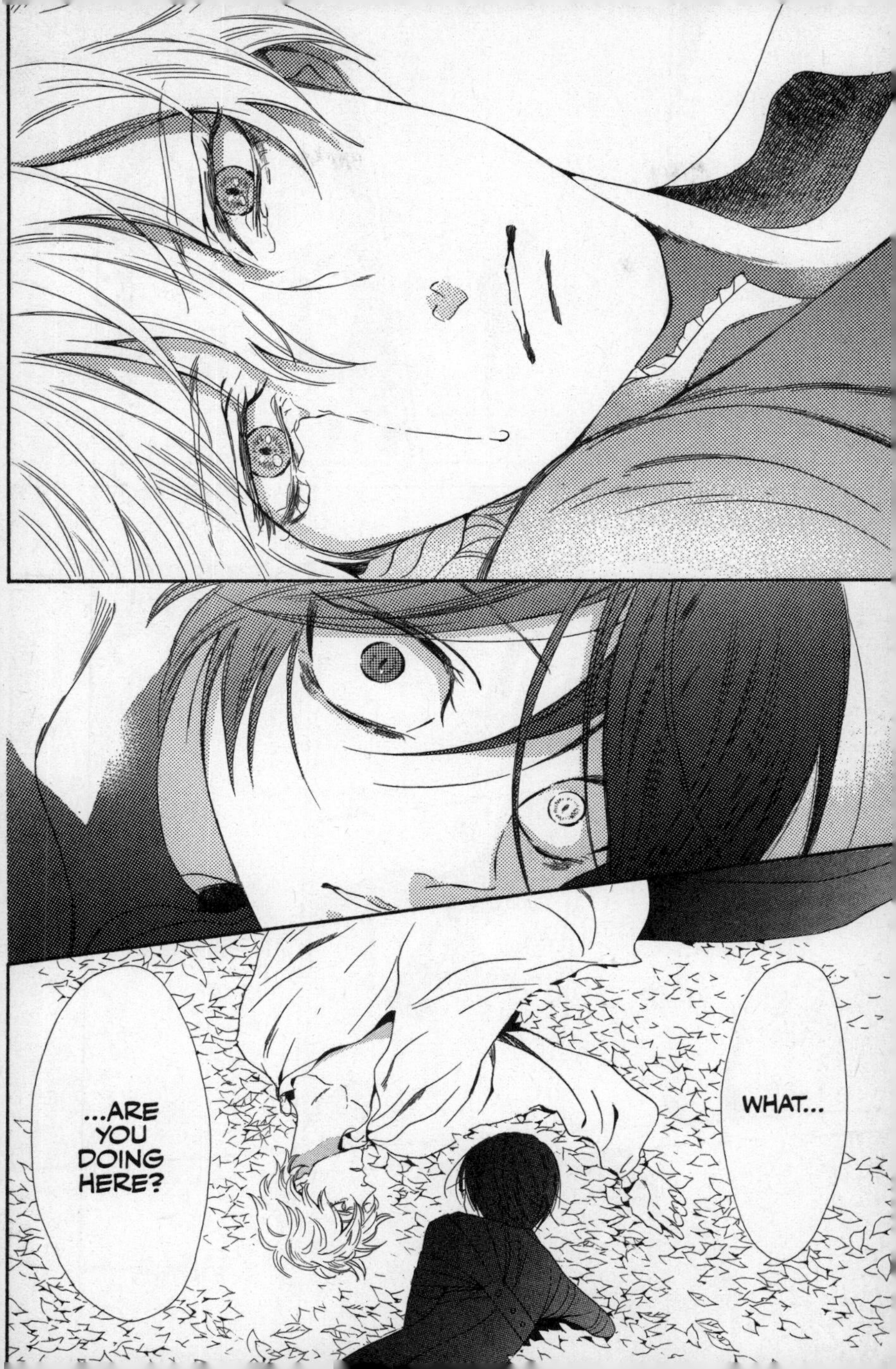
WHAT...
...ARE YOU DOING HERE?

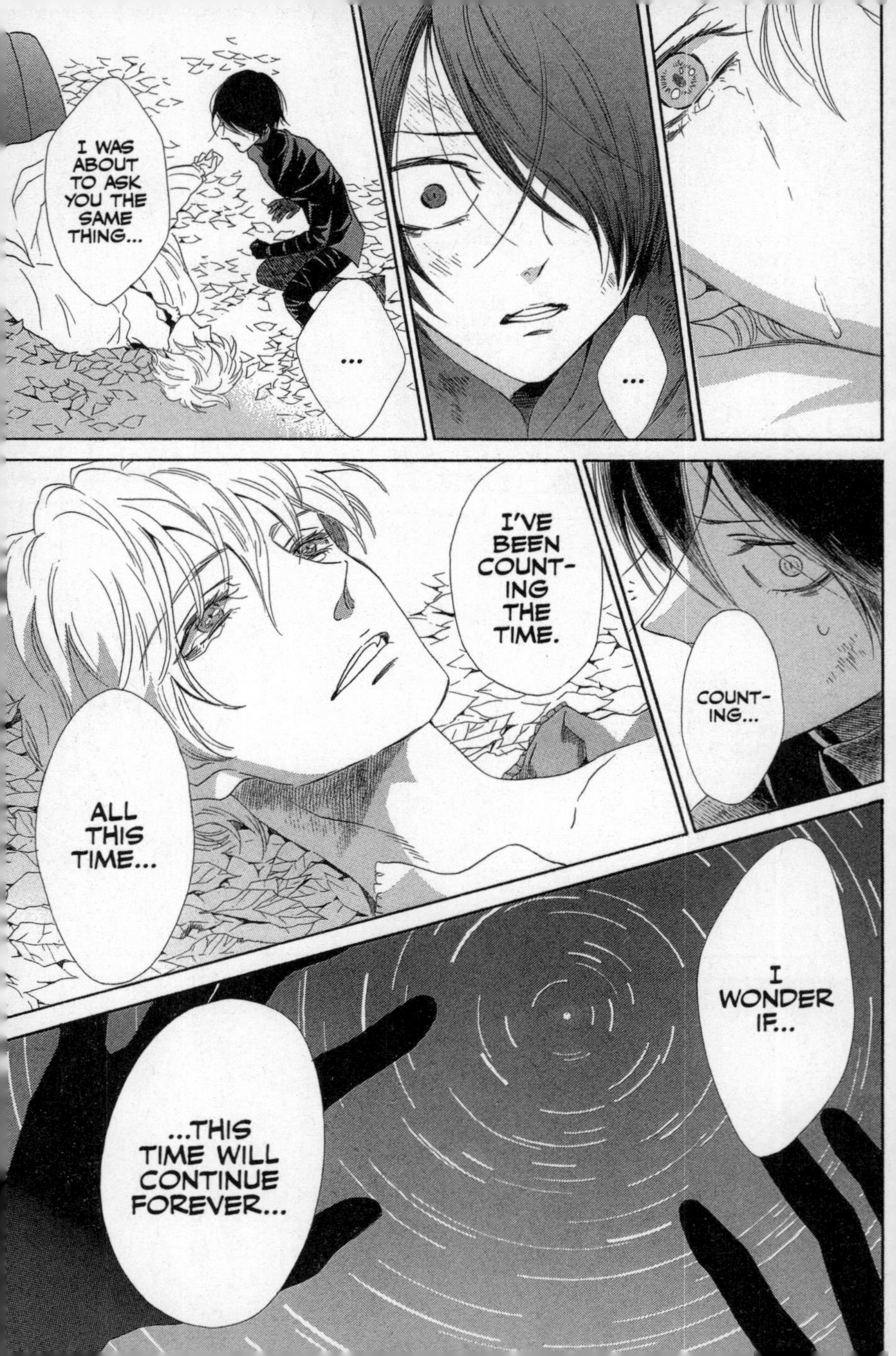
...
I WAS ABOUT TO ASK YOU THE SAME THING...
...
COUNTING...
I'VE BEEN COUNTING THE TIME.
ALL THIS TIME...
I WONDER IF...
...THIS TIME WILL CONTINUE FOREVER...

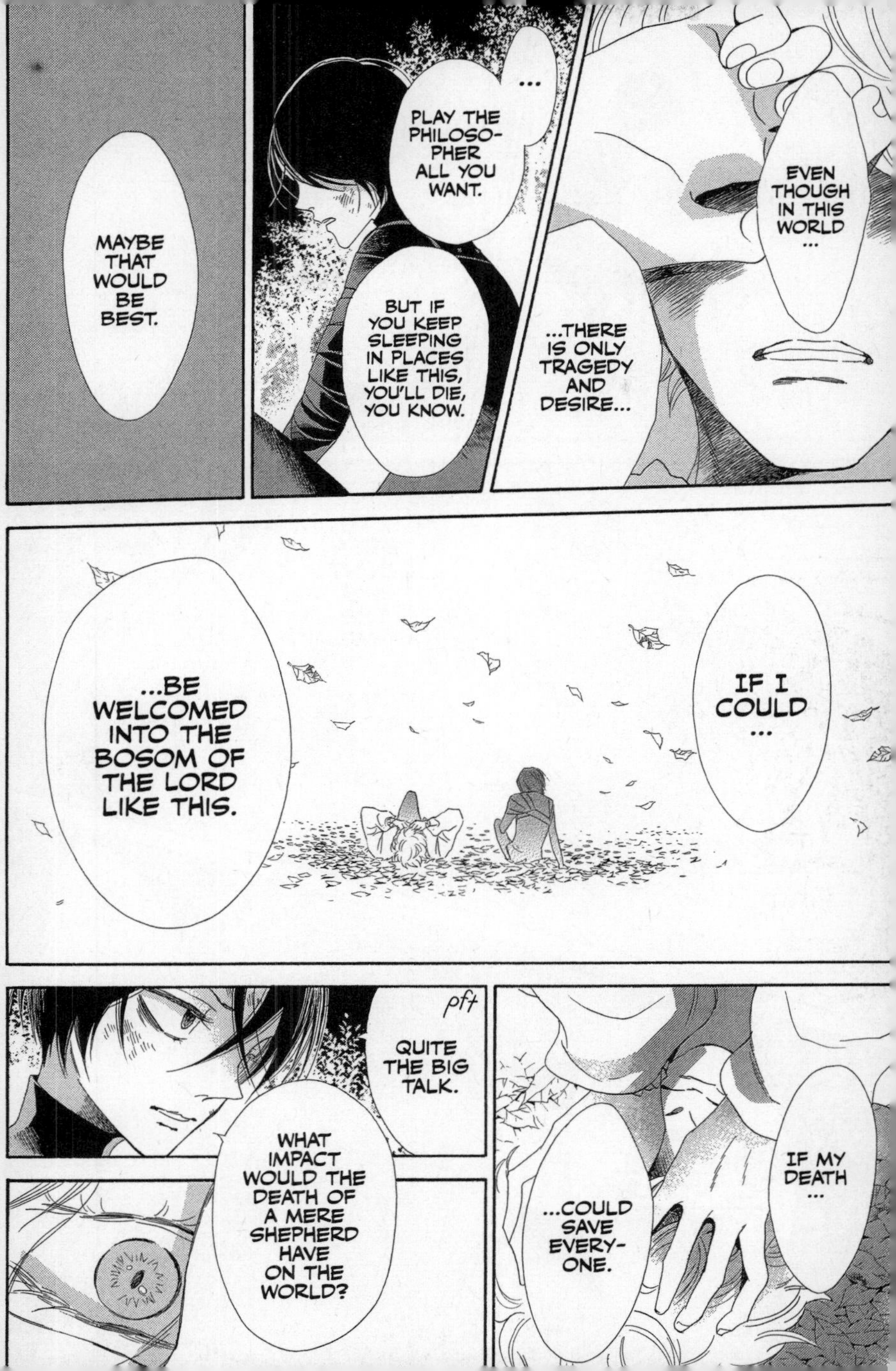
EVEN THOUGH IN THIS WORLD ...
...THERE IS ONLY TRAGEDY AND DESIRE...
...
PLAY THE PHILOSO-PHER ALL YOU WANT.
BUT IF YOU KEEP SLEEPING IN PLACES LIKE THIS, YOU'LL DIE, YOU KNOW.
MAYBE THAT WOULD BE BEST.
IF I COULD ...
...BE WELCOMED INTO THE BOSOM OF THE LORD LIKE THIS.
IF MY DEATH ...
...COULD SAVE EVERY-ONE.
pft
QUITE THE BIG TALK.
WHAT IMPACT WOULD THE DEATH OF A MERE SHEPHERD HAVE ON THE WORLD?

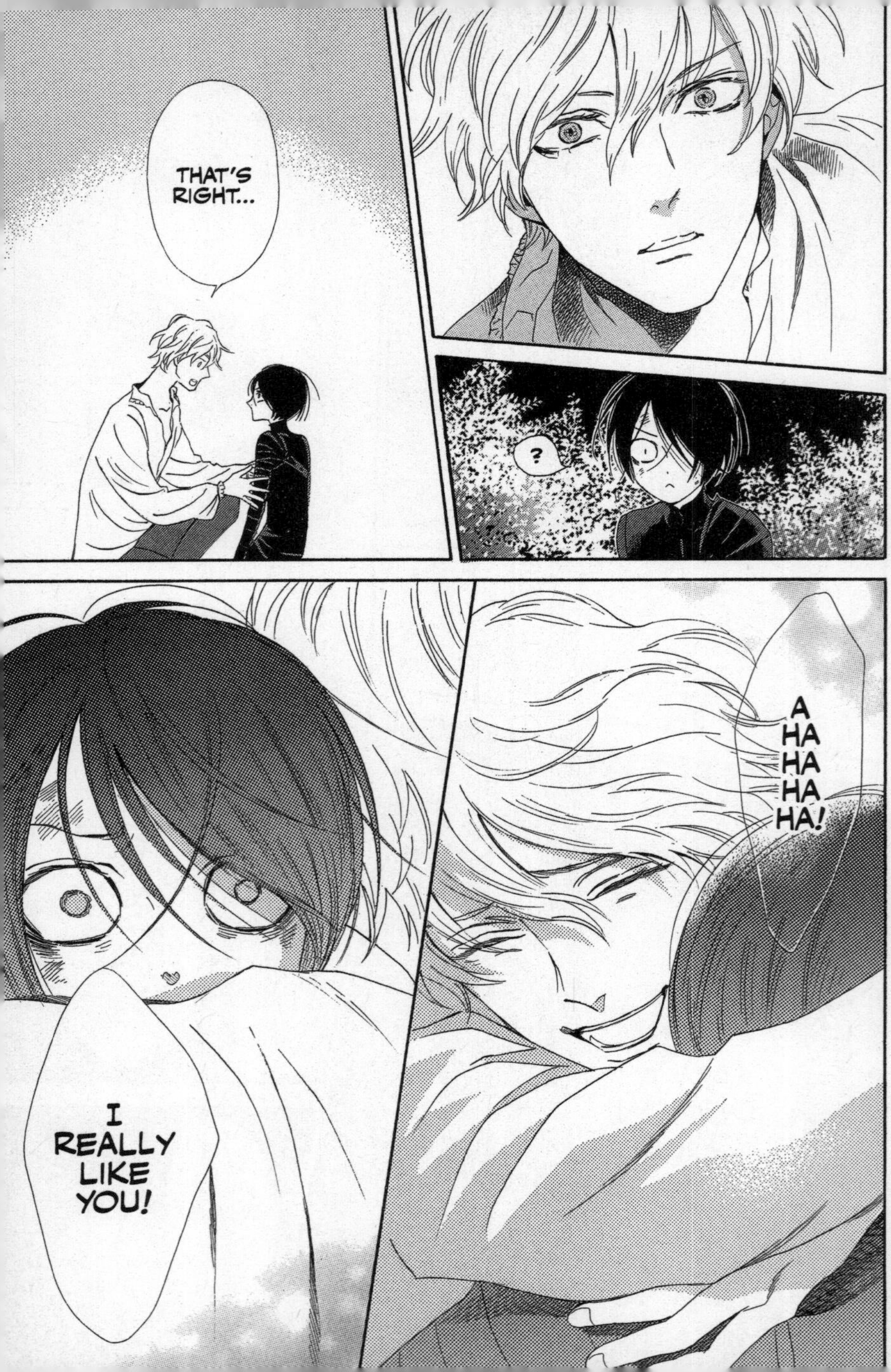
?
THAT'S RIGHT...
A HA HA HA HA!
I REALLY LIKE YOU!

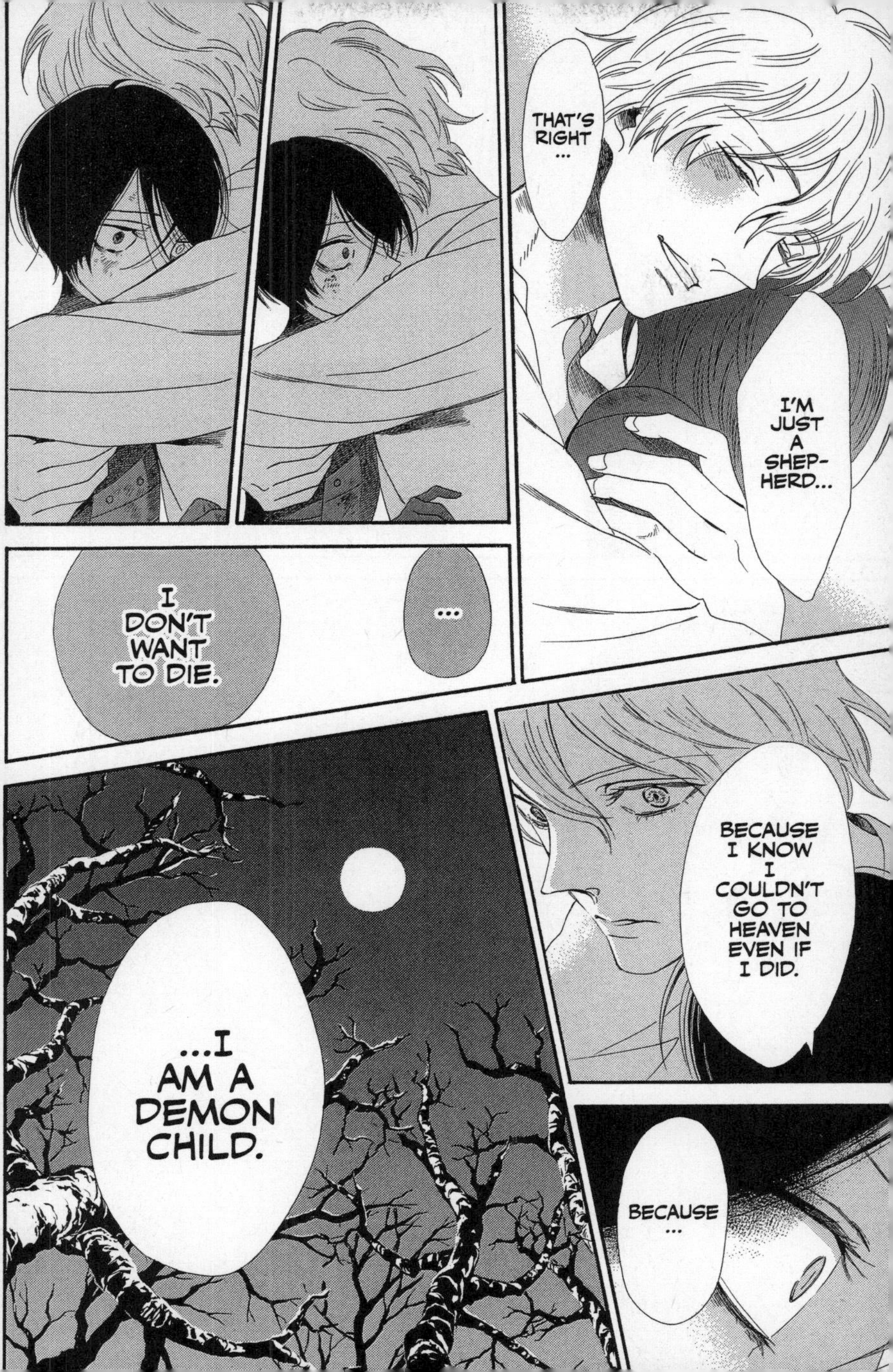
THAT'S RIGHT ...
I'M JUST A SHEP-HERD...
...
I DON'T WANT TO DIE.
BECAUSE I KNOW I COULDN'T GO TO HEAVEN EVEN IF I DID.
BECAUSE ...
...I AM A DEMON CHILD.

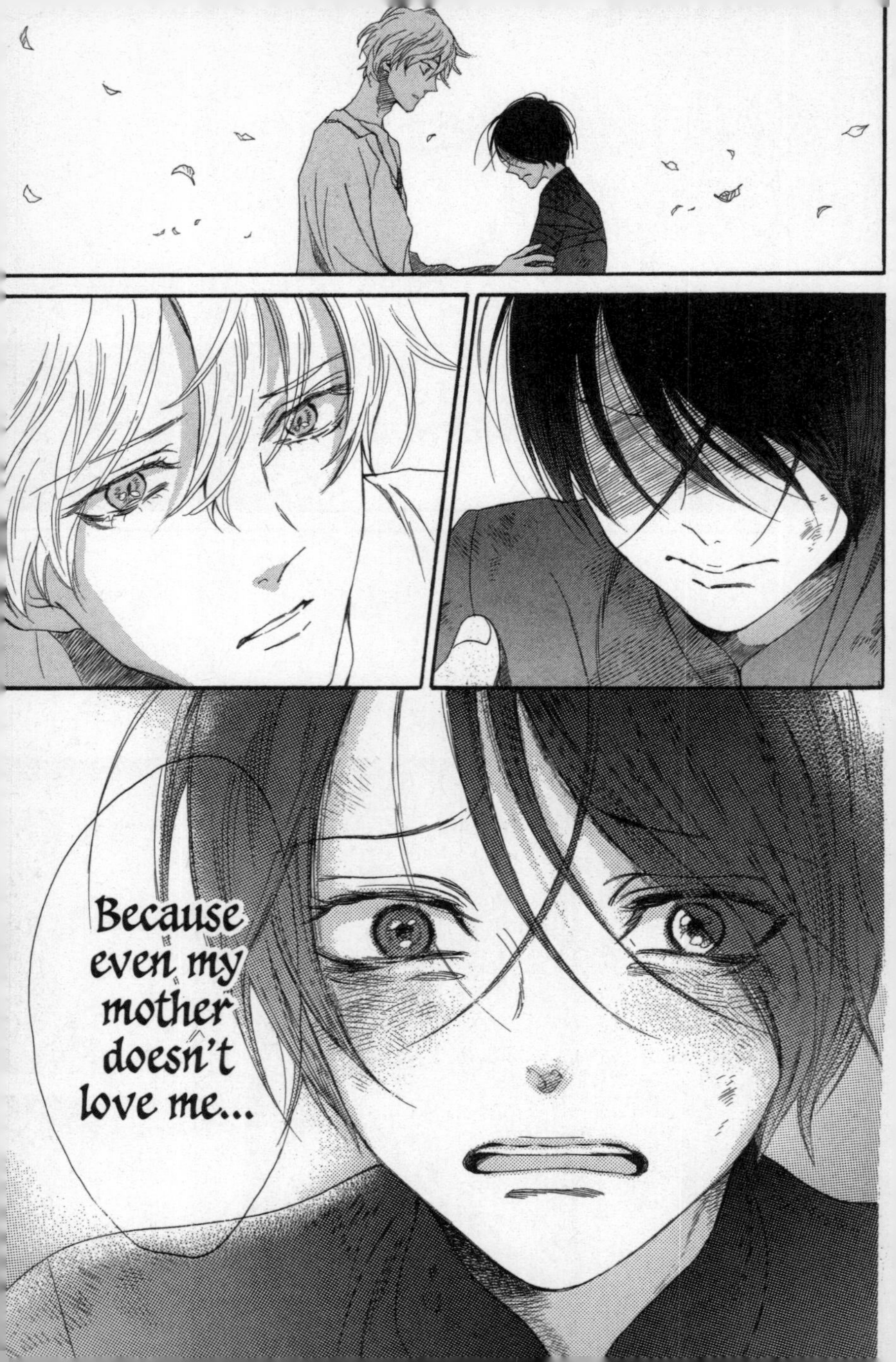
Because even my mother doesn't love me...

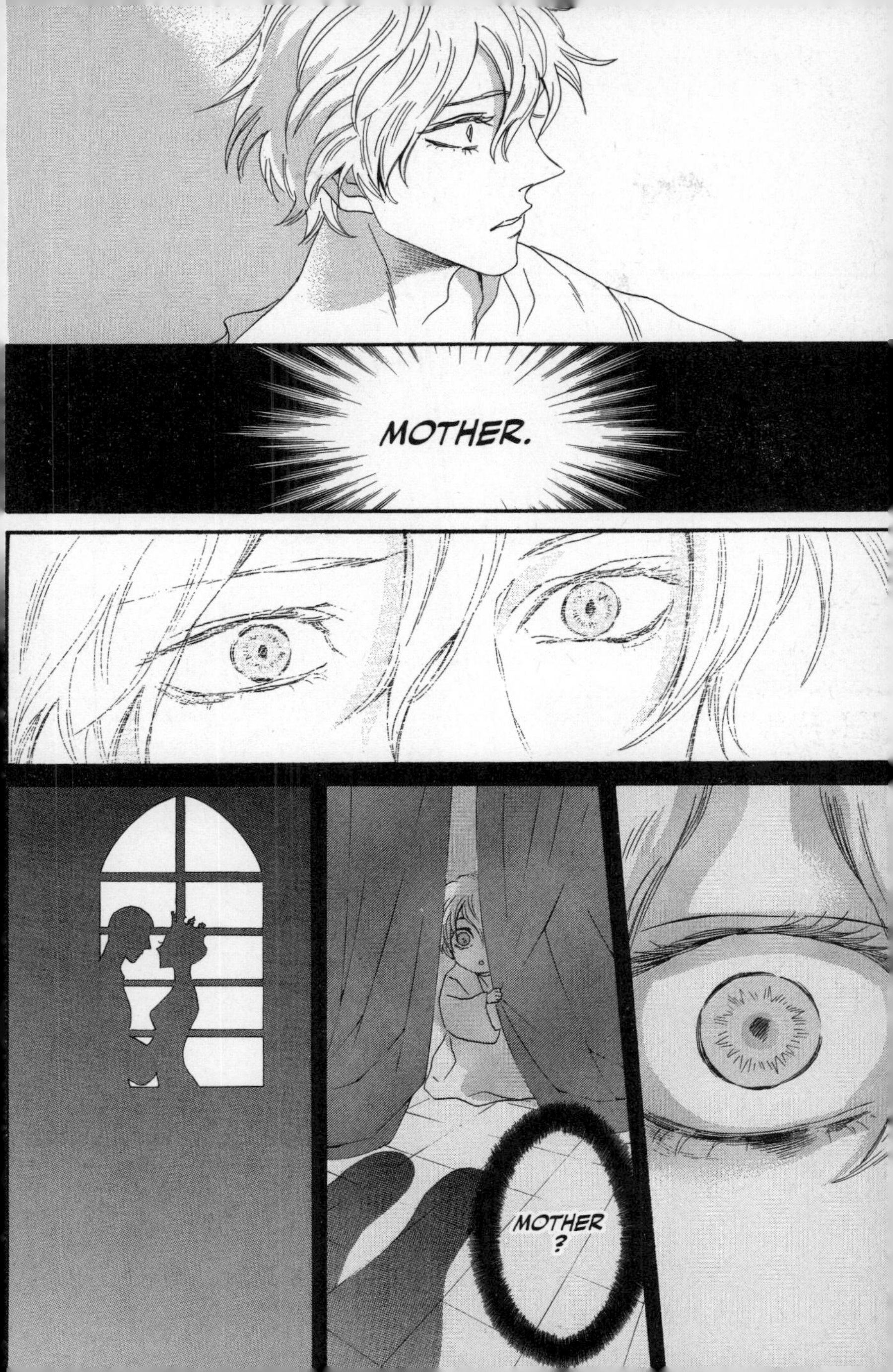
MOTHER.
MOTHER
?

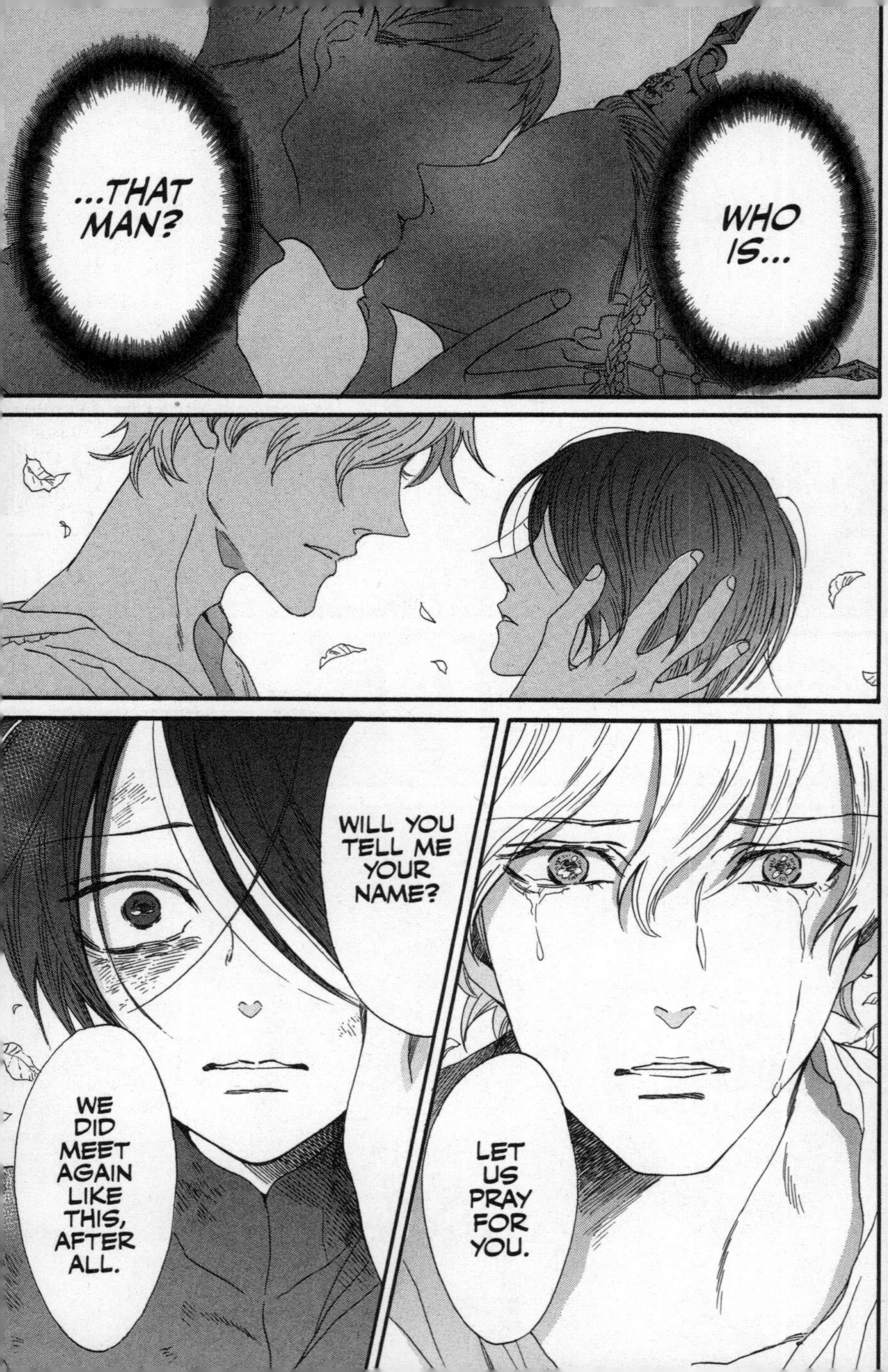
WHO IS...
...THAT MAN?
LET US PRAY FOR YOU.
WILL YOU TELL ME YOUR NAME?
WE DID MEET AGAIN LIKE THIS, AFTER ALL.

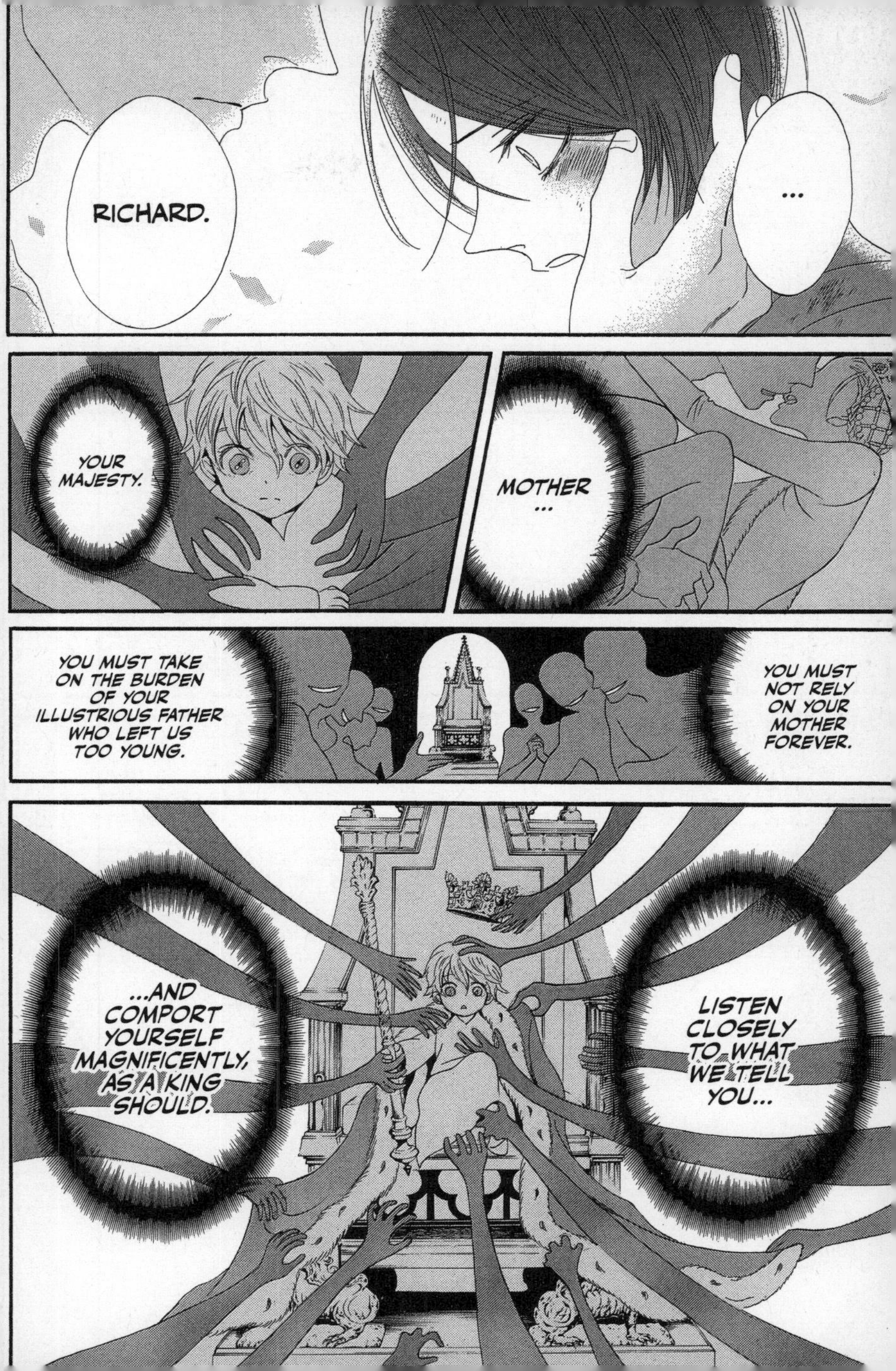
...
RICHARD.
MOTHER ...
YOUR MAJESTY.
YOU MUST NOT RELY ON YOUR MOTHER FOREVER.
YOU MUST TAKE ON THE BURDEN OF YOUR ILLUSTRIOUS FATHER WHO LEFT US TOO YOUNG.
LISTEN CLOSELY TO WHAT WE TELL YOU...
...AND COMPORT YOURSELF MAGNIFICENTLY, AS A KING SHOULD.

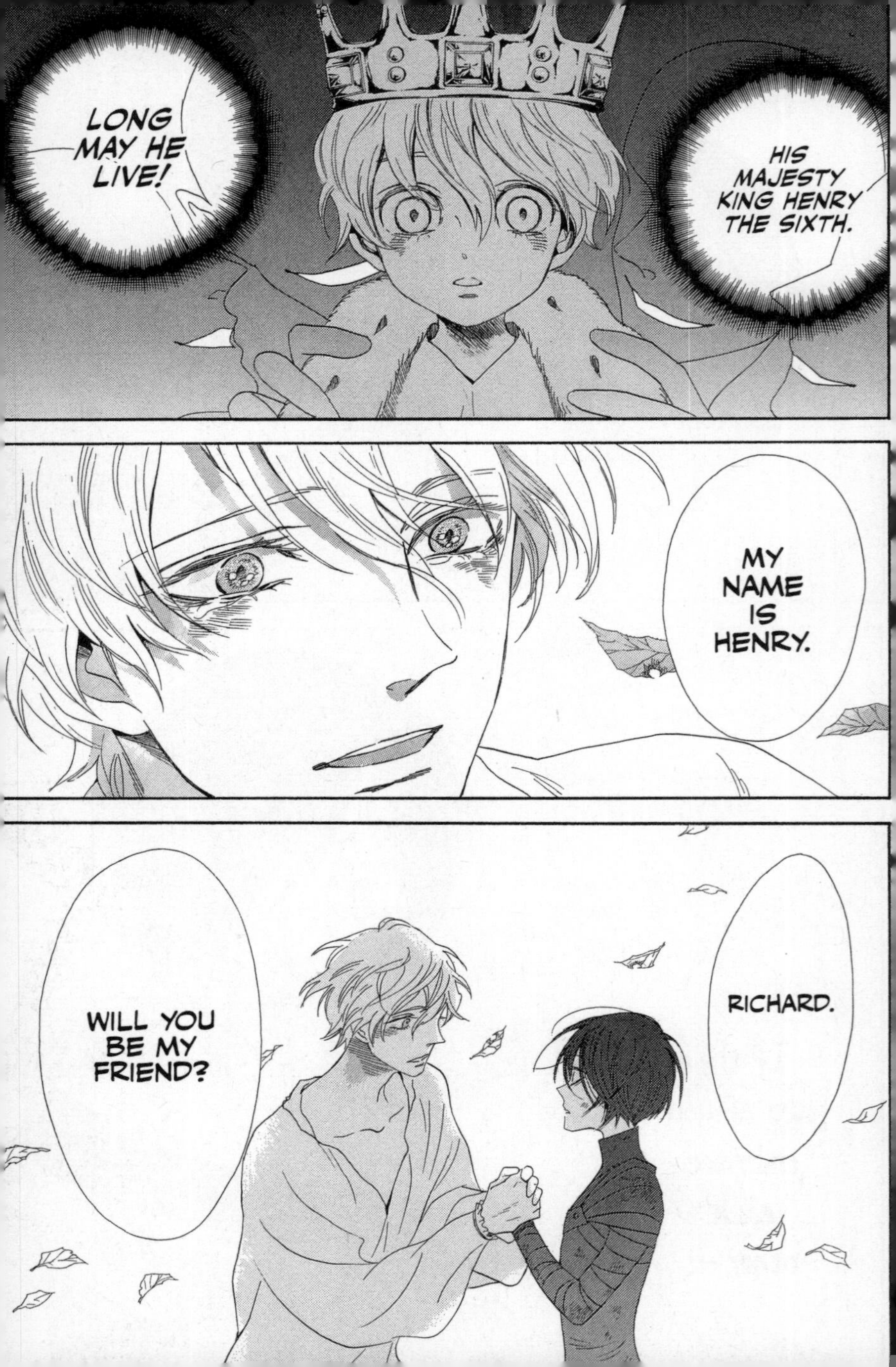
HIS MAJESTY KING HENRY THE SIXTH.
LONG MAY HE LIVE!
MY NAME IS HENRY.
RICHARD.
WILL YOU BE MY FRIEND?

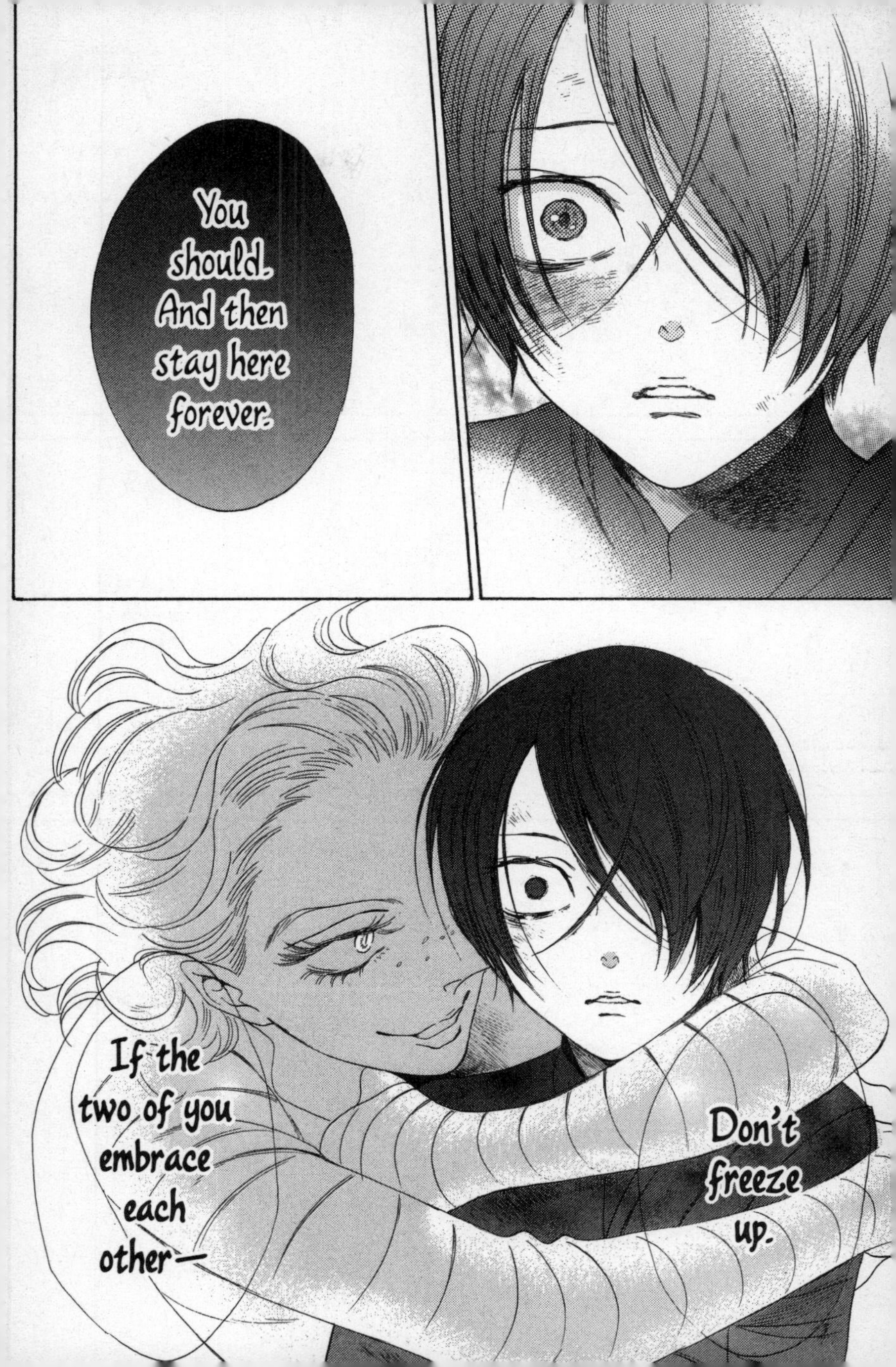
You should. And then stay here forever.
Don't freeze up.
If the two of you embrace each other—

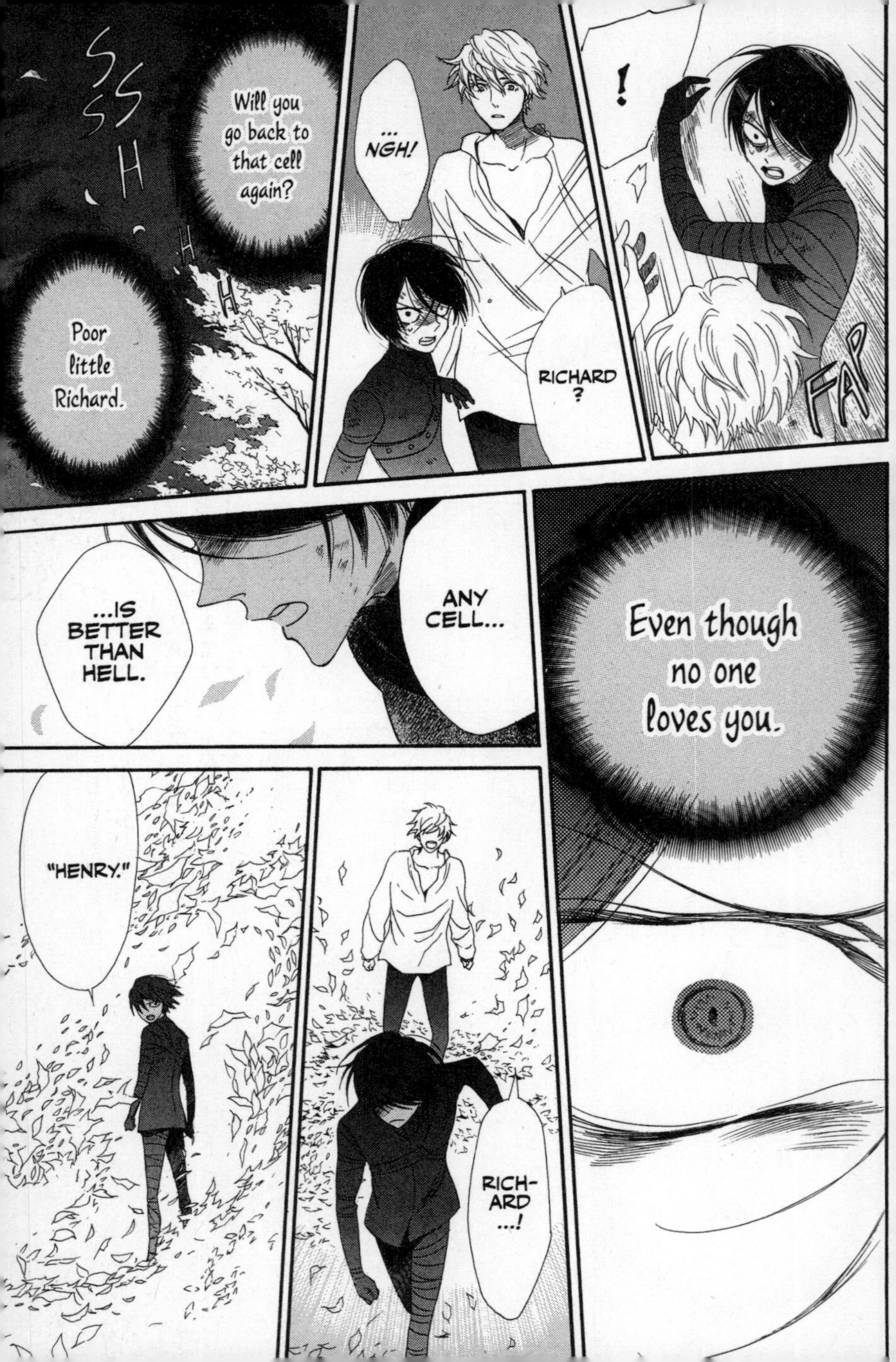

!
FAP
...NGH!
RICHARD?
SSSHHH
Will you go back to that cell again?
Poor little Richard.
Even though no one loves you.
ANY CELL...
...IS BETTER THAN HELL.
RICH-ARD...!
"HENRY."

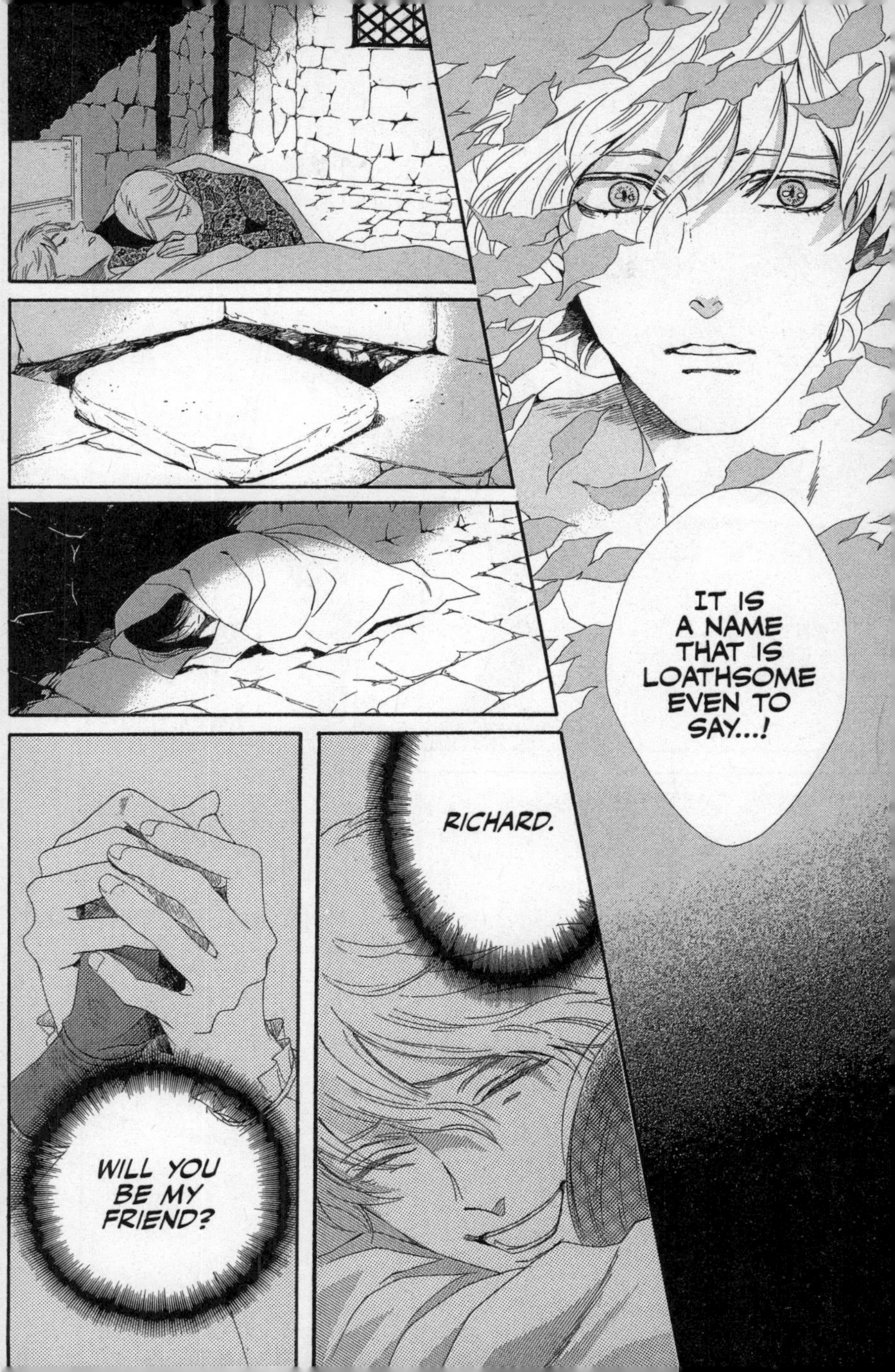
IT IS A NAME THAT IS LOATHSOME EVEN TO SAY...!
RICHARD.
WILL YOU BE MY FRIEND?

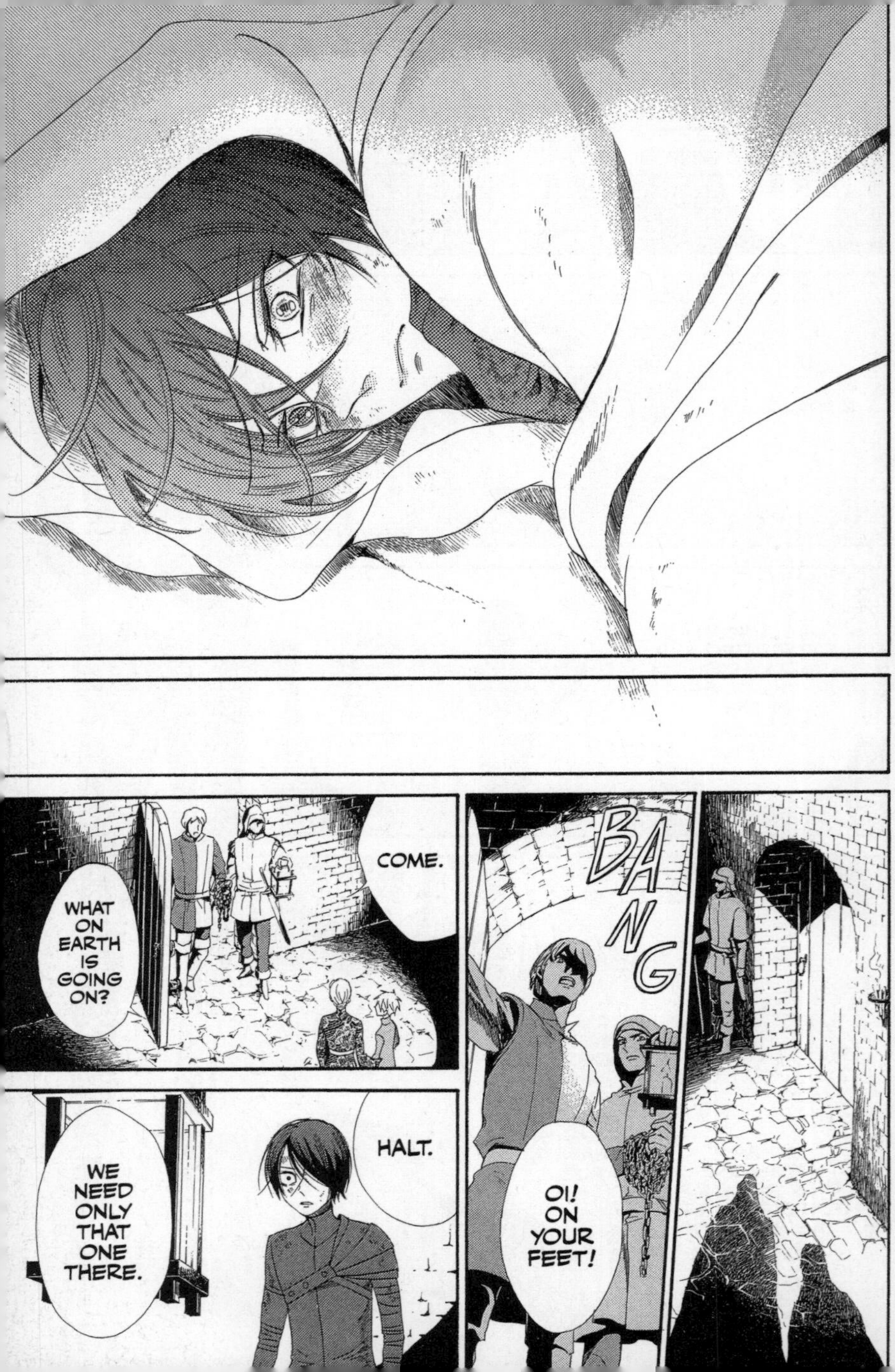
BANG
OI! ON YOUR FEET!
COME.
WHAT ON EARTH IS GOING ON?
HALT.
WE NEED ONLY THAT ONE THERE.

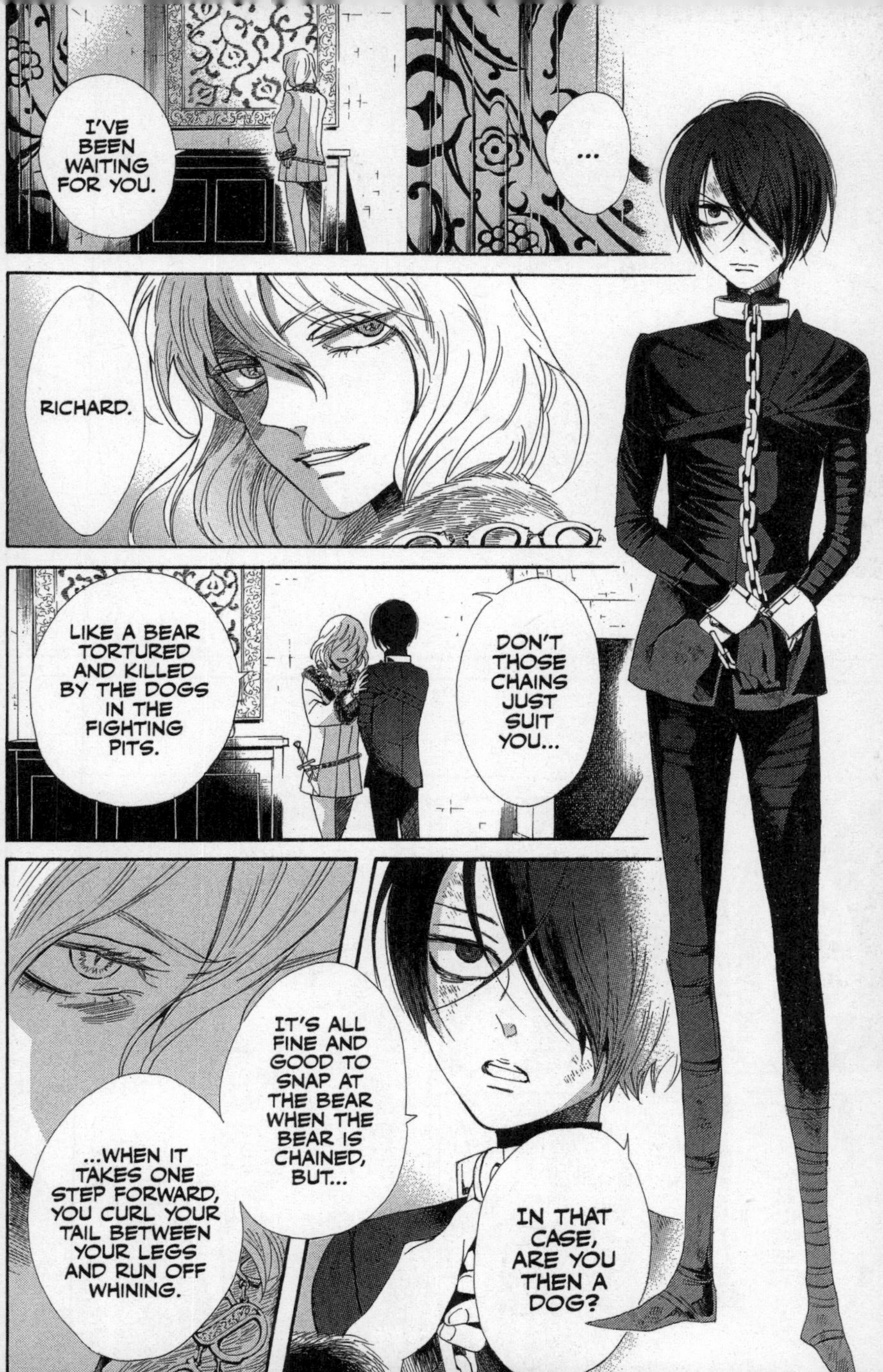
...
I'VE BEEN WAITING FOR YOU.
RICHARD.
DON'T THOSE CHAINS JUST SUIT YOU...
LIKE A BEAR TORTURED AND KILLED BY THE DOGS IN THE FIGHTING PITS.
IT'S ALL FINE AND GOOD TO SNAP AT THE BEAR WHEN THE BEAR IS CHAINED, BUT...
...WHEN IT TAKES ONE STEP FORWARD, YOU CURL YOUR TAIL BETWEEN YOUR LEGS AND RUN OFF WHINING.
IN THAT CASE, ARE YOU THEN A DOG?

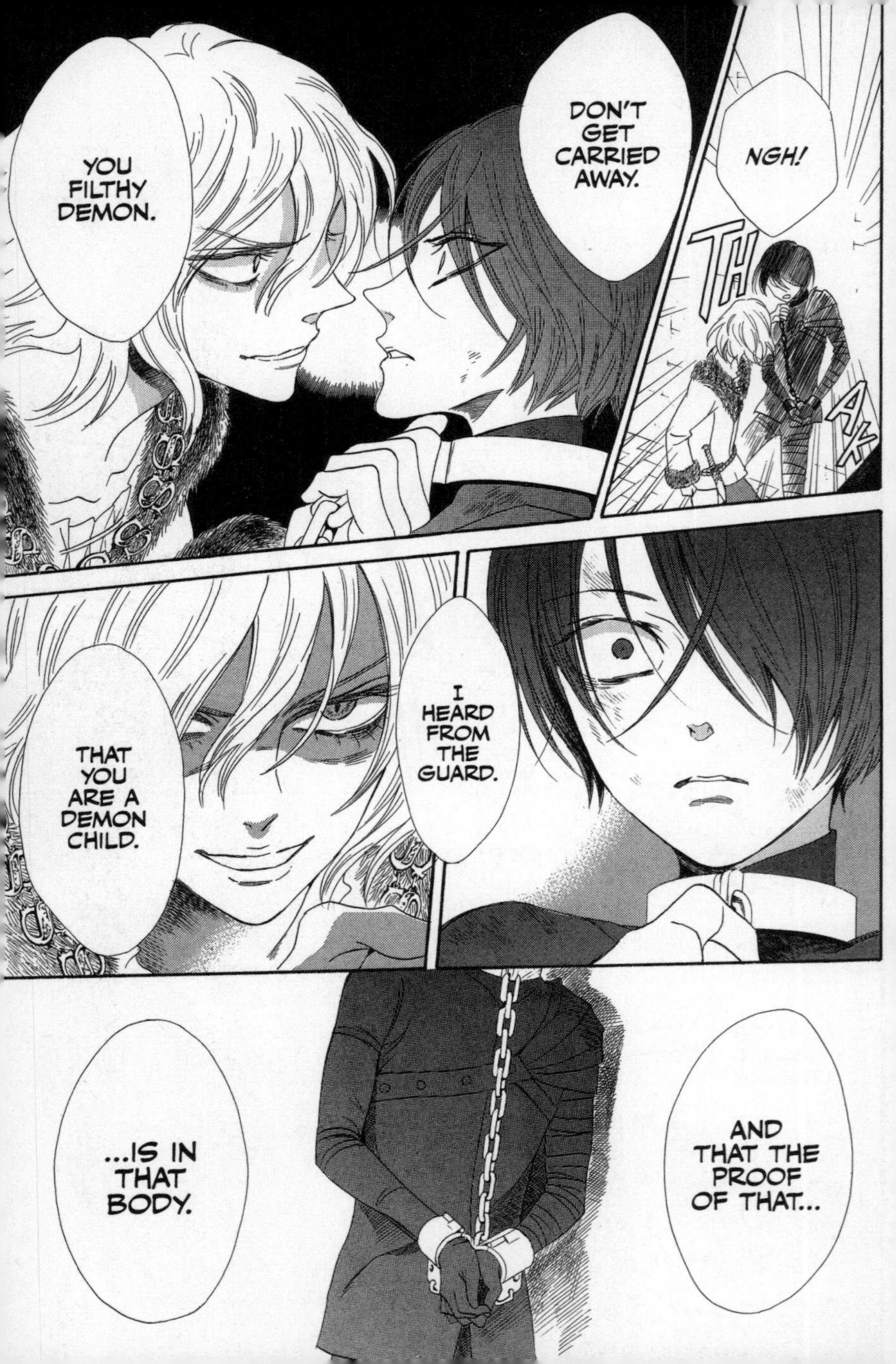
NGH!
THAK
DON'T GET CARRIED AWAY.
YOU FILTHY DEMON.
I HEARD FROM THE GUARD.
THAT YOU ARE A DEMON CHILD.
AND THAT THE PROOF OF THAT...
...IS IN THAT BODY.

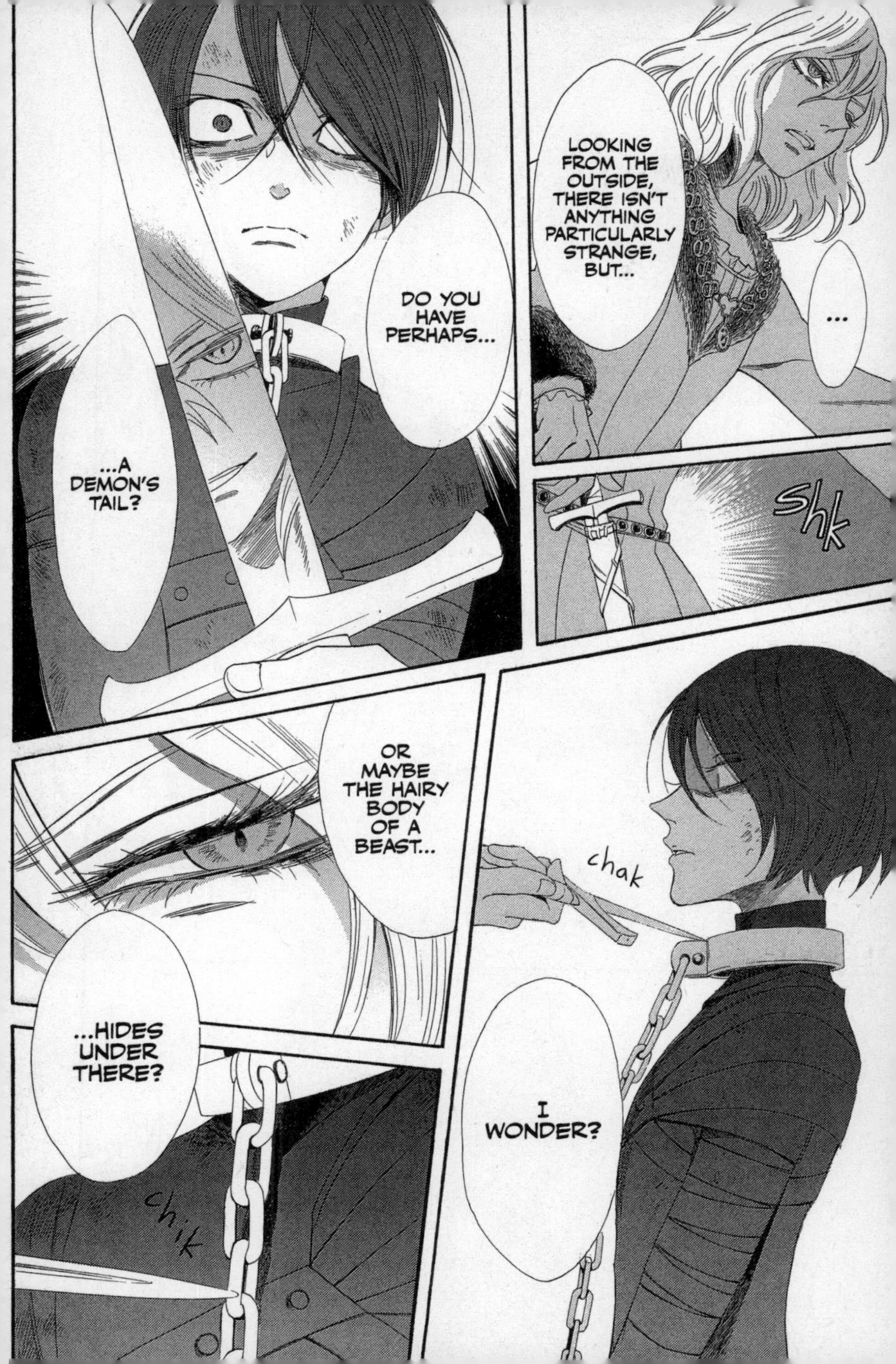
...
LOOKING FROM THE OUTSIDE, THERE ISN'T ANYTHING PARTICULARLY STRANGE, BUT...
Shk
DO YOU HAVE PERHAPS...
...A DEMON'S TAIL?
chak
I WONDER?
OR MAYBE THE HAIRY BODY OF A BEAST...
...HIDES UNDER THERE?
chik

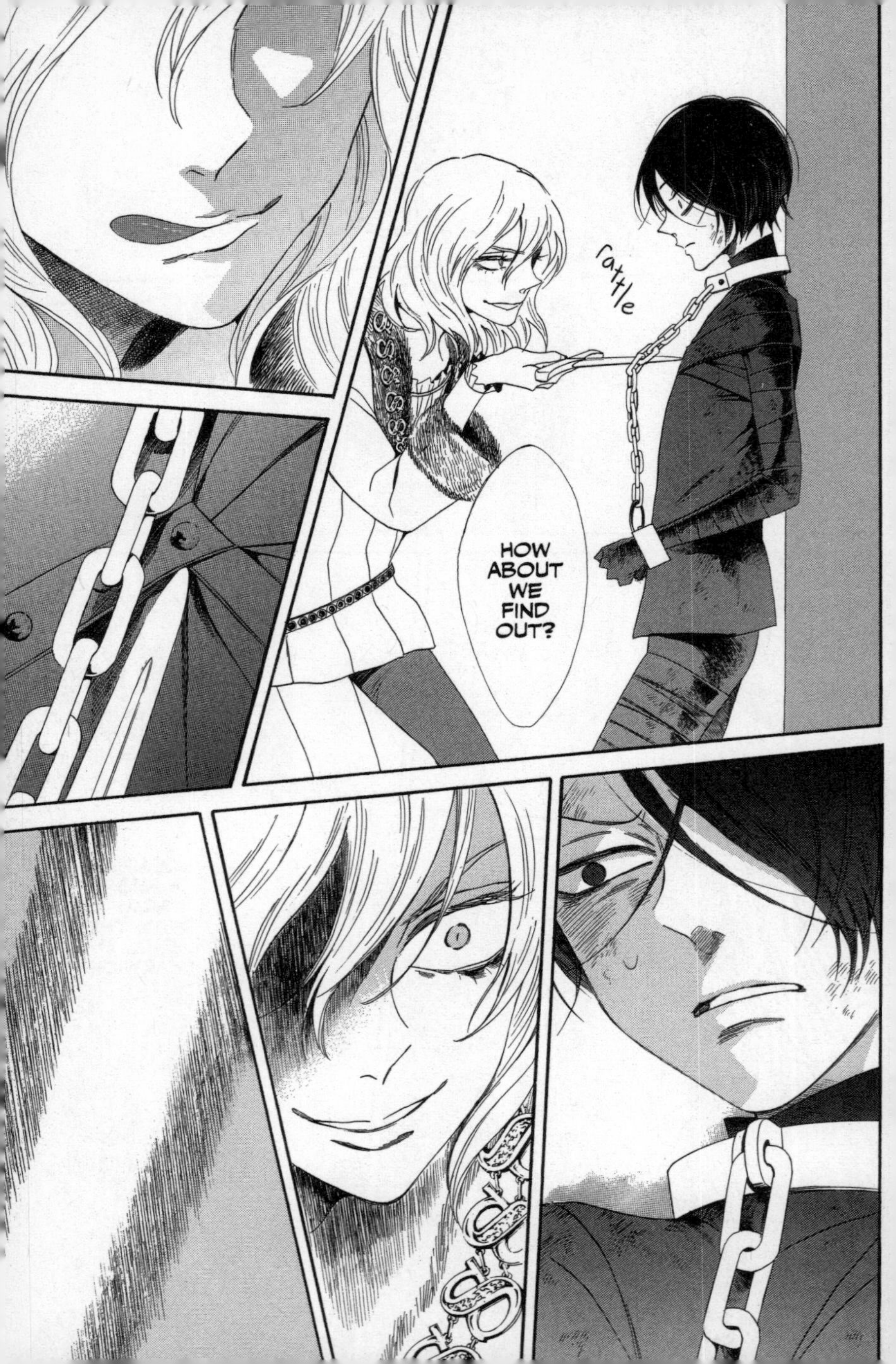
rattle
HOW ABOUT WE FIND OUT?

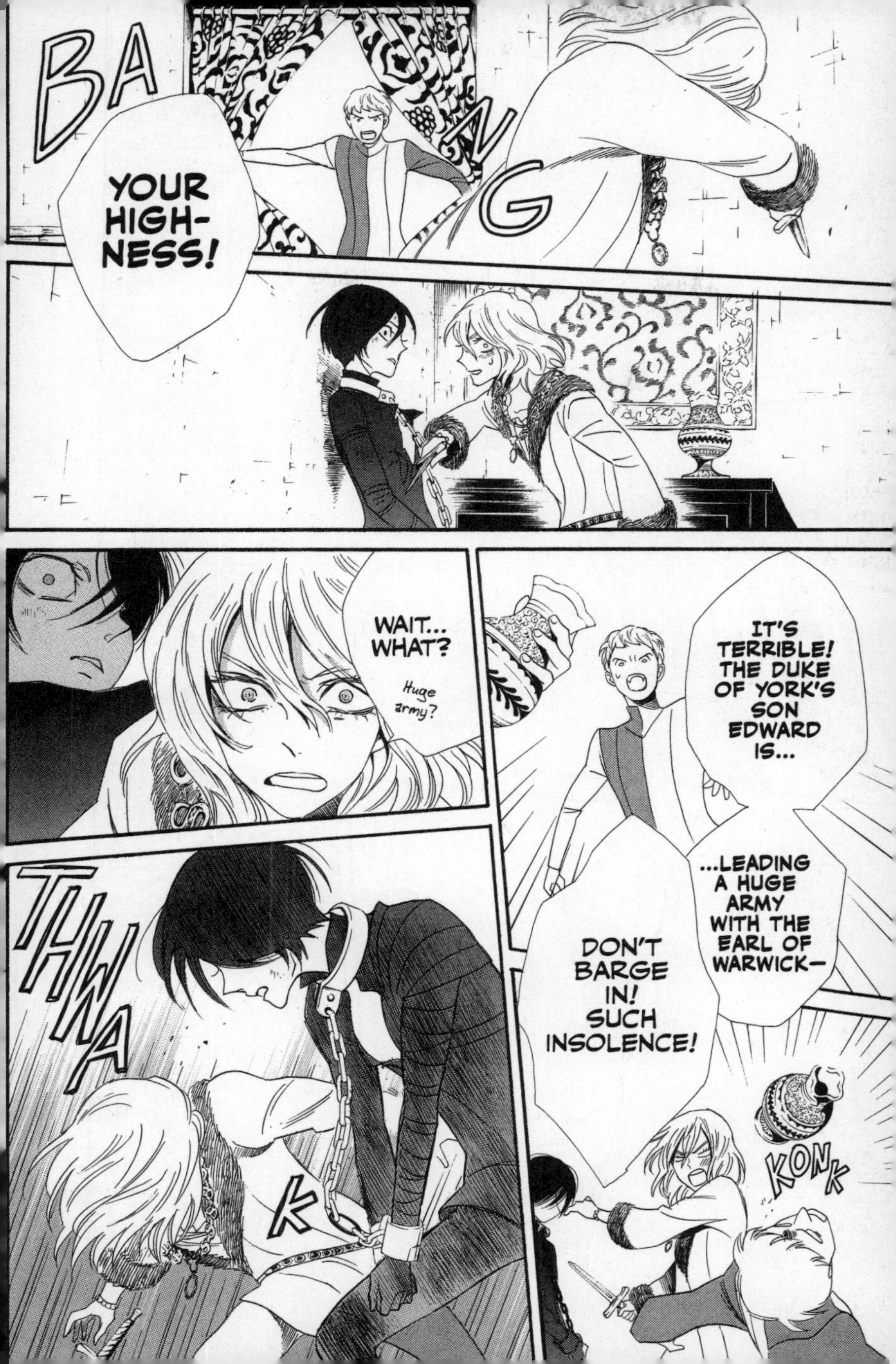
BANG
YOUR HIGHNESS!
IT'S TERRIBLE! THE DUKE OF YORK'S SON EDWARD IS...
...LEADING A HUGE ARMY WITH THE EARL OF WARWICK—
WAIT... WHAT?
Huge army?
DON'T BARGE IN! SUCH INSOLENCE!
KONK
THWACK

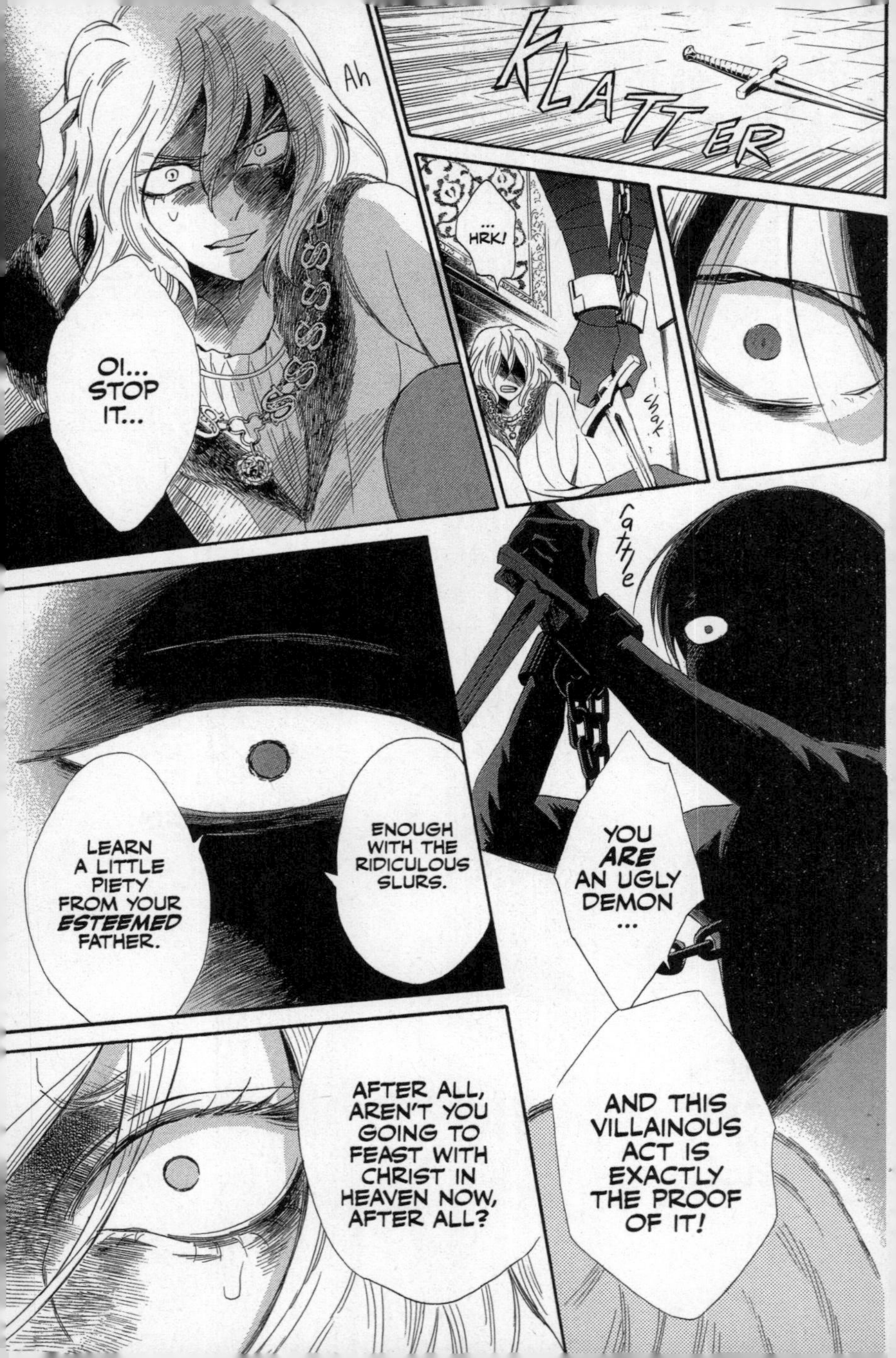
KLATTER
... HRK!
chak
Ah
OI... STOP IT...
rattle
YOU *ARE* AN UGLY DEMON ...
AND THIS VILLAINOUS ACT IS EXACTLY THE PROOF OF IT!
ENOUGH WITH THE RIDICULOUS SLURS.
LEARN A LITTLE PIETY FROM YOUR *ESTEEMED* FATHER.
AFTER ALL, AREN'T YOU GOING TO FEAST WITH CHRIST IN HEAVEN NOW, AFTER ALL?

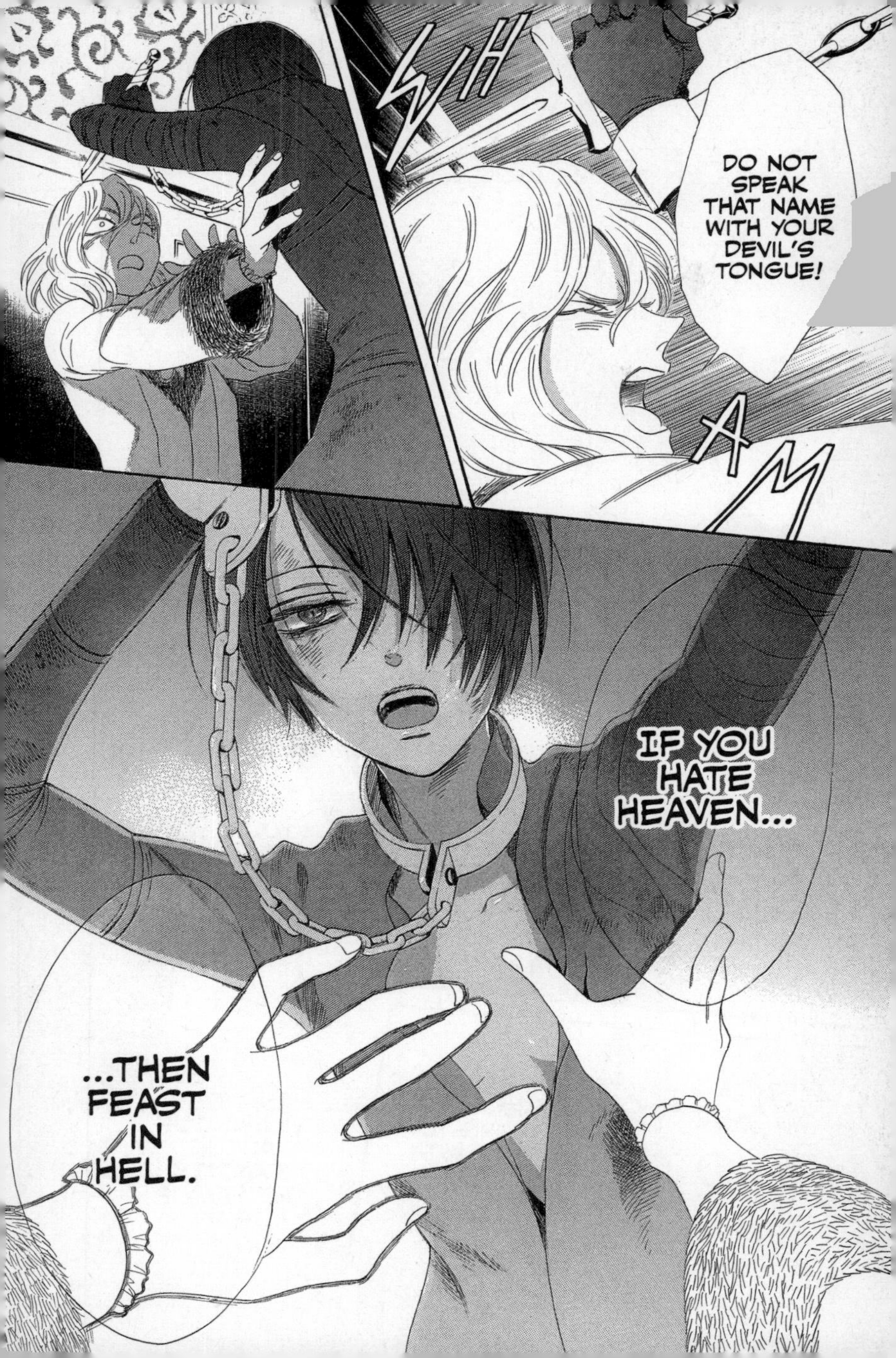
WH
AM
DO NOT SPEAK THAT NAME WITH YOUR DEVIL'S TONGUE!
IF YOU HATE HEAVEN...
...THEN FEAST IN HELL.

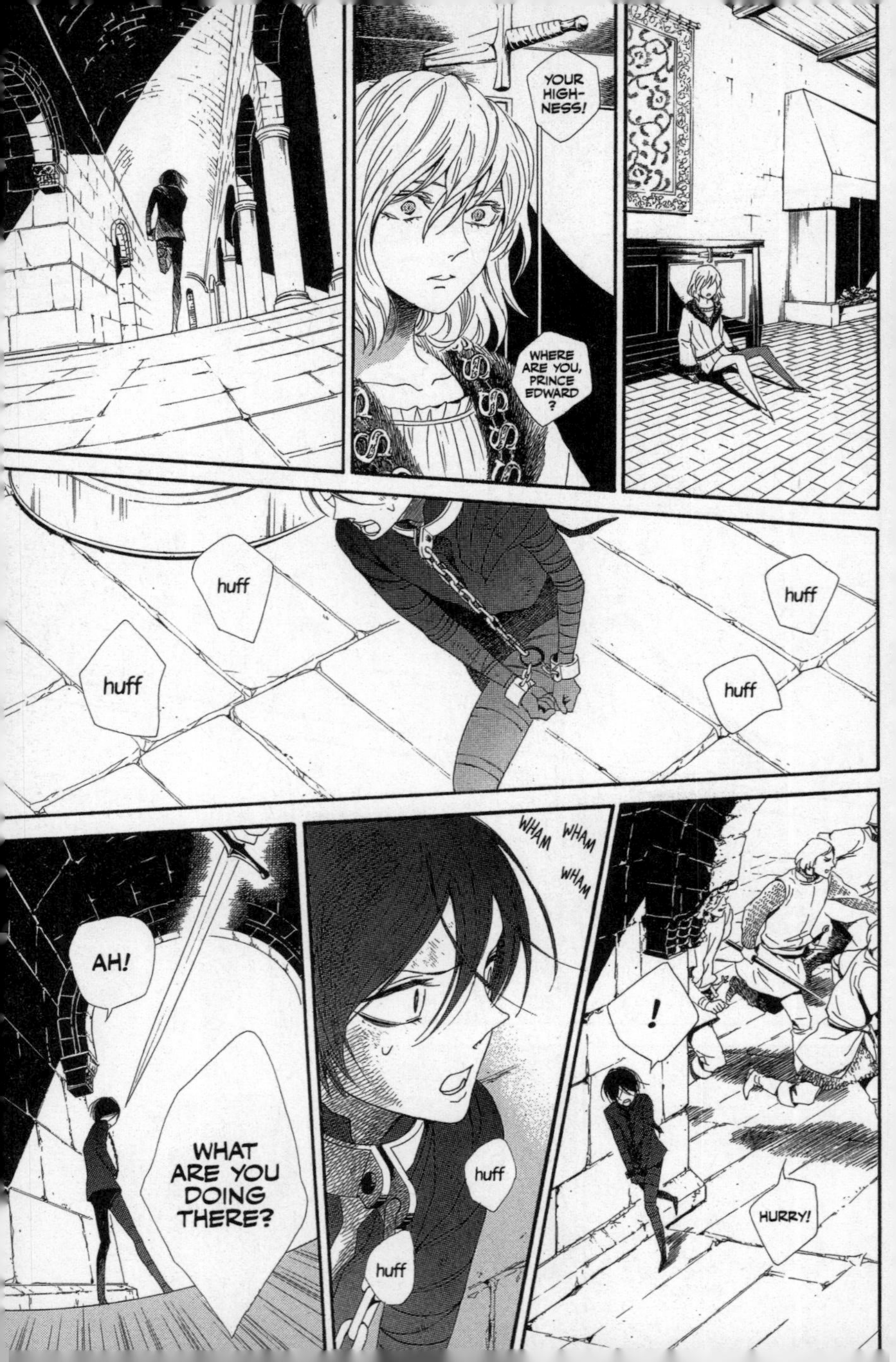

YOUR HIGHNESS!
WHERE ARE YOU, PRINCE EDWARD?
huff
huff
huff
huff
WHAM
WHAM
WHAM
!
HURRY!
huff
huff
AH!
WHAT ARE YOU DOING THERE?

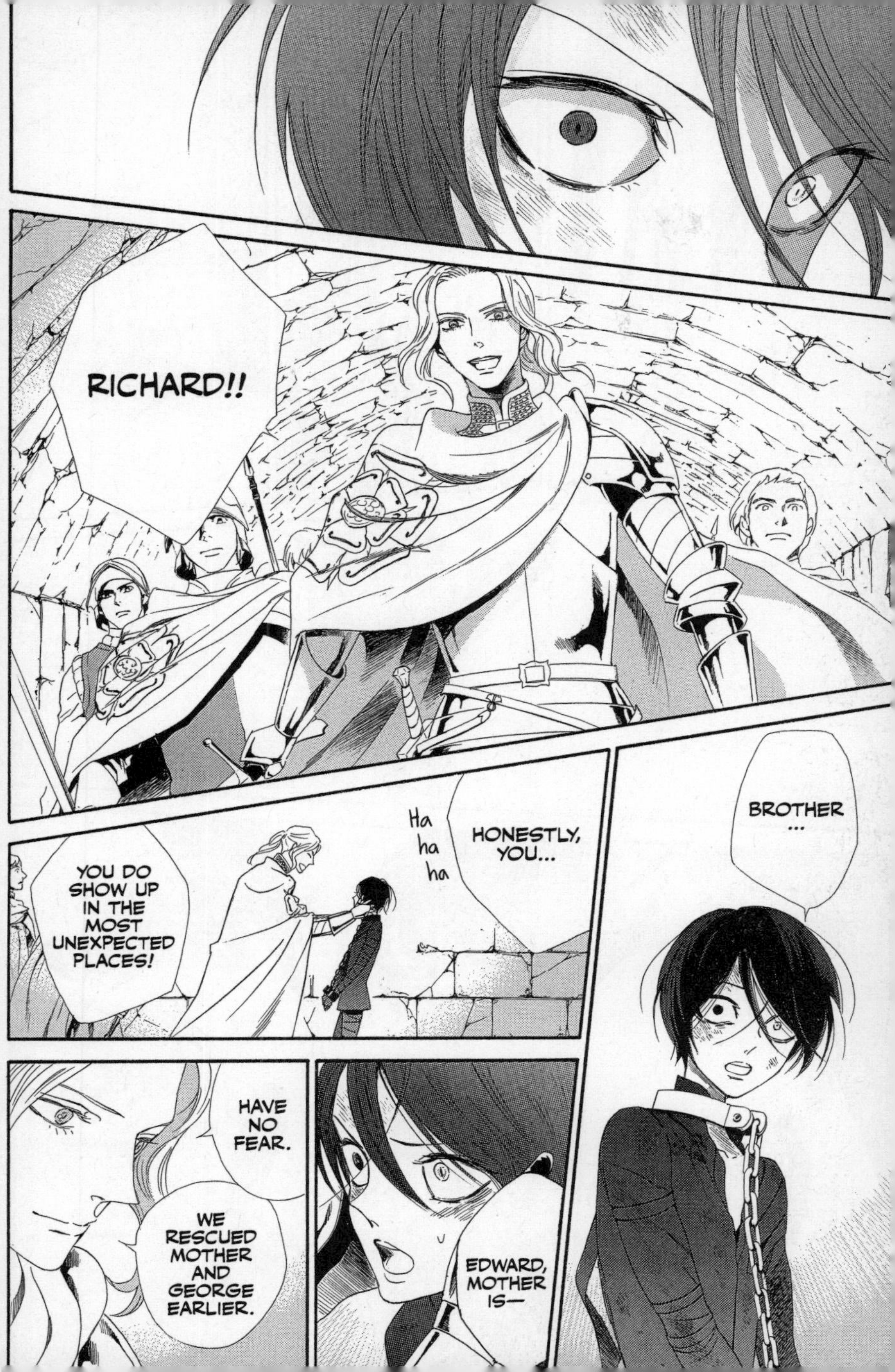
RICHARD!!
BROTHER...
HONESTLY, YOU...
Ha ha ha
YOU DO SHOW UP IN THE MOST UNEXPECTED PLACES!
EDWARD, MOTHER IS—
HAVE NO FEAR.
WE RESCUED MOTHER AND GEORGE EARLIER.

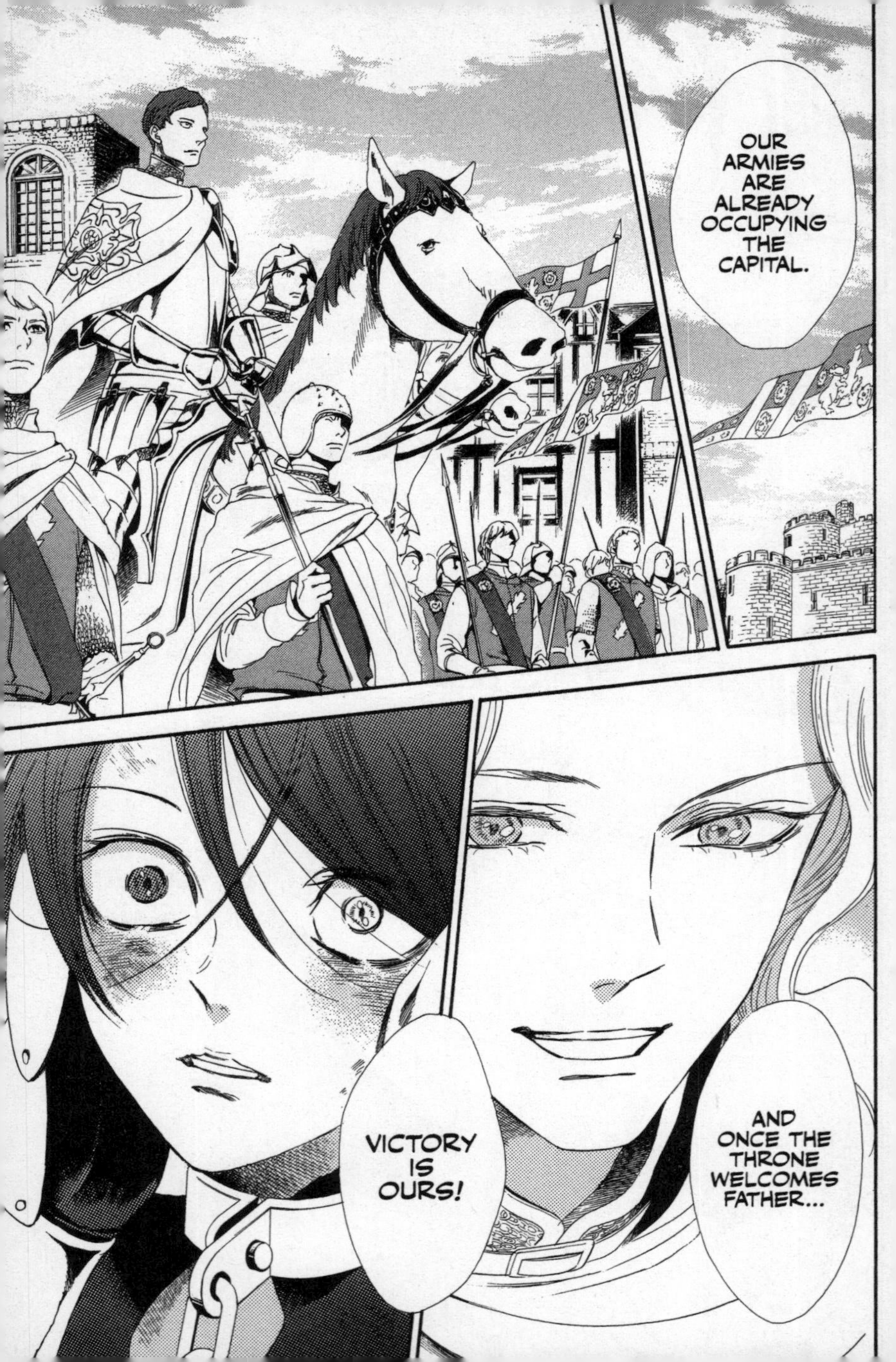
OUR ARMIES ARE ALREADY OCCUPYING THE CAPITAL.
AND ONCE THE THRONE WELCOMES FATHER...
VICTORY IS OURS!

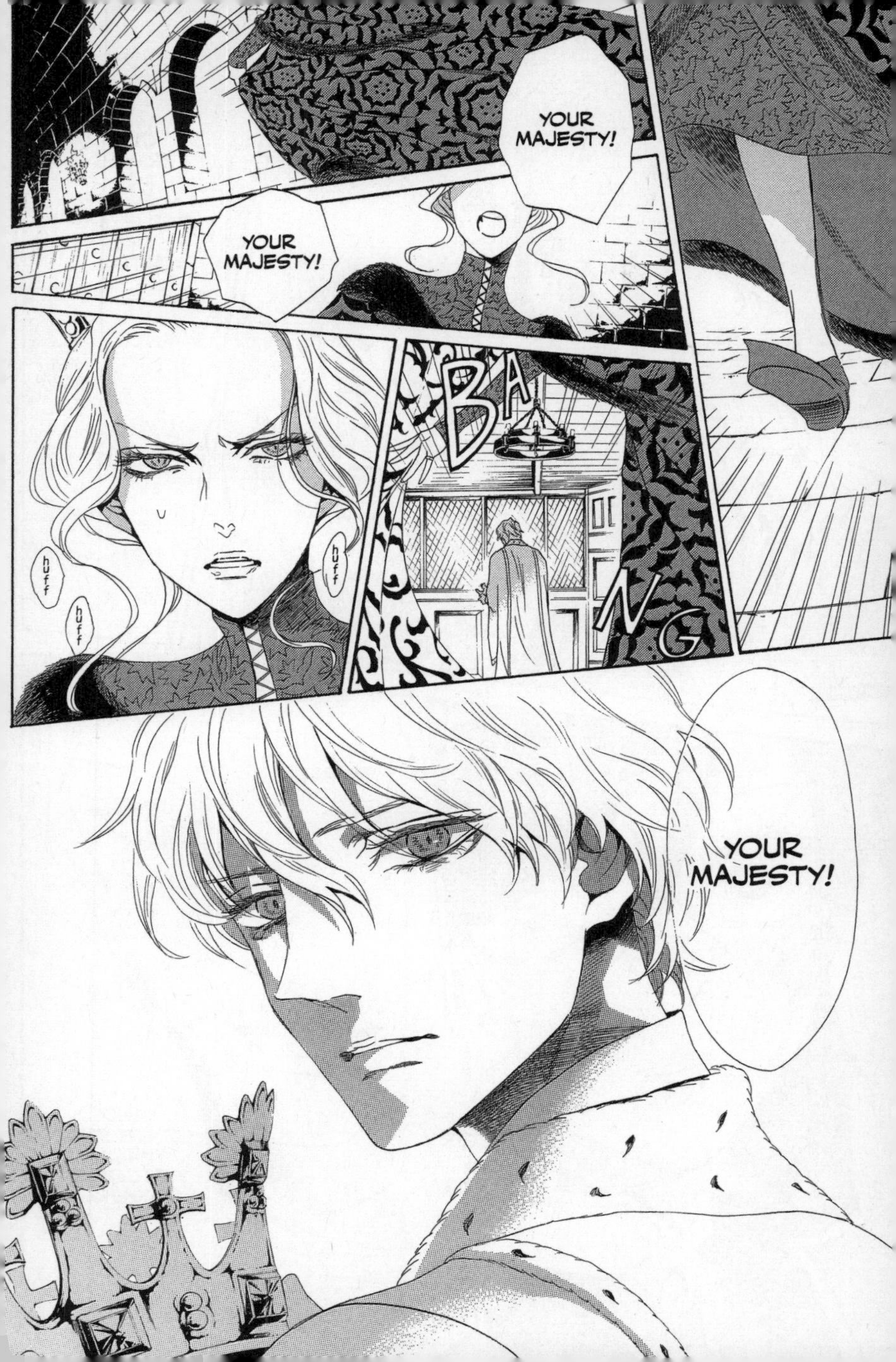
YOUR MAJESTY!
YOUR MAJESTY!
BANG
huff
huff
huff
YOUR MAJESTY!

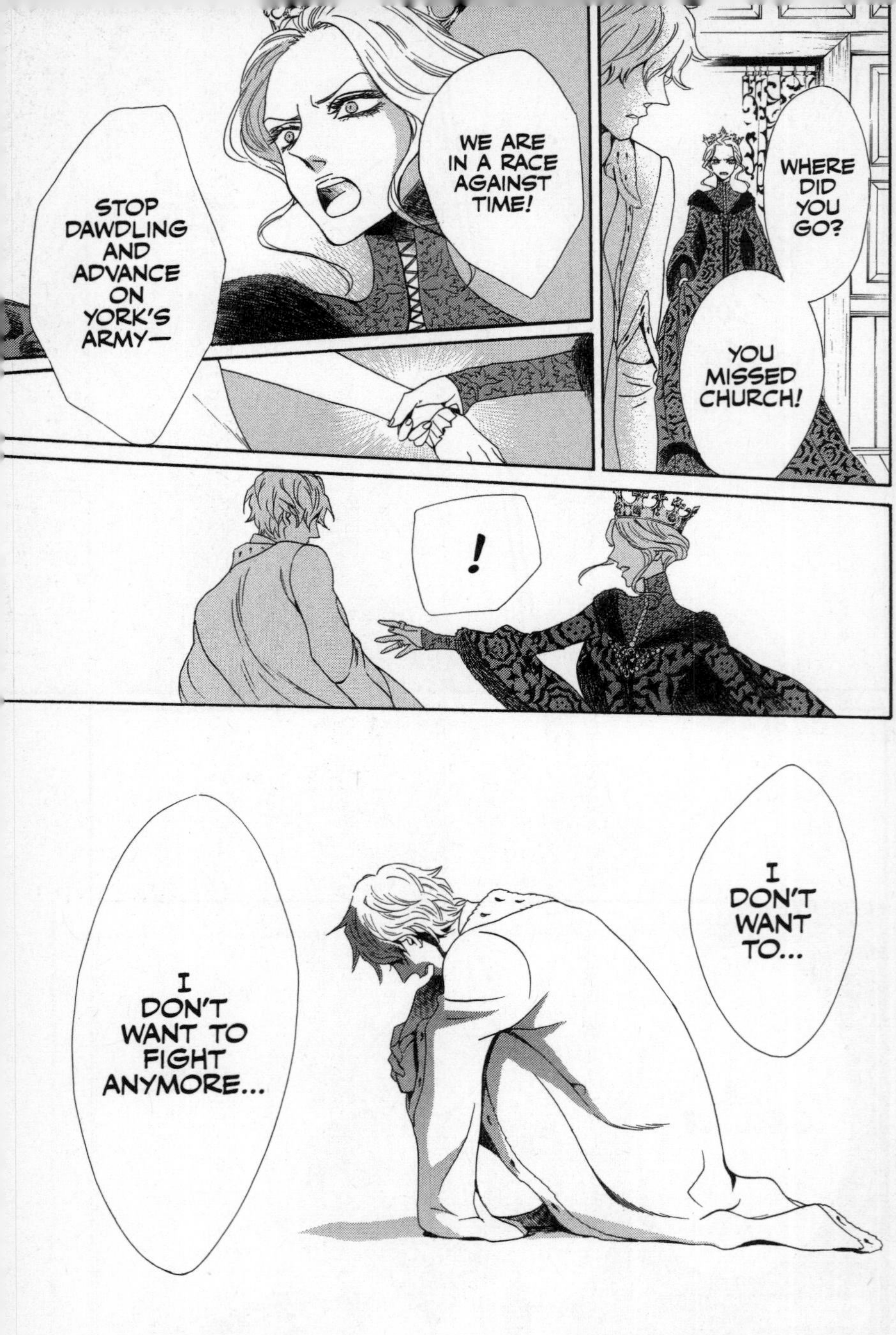
WHERE DID YOU GO?
YOU MISSED CHURCH!
WE ARE IN A RACE AGAINST TIME!
STOP DAWDLING AND ADVANCE ON YORK'S ARMY—
!
I DON'T WANT TO...
I DON'T WANT TO FIGHT ANYMORE...

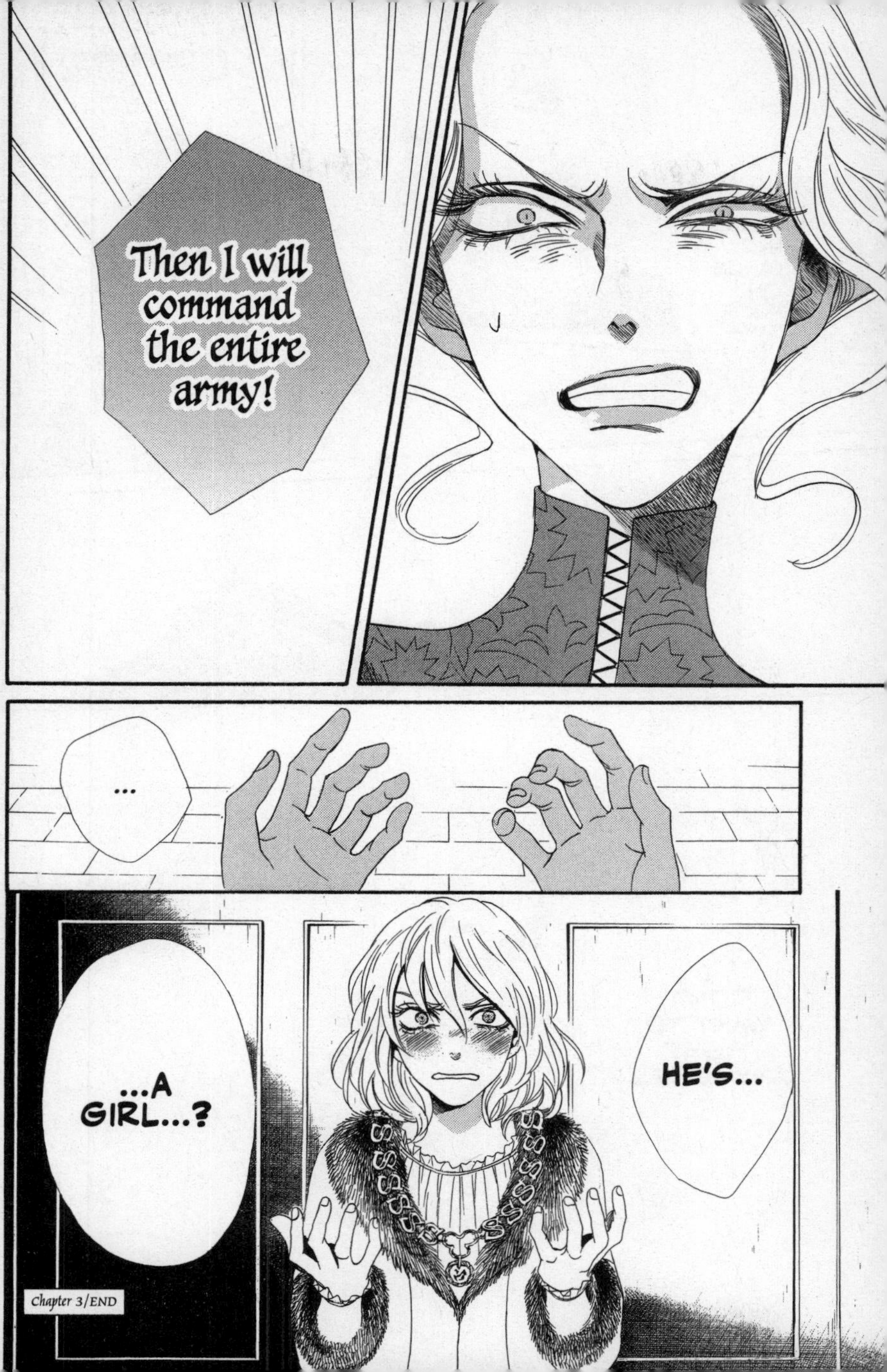
Then I will command the entire army!
...
HE'S...
...A GIRL...?
Chapter 3/END

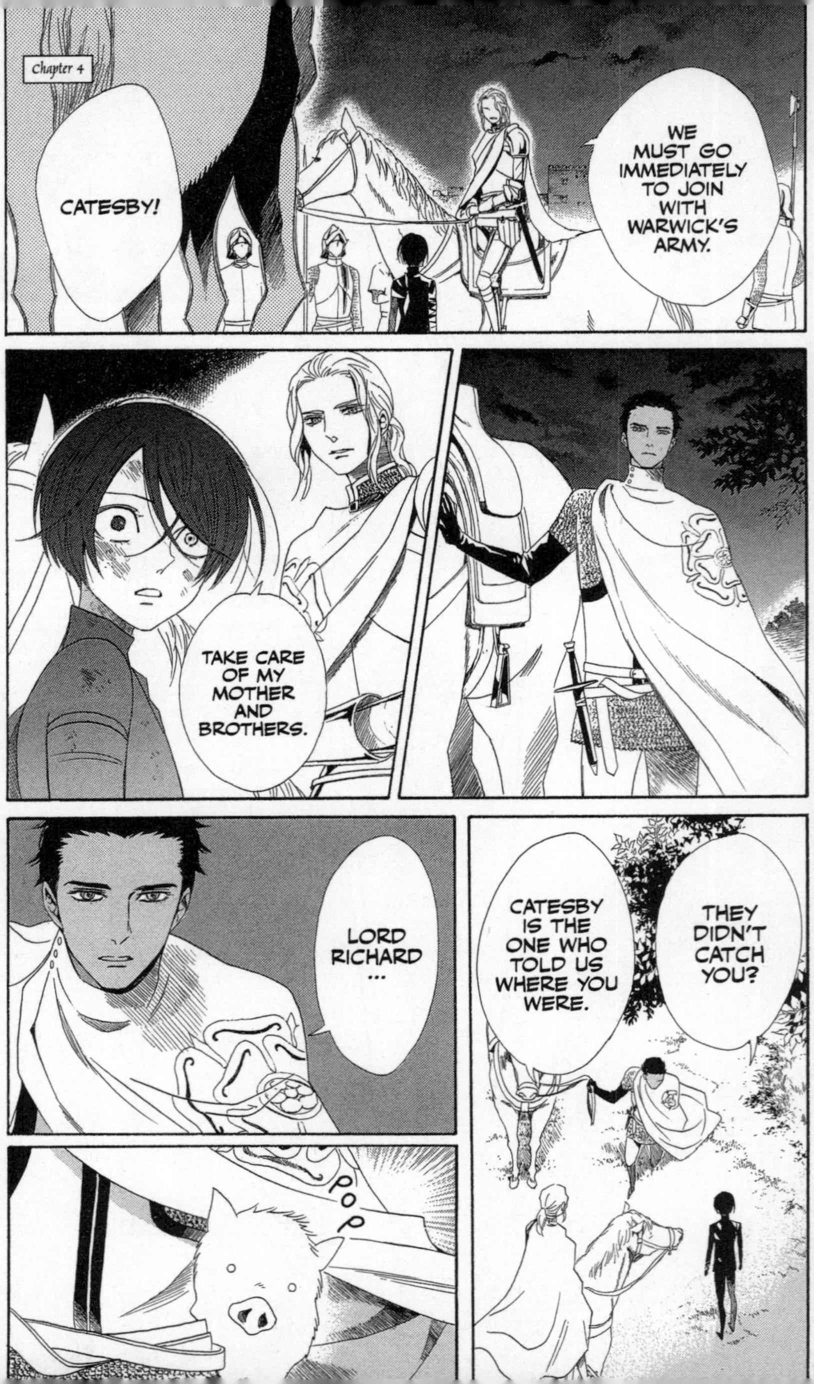
Chapter 4
WE MUST GO IMMEDIATELY TO JOIN WITH WARWICK'S ARMY.
CATESBY!
TAKE CARE OF MY MOTHER AND BROTHERS.
THEY DIDN'T CATCH YOU?
CATESBY IS THE ONE WHO TOLD US WHERE YOU WERE.
LORD RICHARD ...
POP
POP

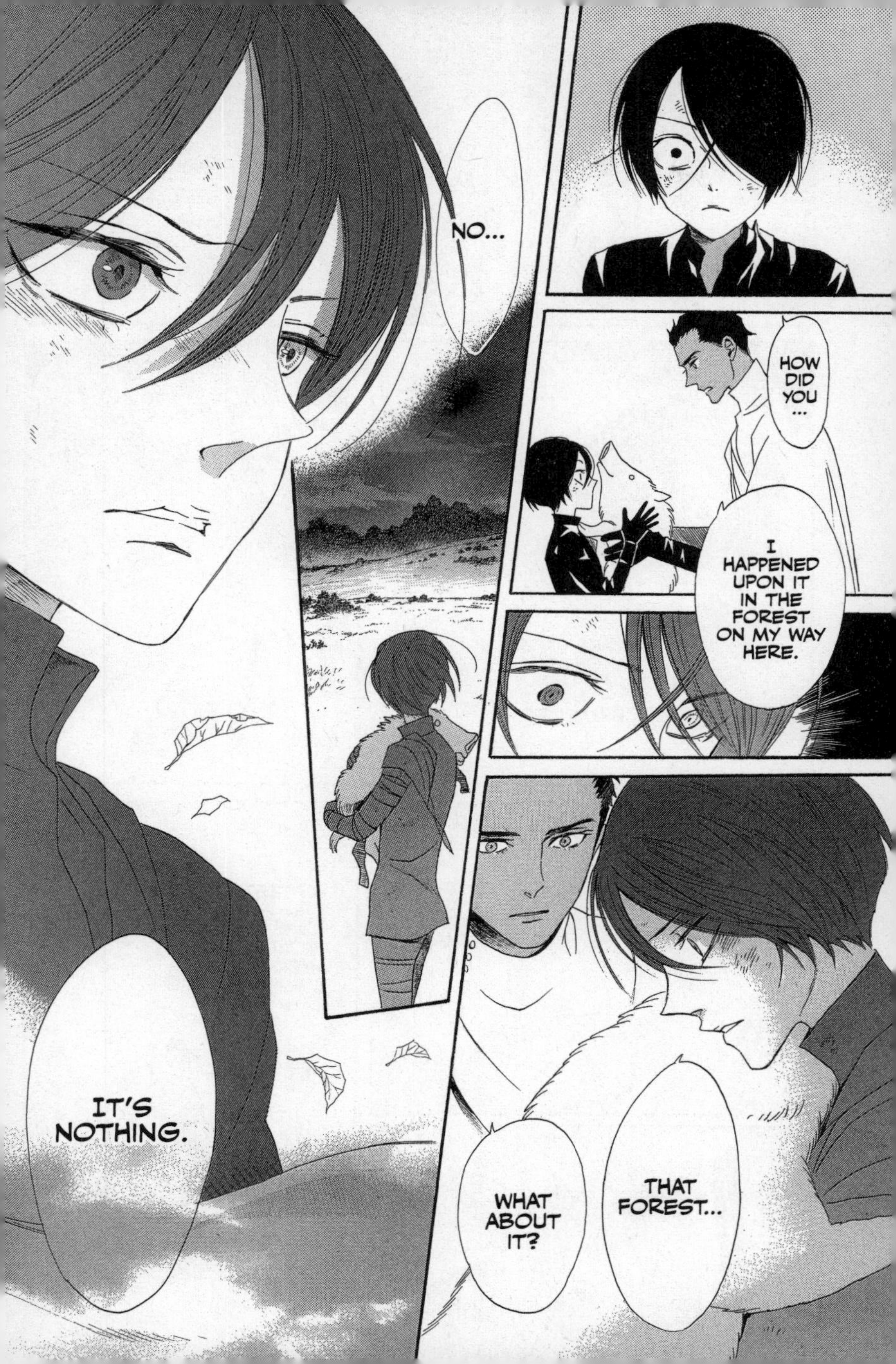
NO...
HOW DID YOU ...
I HAPPENED UPON IT IN THE FOREST ON MY WAY HERE.
THAT FOREST...
WHAT ABOUT IT?
IT'S NOTHING.

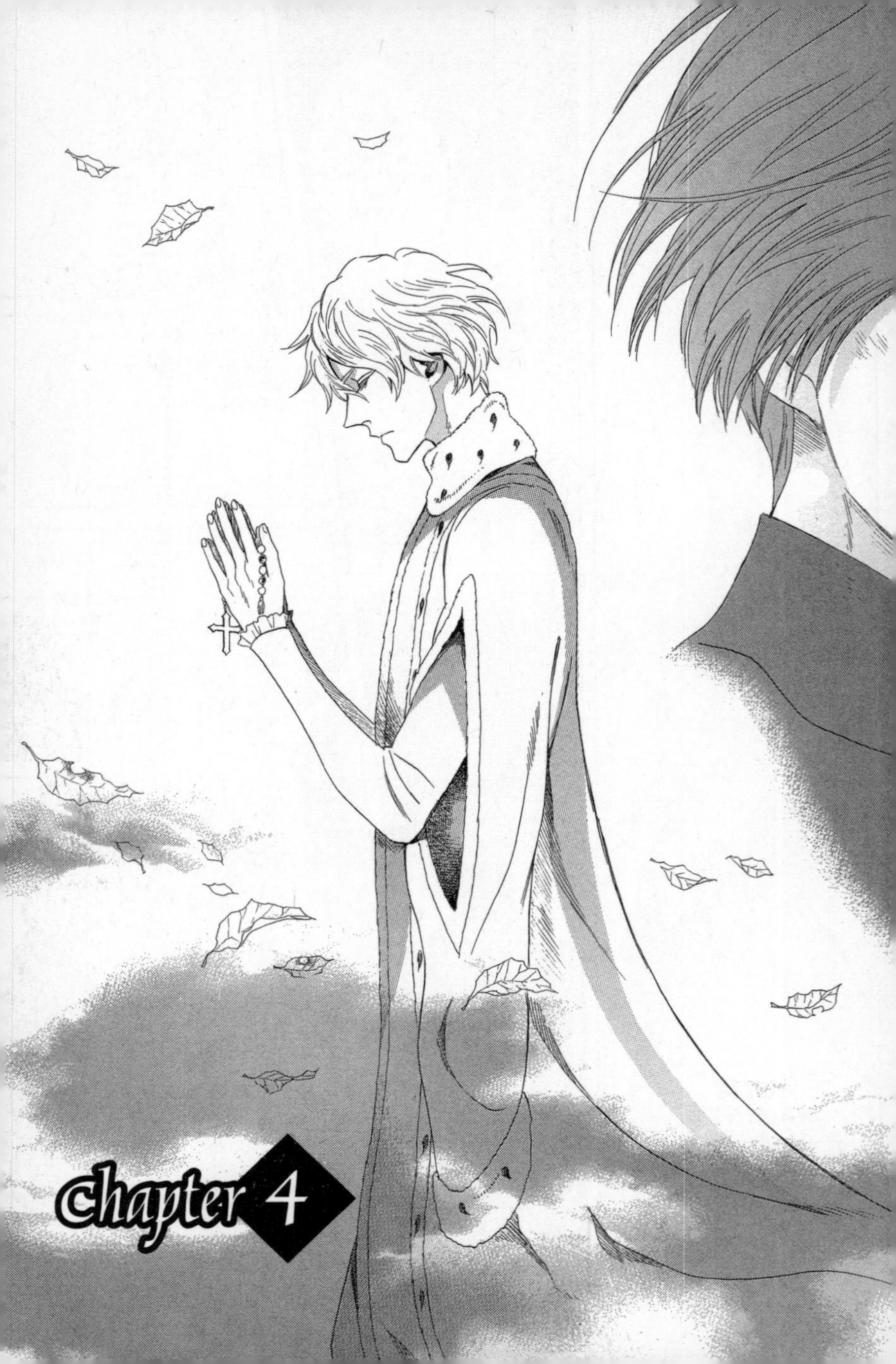
Chapter 4

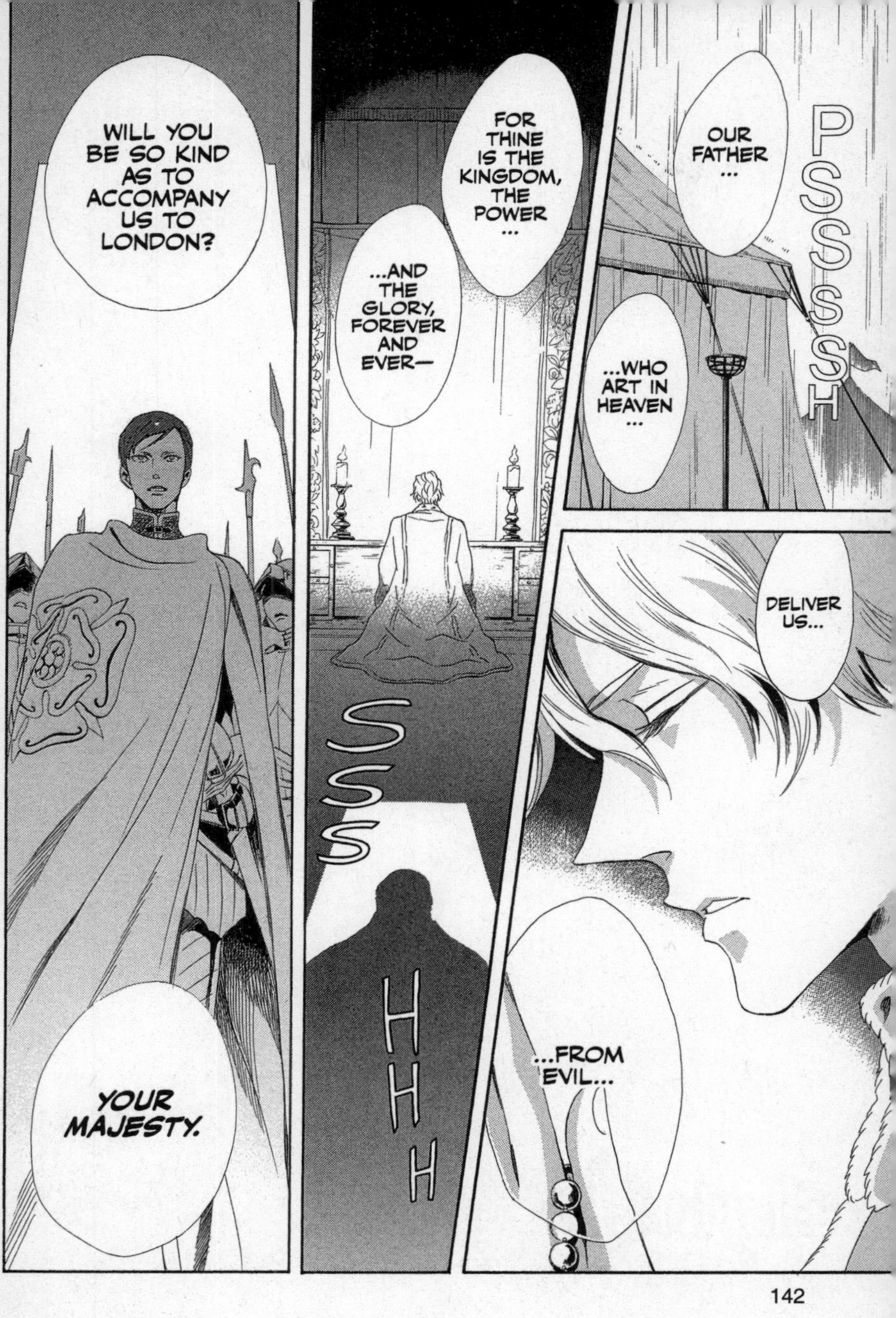

OUR FATHER ...
...WHO ART IN HEAVEN ...
PSSSSH
DELIVER US...
...FROM EVIL...
FOR THINE IS THE KINGDOM, THE POWER ...
...AND THE GLORY, FOREVER AND EVER—
SSSHHH
WILL YOU BE SO KIND AS TO ACCOMPANY US TO LONDON?
YOUR MAJESTY.

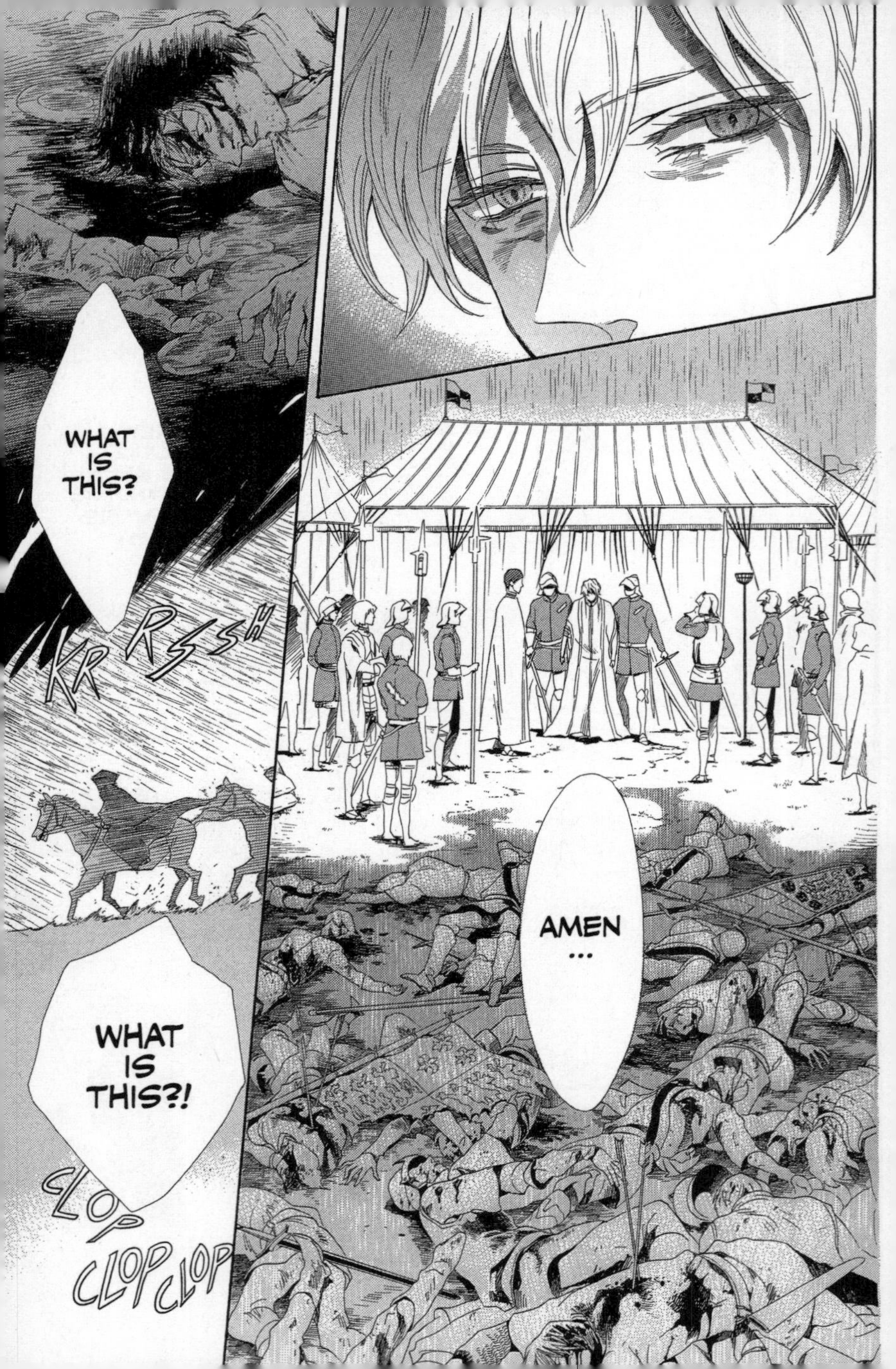

AMEN ...
WHAT IS THIS?
KRRSSH
WHAT IS THIS?!
CLOP CLOP CLOP

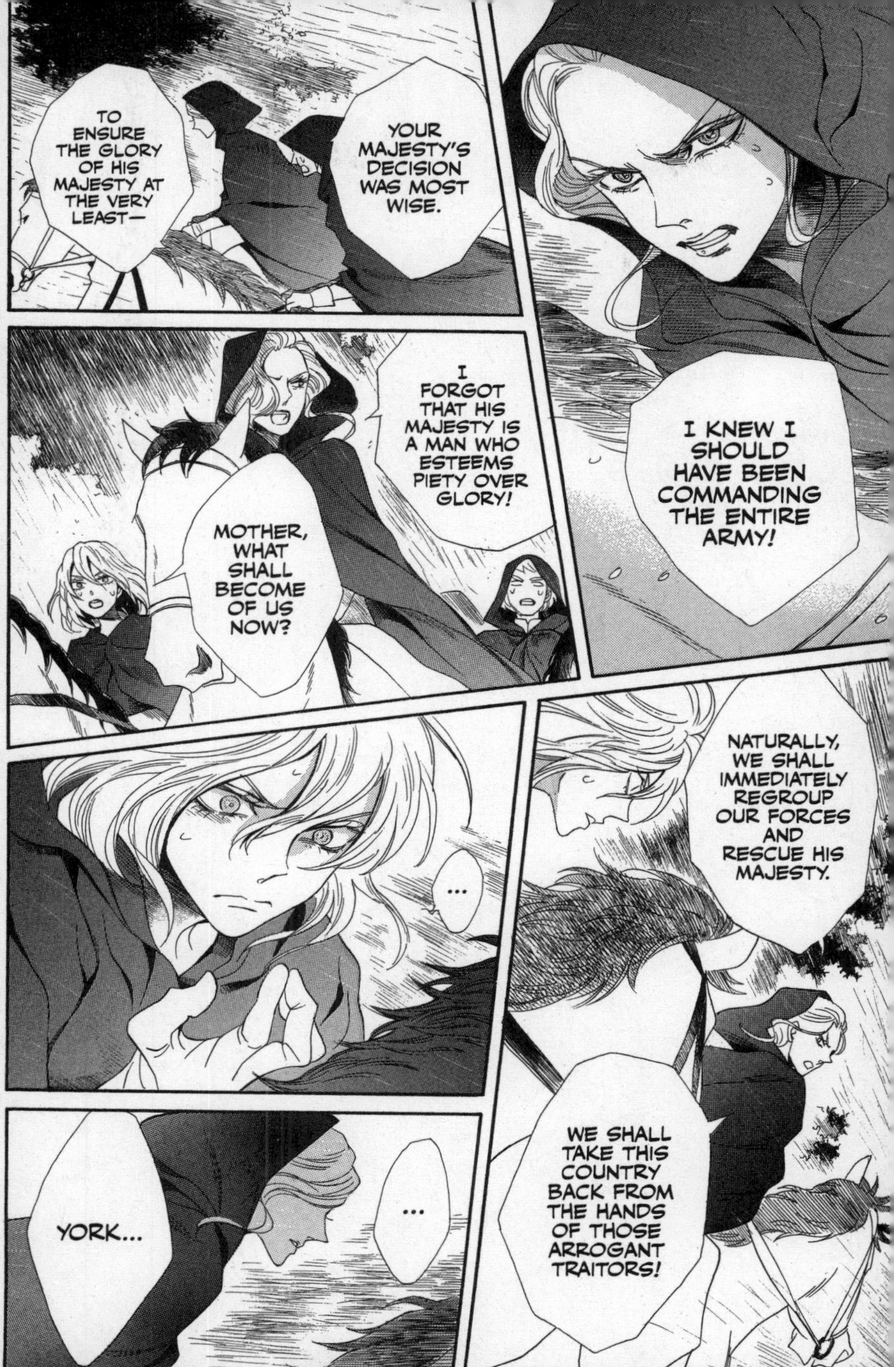
I KNEW I SHOULD HAVE BEEN COMMANDING THE ENTIRE ARMY!
YOUR MAJESTY'S DECISION WAS MOST WISE.
TO ENSURE THE GLORY OF HIS MAJESTY AT THE VERY LEAST—
I FORGOT THAT HIS MAJESTY IS A MAN WHO ESTEEMS PIETY OVER GLORY!
MOTHER, WHAT SHALL BECOME OF US NOW?
NATURALLY, WE SHALL IMMEDIATELY REGROUP OUR FORCES AND RESCUE HIS MAJESTY.
WE SHALL TAKE THIS COUNTRY BACK FROM THE HANDS OF THOSE ARROGANT TRAITORS!
...
...
YORK...

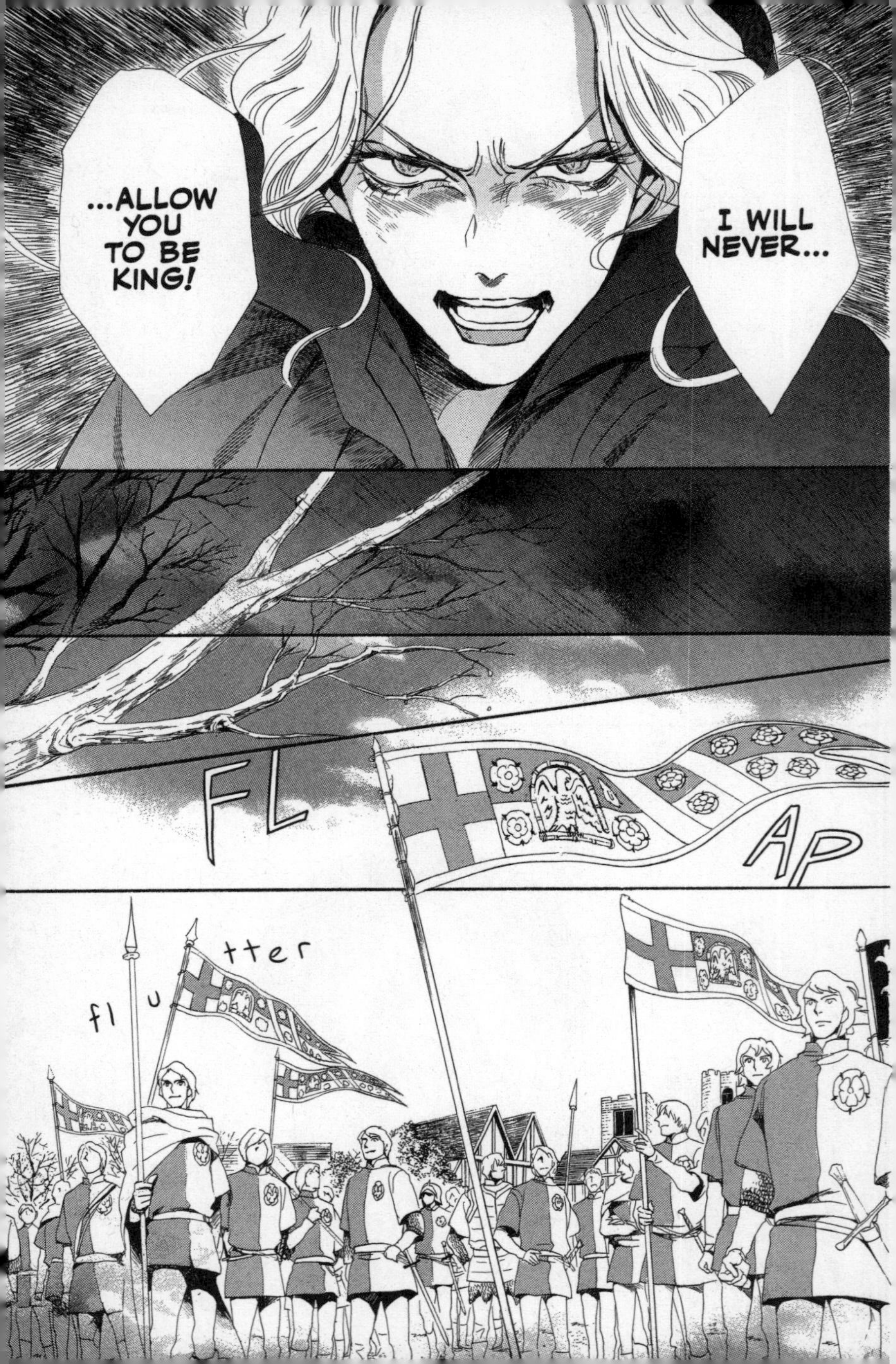
I WILL NEVER...
...ALLOW YOU TO BE KING!
FLAP
flutter

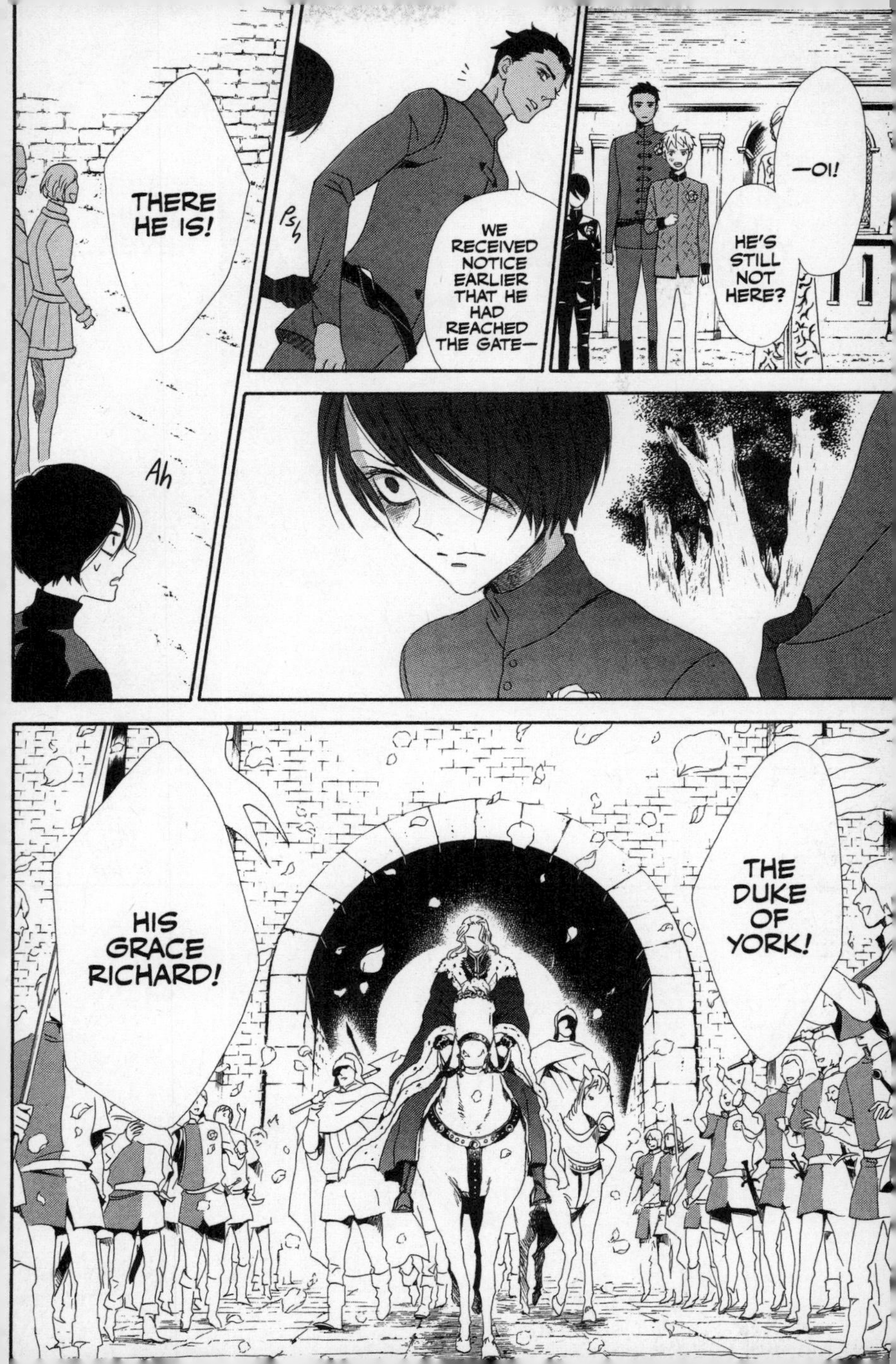
—OI!
HE'S STILL NOT HERE?
WE RECEIVED NOTICE EARLIER THAT HE HAD REACHED THE GATE—
Psh
THERE HE IS!
Ah
THE DUKE OF YORK!
HIS GRACE RICHARD!

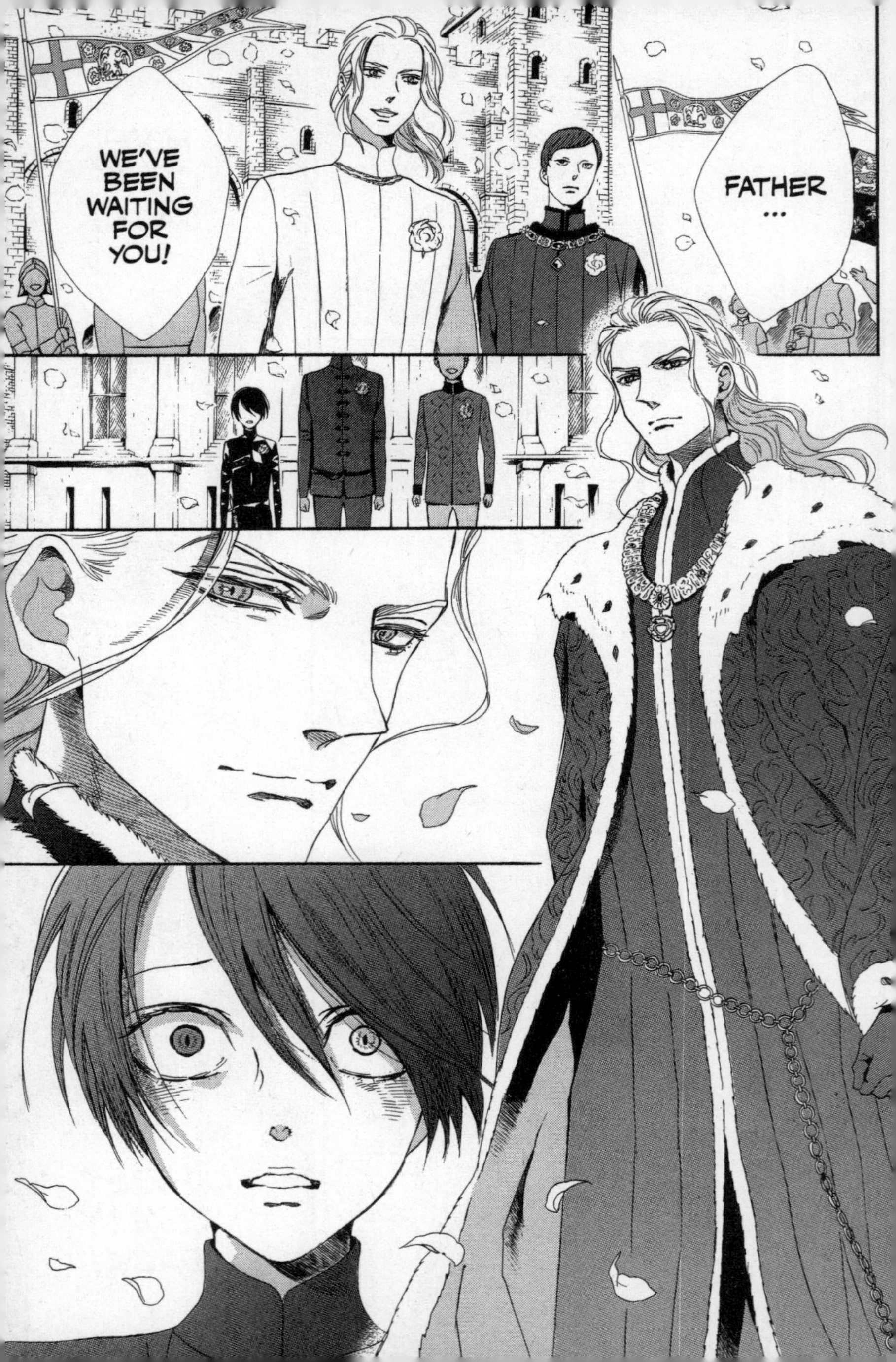
FATHER...
WE'VE BEEN WAITING FOR YOU!

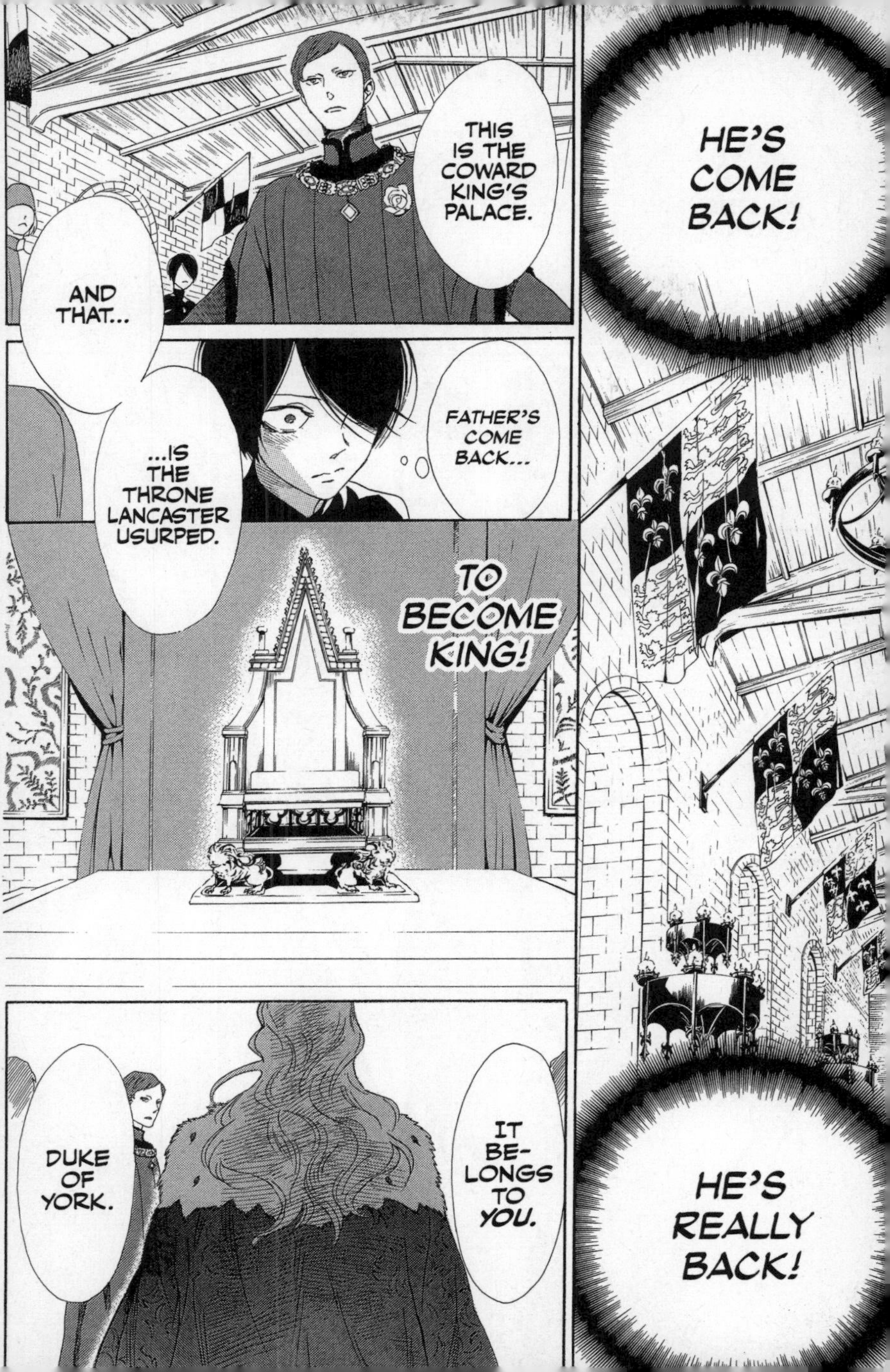
HE'S COME BACK!
HE'S REALLY BACK!
THIS IS THE COWARD KING'S PALACE.
AND THAT...
FATHER'S COME BACK...
...IS THE THRONE LANCASTER USURPED.
TO BECOME KING!
IT BE-LONGS TO *YOU*.
DUKE OF YORK.

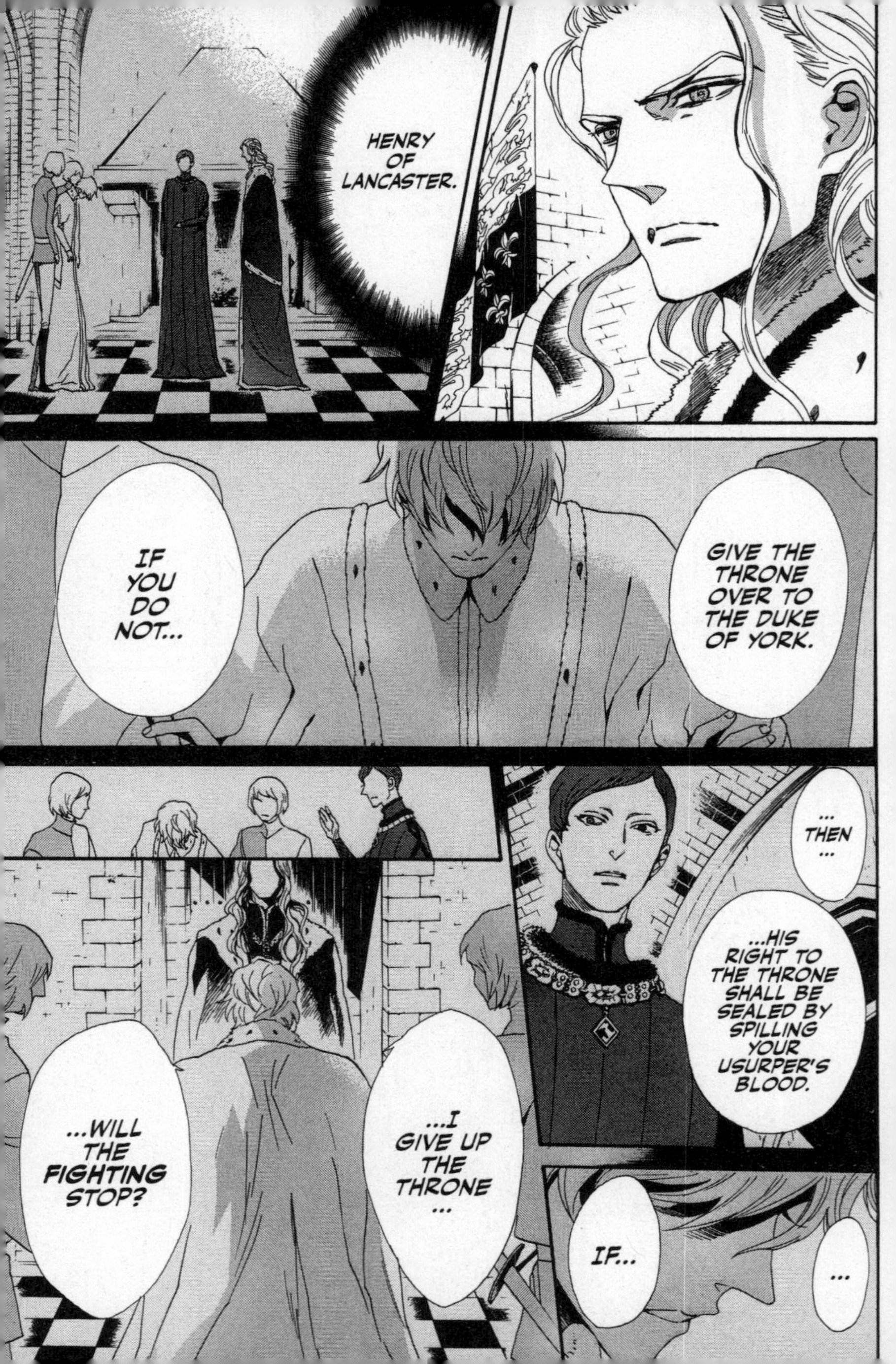

HENRY OF LANCASTER.
GIVE THE THRONE OVER TO THE DUKE OF YORK.
IF YOU DO NOT...
...THEN ...
...HIS RIGHT TO THE THRONE SHALL BE SEALED BY SPILLING YOUR USURPER'S BLOOD.
...
IF...
...I GIVE UP THE THRONE ...
...WILL THE FIGHTING STOP?

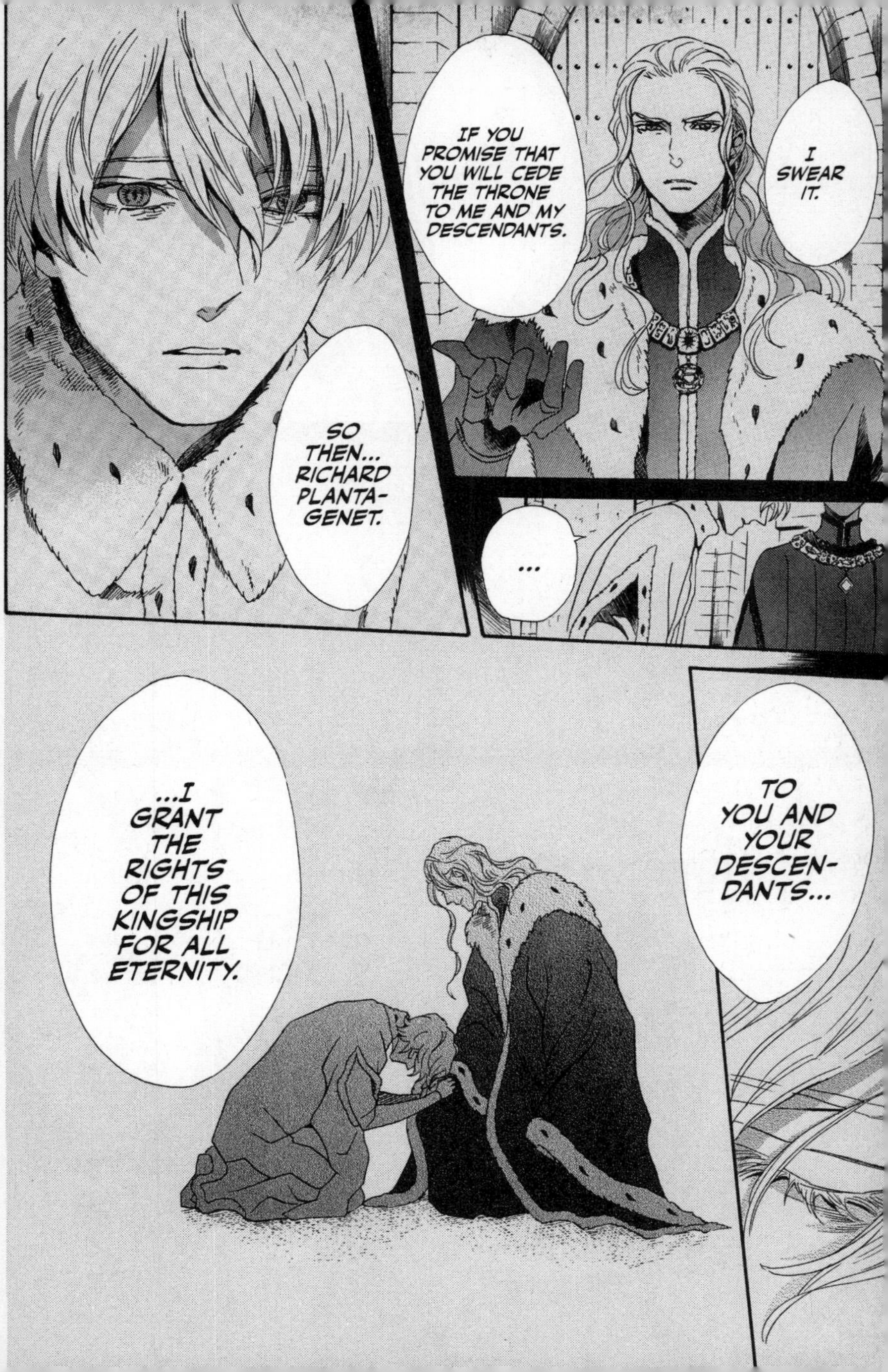
IF YOU PROMISE THAT YOU WILL CEDE THE THRONE TO ME AND MY DESCENDANTS.
I SWEAR IT.
...
SO THEN... RICHARD PLANTA-GENET.
TO YOU AND YOUR DESCEN-DANTS...
...I GRANT THE RIGHTS OF THIS KINGSHIP FOR ALL ETERNITY.

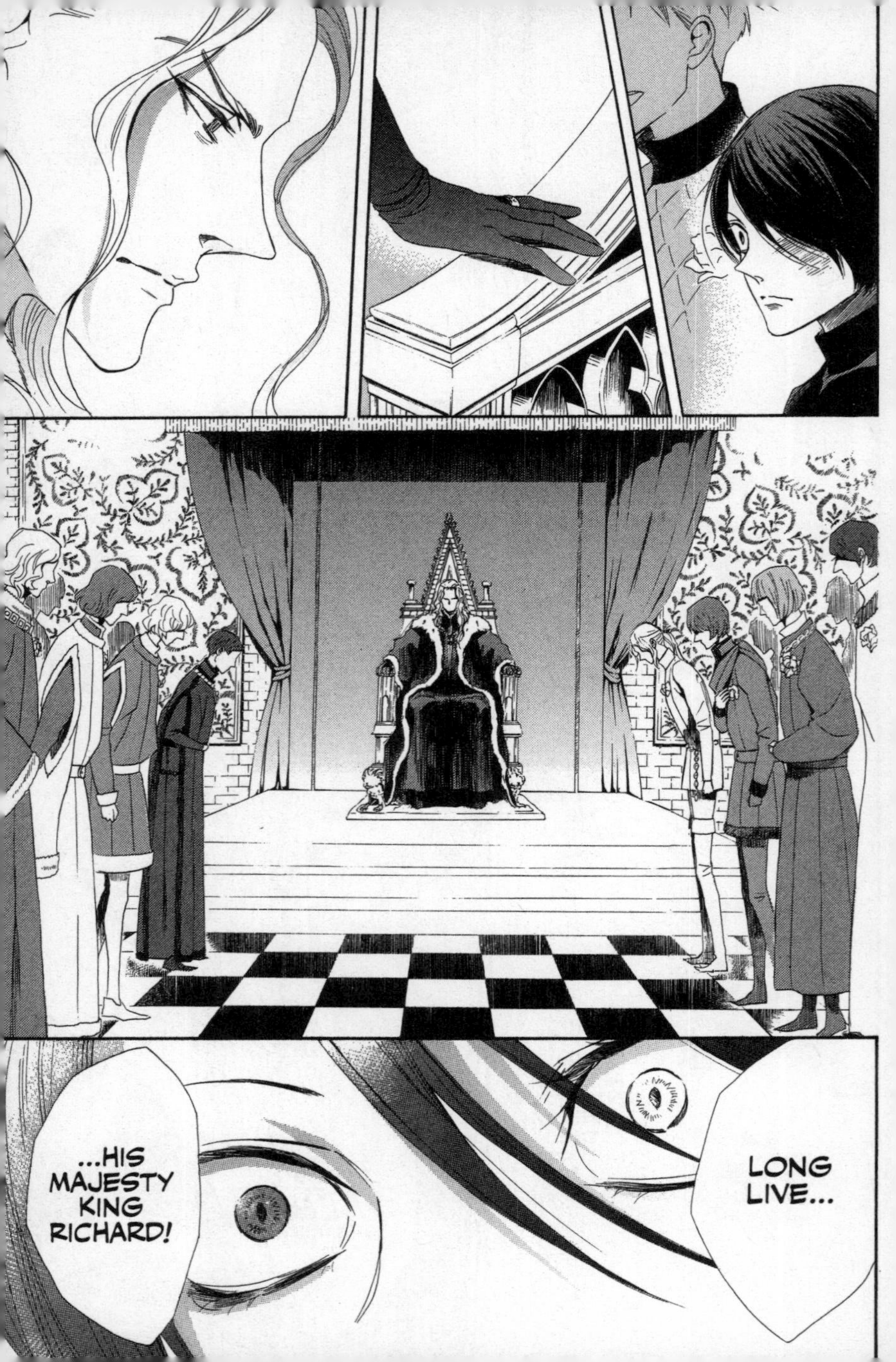
LONG LIVE...
...HIS MAJESTY KING RICHARD!

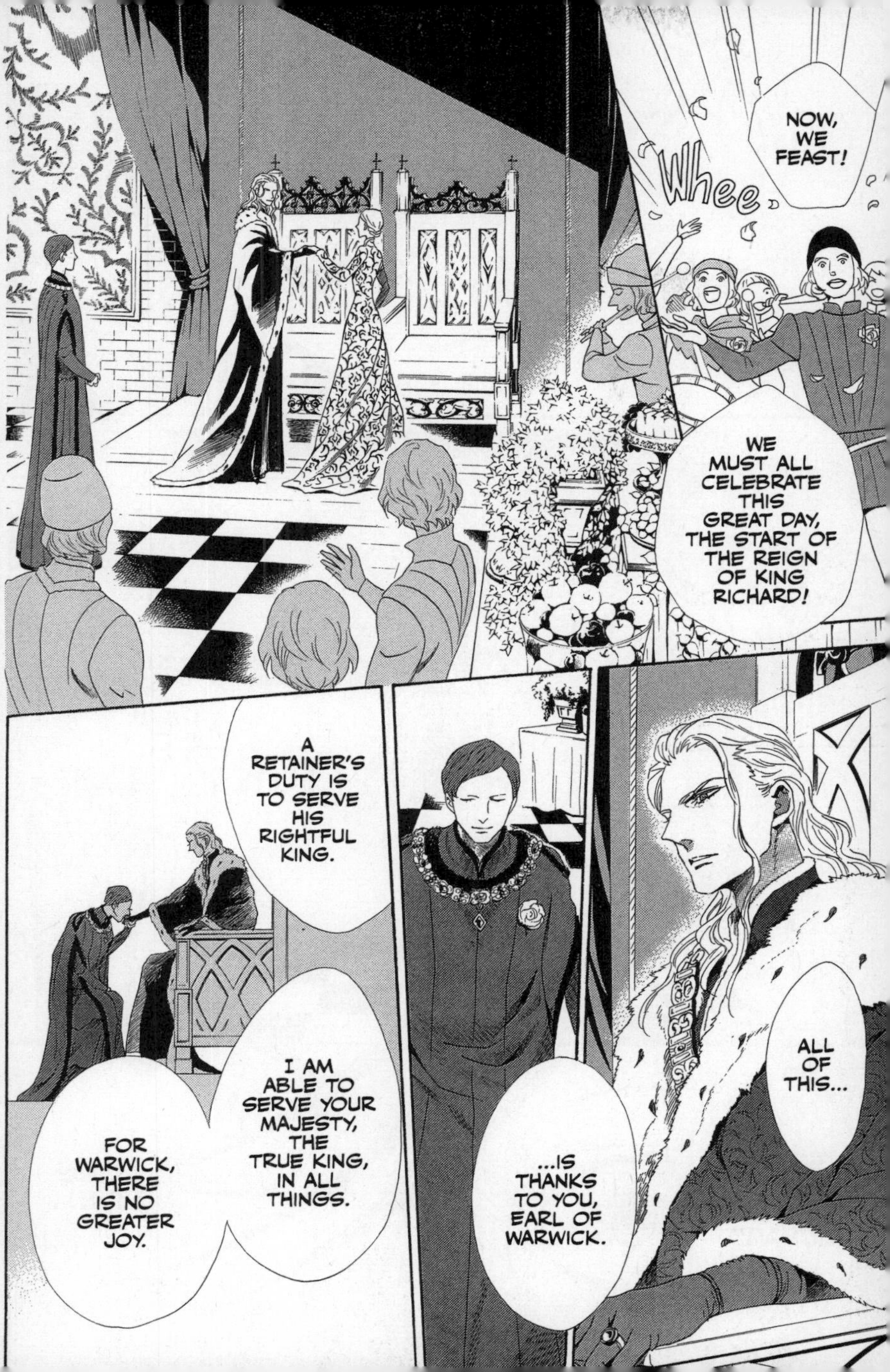
NOW, WE FEAST!
Whee
WE MUST ALL CELEBRATE THIS GREAT DAY, THE START OF THE REIGN OF KING RICHARD!
ALL OF THIS...
...IS THANKS TO YOU, EARL OF WARWICK.
A RETAINER'S DUTY IS TO SERVE HIS RIGHTFUL KING.
I AM ABLE TO SERVE YOUR MAJESTY, THE TRUE KING, IN ALL THINGS.
FOR WARWICK, THERE IS NO GREATER JOY.

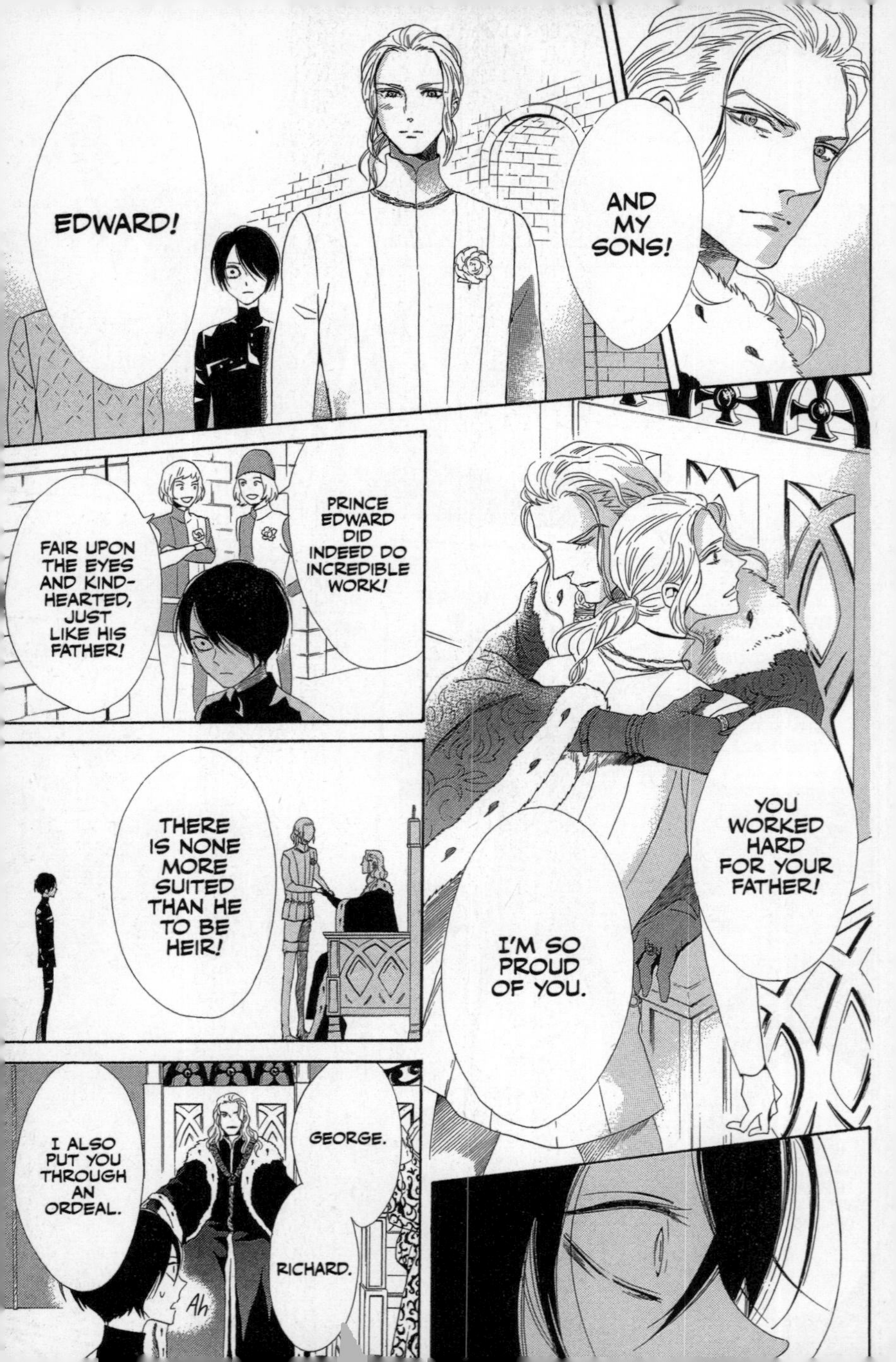
AND MY SONS!
EDWARD!
YOU WORKED HARD FOR YOUR FATHER!
I'M SO PROUD OF YOU.
PRINCE EDWARD DID INDEED DO INCREDIBLE WORK!
FAIR UPON THE EYES AND KIND-HEARTED, JUST LIKE HIS FATHER!
THERE IS NONE MORE SUITED THAN HE TO BE HEIR!
GEORGE.
RICHARD.
I ALSO PUT YOU THROUGH AN ORDEAL.
Ah

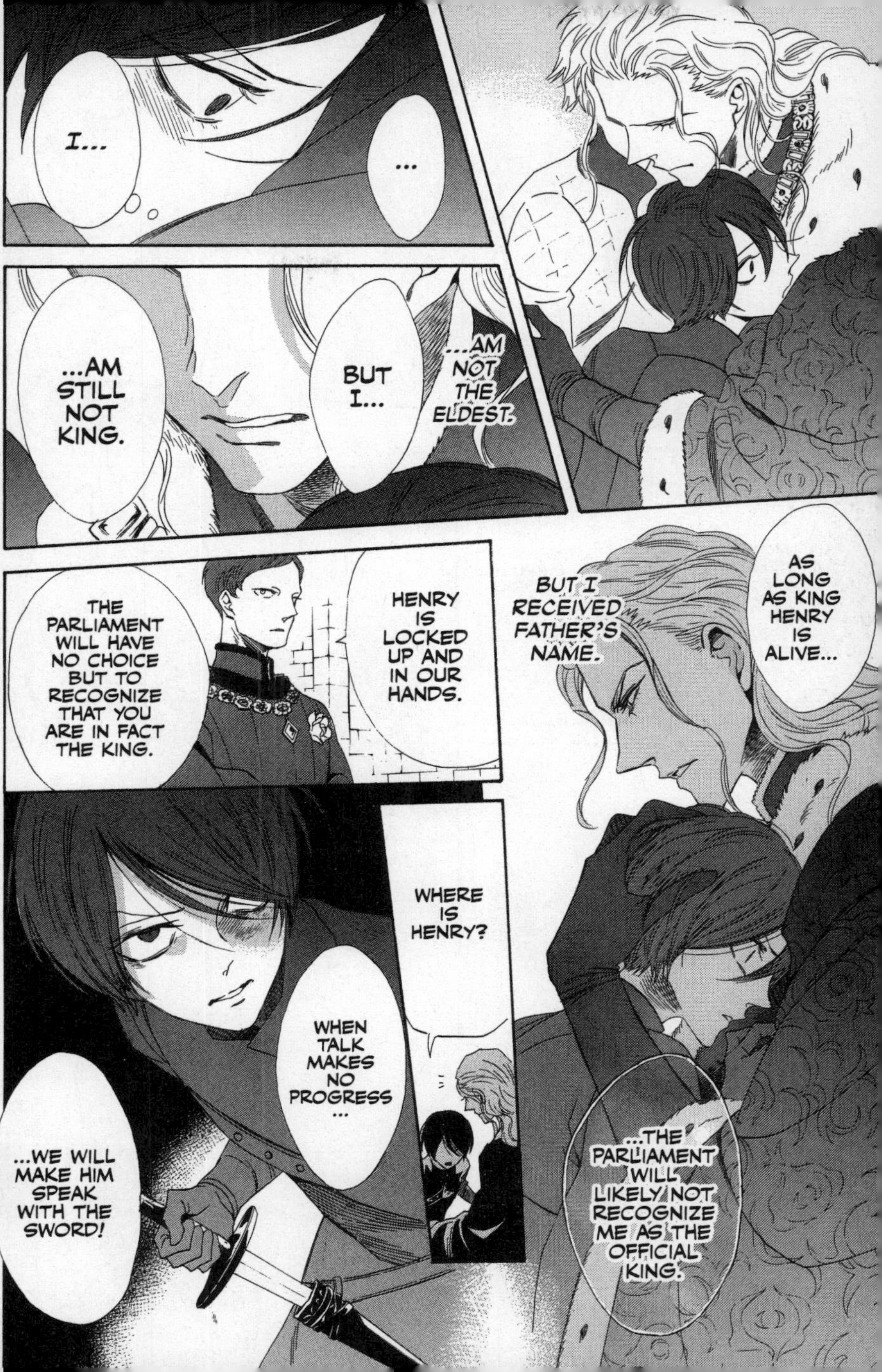

I...
...
...AM NOT THE ELDEST.
BUT I...
...AM STILL NOT KING.
AS LONG AS KING HENRY IS ALIVE...
BUT I RECEIVED FATHER'S NAME.
...THE PARLIAMENT WILL LIKELY NOT RECOGNIZE ME AS THE OFFICIAL KING.
HENRY IS LOCKED UP AND IN OUR HANDS.
THE PARLIAMENT WILL HAVE NO CHOICE BUT TO RECOGNIZE THAT YOU ARE IN FACT THE KING.
WHERE IS HENRY?
WHEN TALK MAKES NO PROGRESS...
...WE WILL MAKE HIM SPEAK WITH THE SWORD!

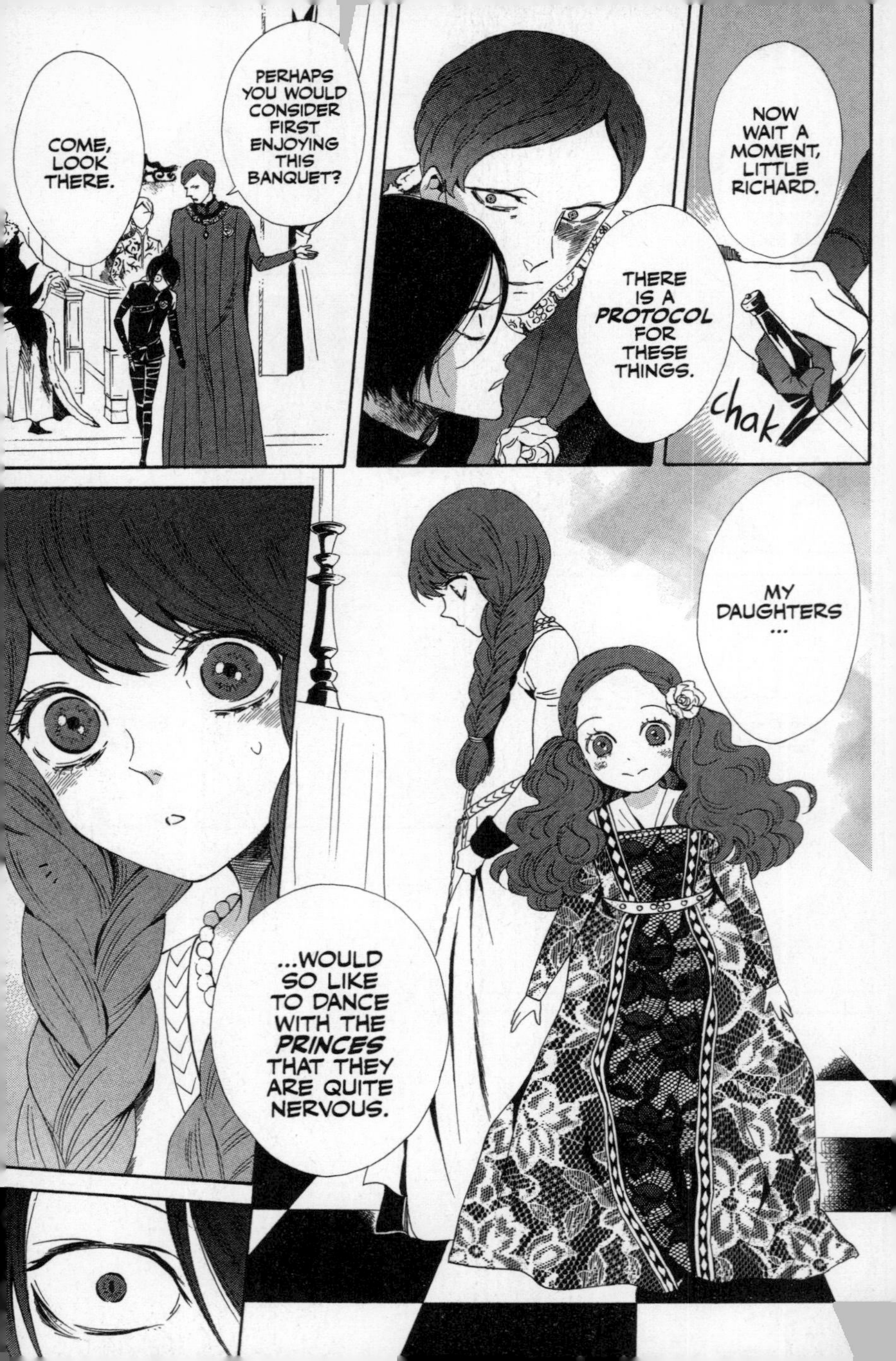
NOW WAIT A MOMENT, LITTLE RICHARD.
Chak
THERE IS A *PROTOCOL* FOR THESE THINGS.
PERHAPS YOU WOULD CONSIDER FIRST ENJOYING THIS BANQUET?
COME, LOOK THERE.
MY DAUGHTERS...
...WOULD SO LIKE TO DANCE WITH THE *PRINCES* THAT THEY ARE QUITE NERVOUS.

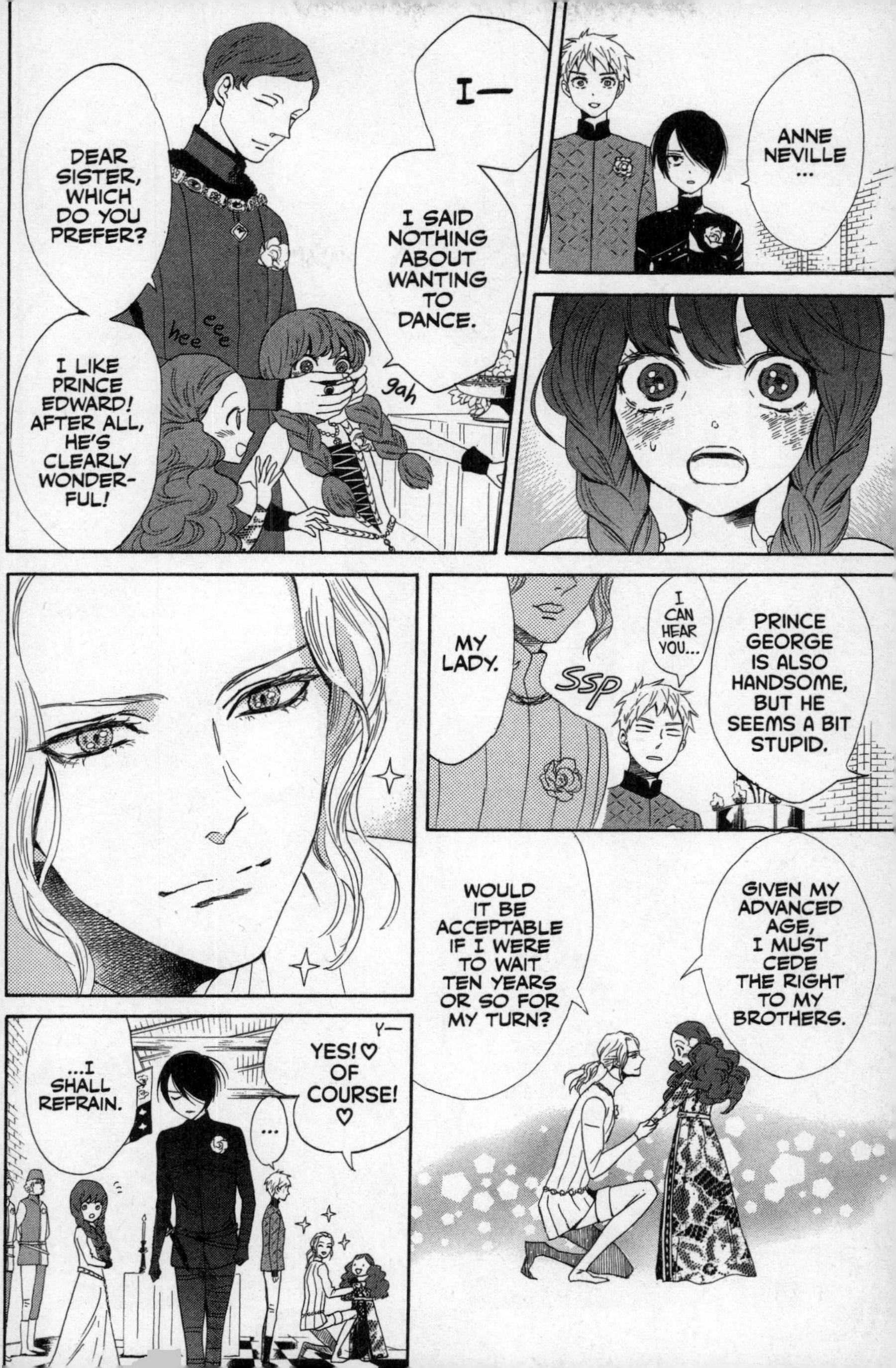
ANNE NEVILLE ...
I—
I SAID NOTHING ABOUT WANTING TO DANCE.
DEAR SISTER, WHICH DO YOU PREFER?
hee eee
gah
I LIKE PRINCE EDWARD! AFTER ALL, HE'S CLEARLY WONDER-FUL!
PRINCE GEORGE IS ALSO HANDSOME, BUT HE SEEMS A BIT STUPID.
I CAN HEAR YOU...
MY LADY.
Ssp
GIVEN MY ADVANCED AGE, I MUST CEDE THE RIGHT TO MY BROTHERS.
WOULD IT BE ACCEPTABLE IF I WERE TO WAIT TEN YEARS OR SO FOR MY TURN?
Y—
YES! ♡ OF COURSE! ♡
...
...I SHALL REFRAIN.

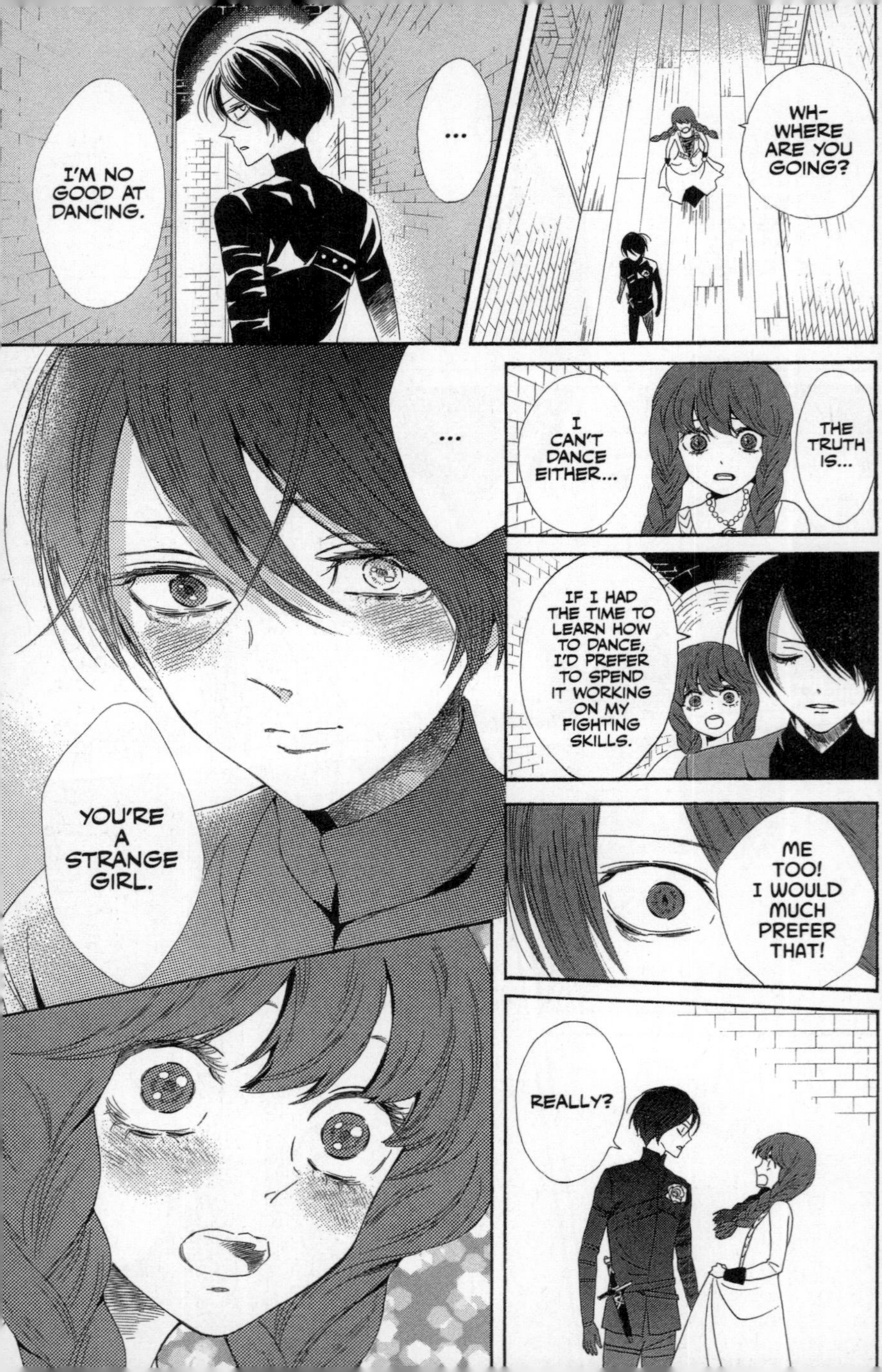
WH- WHERE ARE YOU GOING?
...
I'M NO GOOD AT DANCING.
THE TRUTH IS...
I CAN'T DANCE EITHER...
IF I HAD THE TIME TO LEARN HOW TO DANCE, I'D PREFER TO SPEND IT WORKING ON MY FIGHTING SKILLS.
ME TOO! I WOULD MUCH PREFER THAT!
REALLY?
...
YOU'RE A STRANGE GIRL.

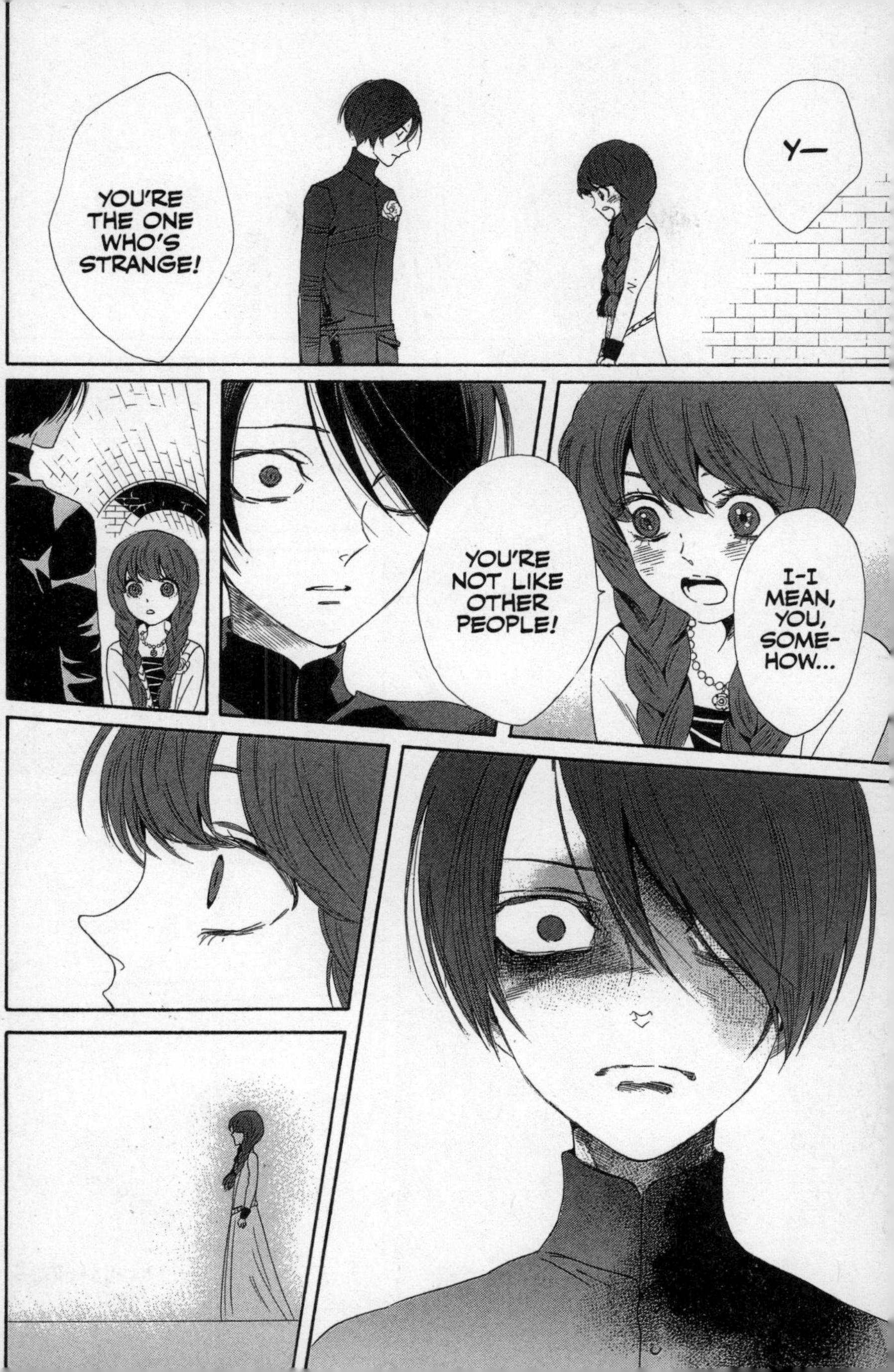
Y—
YOU'RE THE ONE WHO'S STRANGE!
I-I MEAN, YOU, SOMEHOW...
YOU'RE NOT LIKE OTHER PEOPLE!

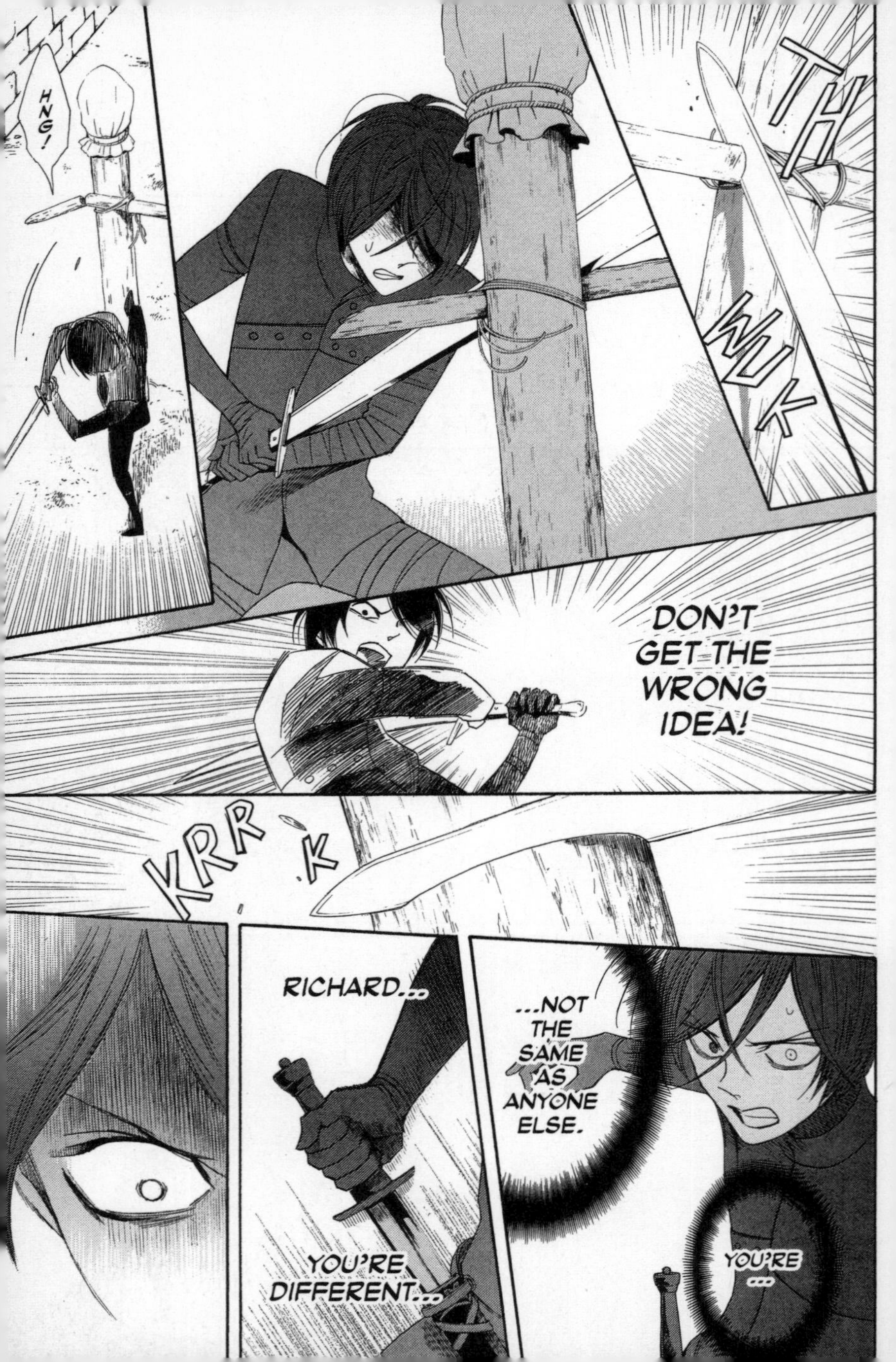
THWUK
HNG!
DON'T GET THE WRONG IDEA!
KRR K
...NOT THE SAME AS ANYONE ELSE.
YOU'RE ...
RICHARD...
YOU'RE DIFFERENT...

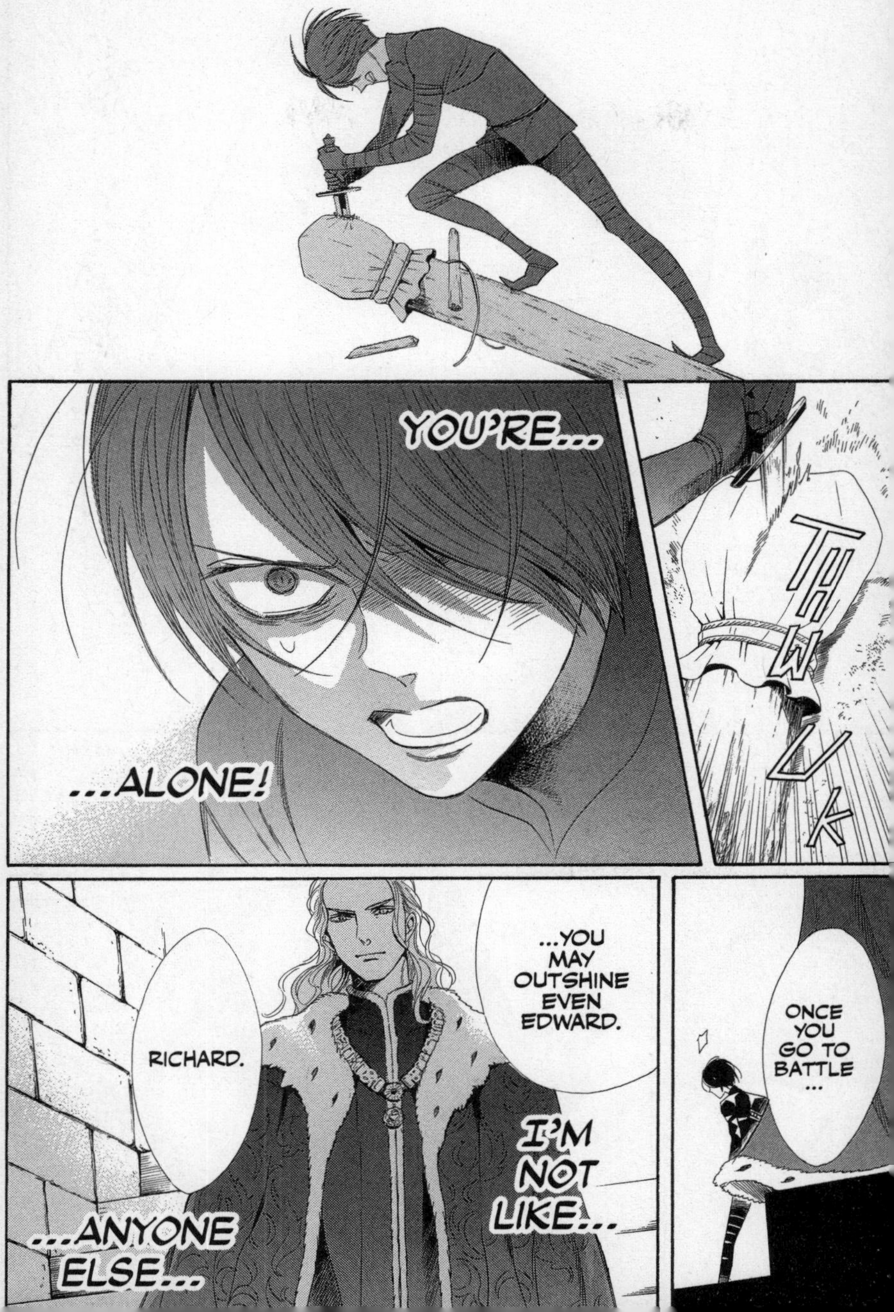
THWUK
YOU'RE...
...ALONE!
ONCE YOU GO TO BATTLE ...
...YOU MAY OUTSHINE EVEN EDWARD.
RICHARD.
I'M NOT LIKE...
...ANYONE ELSE...

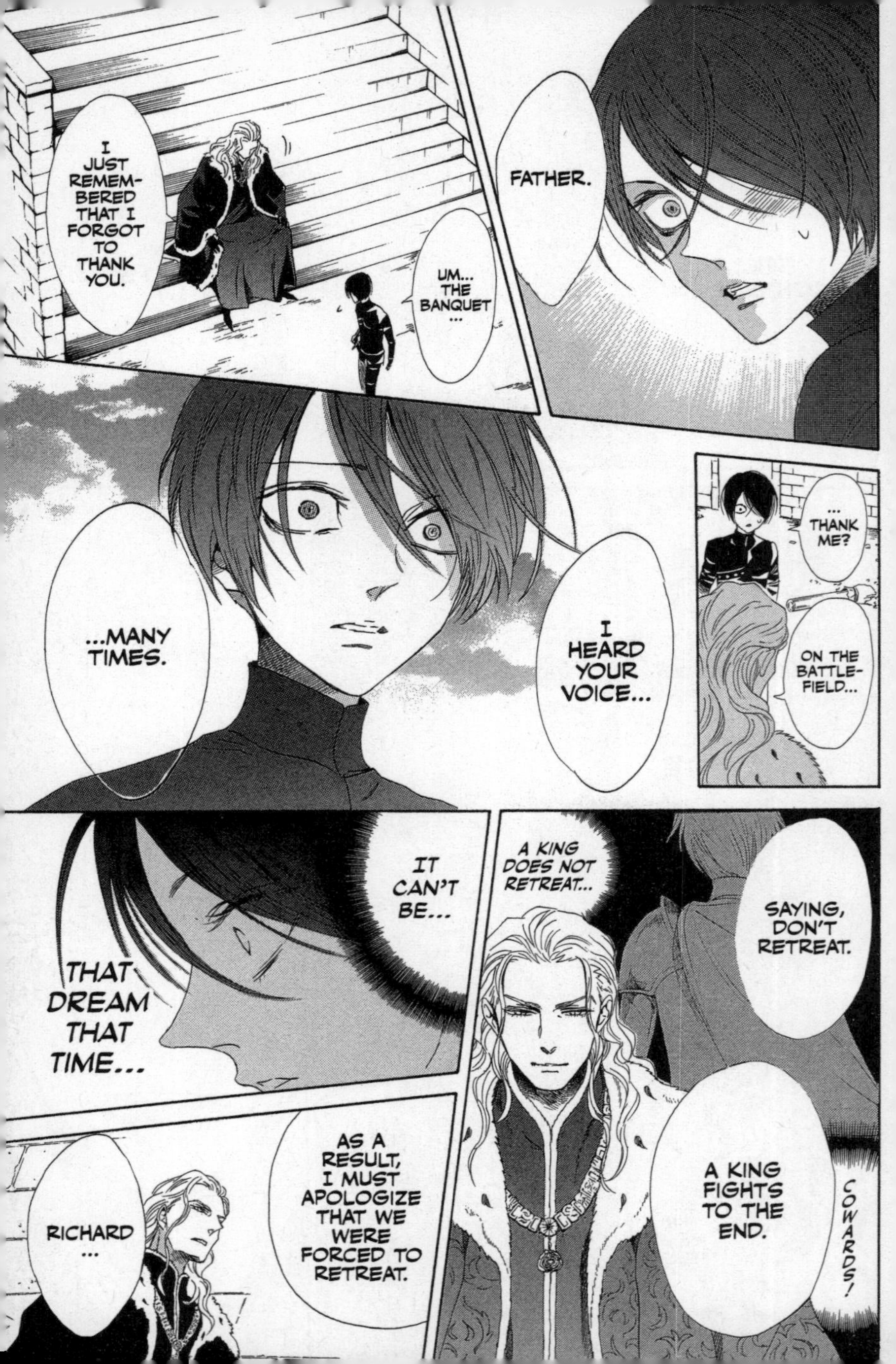
FATHER.
UM... THE BANQUET...
I JUST REMEMBERED THAT I FORGOT TO THANK YOU.
...THANK ME?
ON THE BATTLEFIELD...
I HEARD YOUR VOICE...
...MANY TIMES.
SAYING, DON'T RETREAT.
A KING DOES NOT RETREAT...
COWARDS!
A KING FIGHTS TO THE END.
IT CAN'T BE...
THAT DREAM THAT TIME...
AS A RESULT, I MUST APOLOGIZE THAT WE WERE FORCED TO RETREAT.
RICHARD...

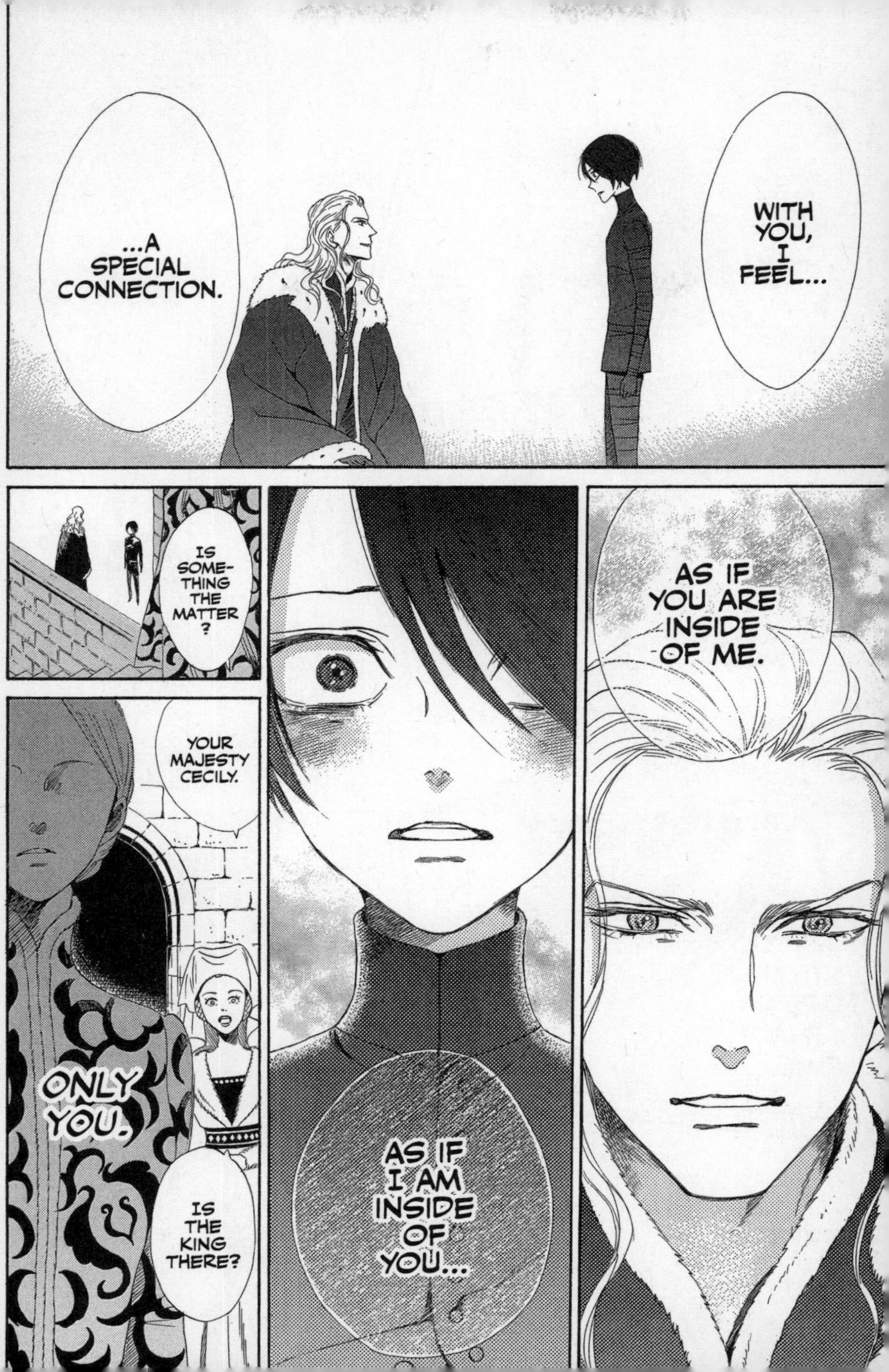
WITH YOU, I FEEL...
...A SPECIAL CONNECTION.
AS IF YOU ARE INSIDE OF ME.
AS IF I AM INSIDE OF YOU...
IS SOMETHING THE MATTER?
YOUR MAJESTY CECILY.
ONLY YOU.
IS THE KING THERE?

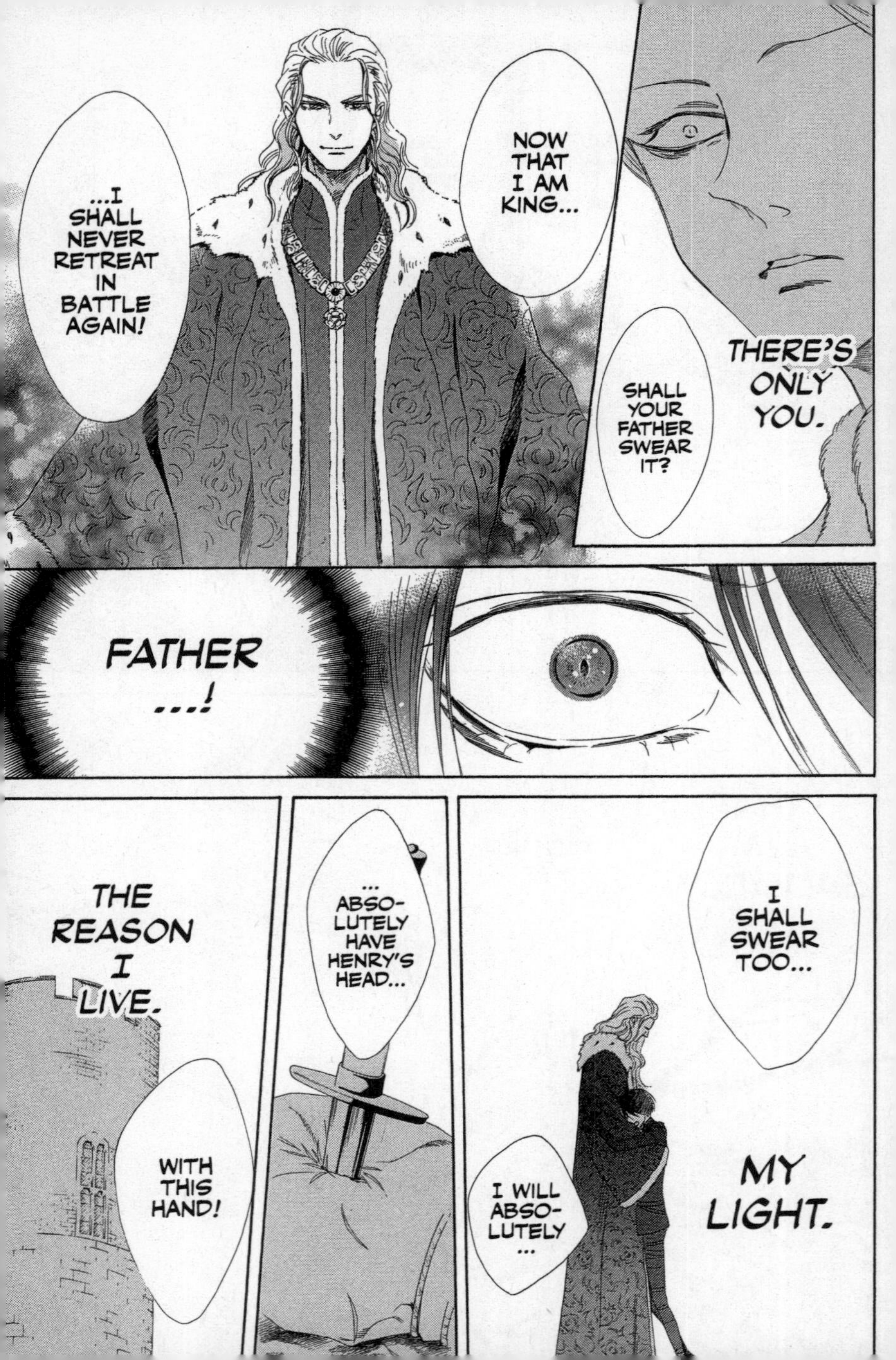
THERE'S ONLY YOU.
SHALL YOUR FATHER SWEAR IT?
NOW THAT I AM KING...
...I SHALL NEVER RETREAT IN BATTLE AGAIN!
FATHER ...!
I SHALL SWEAR TOO...
MY LIGHT.
I WILL ABSO-LUTELY ...
... ABSO-LUTELY HAVE HENRY'S HEAD...
THE REASON I LIVE.
WITH THIS HAND!

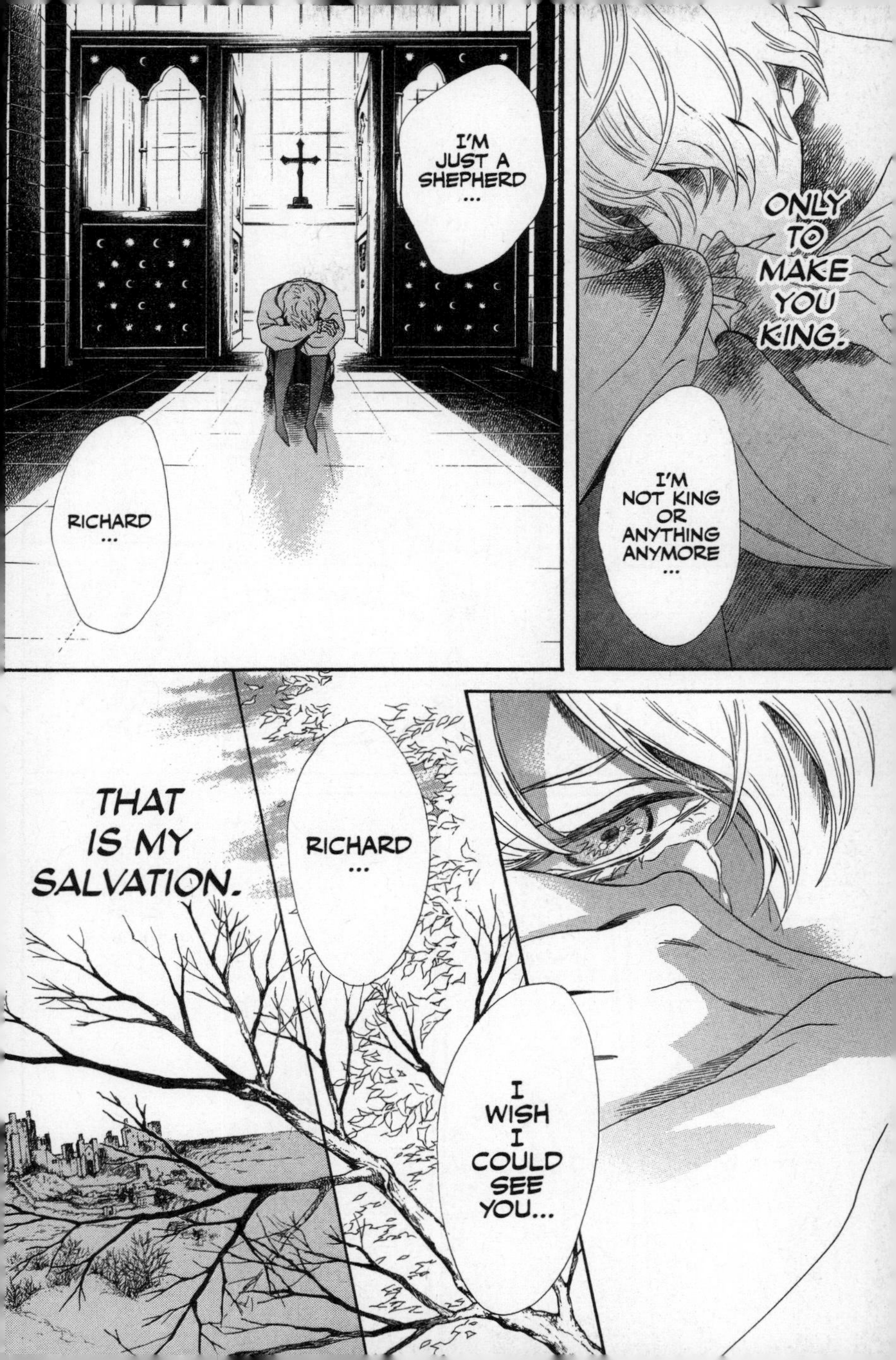
ONLY TO MAKE YOU KING.
I'M NOT KING OR ANYTHING ANYMORE...
I'M JUST A SHEPHERD...
RICHARD...
I WISH I COULD SEE YOU...
RICHARD...
THAT IS MY SALVATION.

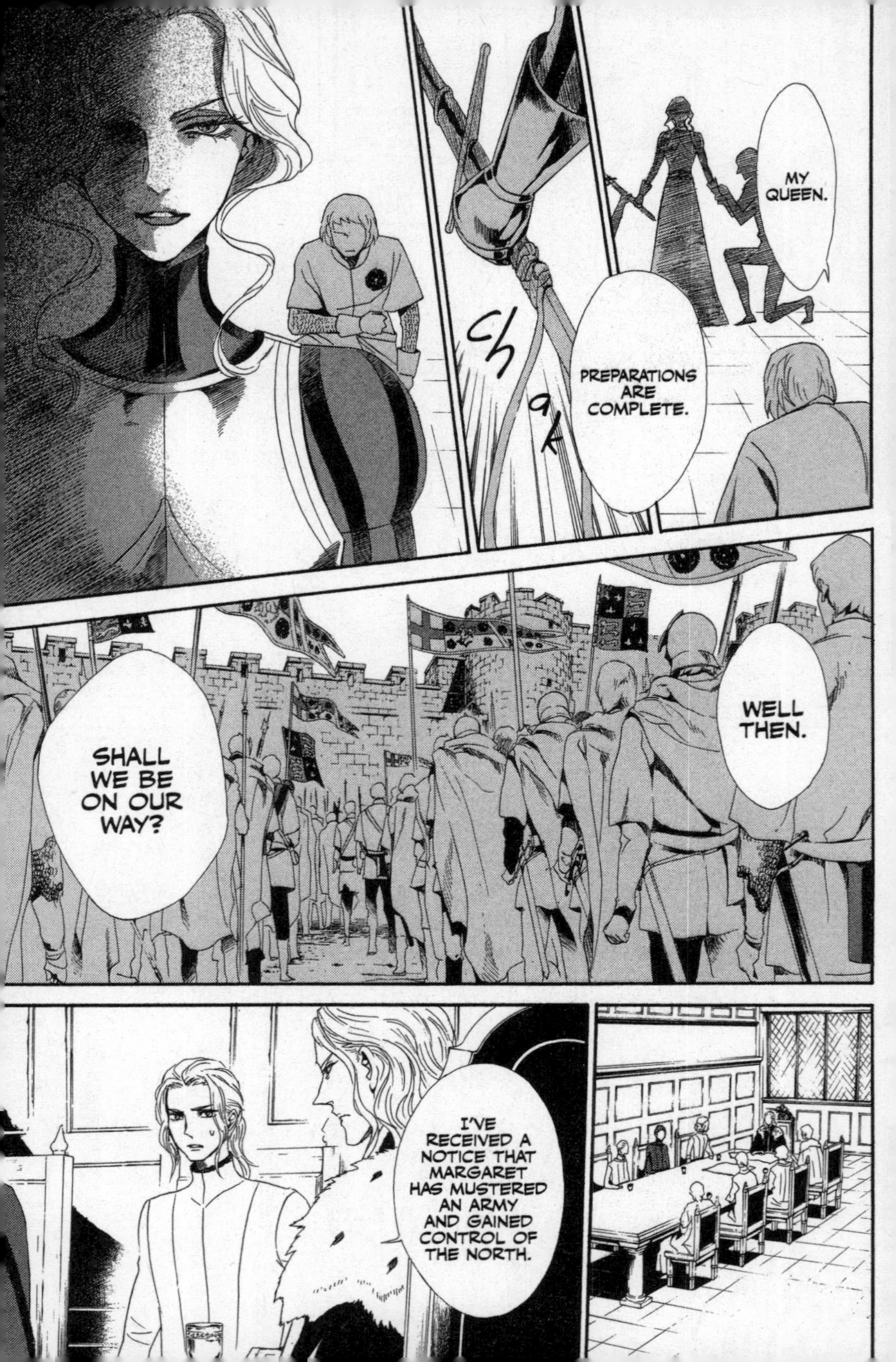

MY QUEEN.
PREPARATIONS ARE COMPLETE.
Chak
WELL THEN.
SHALL WE BE ON OUR WAY?
I'VE RECEIVED A NOTICE THAT MARGARET HAS MUSTERED AN ARMY AND GAINED CONTROL OF THE NORTH.

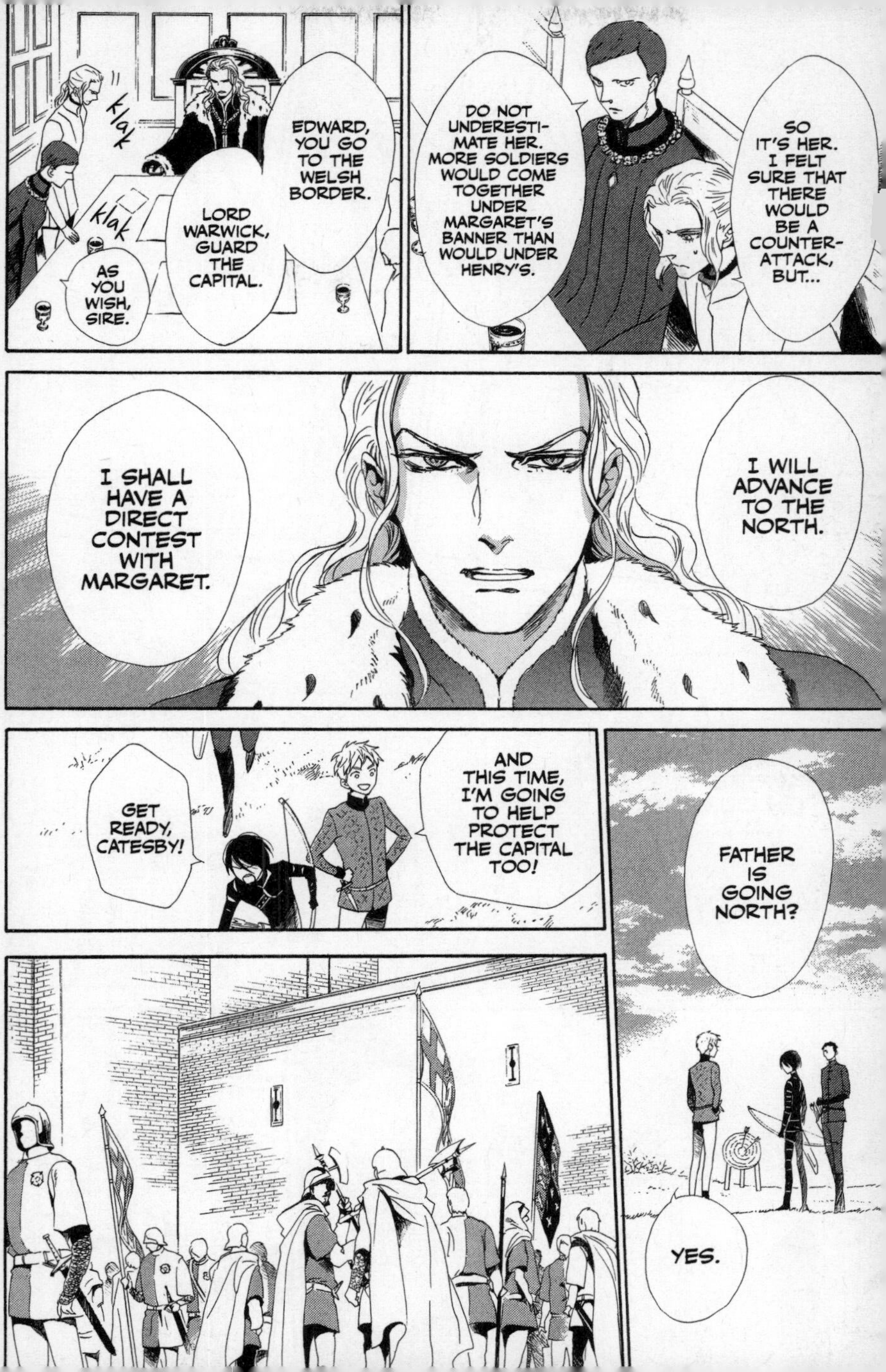
SO IT'S HER. I FELT SURE THAT THERE WOULD BE A COUNTER-ATTACK, BUT...
DO NOT UNDERESTIMATE HER. MORE SOLDIERS WOULD COME TOGETHER UNDER MARGARET'S BANNER THAN WOULD UNDER HENRY'S.
EDWARD, YOU GO TO THE WELSH BORDER.
klak
LORD WARWICK, GUARD THE CAPITAL.
klak
AS YOU WISH, SIRE.
I WILL ADVANCE TO THE NORTH.
I SHALL HAVE A DIRECT CONTEST WITH MARGARET.
FATHER IS GOING NORTH?
YES.
AND THIS TIME, I'M GOING TO HELP PROTECT THE CAPITAL TOO!
GET READY, CATESBY!

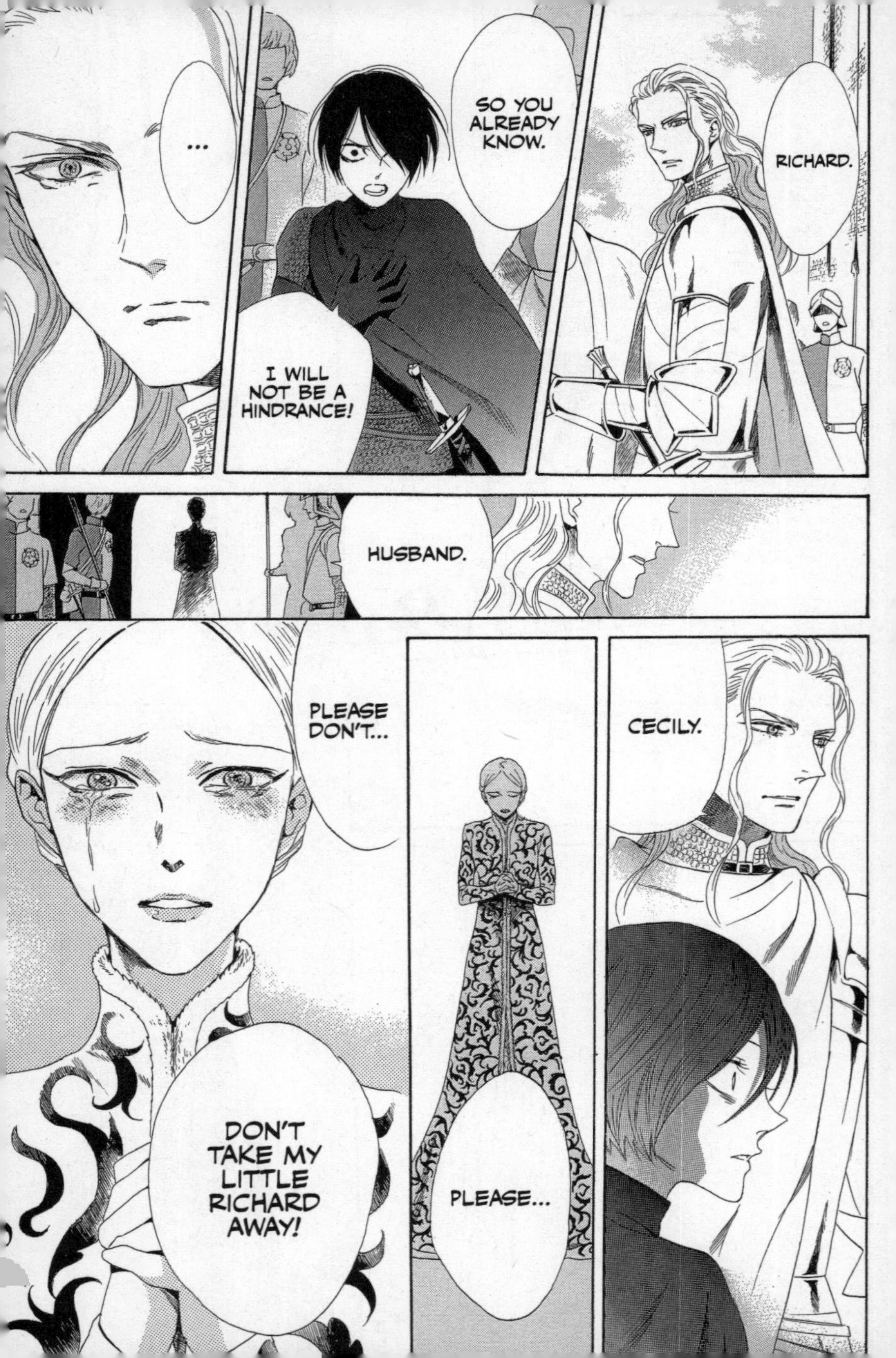
RICHARD.
SO YOU ALREADY KNOW.
I WILL NOT BE A HINDRANCE!
...
HUSBAND.
CECILY.
PLEASE...
PLEASE DON'T...
DON'T TAKE MY LITTLE RICHARD AWAY!

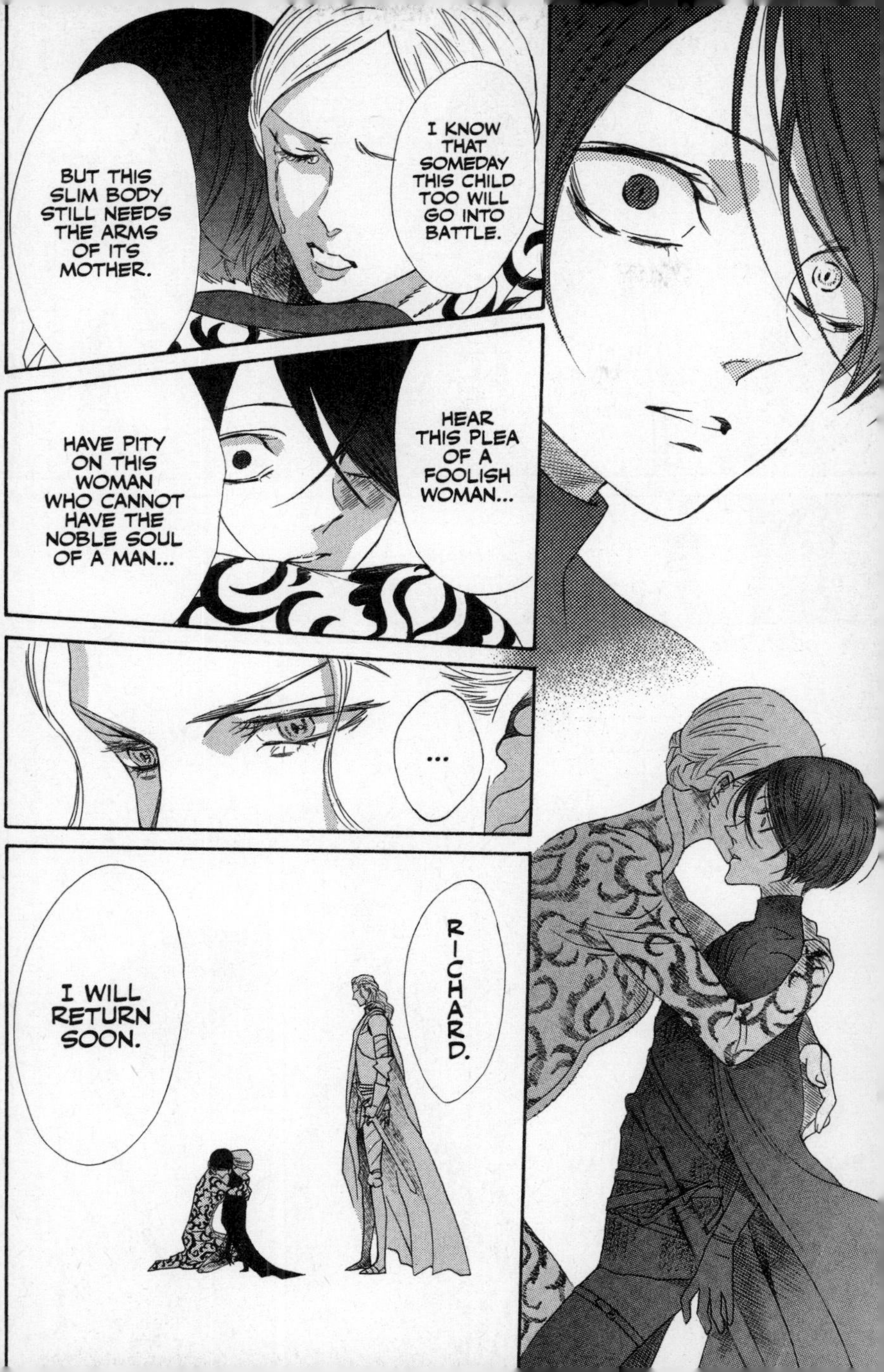
I KNOW THAT SOMEDAY THIS CHILD TOO WILL GO INTO BATTLE.
BUT THIS SLIM BODY STILL NEEDS THE ARMS OF ITS MOTHER.
HEAR THIS PLEA OF A FOOLISH WOMAN...
HAVE PITY ON THIS WOMAN WHO CANNOT HAVE THE NOBLE SOUL OF A MAN...
...
RICHARD.
I WILL RETURN SOON.

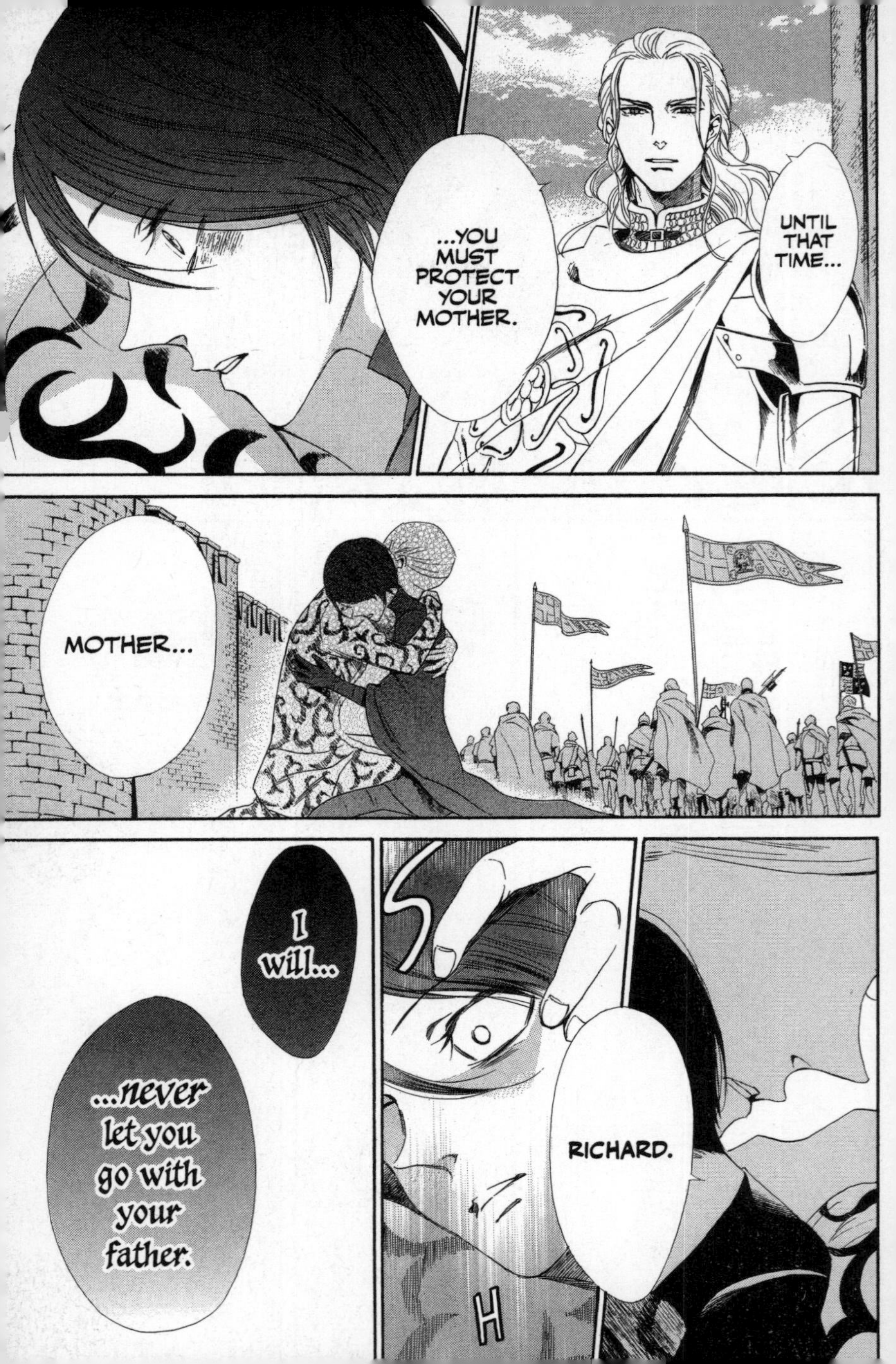

UNTIL THAT TIME...
...YOU MUST PROTECT YOUR MOTHER.
MOTHER...
RICHARD.
S
H
I will...
...never let you go with your father.

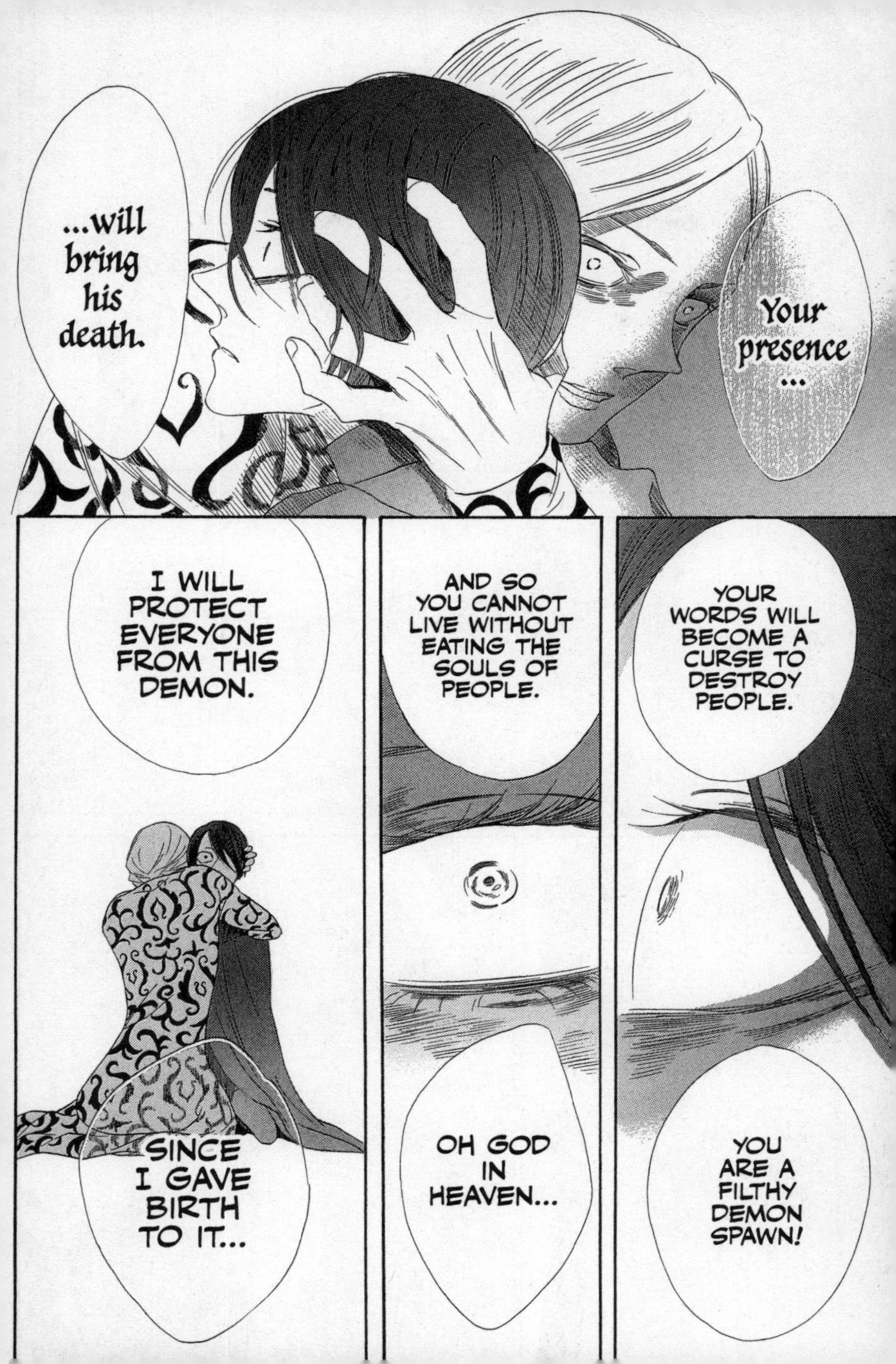
Your presence ...
...will bring his death.
YOUR WORDS WILL BECOME A CURSE TO DESTROY PEOPLE.
YOU ARE A FILTHY DEMON SPAWN!
AND SO YOU CANNOT LIVE WITHOUT EATING THE SOULS OF PEOPLE.
OH GOD IN HEAVEN...
I WILL PROTECT EVERYONE FROM THIS DEMON.
SINCE I GAVE BIRTH TO IT...

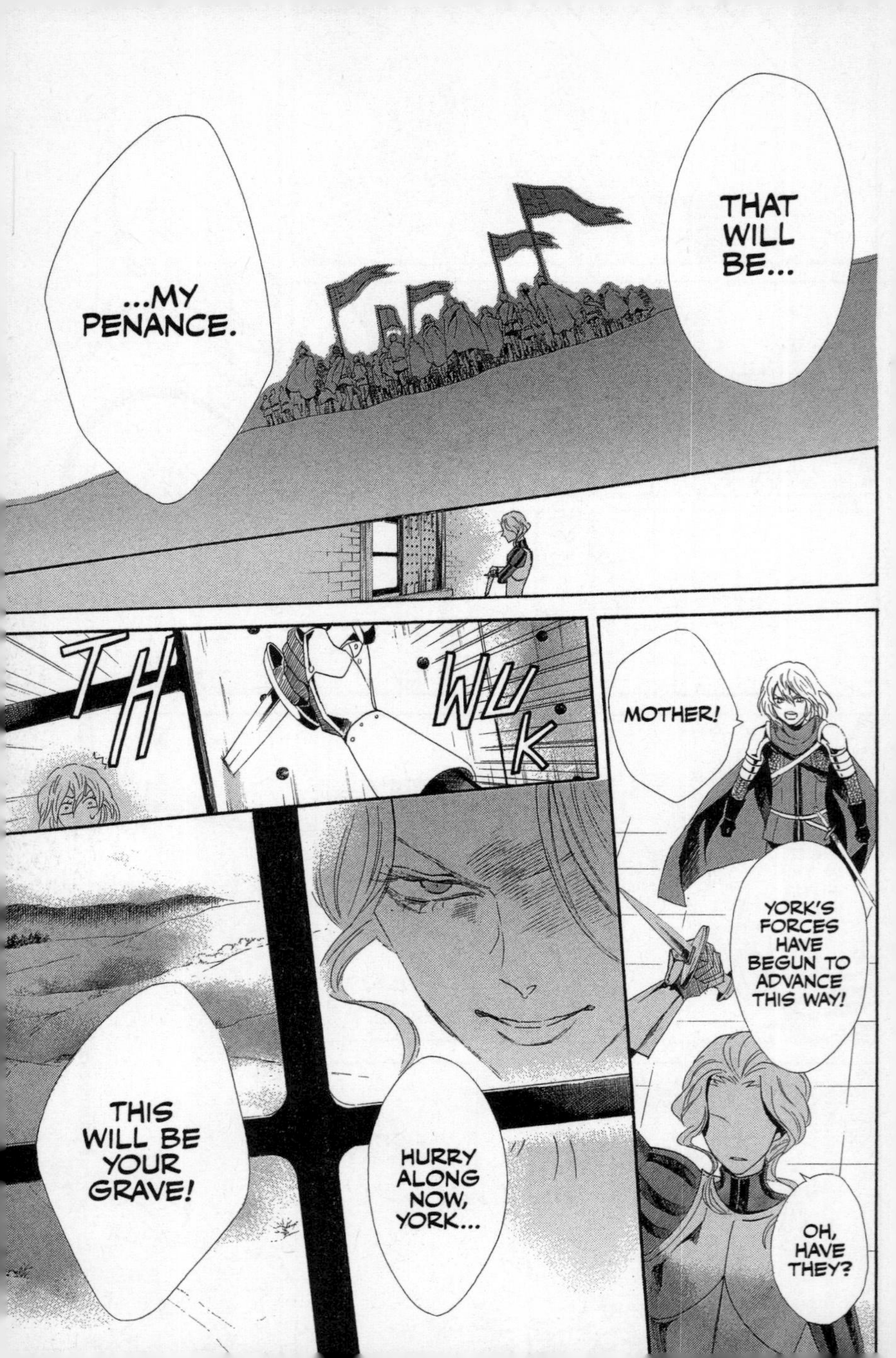
THAT WILL BE...
...MY PENANCE.
MOTHER!
YORK'S FORCES HAVE BEGUN TO ADVANCE THIS WAY!
OH, HAVE THEY?
THWUK
HURRY ALONG NOW, YORK...
THIS WILL BE YOUR GRAVE!

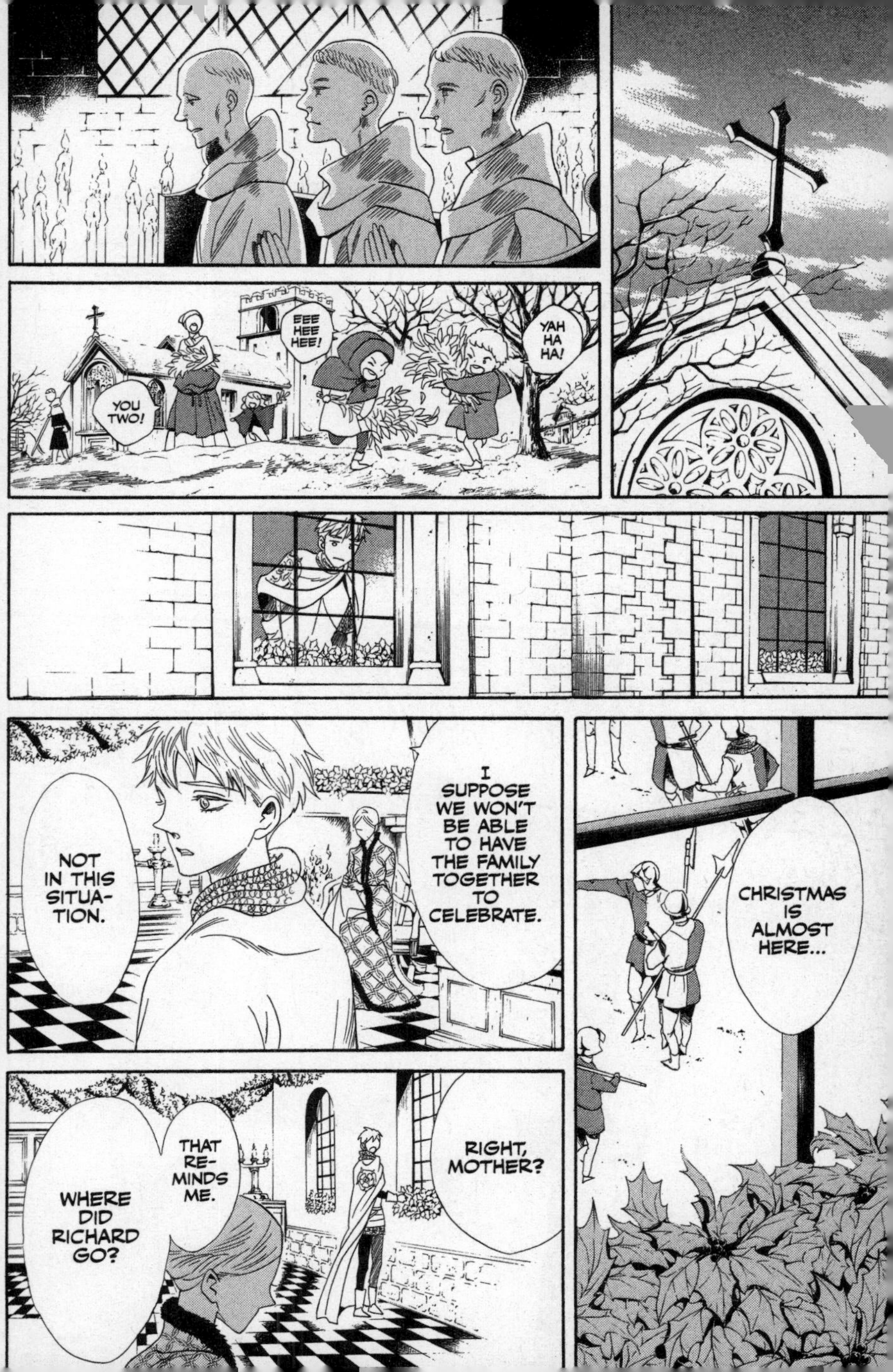

YAH HA HA!
EEE HEE HEE!
YOU TWO!
CHRISTMAS IS ALMOST HERE...
I SUPPOSE WE WON'T BE ABLE TO HAVE THE FAMILY TOGETHER TO CELEBRATE.
NOT IN THIS SITUATION.
RIGHT, MOTHER?
THAT RE-MINDS ME.
WHERE DID RICHARD GO?

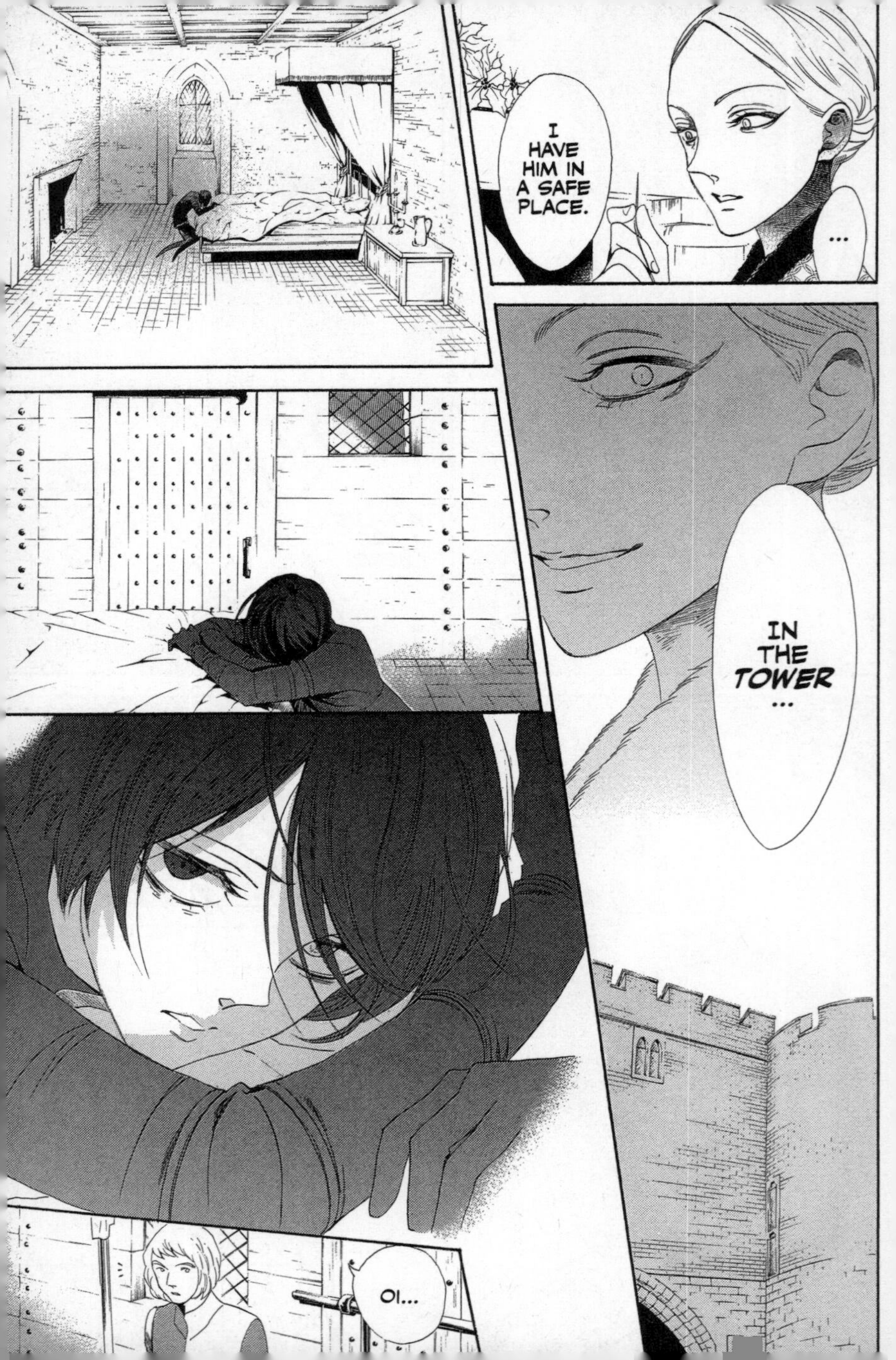
I HAVE HIM IN A SAFE PLACE.
...
IN THE *TOWER* ...
OI...

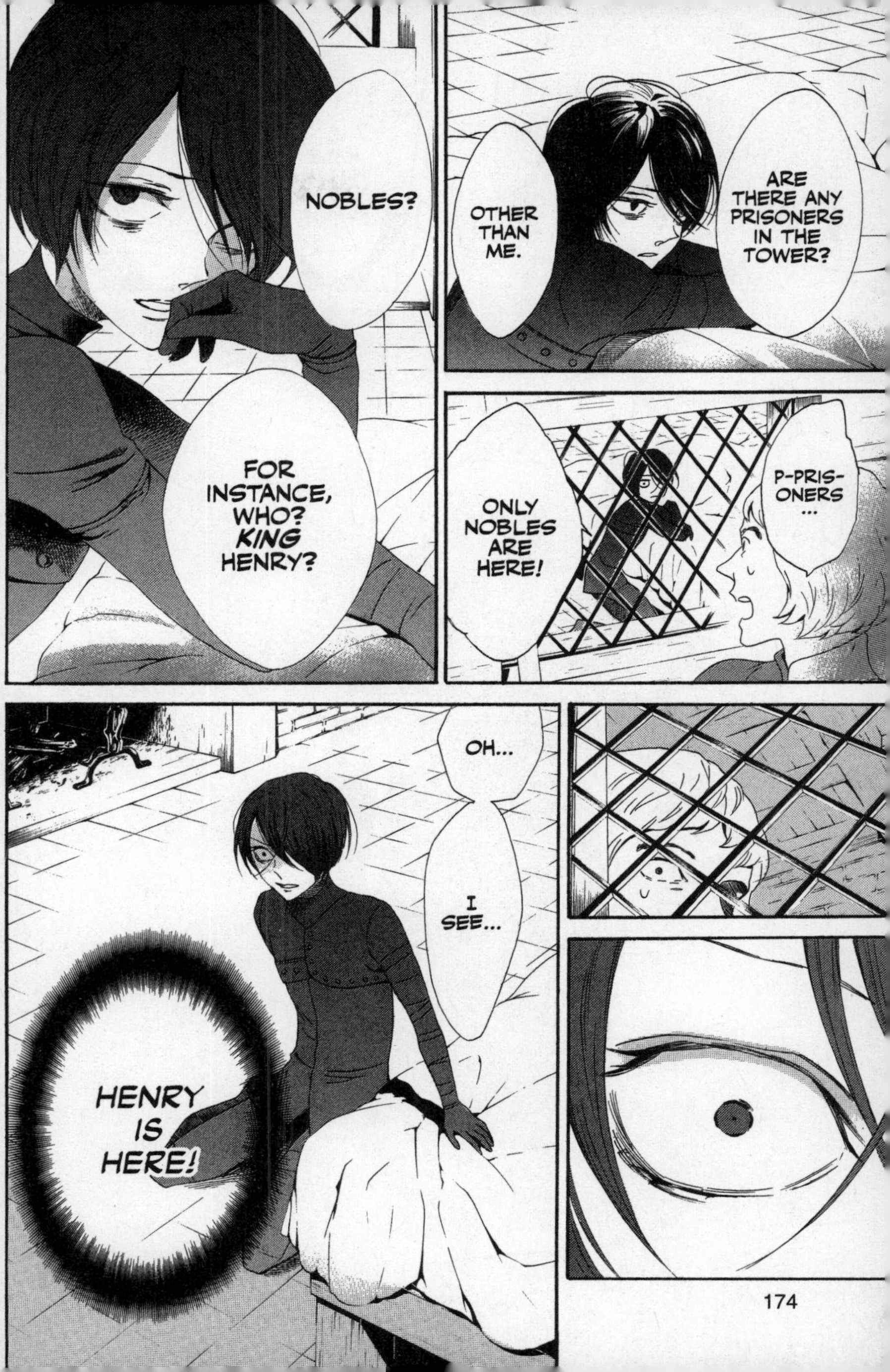
ARE THERE ANY PRISONERS IN THE TOWER?
OTHER THAN ME.
P-PRISONERS...
ONLY NOBLES ARE HERE!
NOBLES?
FOR INSTANCE, WHO? *KING* HENRY?
OH...
I SEE...
HENRY IS HERE!

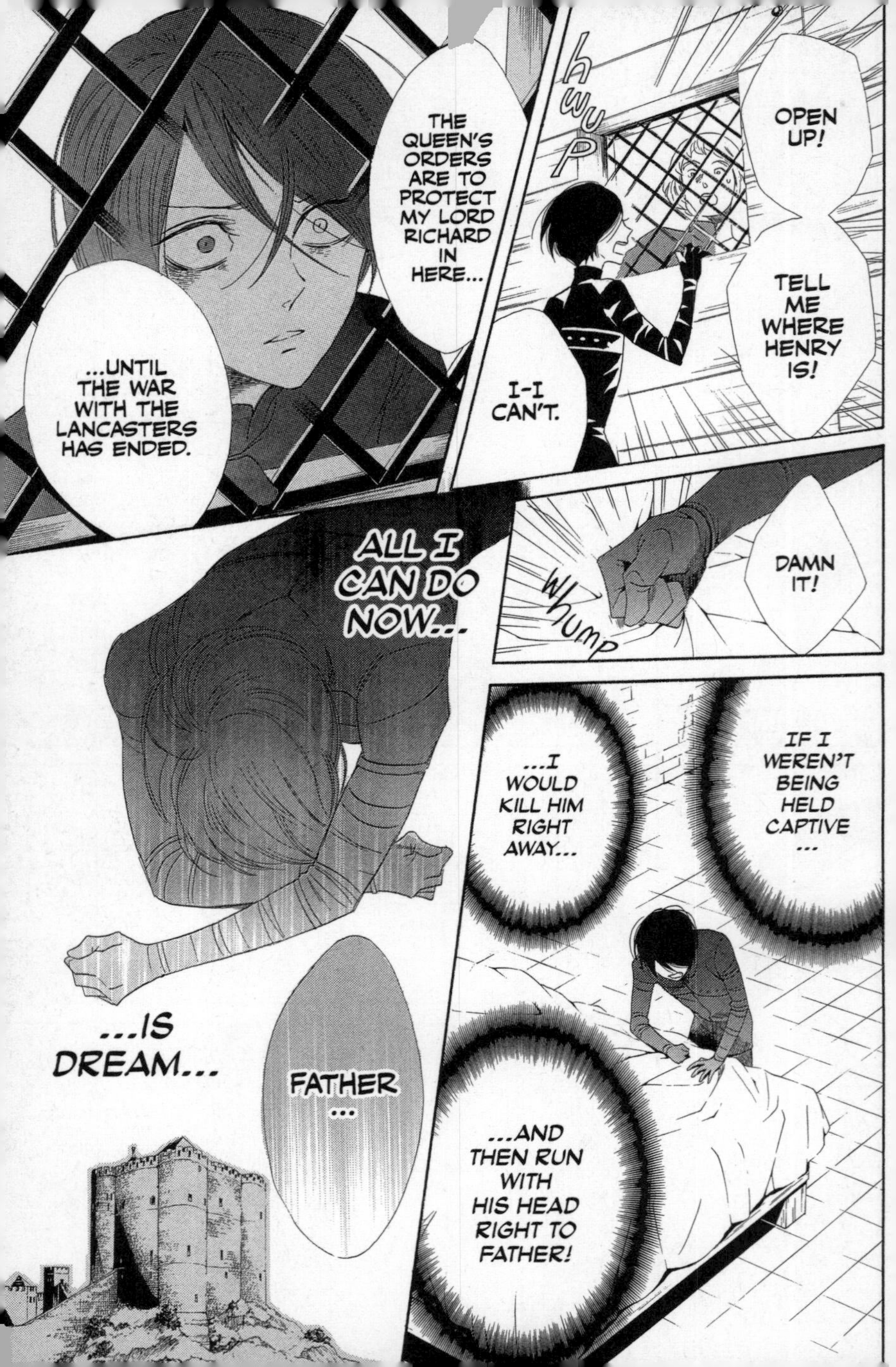
OPEN UP!
hwup
TELL ME WHERE HENRY IS!
I-I CAN'T.
THE QUEEN'S ORDERS ARE TO PROTECT MY LORD RICHARD IN HERE...
...UNTIL THE WAR WITH THE LANCASTERS HAS ENDED.
DAMN IT!
whump
IF I WEREN'T BEING HELD CAPTIVE...
...I WOULD KILL HIM RIGHT AWAY...
...AND THEN RUN WITH HIS HEAD RIGHT TO FATHER!
ALL I CAN DO NOW...
...IS DREAM...
FATHER...

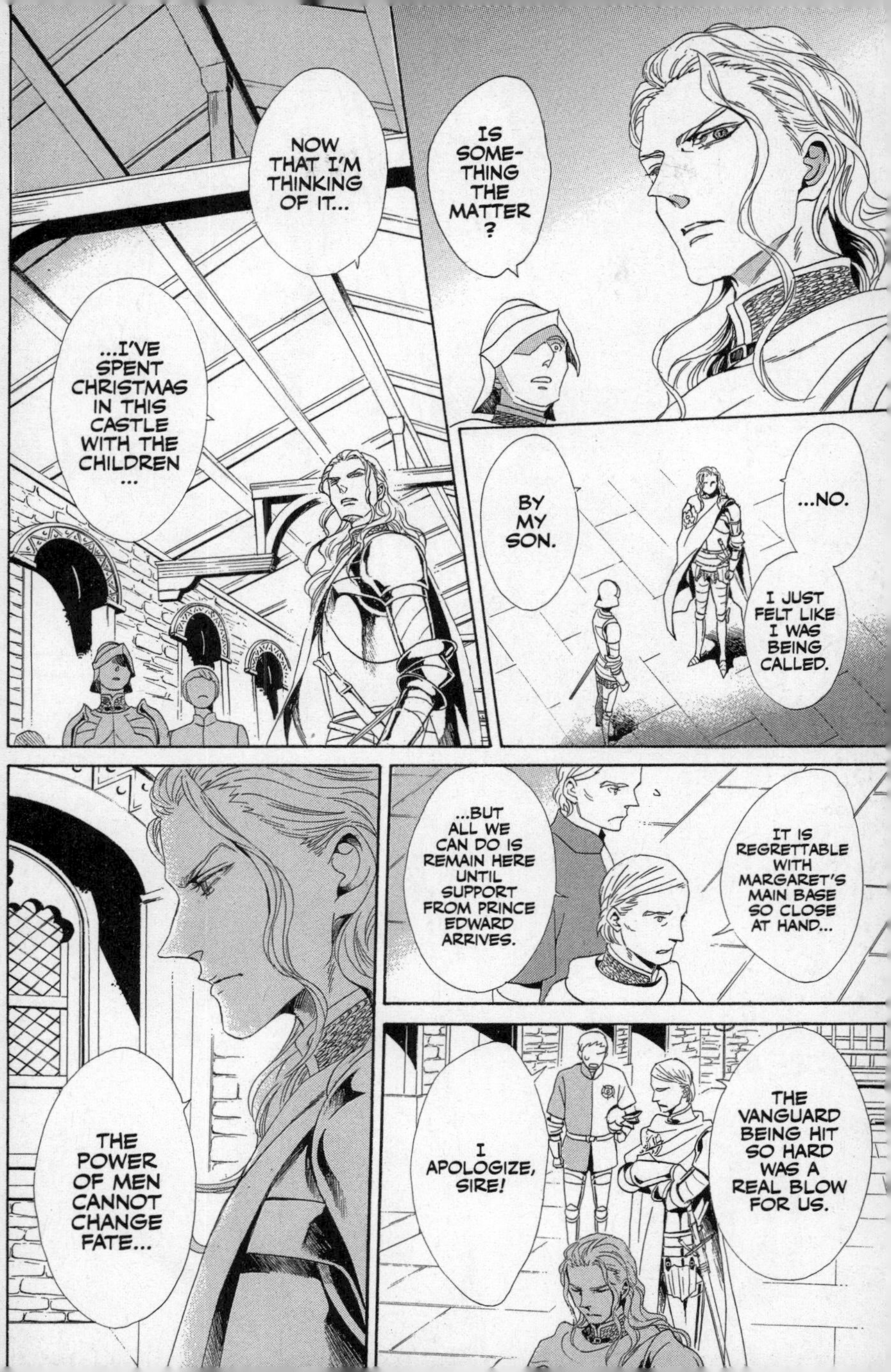
IS SOMETHING THE MATTER?
...NO.
I JUST FELT LIKE I WAS BEING CALLED.
BY MY SON.
NOW THAT I'M THINKING OF IT...
...I'VE SPENT CHRISTMAS IN THIS CASTLE WITH THE CHILDREN...
IT IS REGRETTABLE WITH MARGARET'S MAIN BASE SO CLOSE AT HAND...
...BUT ALL WE CAN DO IS REMAIN HERE UNTIL SUPPORT FROM PRINCE EDWARD ARRIVES.
THE VANGUARD BEING HIT SO HARD WAS A REAL BLOW FOR US.
I APOLOGIZE, SIRE!
THE POWER OF MEN CANNOT CHANGE FATE...

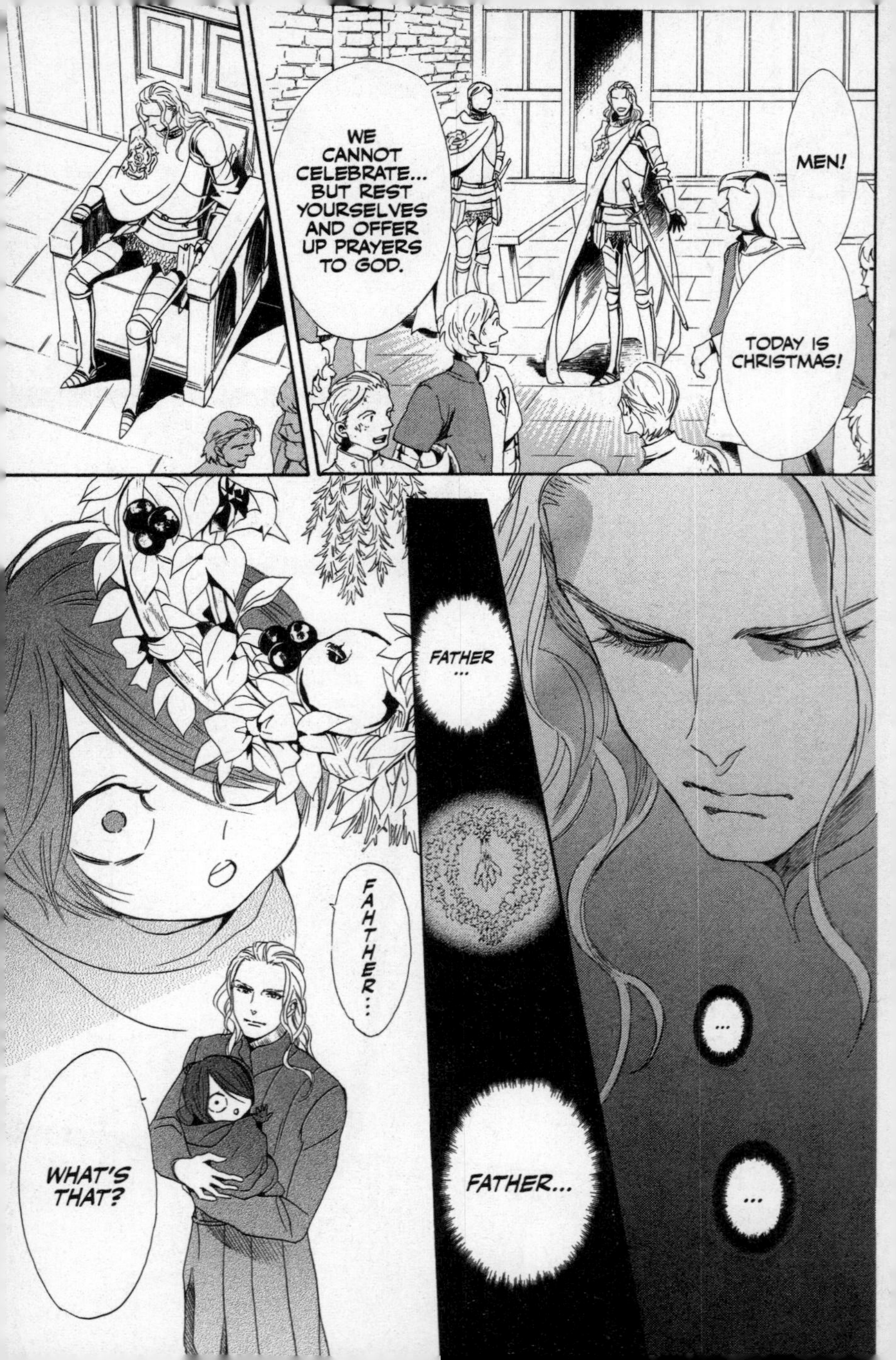
MEN!
TODAY IS CHRISTMAS!
WE CANNOT CELEBRATE... BUT REST YOURSELVES AND OFFER UP PRAYERS TO GOD.
...
...
FATHER ...
FATHER...
FAHTHER...
WHAT'S THAT?

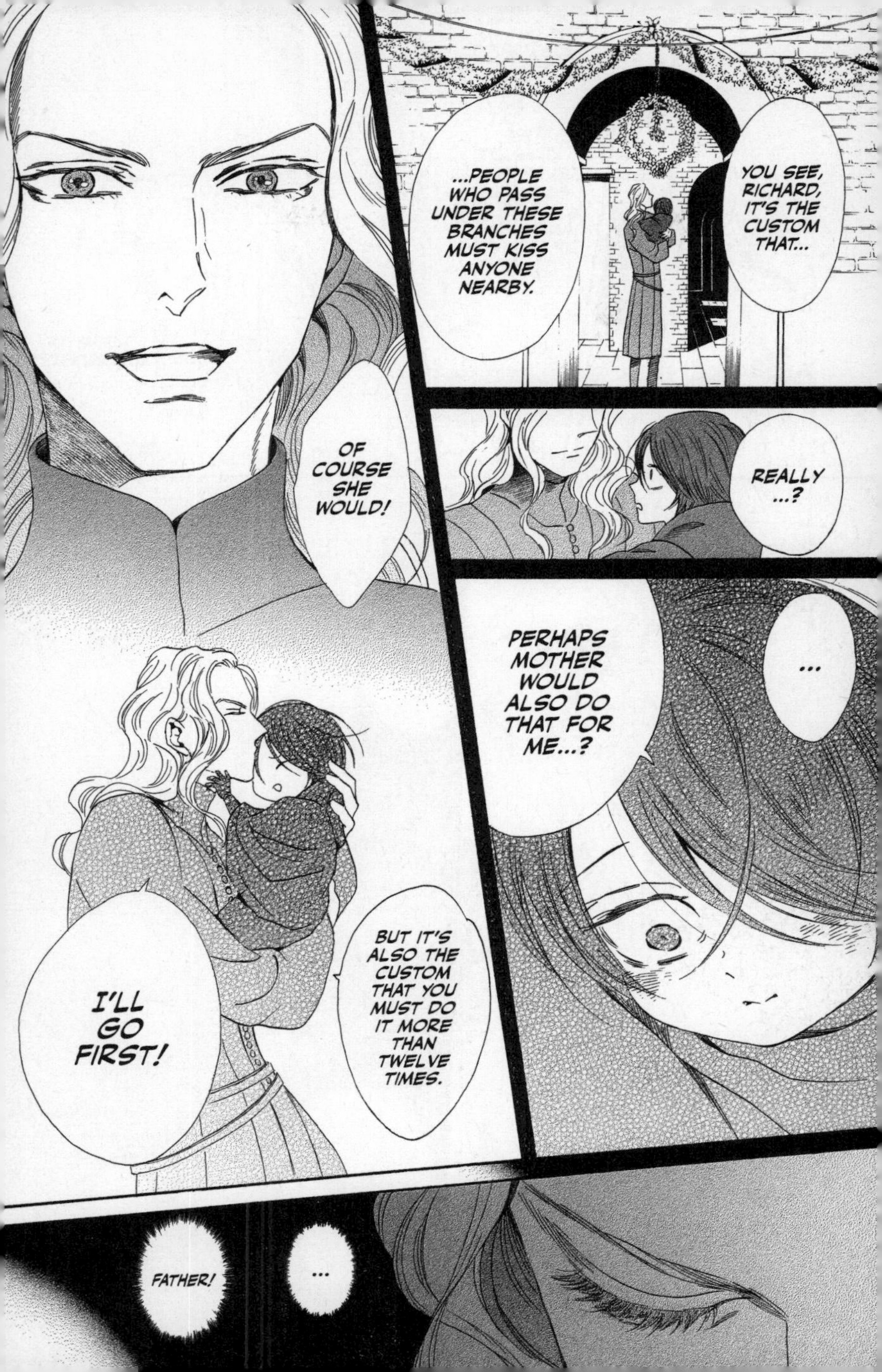
YOU SEE, RICHARD, IT'S THE CUSTOM THAT...
...PEOPLE WHO PASS UNDER THESE BRANCHES MUST KISS ANYONE NEARBY.
REALLY ...?
...
PERHAPS MOTHER WOULD ALSO DO THAT FOR ME...?
OF COURSE SHE WOULD!
BUT IT'S ALSO THE CUSTOM THAT YOU MUST DO IT MORE THAN TWELVE TIMES.
I'LL GO FIRST!
...
FATHER!

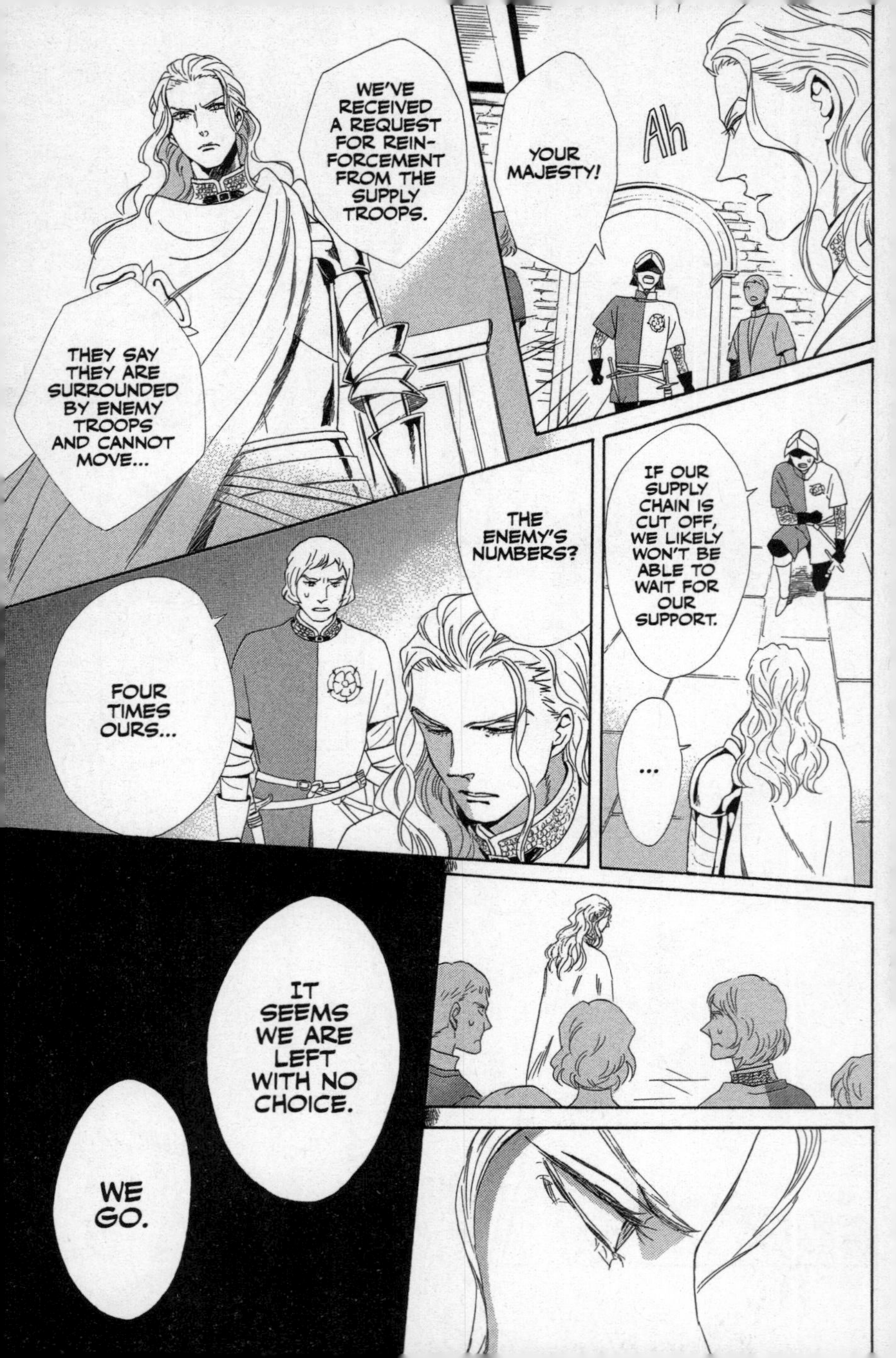
Ah
YOUR MAJESTY!
WE'VE RECEIVED A REQUEST FOR REIN-FORCEMENT FROM THE SUPPLY TROOPS.
THEY SAY THEY ARE SURROUNDED BY ENEMY TROOPS AND CANNOT MOVE...
IF OUR SUPPLY CHAIN IS CUT OFF, WE LIKELY WON'T BE ABLE TO WAIT FOR OUR SUPPORT.
...
THE ENEMY'S NUMBERS?
FOUR TIMES OURS...
IT SEEMS WE ARE LEFT WITH NO CHOICE.
WE GO.

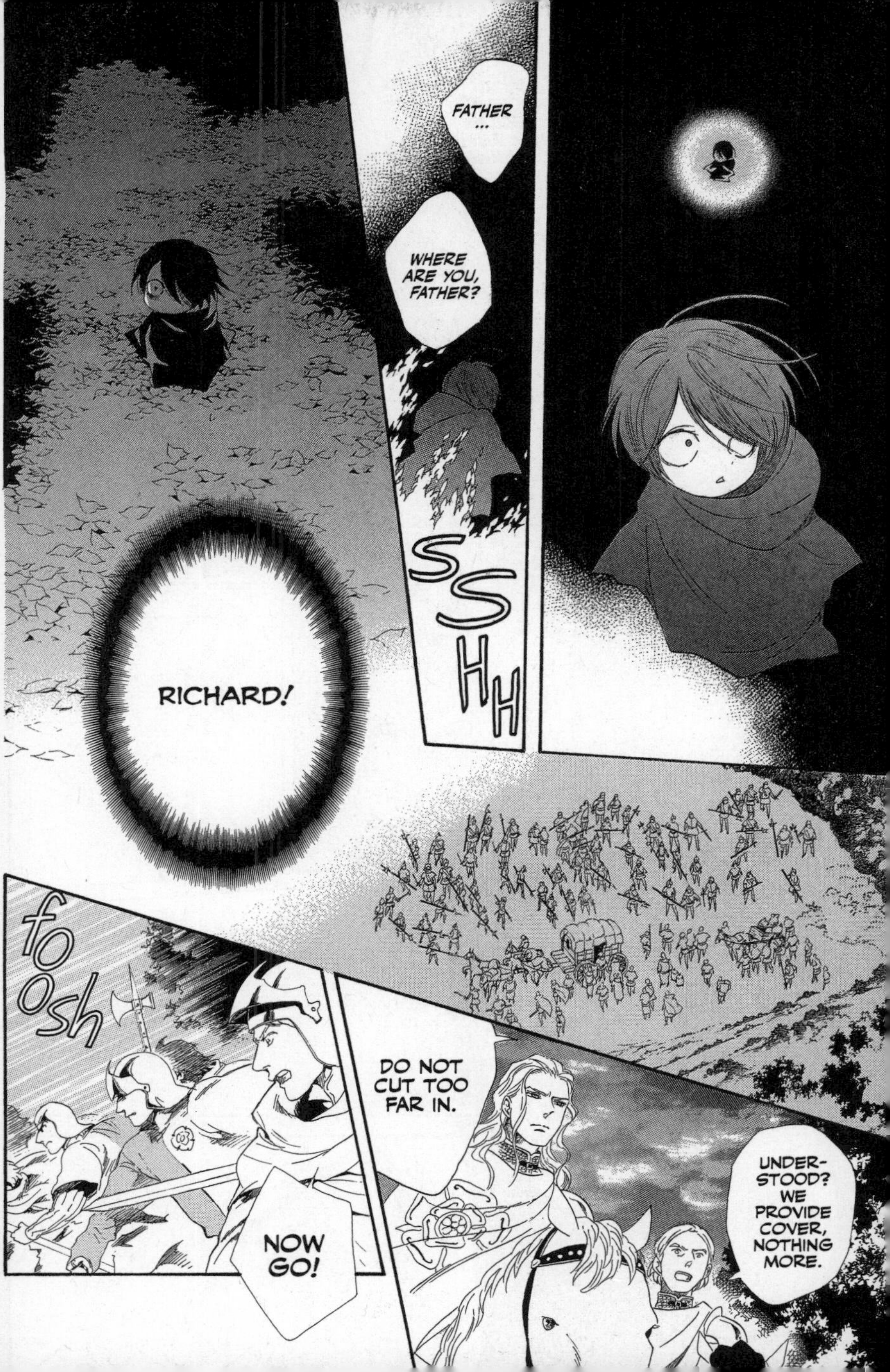
FATHER ...
WHERE ARE YOU, FATHER?
SSHH
RICHARD!
DO NOT CUT TOO FAR IN.
UNDER-STOOD? WE PROVIDE COVER, NOTHING MORE.
foosh
NOW GO!

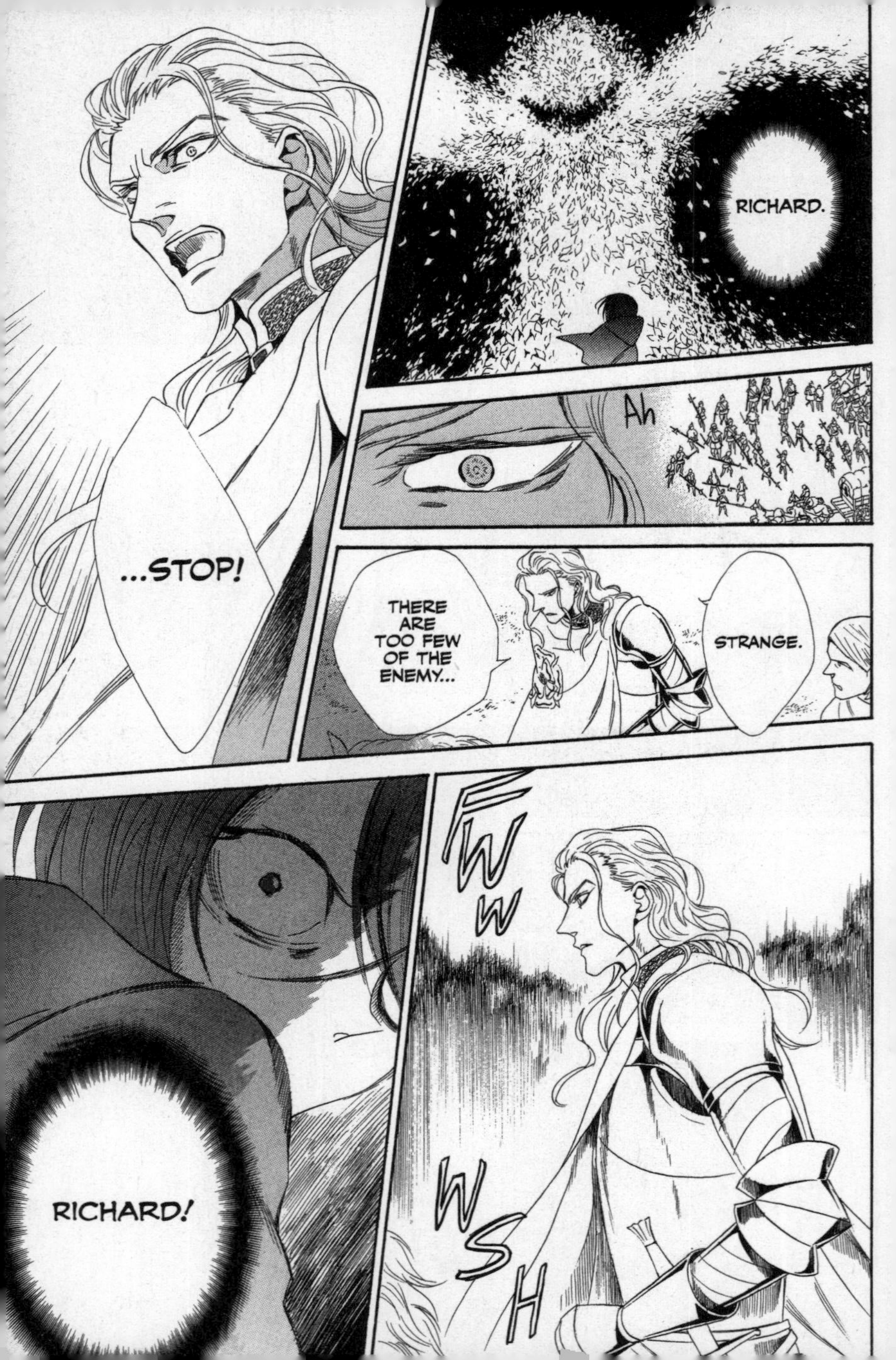
RICHARD.
Ah
STRANGE.
THERE ARE TOO FEW OF THE ENEMY...
...STOP!
FWWWSH
RICHARD!

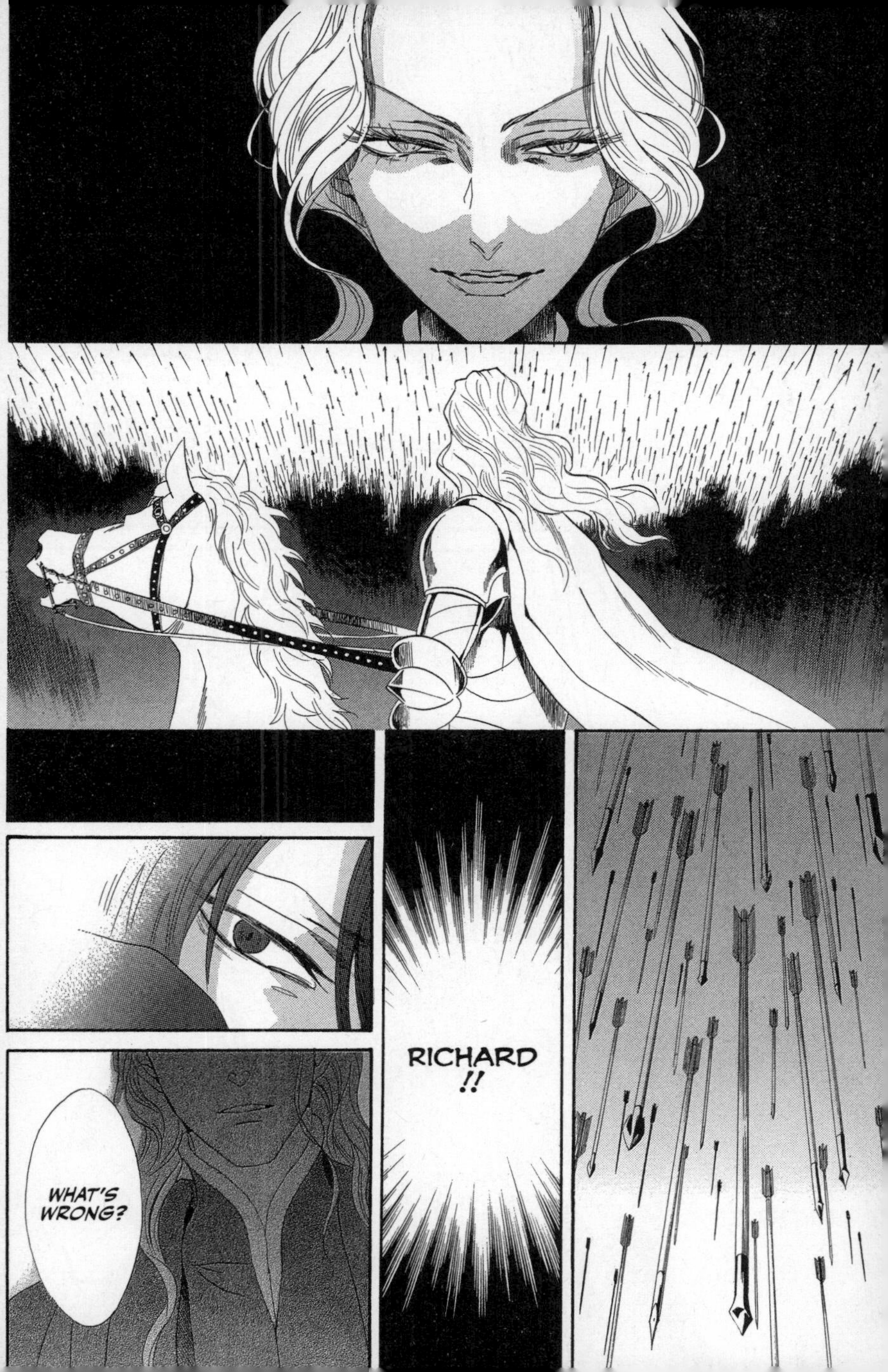
RICHARD !!
WHAT'S WRONG?

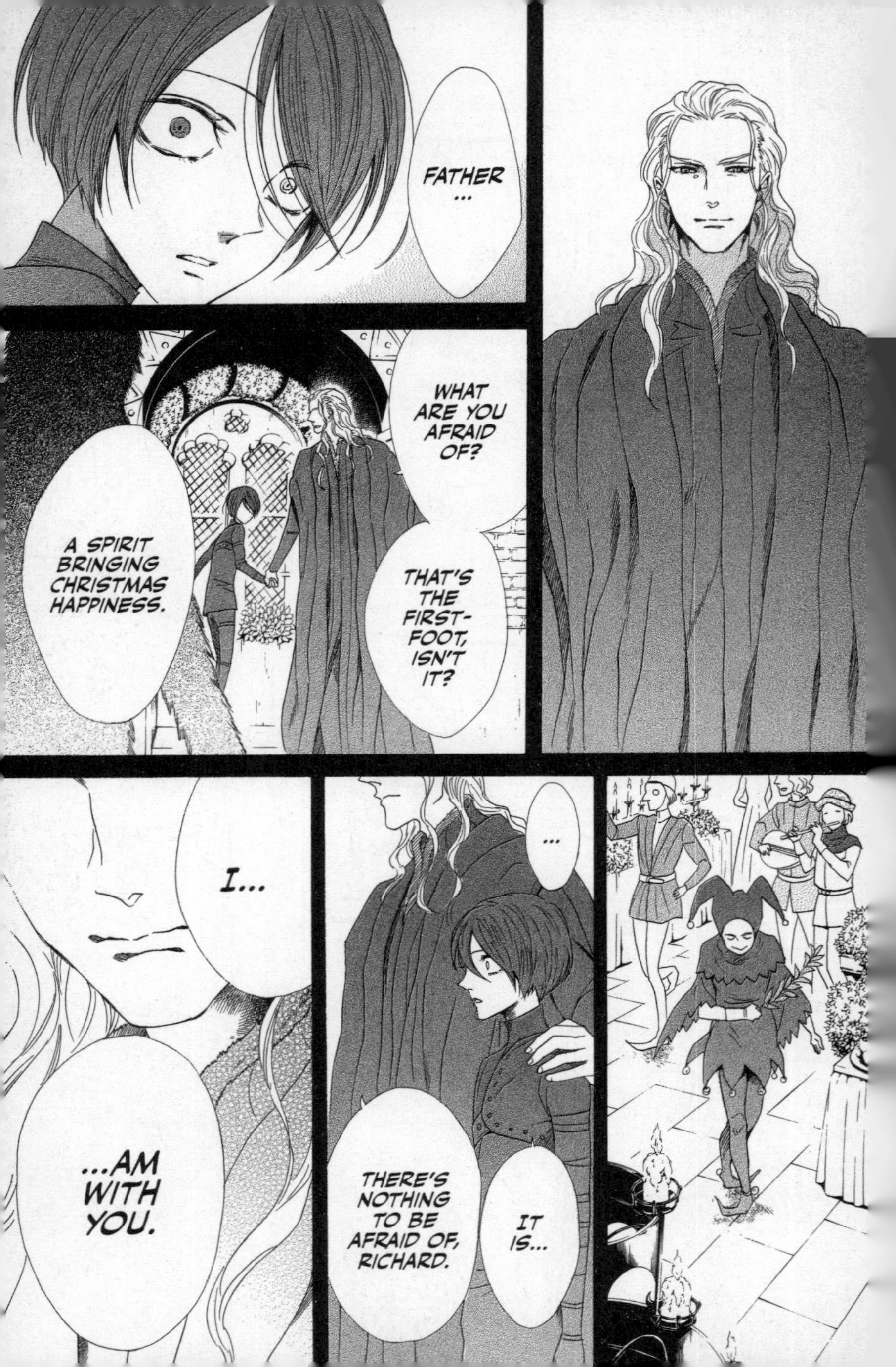
FATHER ...
WHAT ARE YOU AFRAID OF?
THAT'S THE FIRST-FOOT, ISN'T IT?
A SPIRIT BRINGING CHRISTMAS HAPPINESS.
...
IT IS...
THERE'S NOTHING TO BE AFRAID OF, RICHARD.
I...
...AM WITH YOU.

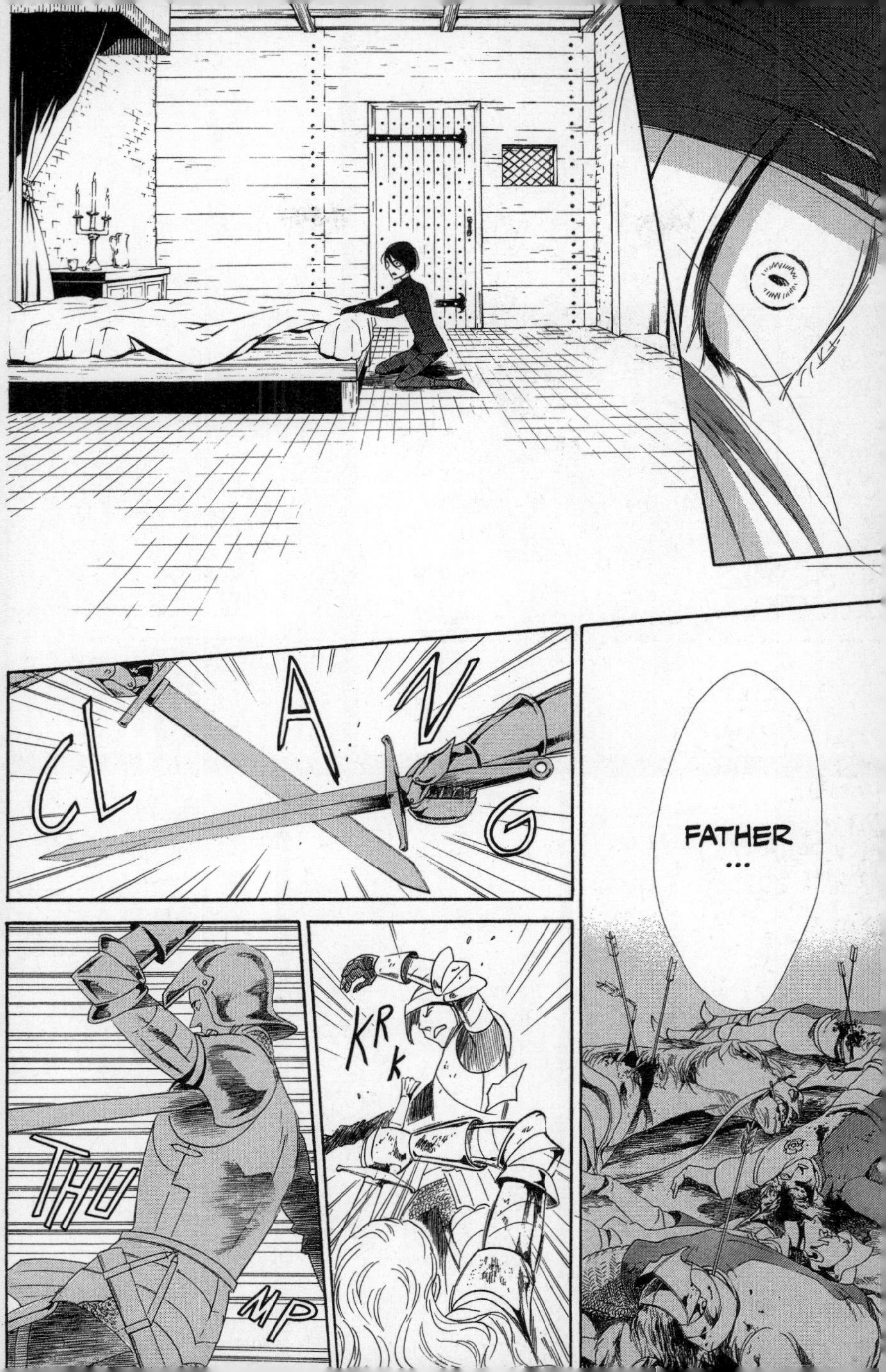
FATHER ...
CLANG
KRK
THUMP

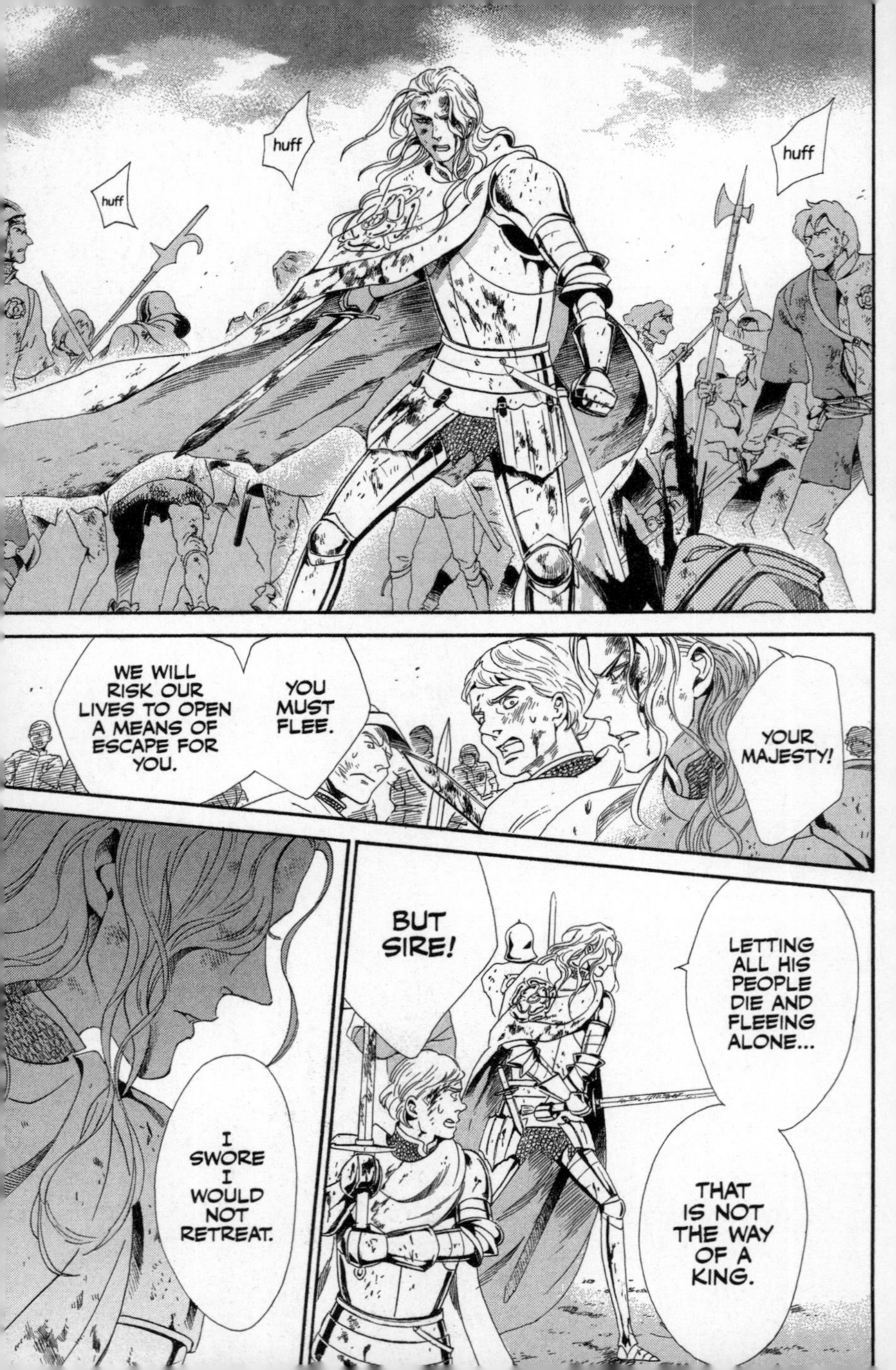
huff
huff
huff
YOUR MAJESTY!
YOU MUST FLEE.
WE WILL RISK OUR LIVES TO OPEN A MEANS OF ESCAPE FOR YOU.
LETTING ALL HIS PEOPLE DIE AND FLEEING ALONE...
BUT SIRE!
THAT IS NOT THE WAY OF A KING.
I SWORE I WOULD NOT RETREAT.

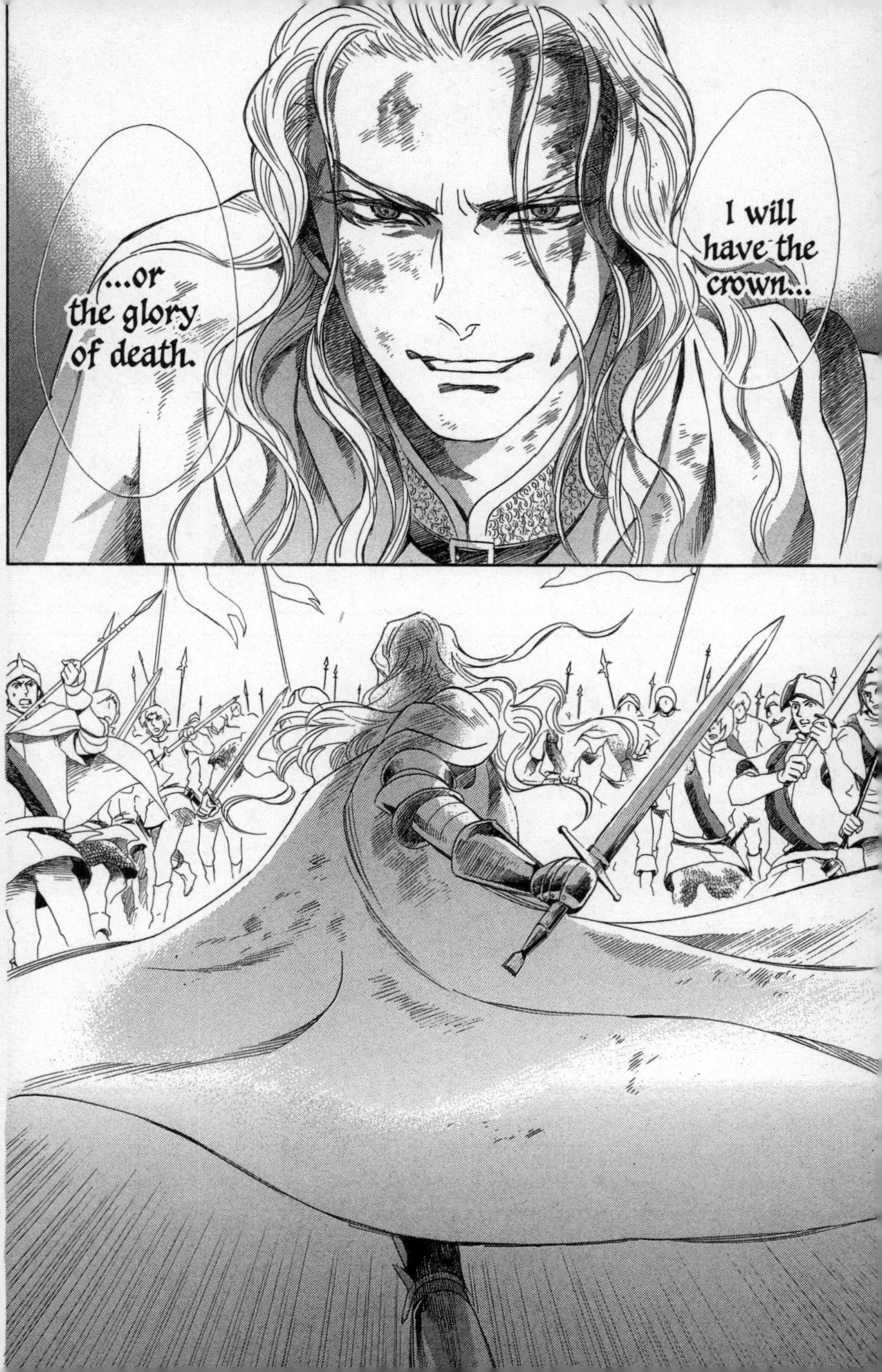
I will have the crown...
...or the glory of death.

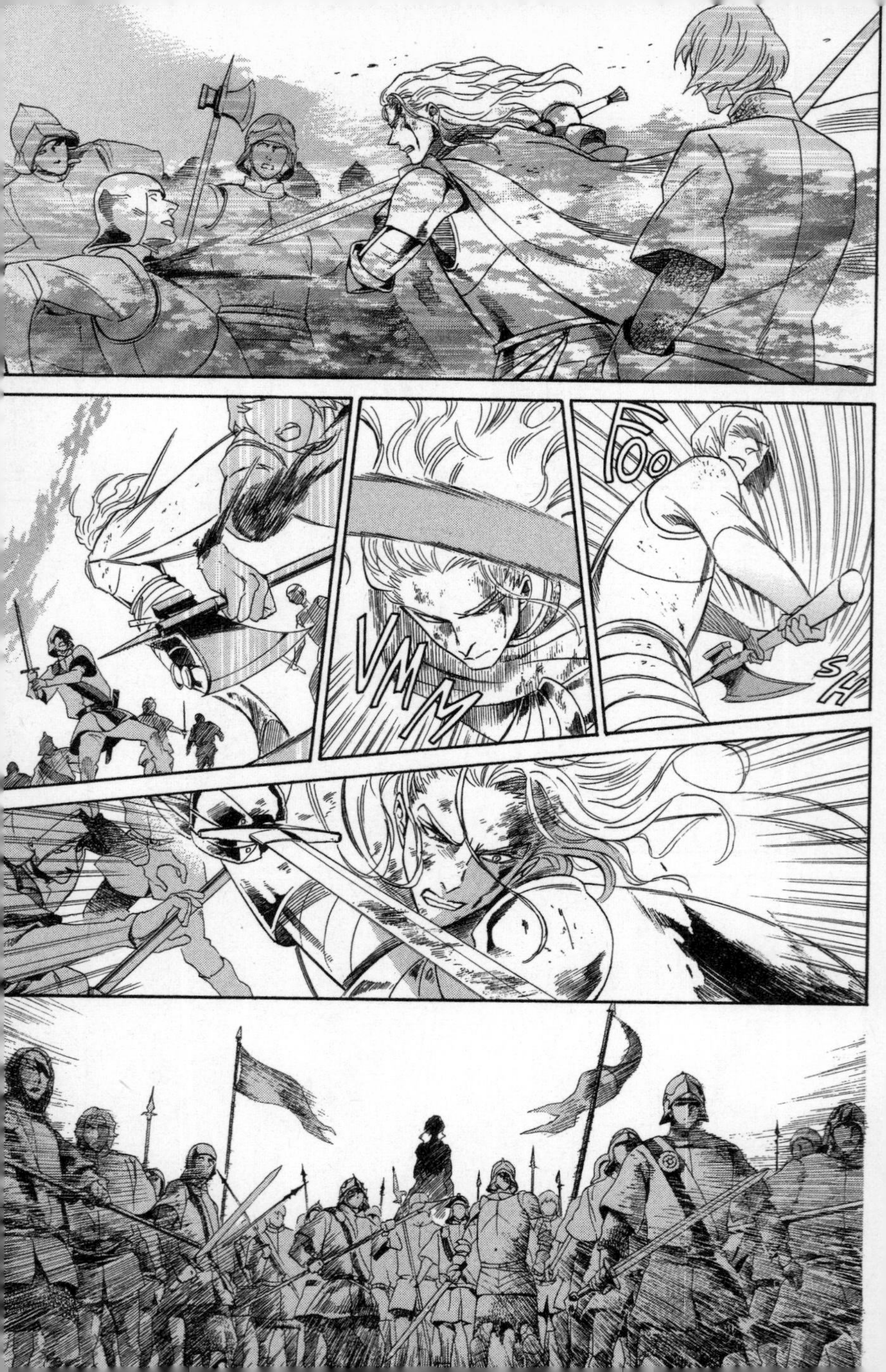
FOO
SH
VMM

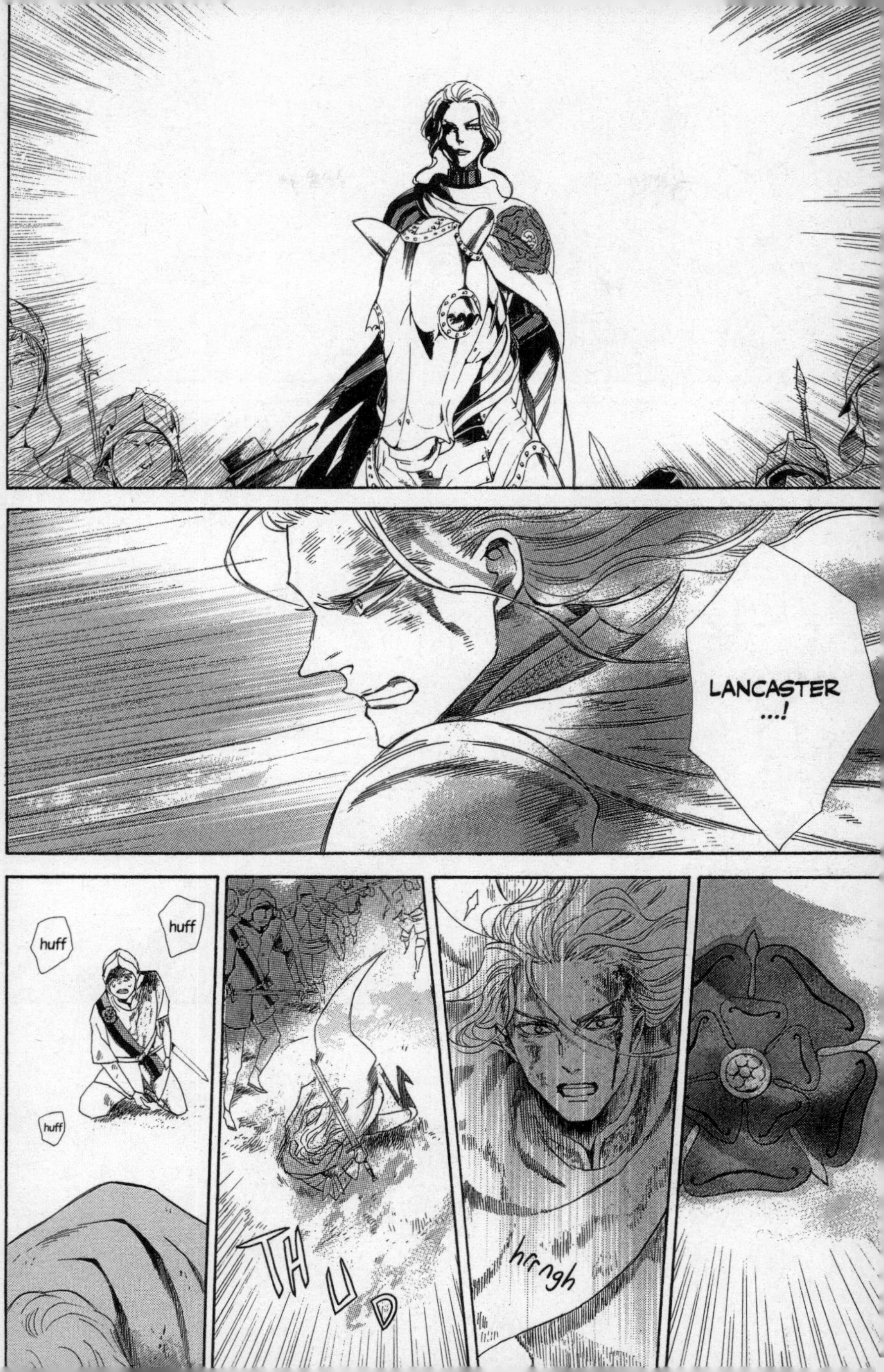
LANCASTER ...!
hrrngh
THUD
huff
huff
huff

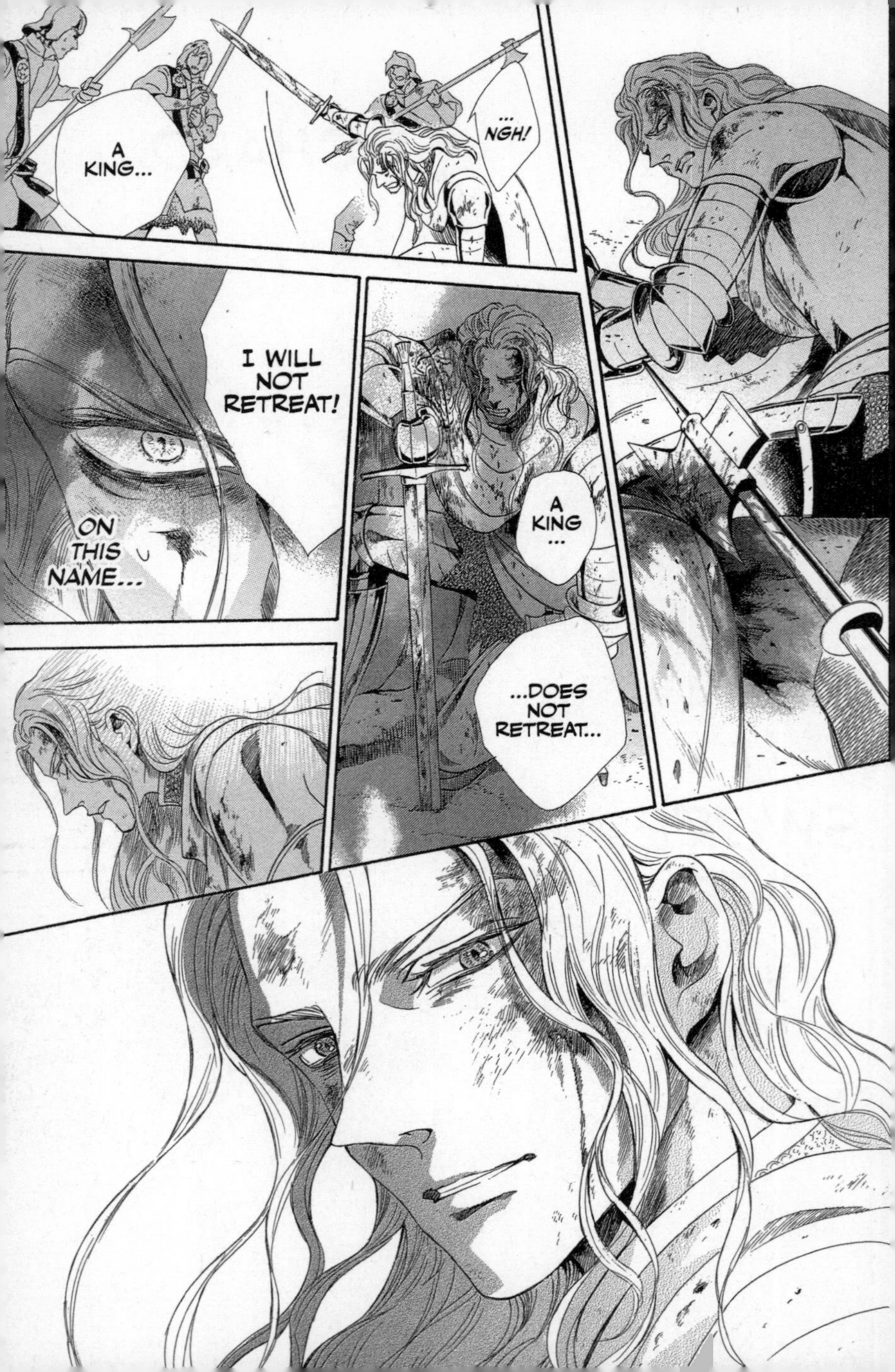
... NGH!
A KING...
A KING ...
...DOES NOT RETREAT...
I WILL NOT RETREAT!
ON THIS NAME...

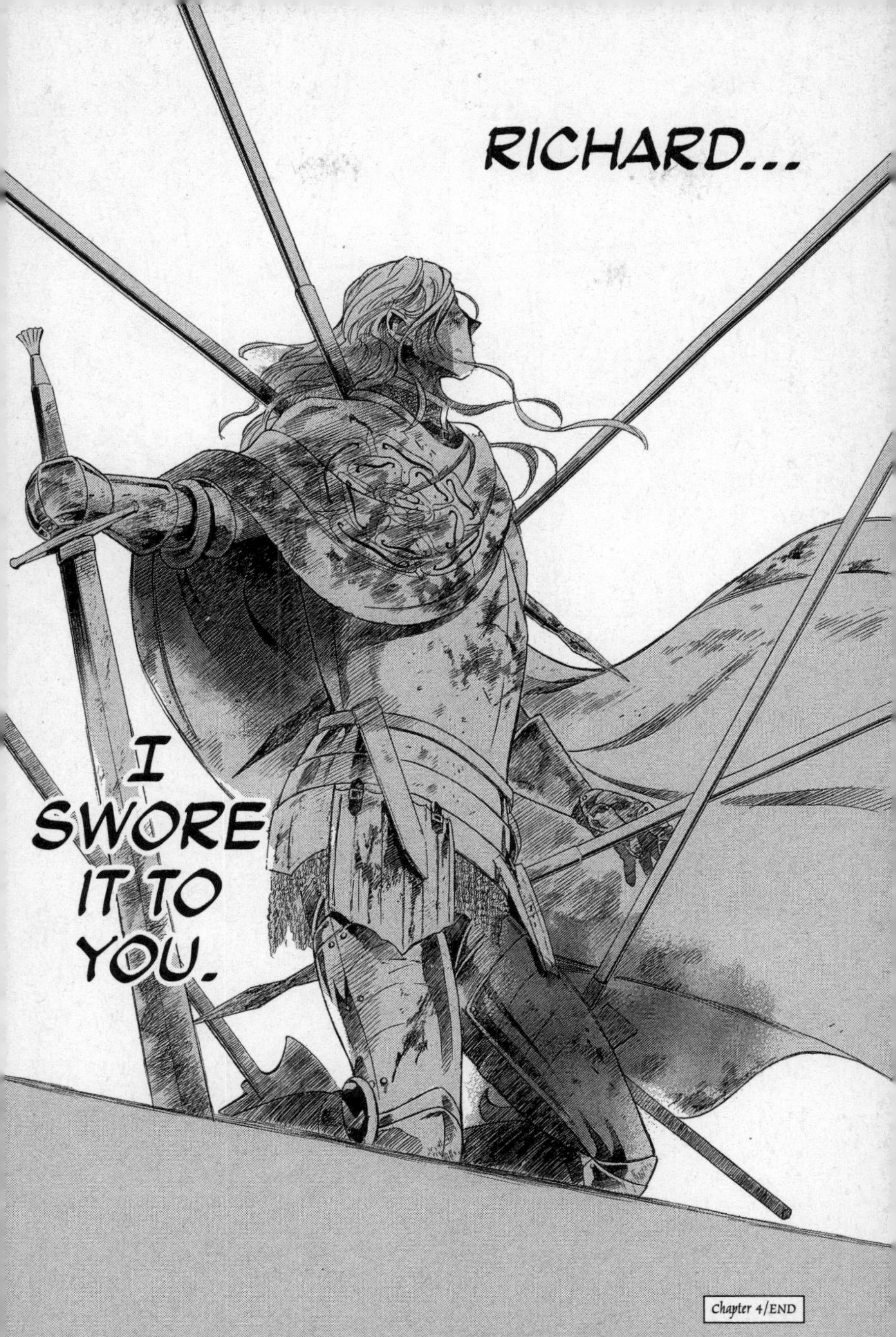
RICHARD...
I SWORE IT TO YOU.

Chapter 4/END

I've remixed in my own way the dialogue, settings and characters of my beloved *Henry VI* and *Richard III*. For the dialogue, I mixed my own translations into Shoyo Tsubouchi's. The original was a bit grandiose, so I ended up doing my own thing. The story turned out fairly different from the original, but I'll be happy if you enjoy it, whether or not you know the original works.

Aya Kanno

was born in Tokyo, Japan. She is the creator of *Soul Rescue*, *Blank Slate* and the *New York Times* best-selling series *Otomen*.

REQUIEM
OF THE
ROSE KING

VOLUME 1
VIZ MEDIA EDITION

STORY AND ART BY
AYA KANNO

TRANSLATION | JOCELYNE ALLEN
LETTERING | SABRINA HEEP
DESIGN | FAWN LAU
EDITOR | JOEL ENOS

BARAOU NO SOURETSU Volume 1
© 2014 AYA KANNO
First published in Japan in 2014 by AKITA PUBLISHING CO., LTD., Tokyo
English translation rights arranged with AKITA PUBLISHING CO., LTD.
through Tuttle-Mori Agency, Inc., Tokyo

The stories, characters and incidents mentioned in this
publication are entirely fictional.

Additionally, the author has no intention to discriminate
with any of the depictions within this work.

Printed in the U.S.A.

Published by VIZ Media, LLC
P.O. Box 77010
San Francisco, CA 94107

10 9 8 7 6 5 4 3 2 1
First printing, March 2015

www.viz.com